W9-DBF-869

SOCIAL STUDIES FOR THE TWENTY-FIRST CENTURY

Now in its 5th edition, this popular text offers practical, interesting, exciting ways to teach social studies along with a multitude of instructional and professional resources for teachers. Theory, curriculum, methods, and assessment are woven into a comprehensive model for setting objectives; planning lessons, units, and courses; choosing classroom strategies; and constructing tests for some of the field's most popular and enduring programs. The reflective and integrative framework emphasizes building imagination, insight, and critical thinking into everyday classrooms; encourages problem-solving attitudes and behavior; and provokes analysis, reflection, and debate.

Throughout the text, all aspects of curriculum and instruction are viewed from a tripartite perspective that divides social studies instruction into didactic (factual), reflective (analytical), and affective (judgmental) components. These three components are seen as supporting one another, building the groundwork for taking stands on issues, past and present. At the center is the author's belief that the heart and soul of social studies instruction, perhaps all teaching, lies in stimulating the production of ideas; looking at knowledge from others' viewpoints; and formulating for oneself a set of goals, values, and beliefs that can be explained and justified in open discussion.

This new edition is heavily revised and condensed to promote ease of use. "Build Your Own Lesson" additions to each chapter encourage improvisation and inquiry-based teaching and learning across subjects. A Companion Website offers additional activities, lessons, and resources for pre-service and practicing social studies teachers.

Jack Zevin is Emeritus Professor of Social Studies Education at Queens College, City University of New York, USA.

SOCIAL STUDIES FOR THE TWENTY-FIRST CENTURY

Methods and Materials for Teaching in Middle and Secondary Schools

Fifth Edition

Jack Zevin

Routledge
Taylor & Francis Group

NEW YORK AND LONDON

Cover image: Getty Images

Fifth edition published 2023
by Routledge
605 Third Avenue, New York, NY 10158

and by Routledge
4 Park Square, Milton Park, Abingdon, Oxon, OX14 4RN

Routledge is an imprint of the Taylor & Francis Group, an informa business

© 2023 Jack Zevin

The right of Jack Zevin to be identified as author of this work has been asserted in accordance with sections 77 and 78 of the Copyright, Designs and Patents Act 1988.

All rights reserved. No part of this book may be reprinted or reproduced or utilised in any form or by any electronic, mechanical, or other means, now known or hereafter invented, including photocopying and recording, or in any information storage or retrieval system, without permission in writing from the publishers.

Trademark notice: Product or corporate names may be trademarks or registered trademarks, and are used only for identification and explanation without intent to infringe.

First edition published by Lawrence Erlbaum Associates, Inc. in 2007
Fourth edition published by Routledge 2015

Library of Congress Cataloging-in-Publication Data
A catalog record for this title has been requested

ISBN: 978-0-367-45959-8 (hbk)
ISBN: 978-0-367-45956-7 (pbk)
ISBN: 978-1-003-02623-5 (ebk)

DOI: 10.4324/9781003026235

Typeset in Bembo and Futura Std
by Deanta Global Publishing Services, Chennai, India

Access the Comnpanion Website: www.routledgetextbooks.com/textbooks/_author/zevin/

CONTENTS

ABOUT THE AUTHOR

Jack Zevin (recently emeritus from Queens College) is a lifelong social studies education professor and the author of a widely used basic methods book in the field, "Social Studies for the Twenty-First Century" published by Routledge. Jack received the 2016 President's award by the ATSS/UFT, the New York Association of Teachers of Social Studies, recognizing five decades of service in the metropolitan area for preparing, nurturing, and

encouraging the best teaching among the many graduates prepared at Queens College. His widely published books on geography, history, and teaching include, *Teaching Geography as Inquiry*, co-written with a Chicago colleague, Dr. Mark Newman of National Louis University, (2016) and *Suspicious History* (2021) both published by Rowman & Littlefield. He published two researched books on teaching World and U.S. history, *Mystery* (Routledge, 2010, 2012), with co-author Prof. David Gerwin, that take a strong position on teaching global history as "mystery" to awaken interest and clearly set out three problems that make the teaching of global awareness and understanding so difficult. This book presents history as an ongoing struggle rather than as a simple, settled set of conclusions. Jack is still active in City University of New York, teaching for a term in 2020 for Macaulay College, and serving in the University Senate, as well as co-directing the Taft Institute for Government, a civic education foundation. Jack has also contributed articles, simulations, and role-plays for decades in social studies with the aim of building creative and gifted instruction in across subjects and grade levels.

PREFACE

In his prescription of "requirements for a historian," ibn Khaldun (1332–1406) stated that several things were essential if a historian were to be qualified to deal with historical events and stories:

1. An understanding of the rules of politics and the nature of people.
2. Knowledge of the natural environment and how it differs according to time and place.
3. Acquaintance with the social environments of the various different nations in terms of way of life, morals, incomes, doctrines, and so forth.
4. An understanding of the present time and an ability to compare it with the past.
5. Knowledge of the origins and motives of states and sects, their declared principles, their rules, and major events in their histories.

To achieve a critical understanding of historical events, then, the historian must study the general circumstances of the period with which he is dealing and compare the particular events in which he is interested. He should then explore any similar events that have taken place at other periods along with the general circumstances of these periods. When he has completed these two main stages he should be able to recognize events as reasonable and probably true, or unacceptable and almost certainly false. Certain events need only be studied separately, along with the general circumstances of their periods, to know which parts of them must be true or false.[1]

NOTE

1 Cited in www.philosophynow.org.

PREFACE

For our new 5th edition, we social studies practitioners are living in a changed educational world, one dominated by the Internet, our huge and rapidly growing electronic base of knowledge, junk mail, and unfounded claims. The advantages of this base for social studies offers astounding possibilities for teachers, unheard of quantities of original sources now digitalized, vast troves of lesson plans, and canned versions of almost anything a teacher could desire including aims, lessons, units, courses, texts, tests, scholarly discussions and lectures, and whole websites devoted to history and the social sciences. And let's not forget wonderful media, including online courses, blogs, videos, film clips, interviews, lectures, and music.

All this material is ours for the taking and is very rich and varied; easily found and easily forgotten too.

However, the specter of a knowledge explosion and subject fragmentation haunt the horizon of a virtual reality that seems to be replacing ordinary reality in the secondary school curriculum. There are many problems and issues that have arisen as the Web has expanded, and computers, electronic notebooks, and cell phones have become almost universally available. Problems range from sublime to ridiculous, but the biggest, in my view, is that teaching methods and the curriculum are out of synch with the new electronic opportunities. Students are distracted by glitz and social media, with outcomes both positive and negative.[1]

The Internet Age as Distraction: Underground communication in class!

Certainly, the new C3 NCSS Framework based on Common Core goals bears a deep desire for an 'inquiry arc' rather than data collection as a supreme objective. The Common Core seeks a much richer and deeper kind of instruction for our youth based on decades of accumulated research on teaching and learning.[2]

Despite widespread dissemination of computers and extensive knowledge of websites on the part of most teachers, the sheer quantity available tends to overwhelm both us, and our students. Rather than providing deeper insight and analysis the Web gives so many choices (many not sourced or checked) that research is required simply to choose the one or two sources we hope to get across to our students.

Figure 0.1: Internet Age as distraction.

Credit: Pixnio.com.

Added to the complexity of knowledge expansion and curriculum rigidity and lack of innovation, is the new 'reform' movement that has encompassed and endorsed quite an array of methods and structures to organize goals and content. These reforms run the gamut from the Danielson evaluation system to newly popular C3 Framework, with many attempts discarded or added in between.

In this new world, the authorities (federal, state, and local governments) in conjunction often with private industry have imposed new objectives, and evaluation systems for teachers without a great deal of philosophical consideration about what we really want from ourselves and our pupils as input and results. Educators have seldom been at the forefront of consultations.

The Common Core, a basis for new integrated standards for the social studies, in particular needs careful examination and conversation. It is the dominant set of goals that has been adopted widely across our nation by many professionals, states, and communities. Irony abounds since the deeply analytical Common Core demands complex inquiry behavior while schools operate online, and there are cutbacks and a rather restricted curriculum.[3]

Legislated inquiry and historical habits of mind are on the way in, if not already in place, largely by fiat from above.

Yet as teachers of social studies, we are still left with the same old basic problems and questions: what to teach, how to teach, why this organization of curriculum, and how do we ascertain results? The Web has created unlimited opportunities, but also issues of information overload and identifying and sourcing origins. However, choosing quality data and quality learning methods are even greater problems, since the Internet desperately needs a version of Consumer Reports for educators to sift the wheat from the chaff. There are websites now designed to find other websites.

And above all is that perennial question of what is worth teaching. This question will be our central focus throughout the book, helping you to decide in the light of multiple demands, what is really of value for the youthful citizens of tomorrow, and for ourselves as social studies/history teachers. Must we teach manifest destiny?

You are invited to use this newly revised and updated fifth edition of *Social Studies for the Twenty-First Century* as a guide, framework, and reference for teaching social studies at the middle and secondary levels. Inside is a fair and balanced review of the field using up-to-date and classic curriculum, research, and theory, including important work on history, civics, and economic education.

We will also increase expansion of horizons particularly in global lessons, and extend a welcome to the humanities and sciences. The social studies can draw successfully from a wide array of fields and connect to many subjects for enrichment by film, art, and literature. However, caution must be exercised in making the social studies a conglomeration of facts and ideas without a focus of its own.

We will also employ the concept of 'multiples' to guide us: multiple perspectives, intelligences, sources, strategies, and course conceptions. There are many ways to achieve and exceed the standards, and these techniques will be spelled out clearly and supported with multiple examples.

As in previous editions, I stake out a position on what constitutes excellence in teaching, rooted in the inquiry method proposed by John Dewey and others 100 years ago or more, but still not well implemented in schools. More than ever, I am in favor of deeper and more reflective teaching of history through primary and secondary sources promoting higher order thinking, and the development of empathy as seeing and understanding the world, not only as we see it, but as others view it.

However, social studies and history as well as much of the U.S. curriculum, is facing 'reform' from above, not from teachers themselves, with legislated goals and standards that demand a 'constructive,' 'productive,' 'value-added' core-like curriculum without giving much attention to the nitty-gritty of daily lessons, or course content. The Core asks teachers to advance their skills and promote high levels of historical and language literacy, while curriculum itself is left largely at a standstill.[4]

So, we have problems facing our field that are similar to problems facing most of the other fields as well: issues of content, process, adaptation to audiences (differentiation), knowledge outcomes, measurable results, and emotional satisfaction for teachers and audiences.

Therefore, for the foreseeable future, key questions need consideration include:

1. Deciding what knowledge is of greatest worth in terms of process and content.
2. Deciding how to judge the quality of knowledge, texts, sources, and websites, and their accuracy, fairness, balance, and agenda.
3. Deciding why we adopt and adapt specific lessons chosen for student audiences.
4. Deciding on methods of teaching that may best advance student and teacher growth from lower to higher levels of thinking.

5. Deciding and experimenting with ways of engaging student interest and stimulating ideas about history and social science.
6. Deciding how to bring students into conversations about key emotional and value issues embedded in human history.
7. Deciding when, where, and how to be creative professionals who invent new lessons and strategies.

The social studies is a large and complex field, embedded in what is a rapidly growing electronic world of knowledge seemingly so fragmented, yet very entertaining, so rich, yet distracting, that at times its essence is difficult to grasp. Now and in the future we will need approaches to knowledge as much as knowledge itself.

History is still a primary focus of social studies and always has been, but it is still part of a larger and more complex whole of the social sciences and humanities.[5] There are also new advocates appearing promoting connections to the sciences, math, technology, and even engineering (STEM and STEAM) that make the work of a social studies teacher more demanding than in previous eras.

An integrated concept of the field is best, with improved connections to other fields, but proceed with caution, limiting input. How about talking about the huge problems facing humankind: the decline and exploitation of the environment; the rapid rise of security and decline of privacy; the growing inequality and nationalism in the U.S. and around the globe.

Therefore, throughout this text, consider more thoughtful and realistic history teaching as part of better social studies. An overview of social studies/history theory, goals, curriculum, and everyday practice is offered in terms of three interlocking components: the didactic (information), the reflective (reasoning), and the affective (values). These components of planning are three overlapping spheres of development, each moving into the other and contributing to an overall view that connects facts, reasons, and judgments.

Didactic refers to all teaching and learning activities that revolve around gathering knowledge, from memorizing dates and definitions to tests. Reflective concerns all activities that focus on analyzing and thinking about data, research, and reasoning for which more than one answer is possible and welcomed. Affective deals with those facets of classroom life in which feelings, opinions, values, ethics, empathy, and morality dominate. Thus, each of the three components has a different, although not exclusive, focus: didactic focused on the what, reflective on the why, and affective on decisions about the good. Each component is discussed as contributing to and complementing the others; each enriches classroom discussion and learning.

In addition to offering a basic philosophy of teaching social studies, there are also informative 'boxes' scattered throughout for you to think about. Included are summaries about research studies past and present (Research Reports); items to stimulate curriculum ideas (To Do's and Lesson Plans); and places for you to engage primary sources by designing lessons of your own (BYOL: Bring your own lesson!).

And don't forget that as social studies folks, we have the most powerful justification for our subject as a key subject: we are teaching about the real world where future and present evolves out of past events, and where similar questions, issues, and mysteries appear as perennial companions to human behavior since we left the caves.

NOTES

The Common Core State Standards Initiative: www.corestandards.org.
C3 Framework of the National Council for the Social Studies: www.ncss.org.
Centre for the Study of Historical Consciousness: The historical thinking project: www
    .historicalthinking.ca.

NOTES

1 Cited in: www.philosophynow.org.
2 Gardner, H. and Davis, K. (2013) *The App Generation: How Today's Youth Navigate Identity, Intimacy and Imagination in a Digital Age* (New Haven, CT: Yale University Press).
3 C3 NCSS Framework of the National Council for the Social Studies based on Common Core, www.ncss.org
4 edutopia.org/common-core-state-standards-resources.
5 C3 NCSS Framework of the National Council for the Social Studies based on Common Core, www.ncss.org.

PHILOSOPHY AND HISTORY OF SOCIAL STUDIES

What Is (Are) the Social Studies?

1

SOCIAL STUDIES
Definition, Organization, and Orientation

"If you don't know history, then you don't know anything. You are a leaf that doesn't know it is part of a tree."

Michael Crichton

D1.1.6-8. Explain how a question represents key ideas in the field.
D1.1.9-12. Explain how a question reflects an enduring issue in the field.

C3 Framework, p. 24.

OVERVIEW

This chapter will focus on defining the social studies as a broad field based on history and the social sciences oriented toward a philosophy of inquiry and open-mindedness.

INTRODUCTION

Social studies is one of only two subjects in the secondary curriculum that is a compound of many other disciplines and is about the real world. Most subjects are inventions or organizers of inventions, like math, English, music, and art. Social studies seeks to understand how the world works, and ways that human behavior impacts ourselves, the environment, and others. History and the social sciences seek truth in the sense of explaining people and events, trying to understand where we come from and where we are headed.

Social studies could be defined in multiples, but it functions as a single comprehensive subject.

It is an all-encompassing subject representing a fusion of history and the social sciences with help from the humanities and the sciences. Most teachers, however, are teaching history and civics, a smaller portion geography and economics, and very smaller percentages

DOI: 10.4324/9781003026235-2

devoted to psychology, sociology, and anthropology. In a time of pandemic, there is often only a screen contact with other teachers and students that tends to diminish personal contact and increases content driven presentations rather than critical thinking exchanges.

Different traditions flow within the veins of social studies, one coming from history as a discipline, another from civics, and a third from the social sciences. A result of this fusion is a definition of social studies that includes pretty much everything having to do with human history and society.

Educators have never fully agreed on a common definition of social studies. We have not yet decided whether the subject is singular or plural, a unity, or a collection. We have experienced considerable conflict over goals, and this is ongoing. As a result, all social studies teachers confront certain dilemmas at the outset: what to teach, how to teach, and why to teach it.

A major question is what lies at the heart of the subject: whether to respect historical and verifiable evidence or reinforce popular values and storytelling. Some stress history, some decision-making, and some scientific method.

While there are fissures within the field between and among subgroups nearly all unite around the recently developed NCSS Common Core inspired "College, career, and civic life (C3) Framework for Social Studies State Standards" that calls for 'an inquiry arc' as its overall philosophy, i.e.:

"Social studies prepares the nation's young people for college, careers, and civic life.
Inquiry is at the heart of social studies.
Social studies involves interdisciplinary applications and welcomes integration of the arts and humanities.
Social studies is composed of deep and enduring understandings, concepts, and skills from the disciplines.
Social studies emphasizes skills and practices as preparation for democratic decision-making."

While the C3 Framework provides goals and guidance, teachers must still make decisions about evolving and testing a teaching style that suits their situations and audiences, hopefully within an inquiry philosophy. Creating and practicing a pedagogical style is exactly what this book is designed to help you accomplish. Social studies has a history that can be traced back to philosophical debates about its purpose and place in the curriculum. A deep divide is represented by a split between those who emphasize learning content versus those emphasizing critical thinking and preparation for democratic life.

Many argue that the main goal of social studies is to transmit knowledge about the past, a *didactic goal*—one that emphasizes telling. Others protest strongly that the goal of acquiring knowledge is not enough, and is even less valid with the growing influence of the World Wide Web as a source. Critics point out that information must be digested, analyzed, and applied in order to be useful. Forms of reasoning are a *reflective goal*.

There is also a strong lobby for social studies to serve as an agent of social change, for active citizenship education aimed at achieving social justice. Teaching for justice and freedom builds an affective goal. Citizenship education has its value conflict problems now, as well as long ago. Socrates was a social critic of Athenian life, and an outstanding activist and gadfly who was put on trial in a democracy for corrupting youth and committing impious acts (see Figure 1.1). Many would say Socrates was basically helping youths to think critically and make better decisions.

Could there be such a thing as asking too many questions in a democracy? Which goals work best to promote a coming together of didact, reflective, and affective advocates?

The Complete World of Greek Mythology by Richard Buxton (2004) contains stories from the history of ancient Greece that begin with myths and legends of gods and heroes and end with the conquests of Alexander the Great. The book is accessible and well organized, but it is considerably more detailed than some other introductory texts. Because of its length, we do not recommend it for 5th grade or younger. It is an excellent reference, thoroughly engaging, and a good candidate for a somewhat older student's first foray into Greek history.

Advocates in the activist camp worry about the need for participants in the democratic system, those who vote and pursue an ethical lifestyle for themselves and their society. This we describe as an *affective goal* because it encompasses moral questions, feelings, emotions, judgments, and values. Didactic, reflective, and affective dimensions of teaching social studies form part of everyday school practices and disputes about education theory and philosophy.

In addition to debating goals, some define the social studies largely as the study of history; others see it primarily as a study of the social sciences including: anthropology, economics, political science, psychology, and sociology. Still others suggest that social studies

He drank the contents as though it were a draught of wine

Figure 1.1:   Socrates takes the Hemlock. "He drank the contents as if it were a draught of wine. Artist: Walter Crane (1912)"

Source: From History for Boys and Girls www.wikigallery.org

is a unique field unto itself, offering methods of critical interpretation of society to young people, while a minority views it as useful for building of student self-confidence and encouraging good civic values.

Each view of our field has contributed to the current complexity of the curriculum, however, there are new developments that must be addressed every day we walk into or Zoom into a classroom. First, the Internet has replaced nearly all other methods of research and viewing, expanding into messaging, texting, website research, and reproduction of original sources. Cell phones, iPads, computers, and apps have swept the globe, and especially impacted wealthy technologically advanced societies. As the Internet expands and deepens, vast quantities of data are more easily accessed than ever before, including curriculum. original sources, videos, face-to-face communication online, and current events from many reporters, reliable and unreliable. With the glut of data and the rise of multiple news and views sources, critical thinking and the dependence on and democratization of knowledge collection, teaching how to use information takes preeminence over collection.

In this view, we need to **learn how to find, use, and master data rather than simply memorize and repeat it.** If anything there is an overabundance of information, and a shortage of questioning sources as trustworthy and reliable.

At the secondary school level, our field is usually defined in practice by mandated course content: world and U.S. history, economics, and civics with a very small smattering of social sciences and special electives. Classroom realities even before the COVID-19 pandemic included too much work, public opinion, budget restrictions, and insufficient classroom time that further narrow the range of what is actually offered, and how the subject is taught.

In addition to the usual pressures we have an ongoing pandemic, school being conducted at home on computer screens, along with newer issues like worrying about physical contact, getting into a real school, and the growing dependence on conversation media like Zoom, Blackboard, and Google Meet. Also, don't forget to keep up with your e-mail, texts, tweets, and other inboxes!

Theoretically, social studies may include any topics or issues that concern human behavior—past, present, or future. Content is most typically organized around one of the three dimensions or goals identified. Some educators would add at least two other organizing principles to this list: a philosophy of social action, and a person-oriented humanism that encourage self-regulation, confidence building, and personal growth.

Each of these organizing principles has goals, methods, and curriculum additions, which have grown out of those schools of philosophy that influenced educators over the last 100 years and more. But we are experiencing an era of pandemic and social and economic crisis that is nearly unprecedented, which calls for creative responses to education on every level— kindergarten to college.

What Do You Think?

Which subjects have you studied that *must* be included in social studies? Which will not be missed: Sociology? History of science? Driver training? Marketing? Media? Ancient history? Character education? Service learning?

In this chapter, you are invited to study different definitions of *social studies*, different ways of organizing goals, and a brief look at the competing schools of philosophy that have influenced this field. Throughout the book, you are invited to apply the three intertwined dimensions—didactic, reflective, and affective—to help you decide what, how, and why to teach every day in your social studies classroom.

WHAT IS (ARE) THE SOCIAL STUDIES? DEFINING A DISCIPLINE

A major conflict in the definition of *social studies* is contained in the title of this section: Is the social studies a single, integrated field, or are the social studies a series of related disciplines? Social studies is a relatively new subject in the world of academic disciplines, a product of public school expansion in the late 19th and early 20th centuries. The field of study was originally designed to meet a number of needs, including the preservation of democratic life; the upgrading of skills for an increasingly industrialized, technological economy; and the socialization of vast numbers of new immigrants into the general population.[1]

Given diverse purposes, it comes as no surprise that social studies represent a fusion of several different strands, including history (a classical humanities academic discipline), the social sciences (with roots in empirical, scientific traditions), citizenship training (derived from both nationalism and social criticism), and self-enhancement (with roots in psychological and pluralistic /multicultural traditions).

Edgar B. Wesley's famous definition, "the social studies are the social sciences simplified for pedagogical purposes,"[2] suggests that social sciences form the heart of the discipline—a notion that many would dispute and that does not typically represent the practices of secondary school teachers. More fairly, we can define *secondary school social studies* as the study of history, citizenship, and ethical issues that deal with human history, human behavior, and human values. In short, social studies in the classroom is about how and why people act, what they believe, and where and how they live. It is about actions, ideas, values, time, and place—a series of topics that covers an immense range, but allows tremendous latitude in the selection of materials and methods for teachers.[3]

Although there is and will continue to be considerable debate on a theoretical level about what social studies is and should be, most secondary instruction on a practical level is defined by content and courses mandated by state or local requirements that are basically similar from district to district. In this area, it is always useful to read through landmark thinkers like John Dewey, Jerome Bruner, and Howard Gardner as we all borrow freely from them.

Your style and philosophy, however, are your own. As a social studies teacher, you should understand the different schools of thought and the rationales behind them, and from this understanding, slowly and carefully evolve a philosophy that suits your own view of subject and audience. A key issue here is the choice between eclecticism, an attempt to include many viewpoints, or a commitment to one major approach as your principal guide to action. An eclectic approach that collects many topics, views, and techniques may seem fairer in the classroom, but it may also lead to confusion about goals, inconsistency, and a disorganized approach to content. A consistent approach, however, may produce clear, consistent results, but leave you and your students with a narrower range of ideas.

The social sciences, history, citizenship, social action, and personal development advocates want to give social studies a different 'heart' to supply its body with the sustenance of life, set its goals, and direct action. Each position derives from different philosophic grounds and tends to stress widely varying criteria for the content, methods, and outcomes of instruction. For example, in a reflective social science lesson, students might be asked to analyze the reasons for the rise of dictators rather than focus on any single example such as Mussolini or Hitler. A didactic history lesson might discuss political causes of the American Revolution. Citizenship-centered material might be a debate focused on voting rights and responsibilities in the here and now. A social action approach might typically ask students to study an issue such as world hunger, take a position on how to address it, and implement a plan for action. A lesson stressing personal or character development could involve service learning and social activism asking students to make contributions to the community. Thus a dilemma exists not only of definition, but also of choice: Should you attempt to resolve conflicting conceptions, integrating and fusing them into a united whole? Or should you accept and utilize one of the competing conceptions, the 'arc of inquiry,' to guide all classroom decisions? How can we organize our thinking about a diverse and fragmented field?

LET'S DECIDE

Form a group of at least three colleagues or classmates, write your own definition of *social studies,* and share your views. Is everyone's view more or less alike or different? Why? Do you think history *is* social studies, or do you prefer a civics or social science overall theme? Why or why not?

ORGANIZING PRINCIPLES FROM WAY BACK WHEN: A THREE-PART APPROACH

A number of organizing conceptions of social studies can serve as an aid to understanding the dynamics and pressures of the subject. Barr, Barth, and Shermis, for example, offer a view of social studies as divisible into three traditions: one to promote social science, a second to promote citizenship, and a third to promote reflective inquiry.[4]

The *social science tradition* offers the findings, concepts, and rules of the different social sciences, centering on the scientific method. Organizing ideas might include social class, culture, location, power, or the market system. The social science tradition seeks to give secondary students a sample of the ideas, skills, and data available to social scientists, "reduced to manageable terms for young people."[5] Ultimately, Barr, Barth, and Shermis see the social sciences as supporting citizenship education by encouraging analysis of and generalizations about human behavior.

The *citizenship transmission approach* is teaching goals and expectations for U.S. society, seeking to develop the ideal participant in a democratic society. The desired product is someone who knows and understands the culture and its values and is able to function effectively as an active citizen. The intent of the transmitters is to inculcate within students those democratic beliefs and convictions that will be supportive yet critical of social and political institutions while providing assistance in choosing careers and developing personal capital. Barr, Barth, and Shermis view the purpose of the citizenship transmission tradition as being "to raise up a future generation of citizens who will guarantee cultural survival."[6]

The third tradition, *social studies taught as reflective inquiry*, proposes analysis and decision-making as the heart of a student's classroom life, applied to the content and process of knowing and valuing. Method and content are closely related to conclusions, theories, and judgments subject to critical interpretation. Problem solving and critical thinking are integral to the reflective inquiry tradition; the student is placed in a situation in which she or he must deal with ambiguities and unknowns in order to make sense of the world. Inquiry process, according to Barr, Barth, and Shermis, is one "that involves all of the techniques and strategies that lend themselves to improving the students' ability *to ask important questions and find satisfactory answers*."[7]

The three traditions to correlate purpose, method, and content:

   I: Citizenship/Cultural Transmission/National Values and Heritage Tradition
  II: Reflective Thinking/Inquiry-Problem Solving/Social Criticism Tradition
 III: Social Science/Scientific Method and Empiricism/Search for Truth.[8]

Brubaker, Simon, and Williams suggest a similar organizing scheme that includes citizenship, social science, and reflective inquiry, but adds a student-oriented tradition of a sociopolitical 'involvement' meaning participation in social action.[9] The purpose of the student-oriented tradition is self-enhancement and the building of self-confidence; and it includes cultural awareness. The authors view social studies as a vehicle for building identity and strengthening psychological perceptions of the self, aimed at successful social and family and community relationships. *Sociopolitical involvement* is a label for social criticism and political activism. A major purpose of social studies is to promote political activism, for such goals as social justice, free speech and assembly, international peace, etc.

Note that these earlier analyses of social studies and its traditions has much in common with the three major dimensions: didactic, reflective, and affective. Social science and history can have a heavily didactic purpose. Reflective inquiry and critical thinking are, of course, most like our reflective dimension because reasoning is primary. Civic education clearly involves moral values, social criticism, self-analysis, and public controversy—judgments that fit the affective dimension. Thus, current practices and philosophies have grown out of earlier models picking up new ideas and content as we head into the 21st century age of the Internet.

RESEARCH REPORT

A previous five-dimensional view of social studies was bolstered by a survey of teachers' philosophic preferences by Irving Morrissett for the Social Science Education Consortium (1977). In this study, most teachers surveyed identified one or more of five principal areas that comprised social studies:

1. The transmission of culture and history.
2. The life experiences of personal development.
3. Reflective or critical thinking and inquiry.

4. Social sciences processes and subject matter.
5. The study of social and political controversies with the aim of promoting political activism.

A sample of secondary teachers saw history as a main link for knowledge of the past along with citizenship values. The social sciences overall were viewed as providing a scientific/analytic framework. Reflective inquiry was considered as promoting students' thinking through the investigation of social issues and problem solving. The action approach was viewed as involvement in real political processes and leadership in the world outside as well as in school. Teachers saw the student-centered approach enhancing appreciation and understanding of self and others in society through discussion of personal beliefs and deeply held values.

Source: Morrissett, I. (March 1977) "Preferred Aapproaches to the Teaching of Social Studies," *Social Education*, 41, 206–209.

THE ORIGINS OF SOCIAL STUDIES PERSPECTIVES

Social studies goals, definitions, categories, research agendas, curricula, and pedagogy can be traced wholly or in part to several philosophical movements that have had widespread impact on education as a whole in the U.S. and abroad. Almost every teacher's pattern of behavior, self-concept, and curriculum decisions reflect one or more of these philosophic conceptions.

Often conflicting, sometimes overlapping, while evolving one from another, some systems have had almost universal impact, while others have remained the province of theoreticians and researchers. The major organization for social studies education, the National Council for the Social Studies, reflects the many competing philosophies of education, now drawn together into a single C3 Framework. Some advocate citizenship as central, others claim history as central; some view social studies as a "theory of instruction," whereas others see it as a real "education program."[10]

Multiple views have directly affected the choice of content and practice. Overall, the social sciences and special topics have lost ground. The recent trend has definitely been in favor of history and historical 'habits of mind' but this view certainly falls within an inquiry arc and supports long sought reflective goals (Wineburg, 2001).

Perennialism and Essentialism

Advocates of an ancient influential philosophy labeled perennialism argue that absolute and unchanging truths exist in human history. Social studies educators who adhere to this tenet believe that students need to understand and apply truths to daily life and that studying these truths will produce competent, culturally literate individuals who know and understand their own history capable of transmitting events to others. Perennialists support the study of history with an emphasis on skill development; curriculum centers on the study of Western civilization's classic works, typified by Mortimer Adler's 'Great Books program' that still exists.[11] A perennialist perspective continues in the work of E. D. Hirsch's *Cultural Literacy*. School lessons should consist of two complementary parts: an intensive and an extensive curriculum. "The extensive curriculum is traditional literate knowledge, the information, attitudes, and assumptions that literate Americans share:

cultural literacy." The intensive curriculum "encourages a fully developed understanding of a subject, making one's knowledge integrated and coherent.[12] Hirsch extends his argument for common goals and curriculum, arguing in favor of a standard national curriculum as a key to improving student learning.[13] A Core Curriculum ancestor for sure!

A second school of thought closely allied to perennialism is often referred to as *essentialism*. One advocate, William Bagley, argued that students must know the basics or essentials of knowledge to be truly educated, and that these essentials include a strong dose of skills, concepts, and values drawn from the study of history, government, and economics.[14] Essentialism and perennialism have a classical bent, usually emphasizing rigorous training in traditional disciplines of study. Theodore Sizer, for example, is a more modern exponent of essentialism, directing a movement for school reform through a "coalition of essential schools" that aims to train teachers in asking "essential questions."[15]

Essentialism seeks a primary commitment to the transmission of knowledge as effectively as possible. In a recent work, Sizer made clear that the essential schools movement seeks a "focus on helping adolescents learn to use their minds well," learning to use classical knowledge rather than simple rote memorization.[16] Advocates have probably had a greater impact on social studies content perhaps than followers of any other philosophy.

Scientific Empiricism and the New Criticism

A second approach to social studies education derives from the principles of scientific inquiry. Social scientists have built on the techniques and tools of the scientific method in an effort to identify laws, principles, theories, and rules of human thought and behavior. These "empiricists" studied people as individuals, groups, and across cultures.

In secondary schools, educators sought to emulate empiricism by involving students in the scientific method, creating projects based on experimentation, survey research, and case studies. Students were encouraged to think in terms of probabilities rather than absolute truths, offered different perspective to interpret evidence, and exhorted to be fair, objective, and unbiased in drawing conclusions. This search for solidly grounded data was an all-consuming passion in social science during the 1950s, 1960s, and early 1970s. Toward the end of the 1970s, criticism mounted against attempts to define social science through the scientific method alone, especially against the notion that conclusions and theories could ever be entirely value-free. Strongly influenced by philosophers Jürgen Habermas and Thomas Kuhn, many turned to the so-called "new criticism."[17] These ideas, sometimes termed *phenomenology* or *critical theory*, abandoned, wholly or in part, the concept of objectivity and suggested that science can never be 'fully' free of value claims.[18] Critics in social studies as elsewhere expressed deep suspicion not only about empiricists' conclusions, but also about research designs and methods, arguing that values form a basis for human investigation, and must be examined and made explicit. As Richard Bernstein points out:

> When we examine those empirical theories that have been advanced, we discover again and again that they are not value-neutral, but reflect deep ideological biases and underlying controversial value positions. It is a fiction to think that we can neatly distinguish the descriptive from the evaluative components of these theories, for tacit evaluations are built into their very framework.[19]

Scientific empiricism greatly influenced content and method in social studies curriculum throughout the middle and later decades of the last century. The 'new' criticism has wielded less influence, but has had a considerable impact on academics and administrators who seek to promote student activism and decision-making. Advocates suggest that an awareness of and a willingness to examine policy and value claims should be fundamental to social studies education.[20]

Pragmatism and Progressivism

Pragmatism is a term often applied to the work of John Dewey, a key educational philosopher in the U.S., along with other educational 'progressives' who emphasize the development of students' reasoning and judgment applied to everyday civic life. Dewey saw education as part and parcel of supporting democratic traditions in the United States and around the world. Terms associated with Deweyian philosophy include *problem solving, problem finding, reasoning, reflective thinking, inquiry, critical thinking,* and *creative thinking.* Social studies methods are very strongly influenced by pragmatic or philosophical ideas. Dewey stressed the importance of building links among schools, community, and student experiences.

Relationships are recognized, ideas analyzed, and decisions made through a thinking process that works from a grounding in evidence and inductive and/or deductive logic culminating in conclusions. Conclusions or decisions will then presumably lead to taking action in terms of social commitments, political decisions, and personal growth.[21]

If essentialists tend to be preoccupied with content and traditions, pragmatists and progressives tend to emphasize process.[22]

Pragmatists see the curriculum as an open and flexible system capable of absorbing and applying new ideas, rather than be defined by a list of universal or eternal classics. As might be expected, progressives advocate the building of critical thinking and decision-making skills in the social studies classroom. The product of a progressive social studies education might well be a shrewd consumer, an intelligent and well-informed voter, an active participant in community life, and a life-long seeker of new ideas and new skills. Common core seems very much in a Deweyian mode of thought though giving less attention to social justice or making judgments.

Some educators see pragmatism as including personal growth in a democratic society and use terms like *self-actualization, self-fulfillment,* and *identity* and character education.[23] Service learning is a descendant of this point of view contributing to civic action for the common good, although perhaps rather conservative in terms of political action. Multiculturalism also draws on the same philosophical base because transformative education and social protest are part of good citizenship in a democracy that seeks to correct injustices. Activism against civic and social prejudices is seen as part of citizen responsibility. Overall, pragmatism seeks what might be called a middle ground between essentialism and the more radical reconstructionism.

Reconstructionism and Public Issues

Social justice is a cherished value in Western tradition, and promoted in social studies. For those to whom social justice is a primary goal, social studies education provides a perfect vehicle for encouraging students to take a role in the affairs of the community, the nation, and the world, and to raise their voices in objection to moral lapses, political chicanery, and the destruction of the Earth for economic gain.

George S. Counts, who christened this philosophy "Reconstructionism," argues that the schools must play a role in changing or reconstructing society.[24] Count's work has been eagerly adopted by many, some of whom see schools, especially secondary, not only as sites for discussion of controversial issues, but also as participants in social action projects.[25] Doing good, not just discussing good, is seen as the result of studying history.

Critical pedagogy developed by scholars such as Michael Apple, Henry Giroux, Peter McLaren, and Joel Spring provides a thorough analysis of the relationship between schooling and society, rooted in arguments that social injustice grows in part out of an unequal distribution of skills, knowledge, and resources in schools.[26] The long tradition in favor of discussing controversial issues in social studies also stems from earlier reconstructionist notions of teaching.

Reconstructionism has had a wide-ranging impact on social studies education, especially in the 1930s, in the 1960s and 1970s, continuing to the present reflected in curricula that emphasize current events, mock trials, debates, and simulations, raising judgmental questions about equality, the distribution of goods and services, foreign policy choices, international conflict and peace, plus environmental issues such as famine, exploitation, destruction of wetlands, and air and water pollution. A public issues curriculum reflects a primary concern with current and persisting problems in history.[27]

Reconstructionists have in common with pragmatists their emphasis on critical thinking and decision-making. Adherents teach students to examine their own beliefs in order to decide which ones they would be willing to uphold with action; others frankly seek to indoctrinate students with their own values that they view as ethically correct. Participation, protest, and political action are major goals for social studies because 'social reconstruction' still runs wide and deep within educators at many levels in our field (Riley, 2006).

WHAT DO YOU THINK?

Which of the philosophies or traditions do you find most appealing for a teaching career? Do you enjoy content? Is activism necessary? What are the reasons for your choices?

For you, as a teacher, two worlds—one of day-to-day classroom practice and the other of ideological goals, debate, and research—must always be kept in mind if you hope to make sense of the field. Although the theoretical is often intensely debated by representatives of the different philosophic schools of thought, practical classroom concerns usually reflect professional standards, mandated content, course sequence, testing, subject matter, and student audiences. For better or worse, classroom practice tends to be quite stable from decade to decade, with remnants of all of the earlier philosophies of education still competing with one another for dominance.[28]

The bottom line is still tell and ask later, while we would prefer 'ask, don't tell'!

CLASSIC RESEARCH REPORT

Based on a study of more than 300 junior high and 500 senior high school classrooms, John Goodlad found that, by and large, teaching social studies is and has been geared to present information as fact in a style closer to old-fashioned recitation than to modern democratic discussion. He concluded:

> What the schools in our sample did not appear to be doing was developing all those abilities commonly listed under "intellectual development": the ability to think rationally, to use and evaluate knowledge, intellectual curiosity, and a desire for further learning. Only rarely did we find evidence to suggest instruction likely to go much beyond mere possession of information to a level of understanding the implication of that information and either applying it or exploring its possible applications. Nor did we see in subjects generally taken by most students (including social studies) activities likely to arouse students' curiosity or to involve them in seeking solutions to some problems not already laid bare by teacher or textbook. The traditional image of a teacher possessing the knowledge standing at the front of the classroom imparting it to students in a listening mode accurately portrays the largest portion of what we observed. ... And why should we expect teachers to teach otherwise? This is the way they were taught in school and college.

From your own school experiences and observations, do you agree with Goodlad's 30-year-old findings? Do you see more or less variety than he and his researchers uncovered? What do you believe the "climate" of a secondary social studies classroom should be now to fit C3 standards?

Goodlad, J. (1983) "What Some Schools and Classrooms Teach," *Educational Leadership*, 40, 7, 15.

TO DO

Collect two or three social studies history textbooks.

Find passages on the same topic or period, perhaps World War I, or the Progressive Era, or 9/11. Read and decide whether the lesson represents a fusion of several philosophies or is presented from a single viewpoint. Are facts most important or are questions most important? How can you tell?

SETTING GOALS AS PHILOSOPHIC CHOICES

Virtually every choice you will make as a social studies teacher will be based on the goals or learning objectives that you set for students. Objectives and goals, by their very nature, are drawn from theory and philosophy then translated into practice in the form of topics, goals, and questions.

Goals are the bridge between philosophy and practice, between setting objectives, carrying out the lessons, and evaluating results. Look, for instance, at the following typical objectives:

1. Students will learn the important dates, places, and events of World War II.
2. Students will memorize the definitions of commonly used legal terms.

3. Students will list five issues that divide Israelis and Palestinians.

These goals share a common thread: data collection. They suggest methods, materials, and questions that are didactic, stemming from a cultural transmission approach to social studies.

   Now look at a second set of goals:

1. Students will compare and contrast policy positions of the state of Israel and the Palestinian Authority.
2. Students will discuss some causes and consequences of the rise of rebellions and revolutions, recent and past.
3. Students will use data analysis to produce a theory of economic development for a given nation.

These goals all involve a reflective approach to social studies emphasizing a social science data analysis scientific approach to drawing conclusions.

   Finally, here is a third set of objectives.

1. Students will study and evaluate U.S. foreign policy on Syria and the Middle East.
2. Students will identify the most urgent environmental problem in their area and propose actions to remedy it.
3. Students will debate the political, ethical, and moral ramifications of gun control or the lack of it.

These goals share a commitment to the examination of values and represent different elements of social criticism, social action, and citizenship traditions. All reflect controversial themes and an affective approach to social studies education.

   Objectives are not always as clearly derived from one or another of the major social studies philosophies. However, goals almost always reflect one or more of the three dimensions in some way. Knowledge of philosophical premises and definitions of the dimensions will enable you to choose your goals more effectively and support them with appropriate materials, methods, and teaching strategies.

   There is considerable agreement—although for different reasons and toward different ends—that the development of high-quality reasoning skills is a key goal, but there is considerable disagreement about how much stress should be placed on teaching controversial and current issues, as opposed to teaching the heritage and traditions of the common, dominant culture. Similarly, proponents of virtually all philosophic positions support presentation of accurate content and engaging methods of inquiry: teaching global studies and American history, but argue heatedly about the role of indoctrination versus value-free teaching. If teachers set goals that demand one right answer, in terms of data or values, that limits inquiry and student opportunities to work out their own values. In other words, inquiry demands great care by teachers in speaking their own values or endorsing any one particular interpretation as correct, even when patriotic controversies are raging. Inquiry nurtures young people into the art and science of thinking through and defending choices based on evidence and reasons, not prejudice or loyalty.

   Although philosophical debate breaks out in scholarly journals, what happens in the classroom is considerably more practical and stable. Classroom teachers tend to be preoccupied with mainly historical content, sequence and scope, curriculum materials, strategies, and testing. There is modest attention to civics and economics, with a smattering of other disciplines added here and there. On the whole, studies show that teachers avoid controversy, and fear affective expressions of feelings and values. They avoid one-third of our dimensions, and a great deal of the C3 Framework of objectives. Information and reflection seem a lot safer than walking into contested areas of the curriculum or methodology.

Yet it is important for you to recognize that social studies is a fragmented and dynamic field: A level of uncertainty exists concerning issues ranging from the lack of an acceptable definition through methodology and content. That inherent uncertainty, although problematic, provides us with your most potent tool: freedom to select an individual point of view within the constraints of district or state requirements, and freedom to set at least some goals, design homemade lessons, and choose strategies that build an effective and defensible philosophy of instruction guiding both short- and long-range decisions.

A CLASSIC QUESTION: WHAT DO YOU THINK?

In discussing the NCSS, Shirley Engle, then president of the NCSS, noted that the membership and its leaders are "held uneasily together by a common concern for the social education of children and youth. We avoid definition of our field of competence, confusing social education with the social sciences … and afford our members a kind of smorgasbord of educational goodies and services, throughout which no cogent philosophic or pedagogical position runs, and from each, each according to his own interest or bent, may choose to eat whatever he will … [with] no clear and consistent position on social education and, for that matter, no clear definition of our field."

Shirley Engle, The future of social studies education and NCSS, *Social Education*, 34 (1970), 778–781, 795.

Do you think a clear definition of social studies is possible: An advantage or disadvantage to everyday teaching? Think about your views: How would you define the field? Is social studies defined by Common Core, or C3, or by its multiple traditions, curriculum, and teaching approaches?

PRACTICE

As we have pointed out, social studies objectives, methods, units, lessons, and courses reflect a particular viewpoint or collection of viewpoints about ultimate goals. In practice, however, teachers typically offer students an eclectic collection of materials that is often inconsistent and lacks an overall approach, particularly critical review of multiplying sources. Social studies curriculum is defined more by state, city, or district requirements than by the development of a reasonable, well-planned scope and sequence guided by a philosophy of education. Consider this fairly typical secondary school social studies course plan:

Grade 7: World culture, world history, world geography, state history

Grade 8: U.S. history

Grade 9: World cultures, world history, civics, government, state history

Grade 10: World cultures, world history

Grade 11: U.S. history, American studies

Grade 12: American government, civics and electives or requirements, including anthropology, geography, economics, psychology, sociology, problems of American democracy.[29]

This out of sequence curriculum has not changed substantially since World War II or even earlier. Courses may vary by grade and subjects may change somewhat, but the general pattern has held for decades. Within this often repetitive and illogical sequence, students must frequently contend with lessons derived from conflicting philosophies. They may be asked one day to memorize World War I dates; the next day to analyze the consequences of the conflict for Germany, focusing on hypotheses that explain aggression and its results; and the following day, to examine the morality of trench battles portrayed in Erich Remarque's *All Quiet on the Western Front*.

In addition to the curriculum, many other classroom realities are visited on the social studies teacher. These include: pressures to cover a way-too-large number of topics, too many students packed into small spaces, a sometimes adversarial view of the student audience, insufficient planning and preparation time, and a school culture of isolation from colleagues.[30] As you dash around trying to inform large groups of students— often restless, questioning adolescents—about the entire sweep of American and world studies, including relevant issues, in an even-handed and fair manner during precise 40- to 60-minute periods using textbooks one or two decades old, you may lose track of the perfect social studies lesson. In fact, you may lose track of the subject altogether! There is simply too much information to teach, too many skills to practice, and too little time in the day to do achieve ever y goal that has been set.[31] And this was before the Internet offered us a much larger array of lessons, units, and courses from which to choose our materials. The audience may be restless or obstreperous.

Furthermore, as you try to carry out this mission impossible, many other demands will emanate from the principal, parents, and colleagues, as well as an occasional bid for attention from state, county, or local boards of education. Old or new goals may become prominent, such as the surge of interest in national standards or diversity needs and issues, calls for improved Science and Technology instruction, higher order reading and writing skills via Common Core, or the clamor for a Common Core inspired better writing 'across the curriculum.' All of this is crammed into an already overstuffed curriculum where time is at a premium and planning at a minimum.

Conditions such as these may very well lead you to believe that there are reasons for less-than-perfect instruction, and you may wonder why people in the field are still fighting about lofty goals, philosophy, and instructional methodology. You may also understand why teachers band together against critics and outsiders who condemn or criticize them in newspapers, through reports and surveys, or in stereotypical and sarcastic portrayals in film and TV

Given all these problems, you must still decide each day what, why, how, and to whom you will offer instruction in social studies. Whether a conscious decision or not, each choice you make, each act you perform, is derived from precedents, traditions, and course requirements from historical roots. Each tradition and topic is the product of values and beliefs that rest on an educational theory or philosophy. Thus, theory has consequences for practice and practice influences theory.[32] If you spend most of your classroom time covering factual material, transmission or didactic theory is guiding your behavior. If you stress in-depth analysis of original sources, primary documents, and so forth, then a reflective or inquiry theory is influencing your decisions. If you promote the examination of values, debate ethical and moral issues, and foster student involvement then an affective, citizenship, or social activist theory directs your teaching. Whatever happens, there is and must be a link between theory and practice, and I will relentlessly offer advice and guidance so you have ideals to strive for, even if not always attainable.

Given the complexities of teaching social studies, an ideal balance between lower and higher-order thinking, or among the didactic, reflective, and affective goals, may be difficult to achieve, but impossible if no ideal, theory, or central ideas exist to guide you. The Educational philosophy you adopt will strongly influence your practice, and your choice of curriculum

---

LET'S DECIDE

Get together with at least two or three classmates or colleagues and write a sample goal that bridges theory and practice for a topic of your choice from a civics or economics course. Can civics be taught only as didactic information? Is civics taught as 'reconstructionism' a preference, with a strong dose of making choices and taking immediate action? Are you willing to arouse controversy among students on social and political issues? Why or why not?

SUMMARY

Tensions in social studies have arisen because competing schools of thought, philosophies, and political frameworks seek to implement different goals for the field as a whole.

Those who stress mainly didactic goals seek learning in which students acquire a great deal of knowledge about their traditions, culture, and world. They want this transmitted knowledge to be accurate, reliable, and meaningful. Essentialists stress understanding and intelligent reading skills (like Common Core and C3). They want students to build a sense of what is valuable knowledge to be more than walking encyclopedias, facing problems dealing with a world in which there is too much information, rather than too little. Didactic goals are still treated as very important although the Web, the Internet, has rendered the necessity for memorization questionable.

Those who espouse mainly reflective thinking goals want students to develop a systematic, scientific way of approaching data, a style for solving problems, and an overall sense of critical-mindedness. Social scientists want skillful analysis not a mechanical 'scientific procedure.' Historical skills and social science investigative methods change a bit now and then, but are useful across subject matter and do not fade away like ephemeral knowledge.

Finally, those who fervently endorse affective goals want to encourage students to deal with sensitive moral and ethical issues, to be willing to examine their own values and those of others with an open mind. Social activists want students who will make decisions that lead to purposeful political and social action, not simply young people who go through the motions of expressing their opinions as a polite classroom exercise. Facing issues and promoting balanced discussion is desperately needed but becoming more difficult in a society divided by class, race, status, and political identity.

You, the teacher, must decide how to balance goals and priorities.

To diminish confusion and enhance awareness of educational motives this book offers a view of social studies across didactic, reflective, and affective dimensions, relating and uniting knowledge, reasoning, and judgment between actors and audiences. Use the scheme to organize daily lessons. Evaluate both what you intend to happen and actual student performance in terms of (a) acquisition of knowledge (didactic goals), (b) development and understanding of concepts and reasoning skills (reflective goals), and (c) ability to make and defend moral decisions and judgments (affective goals). Historical and scientific habits of mind is the heart and soul of inquiry, not data.

Choices for classroom practice will be viewed throughout this book as **divisible into three interlocking dimensions:**

the didactic, which concerns lessons and curriculum that have a **predominantly infor- mation-processing** orientation, promoting the acquisition of data and the transmis- sion of knowledge as major goals;

the reflective, which encompasses lessons and curriculum that have **a predominantly problem-finding and problem-solving orientation**, fostering reasoning skills with the formation and checking of hypotheses; and

the affective, which includes lessons and curriculum that have **a predominantly moral and policymaking orientation**, encouraging an examination of values and the test- ing of beliefs and belief systems.

These three dimensions should be viewed as related, overlapping, and interactive parts of a holistic way of understanding social studies, both theoretically and as taught and expe- rienced in classrooms. Each dimension may be used to generate goals, lesson plans, questions, textual narratives, group projects, lectures, and tests. Taken as a whole, this three-part conception can guide your planning for a particular student audience, as well as assess curriculum choices and student productivity. Think about a powerful lesson as achieving a balance among the three dimensions so proper attention is given to each within a framework of several shared goals during a typical classroom period.

Barr, Barth, and Shermis first suggested three dimensions of teaching and learning that I call the **didactic, reflective,** and **affective** flexible enough to incorporate most the different philosophic viewpoints that have influenced on our field's evolution. Each dimension may be used to guide lesson planning and classroom performance. The three dimensions offer a plan for choices of specific materials and teaching strategies. Given the complexities of social studies, its competing interests, and students' needs, most les- sons have elements of each dimension embedded. However, a lesson is usually given direction by one or two dominant goals that stresses didactic, reflective, or affective purposes.

One goal is usually dominant in directing the path of a lesson, whether discussion, lecture, role-play, simulation, or research project, and tends to reduce the importance of other goals. A lesson that tries to do too much or has conflicting goals usually loses direc- tion and confuses students, whereas a lesson that focuses on limited tasks (e.g., collecting data) produces boredom and disinterest. Like too many screens and too many devices feeding in data, one can easily drown in a sea of information going in different directions.

The point is that we should teach lessons that harmoniously combine and balance all three dimensions, equivalent to the 'arc of inquiry,' LOT+ MOT + HOT (lower, middle, and higher order thinking).

Each dimension, therefore, may be viewed as an organizing idea for planning, choosing content, and evaluating student learning. For example, a lesson in which students are studying the dates of the Mexican Revolution may be safely placed in a didactic dimension. A session in which students analyze Machiavelli's ideas about 'the circle of government' and compare them to U.S. democracy would undoubtedly sit in the reflective dimension. A debate about which U.S. or local government environmental policies and actions that are best for society would belong, for the most part, in the affective dimension. It is quite conceivable that a lesson, unit, or course could shift in direction and character, combining two or all three dimensions in complex ways, even demonstrating an almost perfect balance among the three categories.

The best social studies lessons combine didactic, reflective, and affective purposes to meet an overarching arc of inquiry, the type of teaching and learning we hope to foster with this book, and others like it.

TO DO

If possible, observe several social studies lessons on the same topic. Take notes on the key activities, questions, and answers you observe. Can inquiries and responses be categorized as affective, reflective, or didactic? Is this distinction easy or difficult to determine? Why? Can you improve the distinctions?

LET'S DECIDE

How can you tell whether you have taken a position or chosen a philosophy that supports choices for a sequence of topics, questions, and tests? How would you judge someone who 'just goes along with department plans or district guidelines?' Are guidelines or a formal curriculum enough for quality? Do we need a philosophy and goals of our own? Why or why not? Would you object to teaching methods that impose beliefs on students? Could you follow a philosophy of open-minded inquiry for all?

NOTES

1 Herczog, M. (2013) "Q & A about the College, Career, and Civic Life (C3) Framework for Social studies state standards," *Social Education* 77, 4, 218–219, National Council for the Social Studies.

2 Hertzberg, H. (1981) *Social Studies Reform: 1880–1980* (A Project SPAN Report) (Boulder, CO: Social Science Education Consortium).

3 How some educators have suggested organizing social studies content, see Brubaker, D. L., Simon, L. H. and Williams, J. W. (March 1977) "A Conceptual Framework for Social Studies

Curriculum and Instruction," *Social Education*, 41; Barr, R. D. Barth, J. L. and Shermis, S. S. *Defining the Social Studies, Bulletin*, 51 (Washington, DC: National Council for the Social Studies; and Morrissett, I. "Preferred Approaches to the Teaching of Social Studies," *Social Education*, 41.

4   Barr, Barth, and Shermis (1977) *Defining the Social Studies*.

5   Ibid., p. 63.

6   Ibid., p. 65.

7   Ibid., p. 67.

8   Ibid., p. 68.

9   Fallace, T. (2017) The Intellectual History of the Social Studies. In McGlinn, M. and Bollick, M. (Eds.) *The Wiley Handbook of Social Studies Research* (New York: Wiley & Blackwell), 42-67.

10 Barth, J. L. (1985) NCSS and the Nature of Social Studies. In Davis, O. L. (ed.) *NCSS in Retrospect* (Washington, DC: National Council for the Social Studies), 9–19.

11 Adler, M. J. (ed.) (1984) *The Padeaia Program* (New York: MacMillan).

12 Hirsch, Jr., E. D. (1987) *Cultural Literacy* (Boston: Houghton Mifflin), 127–128.

13 Hirsch, Jr. E. D. (1996) *The Schools We Need and Why We Don't Have Them* (NY: Doubleday.

14 Bagley, W. C. and Alexander, T. (1937) *The Teacher of the Social Studies* (New York: Scribner's).

15 Sizer, T. (1992) *Horace's School: Redesigning the American High School* (Boston: Houghton-Mifflin).

16 Sizer, T. (1996) *Horace's Hope: What Works for the American High School* (Boston: Houghton-Mifflin).

17 Habermas, J. (1988) *On the Logic of the Social Sciences* (Cambridge, MA: Harvard University); Kuhn, T. (1970) *Structure of Scientific Revolutions* (Chicago: University of Chicago Press,).

18 Nelson, J. (1987) "New Criticism and Social Education," *Social Education* 49, 368–371.

19 Bernstein, R. (1983) *The Restructuring of Social and Political Theory* (New York: Harcourt, Brace, Jovanovich), 228.

20 Ibid.

21 Dewey, J. (1933) *How We Think* (Boston: Heath), 28-29.

22 See important books by: Bruner, J. (1966) *Toward a Theory of Instruction* (Cambridge, MA: Harvard University Press); Raths, L., Harmon, M., and Simon, S. (1966) *Values and Teaching* (Columbus, OH); and Maslow, A. (1968) *Toward a Psychology of Being* (Princeton: Van Nostrand).

23 Raths, L. and Simon S., *Values and Teaching*, 12-44.

24 Counts, G. S. (1977) *Dare the Schools Build a New Social Order?* (Carbondale, IL: Southern Illinois University Press) Arcturus paperback reissue of 1932 edition.

25 Hunt, M. P. and Metcalf, L. E. (1955) *Teaching High School Social Studies* (New York). See also, for example, Newmann, F. (1975) *Education for Citizen Action* (Berkeley, CA: University of California Press) and Apple, M. (1979) *Ideology and Curriculum* (London: Routledge & Kegan Paul).

26 Giroux, H. (1983) *Resistance in Education: A Pedagogy for the Opposition* (South Hadley, MA: Bergin & Garcy); McLaren, P., (1988). *Life in Schools* (White Plains, NY: Longman). Also Freire, P. (1973) *Pedagogy of the Oppressed* (New York: Seabury Press).

27 Oliver D. and Shaver, J. (1966) *Teaching Public Issues in the High School* (Boston: Houghton-Mifflin).

28 Goodlad, J. (1983) "What Some Schools and Classrooms Teach," *Educational Leadership* 40, 7, 8–19.

29 Lengel, J. G. and Superka, D. (1982) *Curriculum Organization in Social Studies, The Current State of Social Studies,* A Project SPAN Report, (Boulder, CO), 11–12.

30 Onosko, J. J. (1991) "Comparing Teachers' Instruction to Promote Students' Thinking," *Journal of Curriculum Studies* 22, 5, 443–461

31 Martin, J. R. (March, 1996) "There's Too Much to Teach: Cultural Wealth in an Age of Scarcity," *Educational Researcher* 25, 2, 4–10.

32 Newmann, F. (1990) *Higher-order Thinking in the Social Studies: Education,* Perkins, D. Segal, J. and Voss, J. (eds.) (Hillsdale, NJ: Lawrence Erlbaum Associates).

RESOURCES FOR FURTHER READING

Adler, S. (ed.) (2000) *Critical Issues in Social Studies Teacher Education* (Charlotte, NC: Information Age Publishing).

Apple, M. W. (2019) *Ideology and Curriculum* (New York: Routledge).

Gross, M. H., and Terra, L. (eds.) (2019) *Teaching and Learning the Difficult Past: Comparative Perspectives* (New York: Routledge).

Jorgensen, C. G. (2012) *John Dewey and the Dawn of Social Studies: Unraveling Confliction Interpretations of the 1916 Report: Connections between Theory and Practice, in Informal Reasoning* (Charlotte, NC: Information Age Publishing).

Parker, W. C. (ed.) (2015) *Social Studies Today: Research and Practice* (New York: Routledge).

Riley, K. (ed.) (2006) *Social Reconstruction: People, Politics, Perspectives* (Charlotte, NC: Information Age Publishing).

Schmidt, L. (2018) *Social Studies that Sticks: How to Bring Content and Concepts to Life* (Heinemann Educational Books).

Stern, B. S. (ed.) (2009) *The New Social Studies: People, Projects, Perspectives* (Charlotte, NC: Information Age Publishing).

Waring, S. and Hartshorne, R. (2020) *Conducting Authentic Historical Inquiry* (New York: Columbia Teacher's College Press).

FOR FURTHER STUDY

Apple, M. J. (1982) *Education and Power* (Boston: Routledge & Kegan Paul).

Bakhurst, D. (2011) *The Formation of Reason* (Oxford: UK: Wiley-Blackwell).

Bruner, J. (1962) *The Process of Education* (Cambridge: MA: Harvard University Press).

Davis, O. L. (ed.) (1996) *NCSS in Retrospect.* Bulletin 92. (Washington, DC: National Council for the Social Studies).

Dewey, J. (1922) *Democracy and Education* (New York: Macmillan).

Fenton, E. F. (1967). *The New Social Studies* (New York: Holt, Rinehart & Winston).

Giroux, H. A. (1983) *Theory & Resistance in Education: A Pedagogy for the Opposition* (South Hadley, MA: Bergin & Garvey).

Hirsch, E. D. (1996) *The Schools We Don't Have and Why We Don't Have Them* (New York: Doubleday).

Johnson, E. and Ramos, E. et al. (2020) *The Social Studies Teacher's Toolbox* (Hoboken, NJ: Jossey-Bass / John Wiley & Sons).

Loewen, J. (2010) *Teaching What Really Happened* (Teachers College Press).

Massialas, B. G. and Cox, B. (1966) *Inquiry in the Social Studies* (New York: McGraw-Hill).

National Commission on Excellence in Education (1983) *A Nation at Risk: The Imperative for Educational Reform* (Washington, DC).

National Commission on Social Studies in the Schools (1989) *Charting a Course: Social Studies for the 21st Century: A Report of the National Commission on Social Studies in the Schools* (Washington, DC: National Council for the Social Studies).

Oliver, D. W., and Shaver, J. P. (1966) *Teaching Public Issues in the High School* (Boston, MA: Houghton-Mifflin).

Ross, W. (2014) *The Social Studies Curriculum: Purposes, Problems, and Possibilities* (Albany, NY: State University of New York Press).

Saxe, D. W. (1977) *Social Studies in Schools: A History of the Early Years* (Albany, NY: State University of New York Press).

Stanley, W. B. (1992). *Curriculum for Utopia: Social Reconstructionism and Critical Pedagogy in the Post-Modern Era* (Albany, NY: State University of New York Press).

Starko, A. (2013) *Creativity in the Classroom* (New York: Routledge).

Zevin, J. (2021) *Suspicious History* (Lanham: MD: Rowman & Littlefield).

SOCIAL STUDIES: DEFINITION, ORGANIZATION, AND ORIENTATION

BUILD YOUR OWN LESSON

The challenge: thinking 'on your feet.'

Interact with a new piece of evidence, data, issue, or problem.

Design a lesson of your own using different materials (newly discovered art, music, literature, history, geography, etc.).

Worry not about what you know, but react by thinking about how you would teach the data. Improvise!

Write a didactic, reflective, and affective goal for each document or picture, then add a low, medium, and high order question.

Choose one of the six strategies.

Pick a brief method of evaluating success (verbal, written, and tested).

What questions do the data support? Where do they fit in history?

What is the source and context: time and place? And how does that matter?

Did you find improvisation for the classroom easy or difficult? Why?

Why is it chipped on both sides? Has it been used? How difficult is it to chip a sharp edge on a stone? Is this beautiful?

DOI: 10.4324/9781003026235-3

Figure 1.2: 25,000 year-old Acheulean hand axe (France). Made by Levallois Technique.

Source: Example from La Parrilla, Valladolid, Spain. Jose Benito Alvarez CC: by-SA2.5.1 (2014)

2

THE FIELDS OF SOCIAL STUDIES
Setting Didactic, Reflective and Affective Goals

"History is that certainty produced at the point where the imperfections of memory meet the inadequacies of documentation."

J. Barnes, *The Sense of an Ending*, p. 18.

D1.2.6-8. Explain points of agreement experts have about interpretations and applications of disciplinary concepts and ideas associated with a compelling question.

D1.2.9-12. Explain points of agreement and disagreement experts have about interpretations and applications of disciplinary concepts and ideas associated with a compelling question.

C3 Framework, *p. 23–24.*

OVERVIEW

This chapter describes and integrates all the fields of study that comprise the social studies within an overall philosophic structure of questions and issues using didactic (factual), reflective (analytical), and affective (values and controversies) model.

INTRODUCTION

The social studies is composed of multiples, many subjects, many goals, varied teaching methods, and many shared sources, but is one subject.

Along with our theme of multiples, let's argue for a view of history, geography, and the social sciences as forming a basic body of content that we all share. With the advent of Common Core and the NCSS 3C Framework, we can also share common goals and methodologies, translating the 'arc of inquiry' into exciting everyday lessons.

DOI: 10.4324/9781003026235-4

Social studies teachers have always drawn from many fields, but often viewing each as independent of the others. We might call this a *boxed* approach, each subject neatly defined and walled in, as well as walled out from other related fields. Where is STEM and STEAM? This is a view we hope to overcome so we can move toward greater enrichment from any relevant field.

Actually, the C3 Framework divides fields into a traditional view as separate, while we seek connections between and among subjects. The Framework seems to subscribe to a view of the social studies long gone, that the social sciences are still taught as separate disciplines. In reality, mergers, overlaps, and mixes are prevalent across the social studies, and across the entire spectrum from kindergarten to college.

Over the last few decades there has been a trend toward a fusion of subjects rather than fragmentation, although the recent years have seen a dramatic resurgence of interest in history as the key field, particularly how young people acquire a deeper understanding of the past.[1]

Research on history as seen through the eyes of learners is a most welcome development. These studies provide living examples of conversations, viewpoints, and historical imaginings of children and youth.[2] However, the reawakening of interest in history has also led to proposals that social studies should be subservient to or subsumed under historical studies, an old issue. Geography was once a very important independent subject, a key part of social studies, but it has been largely integrated into the two bread and butter courses that dominate, U.S. and world history.

Although history is and probably should be central, the humanities, the sciences, and particularly the behavioral sciences can be viewed as vital historical elements in a social studies curriculum. Opening up to other subject areas is based on a recognition that many goals are held in common—for example, the development of students' critical thinking skills or interpreting conflicting sources.

Underlying pressures to improve students' reasoning/critical thinking skills are deep philosophical issues about the nature of knowledge and how decisions are made. Integration is facilitated by our conception of teaching social studies as *the intersection* of three major dimensions: (a) the didactic, transmitting factual information; (b) the reflective, fostering analysis and developing reasoning abilities; and (c) the affective, examining issues, taking positions, and deciding whether to take action.

Central to social studies teaching is how we decide to deal with relationships among these approaches (e.g., stress one over the others, balance all three, or fuse them into a single system) and subject matter (approach each discipline separately, proportion time among them according to relative importance, or link them in a general framework). If we view knowledge as fixed truth, our choice of teaching methods and materials will be very different than viewing knowledge as negotiable and open to revision, or as completely subjective and growing out of human perception. How do we deal with fake news, and big lies? Can we simultaneously teach knowledge as fact, view all information as subjective, and make students aware that conclusions are *at best* probabilities—step-by-step approaches subject to human bias and distortion?

WHICH FIELDS MAKE UP THE SOCIAL STUDIES?

Social studies is a school subject firmly grounded in both history and the social sciences. Social studies also has one foot in the humanities and one in the sciences with all that this implies about content and methodology. Although each camp sometimes seeks to control content and alter the curriculum to suit its own interests, no branch has totally dominated the field. With a deep ethical basis, social studies draws from multiple sources to form its goals. During the era of the New Social Studies in the 1960s, Senesh argued that subject integration and borrowing are a necessity:

> Multidisciplinary awareness must include the humanities in the social science curriculum. The humanities reflect our increasing effort to make moral, philosophical, and ethical sense of the world. A society without ethical standards seriously undermines the values widely regarded as providing the optimum social framework. History, literature, drama, art, philosophy, and music (traditional humanities) express and preserve the wisdom of courageous men and women. For writers, artists, and spiritual leaders, the humanities represent a landscape in which human potential can be explored. For scientists and social scientists, the humanities provide a structure of accountability for the consequences of the knowledge they create. At this stage of scientific development, when a lack of moral judgment can lead to global destruction, it is imperative that society guides the use of scientific advances by ethical standards so that knowledge may be used for human betterment and not to destroy.[3]

In the 1950s and early 1960s, teaching social studies was virtually synonymous with teaching history and geography. Major courses and electives were drawn primarily from European or American history, and when teachers strayed into theory or policy, it was either in government, geography, or economics. During the late 1960s and 1970s, a vigorous and expansive reform movement, now referred to as The New Social Studies, attempted to make the social studies much more activist and innovative. This work took several forms:

1. greater attention to persisting and open questions of history applied to daily life, connecting past and present;
2. greater inclusion of a broad swath of social sciences with history (sociology, psychology, anthropology, as well as economics and geography); and
3. greater numbers of modular, topical, and thematic courses centering on key concerns: law studies, women's studies, black history, and multiculturalism.

Classes at the secondary level were expanded to include a wide range of social science disciplines separate from or integrated into the usual U.S., world, or global history and civics courses. There were a number of reasons for the changes. Primary among them is the growing recognition that we all live in a shrinking, interdependent world, where understanding rather than stereotyping foreign cultures is not simply useful, but vital.

At home, too, new immigration from Asia, the Middle East, and Latin America created a diverse mix of students with needs and interests different from those of the students who preceded them. Finally, the social sciences produced a massive flow of research that has borrowed from and influenced the study of history, thereby diminishing the distinctions among fields. The *new social studies*, added material on women, minorities, and cultures beyond North America and Europe, as well as promoting instruction aimed at activating students as consumers and citizens. There was also a concerted effort to help teachers use primary sources and artifacts rather than textbooks as a basis for instruction in history and the social sciences.

This trend has reversed over the last several decades with a renewed emphasis on a more critical history (but surprisingly without much attention to geography or diversity), particularly in the major courses. Change was viewed largely as part of our 'expanded' patriotic heritage. There have been territorial claims (again) for the superiority of history above all other subjects accompanied by investigations of just how students think about and interpret the past and present as constructions based on primary and secondary sources.[4]

At present, the social studies curriculum is focused mainly on three major courses: U.S. History, Global/World History, Government/Civics, with Economics as a low bidder to join the top three. This is a national trend toward consolidation. Thematic, specialized courses are rare now, though Advanced Placement survives in more affluent or ambitious settings. The push for national standards has, in my view, encouraged this development. It is much easier to design tests and standards for a few specified courses than for a wide variety. As we move toward a common (and Common Core) national curriculum and an obsession with math and reading, we also have moved away from variety toward standardization while retaining outmoded state variations based on local prejudices and identities like sensitivity toward gender or race issues. States still pressure textbook companies to write specifically for the story they want locals to value as their identity.

Professional literature for social studies teachers has generally presented different subjects like anthropology as separate entities with their own wholly distinctive concepts and tools.[5]

Some educators show a clear bias in favor of one or another field, usually history is on top, as *the* major foundation for the social studies. History has found new champions in our field, but has actually been the mainstay of social studies education for a century along with extensive borrowing of ideas, materials, and techniques from other fields.[6]

In addition, there is no theoretical consensus concerning history's domain and coverage because history itself has absorbed and contributed to many other fields.[7] Over the last several decades, because of easy and rapid Internet access and widespread dissemination of knowledge from many fields, the distinctions among the disciplines has blurred, and social, historical, and scientific problems have become more interdisciplinary for historians and social studies educators alike. This is healthy since sharing theories and findings like STEM or STEAM from other fields leads to new perspectives and interpretations. But, remember to keep our focus on social studies!

For example, how can economic growth be discussed without historical background, political analysis, and an understanding of the role of science, invention, and technology, to produce social change? How can we approach the story of early humans without drawing upon archeology, geography, biology, and anthropology? How can we understand the stock market without mathematics, economics, and business history?

Assuming that particular disciplines once had entirely distinctive structures (which is questionable), it is hard to defend separate 'boxes' in The Internet Age because historians freely borrow from sociology, biology, and psychology for hypotheses and tools of investigation.[8] As we move further into the 21st century, many scholarly traditions seek more pragmatic and/or holistic approaches to their research and curriculum, tending to apply whatever methods and evidence work best in solving problems. Historically, this development seems entirely justifiable because intellectual dynamism and liveliness are maintained by diffusion of ideas from outside sources. Testing and experimentation, rather than ever-narrowing and exclusive traditions, lead to new theories, changing ideas, and innovative solutions. Social studies as a field has largely resisted change.

Given its past history, social studies will change very slowly to meet new challenge of historical and social science innovation and scholarship. There is a serious lag between cutting-edge research and classroom implementation. Two reasons for pedaling slowly is that our field is beholden to teaching patriotic identity and assigned to build a 'unique' American-centric view of itself and the world.

Innovation in a social studies classroom is limited by several built-in constraints: (a) requirements to impart knowledge in a quantity not suited to audience learning capabilities, (b) a curriculum and methods that are based on coverage of largely unquestioned content, and (c) demands for patriotic and chauvinistic goals that clash with Common Core and C3 goals for critical reading and thinking in American and World society.

Despite these constraints, there is space to maneuver and for change, enhanced by examining a wide variety of fields and sources, as well as a range of analytical tools. Borrowing generously from the sciences, humanities and social sciences, from media and technology, our field can easily fulfill multiple objectives across global studies, U.S. history, civics, economics, and geography. Meanwhile, the steep increase of Internet/Web resources offers endless possibilities for creative lessons. The aim should be to use data to build skills not to increase and store data when the 'cloud' does it easily.

LET'S DECIDE

Do you believe that each subject in social studies is unique, separate, and special? Or do you see each subject as borrowing and sharing? What role does geography play? Should it be a separate course? Should it be taught as a GPS system, or something more?

What makes one subject (e.g., psychology or economics) different or similar? How is history like or not like anthropology? Can science be part of discussions of The Industrial Revolution or the Rise of Cities?

Along with several colleagues or classmates, choose three traditional topics from American studies and three from global studies. Review the content of each lesson. How many describe only events? How many ask questions about character or personality? How many mention cultural values or a cultural setting? Do we add economic conditions or social factors?

HISTORY

History, a major base for social studies, brings to the field a framework and mind-set of its own drawn largely from literary and humanistic traditions that encourage analysis and discussion of narratives, characters, and contexts in a 'particularistic' fashion (specific to a time and place).

In the tradition of the humanities, considerable attention is paid to historical style, symbol, character, meaning, and message, and the dramatic/emotional side of human art and action. Equally important, historians often express generalizations or judgments about the causes and consequences of events. In the tradition of the social sciences, scientific methods are employed to collect sample data sets and subject these to analysis in search of verifiable conclusions about class, race, gender, place, personality, and culture.

Historical study has changed over the last 100 years because of the field's growth in many directions, including a more scientific approach, which has, to a great extent, incorporated social science concerns and methods.[9] Social science has borrowed extensively from history and the sciences to promote research and study, increasing exchanges of data and methodologies.

Although narrative, descriptive historical writing is still prominent, and historians continue to devote a great deal of time and energy to analysis and reanalysis of documentary evidence. Much of this work is now animated by theories and techniques drawn from anthropology, economics, political science, sociology, psychology, law, and philosophy to build a greater World View (Harari, 2016).

In addition, new tools of analysis have grown with digitalization of sources, although this has further to go than the rapid access to information on the Web. Underlying all historical inquiry from time immemorial is a philosophy of authentication of sources and eyewitnesses, that guides our standards for interpretation and judgment.

Any choice of teaching methodology is still motivated by a philosophy, whether consciously expressed or not. History is still a dominant, reinvigorated force in social studies.[10] Whatever the theoretical disputes, social studies at its best has drawn upon 'historical habits of mind' consisting of attitudes and skills, viewed as keys to a critical minded approach to all inquiry.

A report issued decades ago by the Bradley Commission on History in Schools characterizes valued skills that work to:

- understand the significance of the past to their [students'] own lives, both private and public, and to their society.
- distinguish between the important and the inconsequential, to develop the 'discriminating memory' needed for a discerning judgment in public and personal life.
- perceive past events and issues as they were experienced by people at the time, to develop historical empathy as opposed to present-mindedness.
- acquire at one and the same time a comprehension of diverse cultures and shared humanity.
- understand how things happen and how they change, how human intentions matter, but also how their consequences are shaped by the means of carrying them out, in a tangle of purpose and process.
- comprehend the interplay of change and continuity, and avoid assuming that either is somehow more natural, or more to be expected, than the other.
- prepare to live with uncertainties and exasperating, even perilous, unfinished business, realizing that not all problems have solutions.
- grasp the complexity of historical causation, respect particularity, and avoid excessively abstract generalizations.
- appreciate the often tentative nature of judgments about the past, and thereby avoid the temptation to seize on particular 'lessons' of history as cures for present ills.
- recognize the importance of individuals who have made a difference in history, and the significance of personal character for both good and ill.
- appreciate the force of the non-rational, the irrational, and the accidental in history and human affairs.
- understand the relationship between geography and history as a matrix of time and place, and as a context for events.

- read widely and critically to recognize the difference between fact and conjecture, between evidence and assertion, and thereby to frame useful questions.[11]

Notice that many other fields are listed in this set of objectives and that great importance is given to distinguishing 'fact from conjecture,' a goal similar to favorite social studies lessons aimed at separating fact from opinion. Also note the caution at generalizing, and particularly judging, the past without a deep knowledge base. History has always been a rather cautious field, at least in terms of stated principles, as Ibn Khaldun reminded us in 1377.

History is a large and complex field, not easily summarized in terms of interests and method, subject to open and hidden agendas, borrowing methods from the social sciences and the humanities. So, experiment, but be careful generalizing and judging, in social studies. The pursuit is what counts above all, and the methods of inquiry, not settling conclusions quickly. There is always room to review and revise.

TO DECIDE

Some historians like Hugh Trevor-Roper and Gertrude Himmelfarb see the power of historians as imaginative and insightful, arguing that it is an art, more literature than science. Others like Gerhard Ritter associated with the Annales school of French historians developed quantitative history employing raw data to track the lives of ordinary people. Intellectual historians such as Herbert Butterfield, have argued for the significance of ideas in history. Many American historians, like Eric Foner, have developed social history focusing on formerly overlooked ethnic, racial, and socio-economic groups.

There are also Marxist historians like Eric Hobsbawm who view history in an economic framework of class struggle and imperial dominance.

If you read samples of a wide swath of historians, one from each 'school of thought,' decide which fields their views and methods have been borrowed from: Do all agree on goals, methods, and conclusions, or is there widespread disagreement? Why?

TO DO

Develop your own definitions of the following terms: archeology, history, social studies, scientific method, culture, psychology, philosophy, and geography.

Do you see history, philosophy, and culture as part or outside of social studies? Do you see social studies as part of history? If you work out a web or Venn diagram of the relationships among history, philosophy, culture, and the social studies, what would it look like: concentric circles, connected circles, or linked circles? Draw your own conception. Does it agree or disagree with the one we suggest? Why or why not?

THE SOCIAL SCIENCES

A second major base for social studies is the social sciences, many grown out of the biological sciences and mathematics sharing a scientific cast of mindfulness. A premium is placed on building and testing theories and generalizations through observation and experimentation. Hypotheses are usually defined operationally in the social sciences, and evidence is sampled through a plan or design using research tools that are increasingly statistical. The goal is to validate a theory that explains some aspect of human action or psychology. Social science research follows a model drawn for the most part from the hard sciences seeking objective, replicable, valid, and reliable results.[12] Social scientists are frequently interested in studies that cut across cultures, times, and places to identify laws or principles that guide human behavior. In fact, the whole concept of empirical laws and provable theories in the biological sciences is repeated in the social sciences (e.g., the law of supply and demand, the theory of cognitive dissonance), with the aim of validating concepts and rules that can be applied to numerous examples and cases, past, present, and future. An overall orientation is to identify universal patterns (an ideal not always attainable) through the collection and analysis of data acquired by standardized methods that are open to verification and error control.[13]

In contrast, history and the humanities emphasize particular works, events, and people seen as unique to a social context in history. There is wariness at drawing generalizations in history, though this is continuously done. But there is also an increasing mix of theories and methods among and between the social sciences, history, and the humanities. However, differences should not be exaggerated. For instance, there are historians who seek large underlying causes for what happens—that is 'laws of history.' This includes historians such as Immanuel Wallerstein with his view of history as an economic "modern world system,"[14] as well as innovators like historian Fernand Braudel's 'civilizations' and William McNeill's idea about the "human condition."[15]

WHAT DO YOU THINK?

Historians are careful to generalize about history and judge people and decisions, backing their views with evidence and reasons. A high proportion of social scientists seek objective, value-free generalizations, but also come to forthright conclusions that they defend with reasons and research data. Thus approaches to knowledge have much in common. Most historians and social scientists now view the problem of bias and value judgment as generic to all discussion and analysis of human behavior. Across the fields, there is an awareness of the need to identify assumptions and control bias, especially as the pace of disciplinary ex-change and Internet access grows. Seeking truth runs through all contributors to social studies education. The social sciences stress different lines of inquiry, but they all share similar philosophic bases, theories, and investigative approaches. Different goals and concepts for various social sciences may be summarized as follows:

Social Science	Major Concepts and Interests
Anthropology	Culture, Family, Kinship, Belief System
Economics	Markets, Resources, Supply and Demand, Opportunity Cost, Productivity, Exchange System
Geography	Landforms, Ecology, Human–Land Interactions, Place Peoples
Political Science	Power, Government, Interest Groups, Nations
Psychology	Personality, Learning, Individual Psyche, Motivation Deviance
Sociology	Class and Caste, Social Groups, Social Control, Ethnicity and Race
Jurisprudence (Law)	Justice, Order, Equity, Freedom

The ideas of viewing people in systems, factoring in politics, economics, social class, or culture, and analyzing the roots and consequences of actions run through related fields.[16] The how and why of decisions and actions are common threads in social science investigations and history, whether on a personal, group, national, or international level. How we perceive and know is a key question in designing studies and interpreting results.

Thus, major elements of a social science mind-set include:

- identifying and testing broad generalizations and theories against experience, data, and logic.
- acquiring an understanding of the scientific method: a problem is recognized, evidence collected, alternative theories constructed tested, and a solution tested.
- questioning the relation of theory to evidence and to practice: Does the evidence prove a theory enough to justify or support an action?
- understanding that errors exist in all knowledge; estimating size, type, and means of control.
- being ready to admit doubts, ambiguities, and uncertainties, developing a range of probabilities and tests to estimate truthfulness.
- evaluating knowledge claims based on explicit criteria and accurate evidence.
- understanding relationships between and among economic, political, cultural, social, environmental, and historical factors.
- assessing the ways information was collected and reported, noting the credentials and affiliations of witnesses.
- comparing and contrasting categories of events and classes of behavior in order to generate an explanatory theories.
- showing sensitivity to bias, avoiding ethnocentrism and distortion in reporting about people, places, events, and institutions, separating, as much as possible, prejudices, chauvinism, and egocentrism from well-supported conclusions.
- empathizing with others' points of view as a step toward coming to grips with unpopular, unusual, and unfamiliar ideas and feelings.
- developing research skills that include observer techniques, survey design and polling, experimentation, and meta-analysis.

WHAT DO YOU THINK?

Which is your favorite social science? Why did you study it? Did the social science contribute anything to your understanding of human behavior that history did not? Did history assist your study of the social sciences?

Compare the historical and social science mind-sets described earlier. What are the similarities and differences? Do any elements recall scientific method, for example, 'understand that errors exist in all knowledge,' or 'grasp the complexity of … causation?' Go for it.

As discussed in this chapter, history and the social sciences have a great deal in common as methods of inquiry and as subject matter with considerable overlap. Social scientists and historians apply each other's theories and techniques to their own research. Sometimes, borrowing from the humanities and/or the 'hard' sciences enriches the ways subject matter is interpreted. From a social studies perspective, if several disciplines can enhance a student's understanding of human behavior, now or in the past, how might this help them to integrate ideas and build an interpretation, including their own experience, e.g., past plagues and pandemic and COVID-19.

LET'S DECIDE

After examining the historical and social science mind-sets, decide whether they arise from common or different philosophic concerns. Read and discuss your decision with classmates or colleagues, allowing time for questions and answers. What does your decision imply for social studies: different fields or as unified around common questions?

A FUSION MODEL

The methods and ideas of history and the humanities can be merged with those of the social sciences into a single framework generating ideas for curriculum and instruction. Rather than viewing each subject as separate, a discipline, think about them as complementary, e.g., art and history, history and biology, overlapping and connected, providing a rich body of theory and method to apply in teaching.[17]

TO DO

Write your own lesson on any topic as story and as history, as dramatized fiction and as narrative fact. Is it possible to study a topic from only one dimension? Is it possible for a topic to incorporate two or more dimensions?

A unified or holistic approach focuses attention on selecting theories, research methods, and teaching strategies that help us conceptualize a question and/or solve a problem. A single-minded approach tends to pigeonhole topics—Napoleon's character, the teachings of Confucius, the Spanish Civil War, or the COVID-19 pandemic—into neat categories where questions and answers so there is little to disturb our thoughts.

In contrast, the relationships of history and the social sciences, the humanities, and sciences can be conceived as spokes in a wheel that draw on the strength of each to provide 'axle power' to a center.

Think about developing a unit on the Digital/Electronic Revolution that is global in perspective that including innovations as a central idea to review case studies of social adjustment and news feeds. Research the origins and meaning of the Internet, cell phones, tweets and texts, and connectivity. Where and why were these words created and why are they now part of our historical vocabulary?

The fields of study are encompassed below in broader, underlying questions of philosophy, motivation, and expression of ideas illustrated in Fig. 2.1.

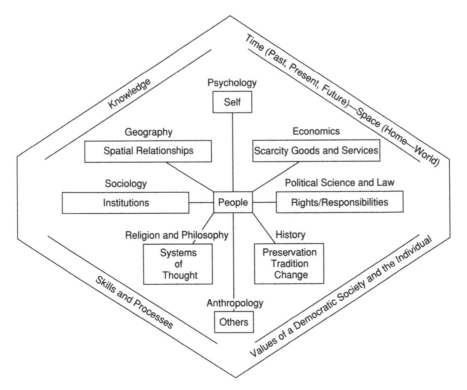

Figure 2.1:   A fusion model for social studies.

PHILOSOPHY AND BELIEF SYSTEMS IN SOCIAL STUDIES

Ultimately, social studies, like history and social science, draws from philosophic concepts to justify what is taught, to whom, and by which method. Social studies is riddled with conflicts about the most profound questions of meaning and judgment Each disagreement can throw light on or engender doubts about nearly every conclusion we hold dear and consider true.

This is why educational questions in social studies often revolve around philosophical issues both ancient and modern, resulting in a search for ways to organize thinking that helps us understand our world. However, most teachers prefer to avoid the tough philosophical questions because these take a lot of discussion and eventually demand judgments. Issues are actually the lifeblood of social studies, not data collection. Issues continue to live forever while facts fade away into the Cloud along with our photo collections.

Perhaps the deepest and most difficult of these issues concerns fact and truth. Social studies is often taught as 'received knowledge,' assumed to be accurate and truthful. Narrators write texts as though they were telling a story from on high as omniscient beings, without bias or personality or context. Didactic goals reinforce fact acquisition, avoiding key questions of selection, perception, honesty, and consistency. Yet from the point of view of modern philosophy, knowledge and definitions are products of theory and all theory is open to debate and discussion. That is what philosophy is supposed to do: change the way we think about basic definitions, about human goals, the way we investigate and accumulate knowledge.

Interpretation, how and why we arrived at a view or conclusion is basic.[18]

Philosophy raises problems concerning how knowledge is selected and collected even now with our vast archives on the 'web'. How do we know we have chosen the relevant data and have not missed out by asking poor questions? How do we know what is reliable, who are keenest eyewitnesses, and who are the biggest fools? How do we know when drama has taken over description? Aren't we the products of a time, place, and culture that has shaped our thinking, our emotions and view of the world? Is there really a universal, objective, verifiable 'truth'?

Perception and theory clearly play a large role in how people absorb and process information. Sometimes theory helps us organize and understand our data, but at times it may blind us to what is really happening. For example, what did the much-celebrated Christopher Columbus actually discover? Wasn't someone 'already here'? What did he really accomplish? How would the Native Americans whom Columbus contacted feel about him (and how do Native Americans feel now?) How easy or difficult would it be to portray Columbus in a negative or positive light? Would our arguments be based on the same 'facts'?

As you can surmise from this example, the same facts and accounts can be turned upside down depending on your theory of culture contact, sympathies, or political philosophy concerning conquest and freedom. A reasonable way out of the dilemma of truth versus perception, objectivity versus subjectivity, is through a critical-mindedness that accepts answers as tentative and open to further examination rather than true for all time.

Both data and process can and should be consistently questioned. Teachers should be wary of hard and fast conclusions, and subject claims to consumer reports style testing. Above all, in the Internet Age and the Time of Division, we need a new kind of data literacy to approach anything and everything from the middle and both ends of the spectrum. A frightening aspect of human beings is their ability to see only what they want to see, regardless of grounded facts.

LET'S DECIDE

By simplifying events, do we introduce inaccuracies and distortions? Yes. By presenting events in all their complexity, do we frustrate and confuse? Yes, again. If you and your colleagues had to choose a best plan for social studies, would it be to include multiple, if clashing, sources or one agreed upon narrative?

Difficult questions of value or meaning are deeply embedded in philosophy and consciously or unconsciously shape our conception of different fields, social studies included.[19] Content and methodology reflect and will continue to reflect many layers of choice, from the data selection to the most complex issues of universal right and wrong.[20]

It is you, the teacher, who must unify the subject in some meaningful way. Usually, the more universal the concept or value, the more power and interest a program will have; conversely, the more specific the issue the faster it's outdated. Whether a lesson is derived from history or social science, some philosophical questions about knowledge issues run throughout the social studies. For example:

Knowledge Questions and Issues

1. What is most worth knowing and who decides?
2. What is truth? Falsity? Can we easily separate the two?
3. Can we identify methods for testing for truth?
4. Can language be trusted or does it beguile us into accepting ideas that are open to question? How can we be taken in by language, image, sounds?
5. Is knowledge absolute, probabilistic, or based only on perception?
6. Is human action determined by environment, social values, genetics, free will, or some combination.
7. What is right and wrong as interpretation, as moral thinking? Is universal acceptance possible or are we culturally bound?
8. Can competing values and viewpoints be treated fairly and a reasonable judgment made?
9. Are there universal rules governing human life and development or are conclusions specific to time and place?
10. How can we judge fairness and justice reasonably?[21]

Tensions in the social studies begin from different philosophies—believer, patriot, good citizen, critical thinker, historian, scientist affecting everyday teaching in important ways. For instance, **those who stress mainly didactic goals and one subject usually want students to acquire knowledge about the world**, but they also want this to be accurate, reliable, and meaningful. The overall goal is collecting solid information.

Those who argue for reflective thinking goals want students to understand evidence, to be critical thinkers using a variety of fields, working to develop systematic inquiry, insight, and interpretation. Reflection demands multiple ways of solving problems. The overall goal is a sense of critical-mindedness.

Finally, **those who fervently endorse affective goals want students to use data, and employ reflective reasoning to probe sensitive issues, to reach defensible judgments**. Affective goals call upon learners to freely express and negotiate views and opinions as a method for sharing perspectives and views with others. The overall goal is to come to judgment, take a stand, negotiate agreements!

A long run goal across all three dimensions is to help everyone in a democratic society tolerate conflicting viewpoints taking steps toward **peacefully working out agreements** most can support for a more smoothly and freely functioning political system. Students are encouraged to examine values, choose, and act upon cherished beliefs, but with the proviso that they defend choices reasonably and accurately, as well as passionately, drawing opponents into conversation and debate.

A wide variety of fields and disciplines contribute to the overall effort as you slowly move through richer and more meaningful questions within each dimension, didactic, reflective, and affective, connecting facts, evidence, reasons, and theories to conclusions, choices, and finally, public action.

APPLYING DIDACTIC, REFLECTIVE, AND AFFECTIVE GOALS

After expressing a good deal of dissatisfaction with the development of social studies, Richard Gross describes "the vision ... that should have been" as "an inclusive single-subject; … essentially thematic and issue-centered; … offered every year of school-ing." He goes on to argue for a social studies that "will have balanced content emphases divided among three sources: societal needs and essentials, student concerns and values, and prime skills, concepts, and generalizations from the social sciences, history, and related subjects."[22] Is this a vision similar to or different from the fusion approach I advocated? Is it a view you approve or disapprove of? Why?

SUMMARY

The big issue for social studies is not its many fields, but the relationship between theory, goals, and practice. Practice without theory tends to reduce every philosophy and tradi-tion to a set of how-to-do-it formulas for content and process but with no inkling about the reasons for conclusions. Theory without practice conveys a set of ideas so lofty and out of touch with real life that most students feel their studies are irrelevant. Ideally, a balance must be struck between theory and practice, philosophy and curriculum, and history and social science to encourage more aware, critical, and sensitive students.

Social studies can be viewed as a subject that rests mainly on history and the social sci-ences for data and theory, but draws on the humanities and 'hard' sciences for ideas. The nature of knowledge is a central problem in teaching social studies. Is knowledge basi-cally verifiable, probabilistic, or perceptual? Tools of analysis can and should be as broad as possible.

The questions we pose as teachers can and should be informed by many disciplines, viewpoints, and sources.

For example, with a slight shift of perspective, Columbus' expedition can be discussed as a cultural conflict and an economic adventure not just an heroic exploration by European adventurers seeking exploitation; the Buddha's Sermons can be discussed as literature and story, as well as religion; the Bill of Rights can be viewed as an expression of 18th century Enlightenment philosophical values, not merely laws; and the idea of nationalism can be studied in long-range historical perspective instead of as a purely 19th-century conception.

Thus, different viewpoints can be used to enrich and extend any lesson. Combining unified or integrated disciplines with social studies goals and methods, we can build from our three-dimensional model of the didactic, reflective, and affective. Link thinking with the three dimensions to build lower, middle, and higher order goals (LOT, MOT, and HOT), see Figure 2.2.

Lower Order Thinking (LOT)
Middle Order Thinking (MOT)
Higher Order Thinking (HOT)

The three dimensions allow us an approach to the curriculum from multiple perspectives and several levels. Any topic or lesson planned or developed 'on the spot' using a historical document you've run across, can be approached as social science, history, literature, and science. Think about reviewing what you know about horses or automobiles from each perspective.

Subsequent chapters discuss goal writing, lesson planning, and all important method-ology, testing didactic, reflective, and affective dimensions, viewing the three as interre-lated, influencing, shaping the others every day in every way.

Higher Order Thinking (HOT)   Middle Order Thinking (MOT)

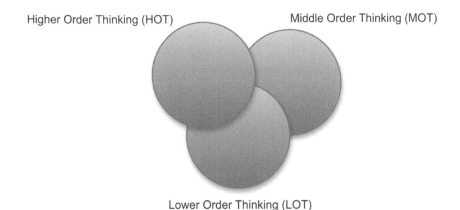

Lower Order Thinking (LOT)

Figure 2.2:   The three dimensions and three orders of thinking.

TO DO

Choose two topics that are commonly taught in middle or secondary school. Develop questions from the perspectives of at least two of our three dimensions and at least two of the disciplines.

The following list may help you generate interesting questions:

1. The Bubonic Plague and COVID-19
2. The American and Haitian Revolutions
3. Colonization of the American Wild West and Siberia
4. Urbanization and Electricity
5. The Seneca Falls Declaration and Role of Women in Ancient Greece and Rome
6. The Rise Speech, and Cell Phones and Communication
7. The American Empire and the re-rise of China in global affairs
8. Novels of WWI and Historian accounts of WWI.
9. Simon Bolivar and Jose San Martin: Latin American Independence in light of Enlightenment thinking and decolonization
10. The Songhai and Mali Empires compared to Roman Empire
11. The Formation of modern India and modern Russia.
12. The 100 Years' War in Europe and the decades long wars in the Near East and Afghanistan
13. Young adult historical literature compared to historical narratives of the American Revolution
14. Global climate change and its deniers

NOTES

1   Van Sledright, B. (2002) *In Search of America's Past* (New York: Teachers College Press).
2   Wineburg, S. (2001) *Historical Thinking and Other Unnatural Acts* (Philadelphia: Temple University Press).

3 Senesh, L. (1967) *The Four Pillars of the Social Science Curriculum*, paper presented at the 1989 General Conference of the Social Science Education Consortium (Boulder, CO), June 1989, 20.

4 Barton, K. C. and Levstik, L. S. (2008) *Research History Education: Theory, Method, and Practice* (New York: Routledge).

5 Morrissett, I. (1966) *Concepts and Structure in the New Social Science Curricula* (New York: Rinehart and Winston).

6 Levstik, L. S. and Tyson, C. (eds.) (2009) *Handbook of Research on Social Studies Education* (New York: Routledge).

7 Van Tassel, D. (1986) Trials of CLIO. In Wronski, S. and Bragaw, D. (ed.) *Social Studies and the Social Sciences: A Fifty Year Perspective* (Washington, DC: National Council for the Social Studies), 1–15.

8 Fenton, E. (1966) A Structure of History. In Morrissett, I. (ed.) *Concepts and Structure in the New Social Science Curricula* (New York: Rinehart and Winston), 38–47.

9 Kammen, M. (ed.) (1980) *The Past Before Us: Contemporary Historical Writing in the United States* (Ithaca, NY: Cornell University Press).

10 Robinson P. and Kirman, J. M. (1986) History, From Monopoly to Dominance. In Wronski, S. and Bragaw, D. (ed.) *Social Studies and the Social Sciences*, 15–27.

11 Bradley Commission on History in Schools (1998) *Building a History Curriculum: Guidelines for Teaching History in Schools* (The Educational Excellence Network).

12 Lambert, K. and Brittan, G. (1970) *An Introduction to the Philosophy of Science* (Englewood Cliffs, NJ: Prentice Hall).

13 Senesh, L., Kuhn, A. and Boulding, K. E. (1973) *Systems Theory and Its Use in the Classroom* (Lafayette, IN: Social Science Education Consortium).

14 Wallerstein, I. (1974, 1975, 1976) *Rise of the Modern World System*, Vols. 1, 2, and 3 (New York: Academic Press); Braudel F. (1995) *History of Civilizations* (New York: Penguin).

15 McNeil, W. (1980) *The Human Condition: An Ecological and Historical View* (Princeton, NJ: Princeton University Press).

16 Kuhn, A. (1975) *Unified Social Science* (Homewood, IL: Dorsey Press).

17 Cherryholmes, C. (1998) *Power and Criticism: Poststructural Investigations in Education* (New York: Teachers College Press).

18 Rorty, R. (1983) *The Consequences of Pragmatism* (Minneapolis: University of Minnesota Press).

19 Dewey, J. (1916) *Democracy and Education* (New York: MacMillan).

20 Senesh, *Four Pillars*.

21 Armstrong, S. (February 2014) "The Revitalization of Social Studies," *Social Education*, 78, 1, 5–6.

22 Gross, R. E., and Dynneson, T. L. (1991) *Social Science Perspectives on Citizenship Education* (New York: Teachers College Press).

FOR FURTHER STUDY

Cuban, L. (2016) *Teaching History Then and Now: A Story of Stability and Change in Schools* (Cambridge, MA.: Harvard University Press).

Dewey, J. (1933) *How We Think* (Chicago: Regnery).

Evans, R. (2004) *The Social Studies Wars* (New York: Teachers College Columbia).

Grant, S. G. (2003) *History Lessons: Teaching, Learning, and Testing in U.S. High School History Classrooms* (Mahwah, NJ: Lawrence Erlbaum Associates).

Hess, D. (2009) *Controversy in the Classroom: The Power of Democratic Discussion* (New York: Routledge).

Muessig, R. H. (ed.) (1980) *The Study and Teaching of Social Science Series: Economics, Political Science, History, Geography, Sociology, and Anthropology* (Columbus, OH: Merrill).

Shaver, J. P. (ed.). (1991) *Handbook of Research on Social Studies Teaching and Learning* (New York: Macmillan).

Sizer, T. R. (1992.) *Horace's School: Redesigning the American High School* (Boston: Houghton-Mifflin).

Stearns, P. N., Wineburg, S. S. and Seixas, P. C. (2000) *Knowing Teaching and Learning History* (New York: New York University Press).

Wineburg, S. (2018) *Why Learn History (When It's Already on Your Phone* (Chicago: University of Chicago Press).

Wronski, S. P., and Bragaw, D. H. (eds.) (1986) *Social Studies and Social Sciences: A Fifty-Year Perspective* (Bulletin 78) (Washington, DC: National Council for the Social Studies).

Zevin, J. and Gerwin, D. (2010) *Teaching World History as Mystery* (New York: Routledge).

Zevin, J. (2021) *Suspicious History: Questioning the Bases for Historical Evidence* (Lanham: MD: Rowman & Littlefield).

THE FIELDS OF SOCIAL STUDIES: SETTING DIDACTIC, REFLECTIVE AND AFFECTIVE GOALS

BUILD YOUR OWN LESSON

The challenge: thinking 'on your feet.'

Interact with a new piece of evidence, data, issue, or problem.

Design a lesson of your own using different materials (newly discovered art, music, literature, history, geography, etc.).

Worry not about what you know, but react by thinking about how you would teach the data. Improvise!

Write a didactic, reflective, and affective goal for each document or picture, then add a low, medium, and high order question.

Choose one of the six strategies.

Pick a brief method of evaluating success (verbal, written, and tested).

What questions do the data support? Where do they fit in history?

What is the source and context: time and place? And how does that matter?

Did you find improvisation for the classroom easy or difficult? Why?

Jim Crack Com'

(1847) [Jim Crack Corn in Vauxhall Comic Songbook, 201–203]

> I sing about de long-tail blue,
> So often you want someting new;
> Wid your desire I'll now comply,
> An' sing about de blue-tail fly.
>   Jim Crack com', I don't care,

DOI: 10.4324/9781003026235-5

Jim Crack com', I don't care,
Jim Crack com', I don't care.
Ole Massa well a-day.

When I was home, I used to wait
On Massa—han' him roun' de plate;
I pass'd de bottle when he was dry,
An' brush'd away de blue-tail fly.
    Jim Crack com', &c

Ole Massa ride in de arternoon,
I follows him wid a kickeribroom;
De pony rear'd when he was dry,
An' bitten by de blue-tail fly.
    Jim Crack com', &c.

De pony jump'd, he rear'd, he pitch'd,
He tumbled Massa in a ditch;
De wonder was he didn't die,
When bitten by de blue-tail fly.
    Jim Crack com', &c.

Dey buried him 'neath a simmon tree;
His paragraph is dere, you'll see;
Beneath de shade he's forced to lie,
All by de means ob de blue-tail fly.
    Jim Crack com', &c.

Ole Massa's dead, so let him res';
Dey say all tings is for de bes'.
I shall neber forget to de day I die,
Ole Massa an' de blue-tail fly.
    Jim Crack com', &c.

What is this song *really* about? What kind of person invented the tune? Would this make a good drama strategy?
    Full lyrics of Dorothy Scarborough's 1925 account in *On the Trail of Negro Folk-Songs* at Archive.org. Origins unknown.

II

TEACHERS AND STUDENTS
A Context for Social Studies Instruction

3

TEACHER ROLES FOR STUDENT AUDIENCES

"Teachers affect eternity; no one can tell where their influence stops."
Henry Adams (1838–1918)

D1.5.6-8. Determine the kinds of sources that will be helpful in answering compelling and supporting questions, taking into consideration multiple points of views represented in the sources.

D1.5.9-12. Determine the kinds of sources that will be helpful in answering compelling and supporting questions, taking into consideration multiple points of view represented in the sources, the types of sources available, and the potential uses of the sources.

C3 Framework, p. 25.

OVERVIEW

This chapter lays out the many roles that teachers can play in classrooms and the nature of the student body, their roles as both interactive teachers and learners.

INTRODUCTION

All of us play roles in life. Teaching is very much a common and vital role, sometimes leading, often dominating, frequently provocative.

As a teacher you are always 'performing' for and with an audience, even when you are being yourself. In this chapter, you are asked to think about the classroom and the school as a stage. Teachers are a key part of the action, but must also juggle audiences and materials to get ideas and feelings across. The actor connects with audiences in much the same way drama does: to educate and entertain.

DOI: 10.4324/9781003026235-7

Teacher-acting, made up of many roles, is defined using our three-part dimensions: (a) didactic (authority, resource, guide); (b) reflective (questioner, scientist, artist); and (c) affective (dramatist, socialization agent, devil's advocate). Understanding these different roles helps you to involve a high proportion of your students in a wide variety of learning activities. Teacher as actor must adapt material to a given student audience, much like presentations in theater. There are many ways to adapt material including role-playing, careful selection of content, and asking exciting questions.

Suggestions are also offered in this chapter for adapting instruction to meet the needs of varied student populations.

Although the majority of your audience may be students of average ability who are basically assimilated into what we have traditionally called *American culture*, more and more frequently individuals come from other cultures with unusual abilities and/or special learning problems. Although excellence in teaching is the foundation on which all adaptations rest, you need to emphasize certain instructional roles for students with special gifts and talents, and others for students with disabilities, some with English as a second language, as well as those who are at risk for other reasons. Look at your potential social studies audience in terms of the roles that you can play to enhance learning. Overall, the focus of this chapter is on how your roles as a teacher help you to connect with your students, as actor to audience, each with particular strengths and weaknesses, to achieve your goals.

INSTRUCTIONAL ROLES

Teachers play many roles in the classroom. Yet seldom do we *consciously* choose from among the many acting possibilities open to us to enhance or create a special effect. Instead, we focus on the subject matter of the lesson, limiting our role to the didactic, providing information. Although knowledge is most certainly a worthy goal of instruction, there are numerous others of equal or greater importance that invite role-play and co-op learning activities. Drama and openness to ideas is a key to exciting teaching of any subject.

Each role has a particular impact on audiences, including getting attention, building self-confidence, reinforcing thinking skills, sparking imagination, and encouraging participation. As in theater, some roles are more dramatic, while others are more involving, but all are related to instruction. When you take on a variety of roles, classroom life becomes more interesting and less predictable than playing only a few parts in the drama.

In preparing and teaching lessons, units, or courses, you can significantly influence student motivation and comprehension by careful selection of roles and approaches to learning styles. Students can be engaged in many ways according to the theory of multiple intelligences first suggested by Howard Gardner.[1] Intelligences should be thought of as overlapping talents and abilities to be drawn upon by teachers to encourage a wide variety of skills in classrooms.

The list includes:

Verbal-linguistic intelligence (ability to use words and language skills)
Logical/mathematical intelligence (ability to use numbers and number concepts)
Visual-spatial intelligence (ability to represent and manipulate spatial relations)
Musical intelligence (ability to think in rhythms, harmony, and patterns)
Kinesthetic intelligence (ability to think and act skillfully in bodily movements)
Intrapersonal intelligence (ability to be introspective and reflective about the self)

Interpersonal intelligence (ability to relate and communicate with others)
Naturalistic intelligence (ability to observe and connect with the natural world)
Existentialistic intelligence (ability to develop and test a philosophy of life)

While there are controversies over experimental proof for multiple intelligences, for our purposes, it is enough to recognize that people have very different abilities that are often restricted by subject matter. For example, history relies heavily on linguistic and spatial (geographic) intelligences but seldom invites musical or visual intelligences, that is art and song. The point is that for social studies, a multiple subject drawing from multiple sources, many skills and talents should be called forth by teachers to lend variety to classroom roles, and to give students with differing abilities the opportunity to shine. You can choose groupings, questions, and materials based on one or more of the multiple intelligences that most effectively achieve didactic, reflective, and/or affective goals. Each role can support one or more aims and intelligences, and you should be able to play a wide range of parts to enhance student growth in knowledge, thinking skills, and the examination of values.

Didactic Roles

Didactic roles usually are designed to convey information. Here the teacher's behavior is geared to provide students with data, 'info in, info out.' As much as possible, these data should be accurate and meaningful material from valuable sources. Three roles suggested to impart knowledge are those of (a) authority, (b) resource, and (c) guide (adviser). Central to all three roles is a didactic concept of teacher as the source of facts, ideas, and conclusions. You present these to learners as predigested (already cooked) information based on your considerable study and examination of sources. Lectures, recitations, and consultations are frequently how knowledge is imparted to students. It is usually assumed (a big assumption) that the information provided is reliable and interesting, contributing to students' stores of material for tests, future courses, and roles as citizens.

As an authority figure, you play a socializing part by simultaneously disciplining a group and sharing knowledge with them.[1] The stress is on giving facts to students who will commit them to memory as part of a base for thinking and valuing. Teachers play the role of data providers by pointing out the documents, scholarly works, references, research techniques, websites and library skills that are necessary to respond to assignments, problems, questions, and hypotheses. Bibliographies may be prepared and used, references and footnotes explained, and information assembled and tested against theories.

How do we encourage students to reflect on songs and images from the past that will build their visual and musical intelligences? What would you focus on in this sheet music from 1904? How do the man and woman view each other? Why does the flag pattern show on both sides of "Her Boy in Blue"? Why are soldiers shown? What does the title, "Her Boy in Blue," mean? Do we still see the same appeals in current wars as in this sheet music? Why or why not? (See Figure 3.1.)

Your role as a guide or adviser is less formal and directive. Although the authoritative aspect remains, the purpose of a guide is more immediate and personal because you are reacting to individuals' problems and needs, aiding them in the development of questions, making challenging statements, and suggesting relevant books and materials. Your word is taken as expert, but students should be expected to check out and reflect on the data.

Figure 3.1: Loss of student interest?

Credit: Photo by Magnet.me on Unsplash.

Therefore, the role of guide or adviser, although seemingly didactic, spills over to reinforce reflective purposes as well.

Thus, you may play several didactic roles: authority, resource, and guide/adviser. Each role presents a somewhat different face to students, more or less formal, more or less aimed at the direct acquisition and testing of knowledge. Overall, however, these didactic roles are central to conveying facts to students needing an information base as a step toward more difficult, demanding, and complex social studies issues.

LET'S DECIDE

Discuss the following questions with two or more colleagues or classmates:

1. Do didactic roles encourage creativity?
2. Do didactic roles promote critical thinking?
3. Do didactic roles engage students in acquiring 'facts' effectively?

Reflective Roles

Reflective roles are designed primarily to promote thinking skills and problem solving. When playing these roles, you stress higher order questions and the formation of ideas, rather than answers per se, or lower order skills such as memorization and comprehension. The essence of reflective roles is fostering students' ideas, for example, producing, revising, and testing hypotheses. Reflective roles may be divided into three major types: (a) catalyst and questioner, (b) scientific inquirer, and (c) artistic interpreter of symbols. Central to all three roles is your commitment to introducing, *but not answering*, problems, questions, mysteries, viewpoints, and issues. As much as possible, reflective roles demand that the

Figure 3.2: WWI song sheet mixing romance and patriotism by popular song-writer Chas W. Duty, 1917.

students take evidence and facts, and interpret these in their own way. It is they who must create theories for explaining an event, topic, or problem. Generally, you as reflective teacher shape, structure, and stimulate ideas by asking questions, redirecting ideas, and challenging hypotheses. Enthusiasm for thinking is the key message conveyed, perhaps more important than the content.[2]

If you interfere with or help students to 'discover' answers, the role-play will shift into the didactic realm and you will lose out on building intra- and interpersonal intelligences. Unlike your performance in authority roles, when you play reflective roles, students question the evidence and its sources. Interpretations are open to attack, revision, and rejection, demanding that meanings or definitions be reformulated and conclusions checked against sources and rules of logic.

The role of questioner is perhaps the most central of all reflective roles because it asks that you act as a philosopher-in-residence.[3] Socrates is still a role model because of his style and ability to ask for clear definitions, present alternative explanations, and call into question hypotheses that most people accept without thinking. You, too, can dig into students' assumptions about any given problem or issue, promoting a good discussion in the process.

Questioning in this sense means that you must poke around into reasoning chains, criticize the degree of objectivity or bias in sources, and act as the skeptic who is not satisfied with neat, clean, pat reasons repeated from a book. Students in the hands of such a questioner must produce and defend ideas they have decided are good, correct, best, or logical. This role is not aimed at helping students amass knowledge. Rather, the point is for them to use knowledge to find and solve problems—how-to thinking. Process rather than product is the key outcome, although product is certainly desirable if students evolve their own responses to a problem.

The scientist role is related to that of questioner, but might be thought of as narrower and more closely focused on scientific reasoning, inductively or deductively.[4] Either way, rules of evidence and logic are followed in a chain of development that strengthens logical and naturalistic intelligences. This chain moves from recognizing and defining a problem through finding alternatives, to developing and testing conclusions, and finally to making a decision. Rules of logic, largely drawn from philosophy, and rules of evidence, largely taken from biology and the social sciences, are used as standards against which the validity is measured. Throughout, you act as the impartial judge who tests student-initiated ideas in the twin crucibles of logic and empirical verification. Your role is to determine whether claims and assertions are indeed proved in terms of scientific probabilities. As scientific inquirer, you can role-play in any number of situations. For example, you can assist in evolving and testing a generalization such as "Levels of community violence increase as the differences between rich and poor populations grow larger." For almost any daily lesson react to student ideas with statements such as, "Can you prove what you say?" or "Where's your evidence for?" "Do we have enough examples to prove our case?" When you ask students to check for proof, limit conclusions, review definitions, or take a look at a rival theory, you and they are playing the role of scientific investigator and bolstering interpersonal intelligence.

The artistic role is also related to that of the questioner, but is focused on personal and creative approaches to problems.[5] These are problems that require interpretation and discussion of meanings and symbols. As an artist-teacher, you can question many aspects of events, sources, and personalities from a humanistic viewpoint that seeks feelings using words, images, and visual representations, visual-spatial intelligences. Deciding on the meaning of something is a major goal of artistic inquiry borrowing methods from historiography and legal reasoning or literary and art criticism. An artist-teacher may turn students' attention to the characters, emotions, and plot of novels such as Amy Tan's *The Joy Luck Club* or African author Chinua Achebe's *Things Fall Apart*, or films such as *All Quiet on the Western Front, El Norte,* or maybe *Legally Blonde.* Connect images and words with social or technological change, very common core.

As additional possibilities, you could bring in or download from the Internet official government photographs of Abraham Lincoln, Jawaharlal Nehru, Sun Yat-sen, Adolf Hitler, Joan of Arc, Hillary Clinton, or Angela Merkel and ask students to compare and contrast leaders in terms of state symbols used in photographs and poses. This could serve as a base for developing generalizations about leaders and leadership in different times and places. Paintings, music, popular songs, and poetry can also serve as motivation for introspection and analysis, with students asked to reflect on the ways in which a time and place may shape culture and ways in which cultural products influence society.

Historiography questions enrich the teacher-artist role by developing student awareness of the way in which history is reported and formulated. Eyewitness reports may be evaluated, with discussion of the different values placed on primary and secondary sources.

The artist role promotes comparison and collation of sources particularly identification of feelings, biases, and assumptions as a story or document is presented. Questioning and analyzing cultural biases and personal feelings lie at the center of the artistic inquirer role.

Thus, reflective roles stresses questioning above all: assumptions, feelings, and biases are challenged and testing hypotheses encouraged. The reflective roles discussed in this section tend to differ in emphasis, but are closely related in purpose and structure. The questioner role stresses philosophic logic: a Socratic style of probing ideas and concepts.[6] The scientist role stresses reasoning based on canons of evidence and logic. The artist role promotes creative problem finding and solving through varied approaches like literary and artistic criticism, historiography inquiry, and examination of values. Reflective roles demand *openness to* innovative ways to study events, people, and places.

TO DO

1. What do you see as the major aims of the reflective role? Which intelligences does reflection support best? Write a statement of this goal in 25 or fewer words.
2. Make a list of 10 activities you could invent or a social studies class that encourages reflective dynamics. Could you plan a lesson that employs five multiple intelligences at the same time?
3. Which type of activity best promotes reflective role development: question-and-answer assignments or playing roles in a mock trial? Why?

Affective Roles

Affective roles are concerned mainly with examination of controversies, contested values and beliefs at personal, social, and philosophical levels. When you play affective roles, you bring values, feelings, and sensitive issues to the forefront of discussion. This should be done in a way that helps students examine their own behavior, as well as the values, beliefs, and actions of others. Affective roles may employ a sense of empathy with audiences and/or build a sense of empathy between audiences and material.

Drawing out emotion is crucial to encouraging students to think about feelings in a history lesson. But teachers often avoid touchy problems for fear that emotions will lead to unruly behavior and lack of resolution. However, studies demonstrate that empathy/feelings have great power in the social studies classroom on a wide range of topics and are actually unavoidable. Could you teach about slavery without emotions or facing history? That is like eliminating rather than coming to grips with subjectivity in the social sciences, while surrounded by feelings.

Affective roles such as dramatist, socializing agent, and devil's advocate seek to awaken students' feelings on a scale that ranges from the beginning of awareness through attitude formation to reasoned judgment.[7] A central goal is the activation and maintenance of decision-making skills that lead students to take and defend positions on a variety of issues. Affective roles channel emotions into a more rational understanding of the different sides in a controversy. Students are pressed to refine and support their own viewpoints by examining the personal and public assumptions offered for each position. Evaluation, judgment, is therefore a strong ultimate component of all affective thinking and role-play.

As a prelude to forming full-scale judgments, you must present enough information for students to use as a base in decision-making. You must question the reasoning underlying their arguments and probe the quality and quantity of evidence to support a position. The overall structure of affective roles is aimed at judgment and decision-making, the formation of defensible value choices, like the greatest good.

To build an awareness of issues and enhance value choices, there are multiple roles to play. First, be the dramatic actor. Second, perform as a socializing agent introducing students to new perspectives. Third, be an agent provocateur or devil's advocate who stimulates debate by switching sides or taking unpopular positions.[8] All three roles work to create a classroom atmosphere in which the free expression of ideas and beliefs, debate, and argument are normal legitimate features of daily discourse. All three roles channel beliefs and emotions through interpersonal relationships that prepare students for public discussion, Because public expression of values and criticism can be sensitive and worrisome to adolescents, affective roles require considerably more skill and attention than do didactic or reflective roles. You should be honest and open to student opinion and careful about making statements before the students have had an opportunity to form views of their own.

In playing the socializing role, you are growing a class structure of orderly, polite, rational arguments and counterarguments following a system to guarantee the largest number of students a chance to participate, building interpersonal skills through group work. To encourage participation, you may use an informal set of guidelines (e.g., speaking in turn, ceding to others, giving recognition to special spokespersons, or assigning student floor managers). More formal involves following Robert's Rules of Order, parliamentary guidelines, or panels. Whatever structure becomes central, it is your role to create a positive feeling toward participation and free expression in a context that allows everyone to have a say in the classroom.[9]

Students are learning to practice democratic methods of participation by involving themselves in the consideration of serious issues. They are developing a commitment to the process of discussion and debate. Naturally, great problems and exciting issues will cause some passion and confusion on occasion. Shouting and a bit of disorder with multiple speakers taking the floor at once should be expected and even cherished as an expression of real caring and commitment. If you have socialized students sufficiently, the disorder (which, it should be noted, is still focused on classwork) will subside. Students will evolve quieter and more organized discussions that encourage thinking and valuing.

CLASSIC RESEARCH REPORT

Teachers should not intervene any more than is absolutely necessary in groups. Most teachers are geared toward jumping in and solving problems to keep 'on track.' With a little patience, cooperative groups often work their way through problems and acquire not only a solution, but also a method of solving similar problems in the future. Choosing when to intervene is part of the art of teaching, and with some restraint you will learn to trust your intuition. Even when intervening, teachers can turn the problem back to the group to solve.

1. When should teachers intervene in activities? When should they refrain? Why?
2. When would you add your ideas to a group discussion? When might you not?

3. Overall, do you think lecture or group problem solving is more effective in promoting student reasoning?

Johnson, D. W., Johnson, R. T. and Houlbec, E. J. (Eds.) (1984) *Circle of Learning: Cooperation in the Classroom* (Alexandria, VA: Association for Supervision and Curriculum Development).

Complementing your role as a socializing agent is an acting job that is common in many repertories. Here you shed a few inhibitions and literally assume a role, perhaps of a famous figure in history, perhaps of a political leader, or maybe that of an expert of some kind, such as a detective, archaeologist, or foreign diplomat. Props may be part of the plan, with visuals aids, costumes, artifacts, posters, or scenery added to gain attention and make a point. The acting role is intended to motivate students and build their awareness of the emotional nuances that might have been part of a situation. For instance, a dramatization, with a script of President Truman's decision to drop the atomic bomb on Nagasaki and Hiroshima could be reenacted with the teacher as director and students playing parts acting as a jury.

Making a verdict. Nearly all levels of affect and interpersonal skills would be developed for a bomb lesson, a valuable exercise in critical thinking aimed at an ethical conclusion on the use of force and the value of human life. Dramatic case studies attract and hold attention, promote participation, and raise awareness of a host of governmental, political, and socio-cultural issues leading eventually to students' reappraisal of their decisions. Case studies also take a great deal of time and preparation and should be treated as special events.

However, you may also dramatize brief cases or issues as these arise on a daily basis in the news, in textbooks, or through other media. Acting can include simply playing the detective and calling attention to an inconsistency in a report or by pointing out a biased remark in a textbook, or portraying another viewpoint. Perform the actor role to create an awareness of beliefs and values of which students were not previously fully conscious by directly calling their emotions into play.

Finally, you can use both socialization and dramatic techniques to develop a third, affective role—that of the devil's advocate or agent provocateur—stressing alternative ideas to whatever students suggest. As devil's advocate, you may probe, redirect, and cross-examine positions as these are placed on the table during a discussion. In this role, you purposely express unpopular, unpleasant, or even untenable (wacky) theories, judgments, and beliefs as a way of testing students' ideas. You can use questions and 'redirects,' or you may offer fully prepared positions to counter and disprove students' claims.

Students unused to devil's advocacy by their teacher may at first feel disoriented and confused, but soon come to enjoy the challenge. They feel particularly successful if you are defeated in argument, which should certainly happen, so plan it that way. As democratic discussion becomes familiar and comfortable, the number of students who frequently ask and answer questions will rise.[10] As the students grow more experienced with you playing roles, they also take on parts, performing tasks usually modeled by you. They may even become self-regulated discoverers!

A provocateur or devil's advocate role is probably most useful when controversial issues are debated and discussed, especially if these are clearly organized into camps or sides that can be reviewed and presented by classmates. More ambiguous problems or moral dilemmas are better approached through the other roles discussed in this section, although some teacher roles such as those of guide, questioner, and socializing agent can probably cut across the distinctions and be useful in many types of classroom activities.

Thus, you have available to you a wide range of roles (and accompanying behaviors) that can have a significant impact on student motivation, thinking, and feeling. In a classroom, use of many roles leads to more thoughtful consideration of the material under study. The various roles—guide, resource, and authority; artist, scientist, and catalyst; actor, socializing agent, and provocateur—affect students by promoting didactic, reflective, and/or affective learning. You have the opportunity to consciously choose and apply one or more of the roles outlined here for teaching varied goals and topics. Furthermore, create a more active, thoughtful, and ethically minded classroom, draw on all roles at different points during the year for variety, enjoyment, and challenge your students.

WHAT DO YOU THINK?

1. Which affective roles do you envision for your classroom? Which do you believe will be most effective? Which do you see as most comfortable? Why?
2. Plan a drama in which you act the role of 'Speaker of the House' while the students must consider several bills that might shut down the government. Assign students to political parties and districts that resemble those in the United States now. Write up at least three different bills: one on immigration, one on gun control, and a third on health care programs. Give these to your congress for debate and discussion. Dress up for the occasion. Be sure to record student votes and announce these publicly.
3. Invent your own role in a class drama, maybe mayor, or Queen and write a script for everyone to follow, leaving sections missing for student improvisation.

YOUR STUDENT AUDIENCE: THE ADOLESCENT AND YOUNG ADULT

Adolescence is a period of rapid physical, social, intellectual, and emotional changes.

Children are becoming young adults. Adulthood entails the experience of physical maturation, including the heightened sexual awareness of puberty. Our audience of young men and women may have experienced significant physical changes beginning as early as age 10 and continuing to age 17 or 18. The average age for the onset of puberty is now 12 to 14. Teachers and classmates, especially in middle or junior high school, often note the bewildering sizes and shapes of the adolescent community, as well as their frequently peculiar or exaggerated social behaviors. Some are very tall, others short, some hungry all the time, others tired, some in a state of emotional tension, others so relaxed you wonder if they are breathing. Although these extremes can be a source of amusement, the behaviors and growth patterns symbolize the dramatic changes of the teen years. An important aspect in dealing with this rapidly, but unevenly, maturing audience is to assure them that their differences will all even out and to see themselves in a positive light. Point out that they are also growing more intelligent every day.[11]

Sexuality is a major interest of your adolescent audience, many of whom can switch in one year from active disregard to passionate interest and physical experimentation. Sexual activity, according to most studies, is quite common by high school, although many schools seem to work at not noticing student involvements unless pregnancies develop. Other schools offer a variety of sex education programs. More important perhaps than the sexual interest and activity is the development of student identities as men and women with distinct sexual preferences, LGBTQ. These are often a source of great anxiety and embarrassment. Your role should be to promote discussion of personal identification, particularly on gender and racial issues, whatever the choices, demonstrating that these topics belong to social studies as important social issues, rather than taboos. Many areas of the U.S. have adopted far more relaxed social norms toward identification than was previously the case, and gay marriage has been legalized throughout the country.

The combination of physical changes, intellectual growth, and sexual awareness makes for a potent brew of problems. Preteen students are usually less self-conscious than the teenage group, oriented more toward peers and the outside world than parents and teachers. These changes often produce sharp alterations of emotions. On occasion, you as teacher may benefit from a 'high' by harnessing student involvement to a lesson that results in sharp insights and quality work. On other occasions, you may suffer from a 'low' that produces negative or cynical feelings toward your subject, foul language, and an overall attitude of hostility toward school discipline and authority.

Although a teacher and a student may really be at odds on an issue, most of the control problems in middle or junior high school are expressions of adolescent difficulties and a desire for freedom from social constraints, rather than personal attacks. As a guide and questioner, working to defuse some of this hostility and cynicism by regularly assessing class feelings or inquiring after individuals' problems, health, and interests. Avoid rushing to judgment on a student's behavior until you have investigated the causes.

Of course, this does not mean that immoral, insensitive, rude, or violent behavior should be overlooked or excused, but you should approach your audience analytically if you can, identifying issues, determining how serious a problem has become. Remember that adolescent growth patterns may render students more emotional, but also more intellectually alive and sensitive than in elementary school. They know a great deal about the world around them, while coming to terms with their own feelings on a wide range of personal, social, and societal issues.

On the intellectual level, most secondary students experience a leap from the concrete to the abstract operational stage, in terms of Piaget's categories of child development.[12] According to Piaget's research, which is widely accepted in education, we can expect the following intellectual changes: The *concrete* stage generally lasts from about age 5 to 11. Students use a hands–on approach to the world and to new events, and they begin to see the reversibility of logic. By about age 11 or 12, students reach the *formal operational stage*, dominated by abstract reasoning and problem solving. This ties in with reinforcing the growth multiple intelligences.

Most secondary students have reached the stage of formal operations, although their abilities are sporadic and uneven; many are more comfortable with the concrete stage, well into the high school years. Although research generally supports Piaget's view of child development, critics have complained about a number of issues.[13] Nonetheless, there is little controversy about secondary students' potential for abstract reasoning. It is up to the teacher and the curriculum to take advantage of this potential by involving students in tasks that open up rather than limit imagination. Thus, in Piaget's terms, all or nearly all adolescents have moved at least partially from the concrete to the abstract levels of reasoning by the time they leave the middle grades and are capable of higher orders of inquiry.

Abstract reasoning abilities present great opportunities for the teacher because this is an audience that has the background and conceptual development to verbalize problems, identify causes, and debate issues while taking others' feelings and arguments into consideration. Logical faculties are fully developed for the vast majority of students by the secondary grades, at levels where they can be challenged to engage in sophisticated reasoning activities involving inference, interpolation and extrapolation, induction and deduction, and judgments. I firmly believe that secondary students need to participate in discussions even if they are a bit immature. They need their views taken seriously even if not fully developed. So play the accepting role.

Your audience has passed childhood in the sense that they are far more sharply aware of themselves and others. They are fully integrated into new technologies and can make decisions on abstract principles and rules. Unfortunately, growth at this age is uneven and may produce less than perfectly satisfying results for you, the teacher, as well as a good deal of disciplinary problems. Nevertheless, it is better to approach the secondary audience as more mature because this contributes to feelings of self-worth, which, in the long run, translate into positive educational outcomes, greater interest in subject matter, and more self-regulated-productivity in school.

In social studies, there are serious credibility problems for adolescent youngsters in dealing with a good portion of the current curriculum.[14] Remember that these young people are in the process of forming individual identities, changing and growing, becoming sexually aware and perhaps active, and undergoing significant intellectual development. They are also seeking to be independent and wish to place some distance between themselves and the authorities around them. The secondary school audience is in the process of seeing others and the world around them in a new light—one that differs from their trusting childhood beliefs and images. To treat this audience as naïve and isolated is a grave error that often leads to cynical attitudes toward the subject, the teacher, and school. It is better to discuss problems and issues than to offer sanitized images of political and social issues, to promote political adult heroes and heroines uncritically, or to avoid or cover up sexual references. Solid evidence, well presented, followed by serious and intelligent debate, should go a long way toward impressing our secondary audience, particularly if their ideas and beliefs are treated with interest and respect. Although unpleasant remarks may be made and topics may encourage heavy criticism and angry emotions, in the long run this process will foster the transition of young people from childhood to adolescence to a true adulthood in which they demonstrate an interest and involvement in public affairs. Learning to engage in frank debate and discussion in secondary school classrooms has been proven to build good citizens.

Therefore, recommendations can be made:

- take advantage of their growing intellectual abilities by encouraging problem solving,
- incorporate student feelings and values into everyday discussions,
- regularly bring up current events and ask how students view the issues of the day,
- empathize now and then with students' emotions and worries,
- utilize increasing awareness of self and the world to reach decisions on controversial personal and social issues,
- be ready to discuss personal problems openly,
- involve students in classroom planning,

- build in opportunities to involve students through panels, debates, games, and socio-drama, and
- be humorous, but refrain from embarrassing your audience as a group or individuals about sensitive problems.

Special Students

Different groups exist within any large population, varying in terms of background, ability, and talent. We are all familiar with young people who exhibit significantly greater skills than others, either physical or intellectual, and with those who display serious emotional or learning problems or endure physical disabilities. In addition, in our economically unequal society, many young people have difficulties adjusting to school because of family poverty, negative attitudes, and other socio-cultural disadvantages.

Social studies teachers, like all teachers, must educate students with special problems and special gifts. Unfortunately, our educational system often cannot provide the resources needed to deal with special groups. Stereotypical attitudes toward young people who are poor, gifted, non-White, foreign-born, or disabled frequently render potentially helpful programs ineffective. Despite these problems, however, social studies can be adapted to the needs of various special groups. Effective instructional techniques can be appropriately adapted for all students, and that your task when teaching students with special needs is to put your effort into those adaptations. Students with special needs may require extra attention, but they should be treated as capable of achieving the same didactic, reflective, and affective goals as their peers, although at different rates and with varying degrees of success.

At-Risk Students

At-risk students are young people who are likely to drop out of school, usually for emotional and/or economic reasons. Many are urban-based people of color, often from groups in the United States with histories of isolation and impoverishment.[15] Many must work to supplement family income; for some, street life is far more attractive than either work or school—neither of which has provided a satisfying experience. A relatively small proportion suffers from mental or emotional disorders, or has a drug or alcohol habit that dramatically reduces their learning ability and reduces their chances of graduating. A fair proportion comes from cultural backgrounds that may add a language and/or customs barrier to their adjustment. Many need instructional approaches and materials with clear and immediate application to the world outside of school, and they need help in developing skills that will allow them to grow and improve in terms of intellectual competence, job opportunities, and, perhaps most important, self- confidence.

Attitudes are an important part of learning. Unfortunately, intellectual skills and classroom accomplishments, social influences, and innate ability are often confused Social prejudices tend to suggest that at-risk students are either lazy or unintelligent; in fact, as a population, at-risk students represent the same normal curve of skills, abilities, and talents as any other group. They frequently perform at lower levels, however, because of low social status, poor self-esteem, or underdeveloped reading and writing skills.

Although you cannot personally change the socioeconomic circumstances of at-risk students, you can adapt teaching to achieve changes in self-image, interest, and achievement.

In general, didactic approaches such as lectures and recitation are less successful with poorly prepared students who are alienated, restless, and skeptical.[16] A number of projects and resources have been developed for at-risk youth, and several professional organizations offer training for teachers as well as curriculum materials. (See Appendix A for a list of these resources and organizations.)

Many instructional adaptations can be effective with at-risk students. Some are particularly useful in raising self-esteem, while others seek to increase prosocial behavior through group projects and peer interaction.[17] Among the suggestions are:

- increased attention and more positive feedback,
- smaller classes and cooperative learning within larger classes,
- activities like role-playing and simulations, including music and rap,
- frequent evaluation of incremental learning,
- integration of students' interests and traditions into the classroom,
- infusion of everyday examples into instruction and an emphasis on analogies to real life in history and social science lessons,
- spontaneity—a willingness to drop scheduled work occasionally to discuss students' problems, current events, and social issues,
- frequent feedback (both written and verbal) with strong encouragement of expression of individual views, and
- a stress on student interaction with the environment outside the school, including field trips.

Students with Physical and Developmental Disabilities

Students with disabilities are a complex group with an enormous range of problems and talents: Some have learning deficiencies, others have physical or emotional problems, but function at high intellectual levels. The behavior of some students indicates multiple learning problems that are difficult to separate and diagnose. There are very bright students who achieve at low levels. Poor performance may arise from lack of interest in a subject or in the total school experience, from inattention growing out of emotional difficulties or physical deficits such as poor hearing or vision, or from poor language and writing skills.

RESEARCH REPORT

"It is helpful if teachers are prepared to understand cultural diversity and get a sense of how their students are thinking, which would help educators understand how to interact with their students." Tan (2011) noted that "in-depth understanding will eliminate guesswork and unrealistic expectations and in the process promote tolerance and acceptance of diversity in ways of knowing" (p. 559). It is especially important in social studies instruction as it tangles with different values and perspectives. What is more, teachers may motivate students' interest beginning from their cultural preference. As the difficulties would be compounded when the students have learning disabilities, teachers should consider all these factors.

In a study of moderately or mildly disabled students, mainstreaming and peer tutoring was found to be superior to segregated classes with specialized approaches to all kinds of disabilities. Mainstreaming tends to improve grades and raise students' self-esteem through enriched programs and contact with peers, and also increases prosocial attitudes toward other racial and ethnic minority groups.

Yang, L. A. (2012) "Comprehensive Look at Social Studies Instruction: Seeking Effective Strategies," *LC Journal of Special Education* 6, 9. www.lynchburg.edu/graduate.

Because of federal legislation over the past two decades—in particular, PL 94–142, the Education of All Handicapped Children Act of 1975, and the Americans with Disabilities Act (ADA) passed in 1990—young people with disabilities now have many more resources available to them in schools, including more accessible physical arrangements, special curriculum programs, and expert diagnosis. In many schools, special classes are available for nearly every type of disabling condition (retardation, developmental and emotional disabilities, sensory loss, etc.) while other schools offer programs for those who can adapt to the regular classroom—an effort usually referred to as *mainstreaming*. Because the ADA mandates "least restrictive environment," many schools and systems are adopting a mixed model in which special education students are integrated into a regular education class that is taught by a team of teachers.

As with at-risk students, your focus in teaching students with developmental or physical disabilities focuses on instructional opportunities to bolster self-confidence as well as skills and intellect.[18] One simple adaptation is to build into coursework examples of people who have dealt with disabilities; such lessons promote self-esteem for students with disabilities and foster tolerant attitudes and respect among their peers.

Secondary students enjoy hands-on activities that involve role-play, map-making, and photograph collecting.[19] Students with disabilities constitute a large and varied group. Those who are physically disabled may be very intelligent, whereas those who are classified as retarded may possess quite advanced sensorimotor skills.

Several national organizations articulate the needs of students with disabilities; a few are broad-based and include all aspects of the exceptional child, whereas others focus on children with particular problems. (See Appendix A for a list of these organizations.)

A number of instructional adaptations have proved effective with students with physical and developmental disabilities, including the following:[20]

- the use of concrete rather than abstract examples of ideas and concepts (e.g., three-dimensional models rather than maps);
- hands-on activities that students must plan, direct, and produce, such as the setting up of a model airplane factory, including assembly line production, production counts, and time limits;
- varied instructional modes that appeal to students with different cognitive levels and respond to different stimuli—visual, auditory, tactile;
- smaller amounts of information in discrete lessons keyed to one or two major points;
- demonstrations—storytelling, speeches, show-and-tell projects, student bulletin boards and posters, songs, plays—rather than lecture; and
- frequent evaluation and feedback on incremental learning, plus positive feedback.

Gifted, Talented, and Creative Students

Gifted and talented students are a diverse group who display outstanding abilities, talents, or skills. Such students may be all-around academic achievers, and show an astonishing talent in a single field like art or mathematics, or may be highly skilled in computer or technology. They may also have behavior problems and be bored by school. Some obtain high standardized test scores, yet receive low grades from teachers; others perform with ease in some areas, but struggle in others. Most students are classified as gifted on the basis of grades, reading scores, teacher recommendations, and/or performances on standardized tests of creativity and intelligence.

Given the structure of most secondary schools and the lack of federal or state funding in support of gifted, talented, and creative programs, many teachers overlook or misdiagnose the needs of these students. Many assume that those who are gifted or talented need little or no special help because they already have advantages conferred on them by birth and/or upbringing. In fact, such assumptions often lead teachers to overlook students from minority or economically disadvantaged backgrounds, or to fail to recognize the special needs of more advantaged students.

Students who are gifted and talented may have problems compounded by a lack of precise diagnostic tools (as compared with those for other exceptional youth). from which reliable judgments can be made. Creativity in particular is difficult to assess: definitions of *creativity* are open to debate, and tests commonly used for evaluation are expensive, time-consuming, and cumbersome. Intelligence tests, by contrast, are well organized and developed, but measure a narrow spectrum of ability— specifically, reasoning skills and knowledge.

Social studies teachers usually view above-average or bright students as candidates for either enrichment activities or acceleration. Schools provide enrichment possibilities, but tend to avoid acceleration (skipping grades) because of potential social problems. Social studies enrichment most often involves an expansion of courses, readings, and coverage, or an in-depth study of one or more topics. Some schools attempt to reach the gifted through clubs, special projects, mini-courses, or subjects that are not part of the regular curriculum. Advanced placement (AP) programs in U.S. and European history are common. Many teachers see enrichment as an opportunity to increase *the quantity* of history or social science offered to students; they overlook the need to build analytical skills.

Gifted, talented, and creative students can certainly move farther, faster, and deeper than most of their peers, but they are also vulnerable to peer and parental pressure just as students with handicaps are—because they are 'different.' Students with intellectual or creative gifts are sometimes seen negatively by some peers out of fear awe, jealousy, or bias. Some may have maladjustments to their social settings or rebel against controls because of what may be intense pressure to succeed; this reaction compounds the universal adolescent problems of maturation, self-definition, and self-esteem. An example is test anxiety, increasingly common at the secondary school level for the brightest students.[21]

High-ability students will be better engaged by a teacher who presents challenges than by one who seeks to cover ground. Gifted and talented need advanced problem finding and problem solving that require them to analyze, synthesize, and evaluate data. They need the opportunity to use their imaginations in mind-stretching activities.[22] For more extensive information on issues, materials, and methods appropriate to education of the gifted, contact to organizations that act as advocates for gifted and creative students. (A list of these is provided in Appendix A.)

Callahan has suggested a number of research-based instructional adaptations for the gifted and talented, including:[23]

- presenting challenges that pique curiosity and provoke imagination—research projects, surveys, or student-designed experiments;
- using popular material (songs, films) to emphasize analysis and judgment;
- focusing on problematic, paradoxical, or controversial issues;
- creative reading assignments involving issues and controversies;
- student participation in and leadership of panels, debates, simulations, or role-playing;
- use of outside resources—talks by area college professors or other experts, field trips;
- longer discussion periods, with an emphasis on critical thinking;
- enrichment through integration of other disciplines—music, art, literature, current events; and
- inclusion of the latest advances in cell phone, iPad, and computer technology, both as a potential research tool and for simulation activities.

Second-Language Students and the Multicultural Classroom

Over the last three decades, the United States and Canada have become the nations of preference for hundreds of thousands of newcomers from around the world. Although immigrants during the 20th century came first from Western Europe and then Eastern and Southern Europe, more recent waves have originated in Asia, Latin America, the Middle East, and parts of Africa. These new populations are reflected in our classrooms, particularly in large urban centers. Most of the new students occupying seats nowadays are from Asia or Latin America. Overall, about 50% of the urban U.S. student population are currently immigrants or minority students. Many of these youth do not speak English as their primary language, although many may speak some English and one or more other languages. Spanish speakers are by far the most important of the second language groups. The 2020 census reports that there are more than 50 million Hispanic residents, old and new, in the United States (about 20% of the total population) and growing fast.

As a result of these population changes, many educators are arguing in favor of altering the social studies curriculum in the direction of multicultural education, usually taken to mean recognition and respect for the diverse groups comprising our society, incorporating their traditions into U.S. culture. This approach, which stresses the acceptance and the celebration of diversity, has been called *cultural pluralism*. Not everyone is happy with this compromise. Some would like to see a return to the view that American traditions are firmly rooted in Western Europe and that English should be the major or even sole mode of communication throughout the nation. Others argue that each group should create its own tradition as a complement to the mainstream culture (e.g., Afro-centric or Hispano-centric education rather than a Eurocentric view).[24]

Although I generally agree with proposals for multicultural social studies education, care should be given to its content and implementation. Changing ethnic populations are an insufficient justification for adopting a pluralistic conception of society. Worldwide changes in communication, the emergence of an international economy, and cultural diffusion of ideas, customs, and artifacts are powerful incentives to respect other cultures even if there were many fewer representatives of those cultures among us. The United States and Canada are moving in the direction of great cultural diversity; the importance of tolerance and global understanding other cultures and migrants has become a high priority.

Second language speakers are one aspect of the more general problem of multicultural education. All the newcomers, including those lacking English, have brought with them prospects for success and cultural enrichment, as well as a variety of social and educational problems. Some are bilingual or multilingual whereas others are monolingual and sometimes illiterate even in their own tongue. Most educators agree that the increasingly diverse mix of immigrants requires acquisition of mainstream language and assistance in understanding and adapting to American customs. There should also be curriculum development so people from a variety of cultures and places see themselves in the textbooks and lessons they study!

Many classroom practices have been suggested to aid second language students.[25] A number of classroom adaptations have been offered to overcome language deficiencies, e.g.:[26]

- motivate interest by using audiovisual materials that are gripping and easy to interpret,
- incorporate key words and phrases from the students' cultures into daily lessons,
- invite students to contribute stories and accounts of their own cultures for others,
- encourage students to translate for each other and back into English,
- allow a few minutes of extra preparation time for answers to questions or to tests and then go over responses in class,
- permit longer response and preparation times than usual and correct errors supportively,
- show respect for and interest in other cultures, inviting shared experiences, and tolerance among groups and individuals.

SUMMARY

Teacher and student roles are similar to roles played by actors and audiences. Actors and audiences were conceived as having a strong interlocking influential relationship. The roles you play as teacher were conceived as following didactic, reflective, and affective goals. Didactic roles include authority, resource, and guide; reflective roles include questioner, scientist, and artist; and affective roles comprise dramatist, socializing agent, and devil's advocate. It was argued that *social studies is an especially inviting field for both teacher and student role-playing* in a wide variety of situations to motivate and involve student audiences with issues and subject matter.

Just as you will find yourself choosing among a number of instructional roles in a middle or high school you will also be faced with learners who vary in many ways. Special groups have received more attention in recent decades, particularly students with language, physical, and developmental disabilities. Other students with special needs—particularly at-risk students and those who are gifted and talented—have received less attention than they deserve. Honors, enrichment, and AP programs are available for the high achieving group at many schools, while there are probably insufficient programs to help the at risk.

It is likely that people of color from diverse cultural backgrounds and second language learners will become more and more of a presence in future classrooms, increasing the trend toward literacy instruction and research promoted by Common Core standards.

Most adaptations (including frequent positive feedback, close reading, selective coverage, critical thinking, examining values and attitudes, the creative integration of other disciplines and of outside resources) constitute the simple act of good teaching for all. If you find yourself confronted with a classroom whose occupants have wide differences in interest, ability, and skill, by all means contact the numerous professional organizations that provide strategies and materials for teaching those with special needs. But remember that every student in your classroom has a special need and talent, and what you bring to each individual student you bring to all of your students.

NOTES

1   Busayanon, K. (2018). "A New 21st Century Classroom Management Model For Pre-Service Social Studies Teacher Development," *Proceedings of Teaching and Education Conferences* 8309722 (International Institute of Social and Economic Sciences).

2   Rosenshine, B. and Furst, N. (1979): "Enthusiastic Teaching: A Research Review," *School Review*, 78, 4, 23–39.

3   Dillon, J. T. (1988). *Questioning and Teaching* (New York: Teachers College Press).

4   Whimbey, A. (1984) "The Key to Higher-Order Thinking Is Precise Processing," *Educational Leadership*, 42, 1, 66–70.

5   Rubin, L. (1985) *Artistry in Teaching* (New York: Random House).

6   Oliver, D. and Shaver, J. (1966) *Teaching Public Issues in the High School* (Boston: Houghton-Mifflin).

7   Krathwohl, D. R. (ed.) (1964) *Taxonomy of Educational Objectives: Handbook II. The Affective Domain* (New York: McGraw-Hill).

8   Singer, A. and Muriel, P. A. (2020) *Supporting Civic Education with Student Activism* (New York, Routledge).

9   Shaftel, A. R. and Shaftel, G. (1967) *Role-Playing for Social Values: Decision-Making in the Social Studies* (Englewood Cliffs, NJ: Prentice Hall).

10 Dillon, J. T. (1983) "Cognitive Complexity and Duration of Classroom Speech," *Instructional Science* 12, 59–66.

11 Arnett, J. J. (2018) *Adolescence and Emerging Adulthood: A Cultural Approach* (New York: Pearson).

12 Piaget, J. (1963) *The Origins of Intelligence in Children* (New York: W.W. Norton Co.).

13 For example: Morra, S., Gobbo, C. et. al (2009) *Cognitive Development: Neo-Piagetian Perspectives* (New York: Psychology Press).

14 Rezan, A. (2006) "School Alienation: Gender, Socio-Economic Status and Anger in High School Adolescents," *Educational Sciences: Theory and Practice*, 721–726.

15 Rumberger, R. W. (1987) "High School Dropouts: A Review of Issues and Evidence," *Review of Educational Research*, 57, 101–21.

16 Winne, P. H. and Hadwin, A. F. (2008) The Weave of Motivation and Self-Regulated Learning. In Schunk, D. H. and Zimmerman, B. J., *Motivation and Self-Regulated Learning: Theory, Research, and Application* (New York, NY: Routledge), 297–314

17 Jacobson, R., Halvorsen, A. et al. (2018) "Thinking Deeply, Thinking Emotionally: How High School Students Make Sense of Evidence," *Theory and Research in Social Education*, 46, 232–276.

18 Grossman, P. (ed.) (2018) *Teaching Core Practices in Teacher Education* (Harvard Education Press).

19 Shah, N. (Spring, 2010) "Into the Mainstream," *Teaching Tolerance*, 46, 37, www.teachingtolerance.org/magazine.

20 Hammond, Z. (2015) *Culturally Responsive Teaching and the Brain: Promoting Authentic Engagement*. Bookshelf by VitalSource, www.vitalsource.com.

21 Sorrentino, R. and Yamaguchi, S. (2008) *Handbook of Motivation and Cognition Across Cultures* (New York: Academic Press).

22 Murdock, M. C. and Keller-Mathers, S. (2008) "Teaching and Learning Creatively with the Torrance Incubation Model: A Research and Practice Update," *The International Journal of Creativity and Problem-Solving*, 18, 2, 11–33.

23 Callahan, C. (2013) *Critical Issues and Practices in Gifted Education: What the Research Says,* 2nd. Ed. (New York: Sourcebooks, Inc.).

24 Banks, J. and Banks, C. M. (2020) *Multicultural Education: Issues and perspectives* (New York: John Wiley).

25 Bennett, C. I. (2019) *Comprehensive Multicultural Education: Theory and Practice*, 7th Ed. (New York: Pearson).

26 Ellis, R. (2008) *The Study of Second Language Acquisition* (Oxford, UK: Oxford University Press).

FOR FURTHER STUDY: TEACHER ROLES/STUDENT AUDIENCE

Banks, J. (2019) *An Introduction to Multicultural Education* 6th Ed. (Boston: Allyn & Bacon).

Banks, J. and Banks-McGee, C. J. (2020) *Multicultural Education: Issues and Perspectives* 10th Ed. (New York: John Wiley & Sons).

Brown, F. (2020) *Instruction of Students with Severe Disabilities* (New York: Pearson).

Conant, J. B. (1961) *Slums and Suburbs* (New York: McGraw-Hill).

Cornbleth, C. (2008) *Diversity and the New Teacher: Learning from Experience In Urban Schools* (New York: Teachers College Press).

Elias, M. J., and Arnold, H. (2006) *The Educated Guide to Emotional Intelligence and Academic Achievement: Social-Emotional Learning in the Classroom* (Thousand Oaks, CA: Corwin Press/Sage Publications).

Gardner, H. (1983) *Frames of Mind: The Theory of Multiple Intelligences* (New York: Basic Books).

Gardner, H. (1993) *Multiple Intelligences: The Theory in Practice* (New York: Basic Books).

Gardner, H. (2000) *Intelligence Reframed: Multiple Intelligences for the 21st Century* (New York: Basic Books).

Howe, W. A. (2013) *Becoming a multicultural educator*. 14th Ed. (Los Angeles, CA: Sage Publications).

Koppelman, K. L. (2020) *Understanding Human Difference Multicultural Education for a Diverse America*, 6th Ed. (New York: Pearson & Co.).

National Academies of Sciences (2018) *How People Learn II: Learners, Contexts and Cultures* (Washington, DC: National Academy Press) www.nap.edu.

Wilson, W. J. (2001) *The Bridge over the Racial Divide* (Berkeley, CA: University of California Press).

Zevin, J. (2013) *Teaching Creatively: In* the Box *out of the Box, and Off the Walls* (Latham, MD: Rowman & Littlefield).

Teacher Roles for Student Audiences

BUILD YOUR OWN LESSON

The challenge: thinking 'on your feet.'

Interact with a new piece of evidence, data, issue, or problem.

Design a lesson of your own using different materials (newly discovered art, music, literature, history, geography, etc.).

Worry not about what you know, but react by thinking about how you would teach the data. Improvise!

Write a didactic, reflective, and affective goal for each document or picture, then add a low, medium, and high order question.

Choose one of the six strategies.

Pick a brief method of evaluating success (verbal, written, and tested).

What questions do the data support? Where do they fit in history?

What is the source and context: time and place? And how does that matter?

Did you find improvisation for the classroom easy or difficult? Why?

What do you notice about the sculpture, neck, headdress, base, pose, expression? What theme would you apply? Which reflective questions might you ask? Is the sculpture designed to entertain, impress, or amuse?

DOI: 10.4324/9781003026235-8

Figure 3.3:   Royal Benin Bronze Figure from 15th Century. What style and adorn-ment indicate status and power?

STRATEGIES FOR SOCIAL STUDIES INSTRUCTION

4

TEACHING STRATEGIES FOR LOWER LEVEL SKILLS

D4.4.6-8. Critique arguments for credibility.

D4.4.9-12. Critique the use of claims and evidence in arguments for credibility.

D4.5.6-8. Critique the structure of explanations.

D4.5.9-12. Critique the use of the reasoning, sequencing, and supporting details of explanations.

C3 Framework, 61.

"Geography has made us neighbors, history has made us friends, economics has made us partners, and necessity has made us allies."

President John F. Kennedy

OVERVIEW

This chapter provides a series of three teaching strategies including data-gathering (easy), comparison and contrast (a bit difficult), and drama (more involving and exciting).

INTRODUCTION

This chapter focuses on three lower-order teaching strategies that foster the acquisition of knowledge and the less complex comprehension and reflective skills such as application, comprehension, and an awareness of value differences. These strategies include data gathering, comparison and contrast, and drama.

The problem-solving demands on students increase with each with drama spilling over into emotion. After all, that is what drama (and much of history and politics) is designed to do.

Drama engages emotion as well as intellect and generates more thought and feeling than data gathering. Comparison and contrast require greater skill at sorting out commonalities

DOI: 10.4324/9781003026235-10

and differences than acquisition of information. Yet all three strategies are interdependent and related to one another because higher levels of thinking must rest on a base of knowledge and understanding. Yes, even now in the Internet Age it helps to have knowledge, especially if digested well, meaning you understand it.

DATA-GATHERING STRATEGY

Data gathering involves collecting information assumed to be valid, reliable, and necessary. Students memorize the 'facts' they need through procedures that involve considerable use of mnemonic devices and organizing categories.

Research makes a distinction between subject-matter knowledge and strategic knowledge.[1]

Subject-matter knowledge, sometimes referred to as domain specific, is composed of 'knowing what' and 'knowing how' in a field—geography, for instance. Defining a peninsula geographically would be 'knowing what,' while using latitude and longitude to locate a place would be 'knowing how.' Strategic knowledge by contrast is a set of general problem-solving skills, like reading maps and graphs, that can be employed in many fields. Strategic knowledge demands more higher order divergent thinking than subject-matter knowledge that usually focuses on more convergent thinking, although this is not a completely sharp division.[2]

Cross-subject strategies, sometimes called *metacognitive strategies* are usually defined as overall ways of thinking, tools of scientific thinking, historical habits of mind. Ideas of context, time, and place in history can be transferred to literature or science to help make sense of an issue. As an illustration, Conrad's story *Heart of Darkness* can be interpreted in a historical context yielding insights into imperialism and prejudice, potential racism and bias, while President William McKinley's speech on Manifest Destiny can be treated as literature and art yielding insights into patriotic images and imperialism.

Usefulness of Data Gathering

A data-gathering strategy is useful but limited since it mainly involves collecting. However, the data gathered is not merely a list, but also a set of meaningful classifications for easy retrieval and application. Vast quantities of historical data are easier to remember if related to concepts—family, gender, government, economy, and culture—than as unrelated bits and pieces.

A data-gathering strategy is a basic element of social studies, encompassing storage of information and tools of organization. With the Internet and Web, data is much easier to find, perhaps too easy, and also can be readily stored on a computer or memory chip, so no need to actually remember anything.

Data *must* be part of any lesson because insights are built on understanding and analysis, of specifics. Facts—specifics—serve as a base for subsequent conclusions and hypotheses suggesting new paths of inquiry. However, facts or data are all too often presented as the entire lesson, and the data do not always relate to theme or topic, and may be less than accurate depending on the source. Because data collection nearly always includes memorization and definitions, a base is provided for the lesson or unit as a whole.

Research has shown that factual learning conforms to well-established psychological principles, one of the most important of which is that facts are more easily remembered if they are related to an overall theme or story. Conversely, data are more easily forgotten if they are unrelated to a question or an idea, or lack an emotional connection.[3]

Problems with Data Gathering

A major problem for students is the amount, sequence, and connections collected, quantity, and topic matter of data.[4] If all items are treated as equal in value, students have difficulty holding on to them for very long. The strategy of data gathering must therefore begin with your recognition that it is impossible to teach *all the facts* on any topic in the time allotted. You should view facts as a selected *sample* of what is known and may have to check sources.

Students should be encouraged to collect, store, and organize facts that appear most reliable and accurate. Teachers should bolster retention by providing students with points of reference, landmarks, ideas, and labels that jog memories and offer opportunities to give positive feedback for good performance.[5]

A data-gathering strategy formulates clear goals that tell students what you expect of them in class, on tests, and for homework assignments. Researchers (situated cognition theory) point out the need to create a situation or atmosphere that data are made to seem valuable and useful. If requirements are clear, students can plan ahead to spark memory, adding new information. Most important, offer students advice on how to organize information using mnemonic devices and categories, headings, and themes.

Keep in mind that the facts themselves are only being accepted for the time being as 'probably' true subject to further checking. Internet sources need to be found and checked for author/artist, date, place, and time just as traditional sources are tested and verified. Otherwise, all of us are simply going along with what is offered, which may be incorrect! Social studies is like science in the sense that we should be skeptical of opinions and results that seem too good, too sure, too quickly discovered.

Data-Gathering Teaching Techniques

Lecture is a time-honored method for presenting data. If a lecture is well organized around a central topic and the subject matter is divided into a logical sequence of reasoning and description, student absorption may be good. Great lectures require considerable preparation, deep homework, enhanced by dramatics and a nice PowerPoint Zoom presentation, so folks don't sleep. As a lecture proceeds, student memorization will take place naturally and need not be forced. A variety of attention-sustaining techniques can enhance student retention.[6]

You may encourage students to acquire information as an Internet research project, but they may get lost in vast canyons of data and wind up at *Star Wars* or *Roblox*. They might research a case study, conduct a survey, or seek expert advice. They may also cooperate in groups/online chat rooms, collecting and sharing large amounts of information, and checking together for source authenticity. Interesting data are signaled by greater richness and a sense of excitement. Even small changes in strategy can make a huge difference to students, limiting your data to key dates big events, rather than exhaustive chronology. Below, Figure 4.1 shows students a set of important dates and actions offering a springboard for questions and discussion of the French Revolution of 1789.

The Timetable of Revolution

5 May Estates General met for first time since 1614, to rescue France from financial collapse.

20 June Tennis Court Oath by Third Estate (commoners) to remain in session until grievances redressed.

12-17 July Rising tension in Paris: riots against customs barrier and troops, culminating in:

14 July Storming of the Bastille

Mid July–August Spread of the Great Fear-rural riots and provincial revolutions.

5 October March of over 10,000 to Versailles demanding an end to bread shortage. Forced Royal family to return with them to Paris.

1790

Consolidation of the revolution. Formation of political clubs including Society of the Friends of the Constitution better known as Jacobins. Formation of provincial "federations" to support the revolution: born from sense of regional autonomy.

19 June Attacks on privilege: Titles declared void; nobles renounced their feudal rights (August 1789)

12 July Clergy "nationalized" via Civil Constitution; church property rights already annexed—November 1789 Reaction: mutinies in navy and army suppressed. Bread riots continued.

27 November Civic oath imposed on the clergy. Many refused to take it.

1791

20 June King Louis XVI and his family flee in secret to join *emigres* over German border; taken prisoner at Varennes and returned to Paris.

Increasing radical pressure.

17 July "Massacre" of the Champ de Mars: mob out of hand fired on by National Guard. Impatience of *sans culottes* with slow pace of change.

Rise of more radical party Girondins— within the assembly, and voices urging war as only solution to threat from royalist *emigres* and their allies—Austria and Prussia.

Royalists promote counterrevolution in the Vendee in western France, and the Midi to the south.

1792

20 April War declared against Austria. Prussia immediately entered as well.

War emergency catalyzed revolution.

Volunteer armies arrived from the *federations*, notably Marseilles.

17 August Mass action by Parisians. A march on Royal Palace of Tuilleries, and massacre of Swiss Guards defending it. King universally held to be in league with Austria.

19 August Defection of hero of 1789, Lafayette, to Austrians. Foreign armies entered France. France now under control of revolutionary government.

2 September Fortress of Verdun fell to Prussia; Paris believed open to invasion. Prisoners in Parisian jails slaughtered.

20 September: Military tide turned by victory at Valmy. Same morning, National Convention met in Paris, replacing the Assembly, lineal descendant of the National Assembly of 1789. Convention purged of possible royalist sympathizers, and took dictatorial powers. The legislative instrument of revolutionary government.

21 September Monarchy abolished.

6 November Victory at Jemappes. Revolutionary armies carried war to the enemy.

1793

21 January King executed.

10 March Revolutionary tribunal established to apply "revolutionary justice." War with rebels in the Vendee.

26 March Committee of Public Safety established; with the Committee of General Security, the executive arm of the revolution.

Provincial revolts by *federations* against the dictatorship of Paris.

Figure 4.1: The Timetable of Revolution.

Source: *The World Atlas of Revolutions.* Copyright © 1983 by Andrew Wheatcroft. Reprinted by permission of Simon & Schuster Inc.

Using chronology, grasp the sequence of events in the French Revolution by applying the concepts of rebellion and social change. Plenty of items on the list imply a beginning, middle, and end, causes and consequences, actions and reactions. But remember that the list of events is itself an edited view of history with a built in selection process.

The following questions can guide examination of the dates and events:

1. According to the Timetable of Revolution, when did the revolution begin and sort of end? What years were involved?
2. Why did the French kings take 175 years to call a meeting of the general Assembly?
3. What happened to the King and Queen and their family?
4. Check out the sources of the Timetable. Is another list possible? Are key events left out?
5. Is there any pattern to the events? Can they be organized in some way? How does the revolution evolve? Why?
6. Which events seem most important and suggest deep causes?
7. Are there enough facts to use, is there data you'd like to have? Is anything important missing? How can you tell? If a timetable is presented, do you trust it totally? Why or why not?
8. Is the timeline too long, too short, just right for your class? How do you decide?

Apply the idea of a revolution and the specifics of 1789 France to the Russian, Chinese, Haitian, Cuban, or American Revolutions. Go Common Core by enriching vocabulary and analyzing meaning. Because many French terms and unusual phrases are used, ask students to identify or define words, events, and phrases including at least those below:

Estates General, Reign of Terror, Tennis Court Oath, Radicals, *sans-culottes coup d'etat*, Royalists Revolutionary Tribunal

Monarchy.. Emigres
Girondins.. Jacobins
Radical.. non-radical

TO DO

Think of data as a challenge. Think of facts as part of 'information literacy'. Go to the American Association of School Librarians @ www.ala.org and read "Evaluating information: An information Literacy challenge" to understand guidelines for judging the quality of data being collected. Metacognition, goals, and many other criteria for judgment are discussed. Pick one criterion and challenge students to evaluate a website or a single picture or document to see if cheating has occurred, or if it has been lifted from somewhere else. Trace knowledge as far back as possible to an original source.

Let's invent our own lesson using an old print of King Solomon deciding a famous case involving a suit by two women claiming a baby as their own. The story goes that the King ordered the baby be sliced in two, half for each mother, but when one mother objected, he gave her the child, not the other one. Now let's face some historical issues, is the picture true to life 2,800 or so years ago? Is the dress, style, and emotional quality right for ancient Israel? Is the story in the Bible or apocryphal? Does the King dress correctly, the women, the Bedouin style elders? How would you present this data?

If time permits, view a popular website like www.worldhistroymatters.org, which provides examples of carefully thought out use of documents on a wide range of subjects. Ask students to use some of 'teacher tap' criteria to examine a document or site for accuracy, honesty, and truthfulness, using criteria like objectivity, authority, authenticity, timeliness, and relevance. If you seek a tough topic, go to 'Did the Holocaust happen?' If you want a funny topic, go to 'snake oil salesmen,' and think about how many hoaxes are believed today!

COMPARISON AND CONTRAST STRATEGY

Comparison and contrast are based on developing, refining, testing, and redefining a set of categories or classifications.[7] Students apply categories to examples and then decide how much the examples are alike or different. This is a familiar and surprisingly effective technique useful in many situations. Comparison and contrast is basic to both a process of understanding and the organization of reasoning—whether A and B 'belong together,' like the old Sesame Street song asks, 'alike or different?', e.g., do all revolutions follow the same or different patterns. The primary engine pushing a comparison strategy is the need to understand likenesses and dissimilarities.

TO DO

Look at Figure 4.3. What kind of event is pictured here? What emotions and facts is the artist trying to portray? Is there going to be violence? Why are there soldiers and onlookers? Is it serious when a King is executed? Why might a King be executed? Does the crowd and soldiers look happy or upset: how can you tell? Who are the men near the King's body? If you used this lithograph in the classroom to teach about the French Revolution, what do you think it tells about the event? How's your visual intelligence?

Usefulness of Comparison and Contrast

Categories and classifications are basic intellectual tools for organizing and analyzing our world. Without agreed-upon definitions, which are categories, communication would be difficult if not impossible? If we could not even agree on definitions of simple objects, a chair or table, how successful can we be with complex concepts, social class, cultural diffusion, or foreign policy choices? Does what we call things and events matter: like the January 6, 2021 events at the Capitol in Washington, DC? Was it a rebellion, invasion, or civic action?

The comparison and contrast processes are crucial to building analogies; these, in turn, are critical to analysis and theorizing that depend on the recognition of patterns or commonalities. Students almost always jump at the chance to compare and contrast because it is interesting and helps them make sense of the world. Sharing definitions is a good group or chat room activity and the audience should work toward agreement.

Figure 4.2: Solomon and Sheba.

Problems with Comparison and Contrast

Teachers frequently ask students to use categories or classifications, but often do not help them toward a complete understanding of the attributes of a category. A category as simple and concrete as 'peninsula' benefits from additional like and unlike examples.

Figure 4.3:   The Execution of King Louis XVI of France (January 21, 1793), German copperplate engraving by Georg Heinrich Sieveking.

This work is in the public domain in its country of origin and other countries. Wikipedia.com.

In French a peninsula is called a 'presque isle,' or almost island. Concrete pictures and photographs also help visualization. For instance, is a long, thin piece of land just barely detached from a shoreline a peninsula or an island? What terms should we apply if there are periodic floods during which the connecting land disappears?

The strategy of comparison and contrast continuously reinforces distinctions. It also encourages students to review their experiences and ideas by building even finer distinctions (identifying more differences) and formulating better analogies (identifying more shared attributes).

For example, Figure 4.3 invites questions about what is happening and why. Even describing the picture takes work because it is detailed, but offers insight into the status of people rebelling. Are the people poor, rich, obedient, violent? Ask students to think of comparable events in other times and places. It is very dramatic with the executioner holding up King Louis XVI's head to the crowd.

Students are less likely to be bored using the comparison strategy than data-gathering. There is intellectual excitement involved in playing with categories and concepts, boosting observational and definitional skills, both very important in social studies.

However, you and the students must learn to ask questions about comparisons, e.g.:

- Do analogies (comparisons) fit the data, and does the data fit the analogy?
- Do the analogies (contrasts) produce interesting conclusions or insights about ideas?
- Which criteria can be used to decide about likenesses and differences?

Comparison and Contrast Teaching Techniques

When two or more examples in a category are part of a lesson, a comparison and contrast strategy is an easy and effective approach for the classroom.

There are two basic variants of comparison. First is an inductive approach in which students derive concepts, categories, or definitions based on a careful examination of evidence. The second is a deductive approach in which one or more definitions is presented for students to apply to examples determining whether or not these fit.

You may plan a lesson or unit around a series of examples that do or don't fit an existing concept or category so that students must test their own concept definitions. For instance, you may show students photographs of "rich and powerful vs. poor and anonymous" people and ask them to identify the attributes that make the two groups alike and those that make them different. Offer students several formal definitions of poverty and wealth—perhaps government guidelines to these two conditions, a philosophical view, and a dictionary definition—and ask the class to discuss the three versions, testing them against one another and outside evidence. The goal is to work toward single standard definition of *poverty* and *wealth* agreeable to all.

Much depends on students' degree of sophistication and maturity in dealing with distinctions and analogies. Middle and senior high school students normally have few problems with lower levels of conceptual development. Classification demands generalization from two or more examples. Klausmeier suggests that there are differences between beginner and more mature attempts at comparison and contrast.[8] The less mature identifies only one or two major differences, and a few examples, whereas a mature approach juggles multiple factors and a greater variety of examples.[9] Secondary school students may start with an easy example, rich and poor, and move on to a more complex problem, like the differences between a democracy and a republic. Steps to an inductive or deductive comparison and contrast lesson or unit are:

Deductive	*Inductive*
1. Set goals for the concept(s) to be learned and the comparisons to be made.	1. Present examples and non-examples.
2. Name the concept(s).	2. Ask students to list attributes that examples have in common.
3. Define the concept in full and present the commonly accepted meaning.	3. Ask students to test their list of attributes, giving reasons, separating examples from non-examples.
4. Present examples and non-examples simultaneously.	
5. List attributes and apply to examples. Ask for reasons in support of the comparisons or contrasts suggested.	4. Ask students to develop a systematic way to judge new examples and revise criteria, if necessary.
6. Develop a systematic way to evaluate new examples.	5. Tentatively define the concept in full and compare with official definition.
	6. Name the concept or concepts.
	7. Give positive feedback throughout the process.

Inductive and Deductive Steps in Reasoning	Inductive Reasoning	Deductive Reasoning
	Evidence/Observations	General Rules/Laws
	Similarities/Differences	Theories
Steps in Two Directions	Generalizations/Conclusions	Generalizations/Conclusions
	Tentative Hypotheses	Tentative Hypotheses
	Theories	Similarities/Differences
	More Evidence/Observations	Evidence/Observations
Conclusions Revisited	Testing and Revision	Testing and Revision

Figure 4.4:   Reasoning: Deductive and Inductive.

As categories are refined, students will become increasingly aware that definitions are even more of a human invention than facts. Use categories or concepts to make sense of the commonalities and differences they discover. Middle or junior high school students who are just beginning to deal with abstract concepts can be asked how sure they are about their comparisons or contrasts.

You might ask questions like:

Does the word *freedom* mean the same thing to everyone who uses it? Does freedom mean doing whatever you like or does it mean respecting community?

Can we define *political freedom* to clearly separate nations into free and un-free states? How much freedom does there have to be in a society to qualify?

Present a selection of real-life examples, some that fit a social science or history definition, some that clearly do not, and some that are in between. Ambiguous and borderline examples drive the comparison and contrast strategy. Historians and social scientists have long used this approach to organize massive sets of data into categories for thinking. An example is Crane Brinton's *The Anatomy of Revolution*, a study that compares and contrasts the best-known revolutions of modern times with the American case to test the concept of revolution.[10]

An Example of a Comparison and Contrast Strategy

In Figure 4.5, an inductive problem is posed to students: a series of artifacts representing three 'mystery' societies, identified only as A, B, and C. On examining the exhibits, students will see that each set of artifacts contains examples that probably have much the same function: a weapon, a tool, and a medium of exchange. Similar in function, but quite different in form, these have contrasting aesthetic design and levels of technology.

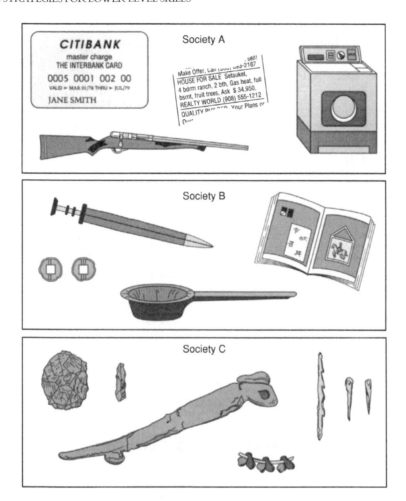

Figure 4.5: Compare artifacts from three societies, A, B, and C.

Themes could be technology, types of exchange media, and/or economic systems. Most participants will probably focus on technological development after the data have been submitted to a process of comparison and contrast. Facilitate the discussion by asking whether the beads, coins, and credit card are some form of money. Do coins represent a much more organized approach than artistic, un-standardized beads? What does the credit card represent? (A still greater level of abstraction in which funds are extended based on the customer's assets and ability to repay a loan?)

Ask which of the implements—the stone tools, pot, or washing machine—represent the greatest change in construction and saves the most labor. Do the students view each implement as a radical departure from what went before (contrast)? Do they note that all share similar functions (comparison) in relation to human social needs? Same questions and conclusions probably hold true for the weapons. Thus, the three artifact sets provide a classification game that propels students toward conclusions about social organization and economic history. Although no single line of thought need prevail as the lesson is strongly suggestive, through *inductive* reasoning procedures, of hypotheses about relationships between technology, social organization, and exchange modes.

The key ideas of technological invention and economic exchange can organize interpretations of the three charts. Comparison and contrast strategies, strongly promotes concept formation and encourages students to test categories and definitions. As students become skillful with new and subtle examples, they will be able to build clearer definitions and meet Common Core standards for determining, "the meaning of words and phrases as they are used in a text, including vocabulary specific to history/social studies" (ELA-Literacy. RH.6-8/4).

TO DO

Set up a compare/contrast lesson on race relations in U.S. history. Choose examples that invite comparison between Reconstruction and the Civil Rights Movement and/or Black Lives Matter that would present the greatest contrasts for student discussion.

Consider your goals in choosing *any* data. What will the information lead students to conclude about U.S. race relations, then and now: should Black Lives Matter be compared to racist opposition groups?

Should *any* facts, widespread miscegenation, be hidden or should there be a frank sharing of historical accounts? Would you include views on slavery held by the founding fathers? Would you include slave owners 'views as well as slaves and abolitionists' perspectives, or feminists, and foreigners?

DRAMA COACHING STRATEGY

Drama coaching views teachers and students as players on a stage. Roles can vary, even between teacher and student. Always there is contact with the people of history, ordinary people as well as leaders.

This is a strategy that promotes the emotional impact of a story, person, and event yielding a sense of involvement and catharsis for the learner. The material being studied, whether primary or secondary attracts students because of excitement generated by the actions performed, or by force of personalities and events.

When students identify, either negatively or positively, with figures and events interest is usually heightened. Topics that elicit a strong emotional involvement and raise awareness of important issues are major components of the drama coaching strategy.[11]

The major aims of the drama strategy are to raise student awareness of the emotional side of history and social science, to make more personal and human the people and events and to increase students' identification with others. Students get to act out roles and teachers get to be stage directors, at least until students can mount their own productions. Try to step into another's shoes, absorb new views, and become immersed in character, plot, and action.

Usefulness of Drama Coaching

Drama coaching is particularly effective in attracting and holding student interest. Students generally enjoy a good story line, especially if it involves adventure, sexual innuendo, and conflict or tension. Crises, attractive or repulsive characters, and outcomes that are comic or tragic usually grip our attention, much as a good mystery or story. The pleasures of theater and literature and film scripts are extended to the classroom!

Drama is useful for teachers who want students to understand historical figures and events in context, viewing them as they might have been in the flesh rather than abstractions. Biographies and autobiographies are excellent tools for filling in the details of historical characters.

Talk show interviews could be scripted with as much faithfulness to the actual events and sources as possible, bringing history to life. Drama as defined here involve role-play of historical figures, election simulations, mock trials, to recapture events. By stressing dramatic elements of social studies materials, you wake everyone up by promoting a feeling for personalities and events. Queen Elizabeth or King Sundiata Keita of West Africa comes to life even if she or he does look exactly like a famous Hollywood actress or actor!

Discuss how you would cast the past!

Problems with Drama Coaching

Emotional involvement might cause students to suspend critical judgment. Students who feel they have become part of a drama may be overwhelmed by the feelings and values in the drama, factual or fictional. As in TV or film, students may trust the evidence as totally accurate, even though invented. Confusing fiction with reality is a serious problem in teaching history. All of us have, at one time or another, been swept away by a drama or film that may be sophisticated propaganda, whether for good or evil, and we accept because of its emotional power, the strength of its characters, and the beauty of its images or language.[12]

Even when we deal with data based on actual occurrences, autobiographies, biographies, diaries, testimony, or speeches, the elements of drama and persuasion are always present. Some educators believe that the whole point of dramatized ideas, fictional or non-fictional, is to touch the emotions. Thus, the strength of the drama strategy is also its most serious weakness—one that you and the students have to neutralize or balance with additional data and criticism. So, keep your critical thinking caps on while being swept away.

Drama-Coaching Teaching Techniques

Creating a sense of drama in social studies is easy and effective.[13]

There are three major techniques that might be described as *scripted, interpretive, and original.*

Scripted follows a written plan of action with relatively little room for invention, but a lot of room for drama. Interpretive means that teacher and audience have considerable latitude in revising, improving, and redesigning classroom performances to meet their own ideas. Original demands that students and teacher use imagination to create a unique product based on historical sources. A first example, builds personal play acting, in which students act out a fully scripted situation with or without props, costumes, and symbols; second, participants interpret the selection of primary and secondary sources that are written with flair and style taking personal points of view that presents an event and/or issue; and third, an original production uses literary and other artistic media that inventing plot, character, images, and language to communicate a viewpoint. Teaching a film takes serious preparation and at least six senses.

You can bring history to life through preplanned or ad hoc presentations that involving period costumes, symbols, and artifacts, or the teacher may play the role of a historical figure using a person's ideas as the basis for a scripted monologue. Sometimes such recreations of the past may seem silly, but for many students, the play is just like play that however amateurish, gets attention. "Teacher-hams" have played a toga-clad Julius Caesar or read the Gettysburg Address wearing a Lincolnesque stovepipe hat. For archeology roles, hide artifacts all over a schoolyard for students to dig up (I did, and it worked!), playing archaeologist and adviser to your junior archaeologist assistants. All of these activities bring a personal, emotive quality that helps students feel special and playful.

Selecting historical news expresses feelings and provides the story as well. For instance, discussing and analyzing a portion of Benjamin Franklin's autobiography is preferable for purposes of building drama to a textbook synopsis. A TV interview with Palestinians and Israelis about their mutual problems will be likely to arouse more interest than a bloodless third-party summary of the issues.

Many novels, short stories, films, paintings, photographs, and theatrical works purposely engage the emotions. Some trivialize an issue, whereas others inflate and distort it, so you must exercise care over classroom choices. You can use distortions and exaggerations to good advantage as spring-boards for discussing bias and feeling in presenting people and issues. Recreate paintings like Picasso's *Guernica* or David's *Death of Socrates* as historically interesting, dramatic, and involving allusions and criticism, the Spanish Civil War and the second for the French Revolution—well worth a classroom discussion.

As noted in Chapter 3, role-play builds a sense of drama. Exercise caution because drama is exciting yet dangerously seductive, sometimes blinding students to others' viewpoints. The problem of students accepting *only one point of view* because of emotional attachment can be counteracted in several ways:

1. switch from one role to another
2. reverse sides in a debate
3. take the unpopular side on an issue
4. play a distasteful character as well as a positive, heroic, noble character
5. ask students to stand in someone else's shoes
6. direct a play or movie that presents a different story than the one we know
7. write and rewrite a script that you think your 'enemy' would like to see
8. think of yourself as a movie director or TV host
9. show conflicting features on different walls at the same time
10. play roles and record on cellphones for discussion.

Encourage students to think about how dramatic language and strong images, taking on roles, can change conclusions, particularly if students swallow a line from author and director. Make sure students have the chance to see the same event from two or more viewpoints. Raise questions about the nature of evidence, the problem of subjectivity, and the relationship of fact to fiction, fiction to fact whenever people, places, and events are 'dramatized.'

Whose version do we believe and how do we know what is truth? Is the fiction seemingly more powerful than the facts? Why?

TO DO

Explore the Famous Trials' website (www.law2.umkc.edu/faculty/projects/ftrials) created by Professor D. O. Linder of the University of Missouri-Kansas City for examples of materials, original sources, and lesson plans for courtroom re-enactments of real trials, all of which were controversial at the time, many of which are burned into historical memory, e.g., John Peter Zenger, John Brown, Nuremberg War Trial, Scopes Monkey Trial, My Lai Courts Martial, and Nelson Mandela.

Choose one to turn into a classroom interpretation asking students to write parts and a script for the trial and set up a courtroom setting to role-play judge, jury, prosecution, and defense, and don't forget the witnesses.

AN EXAMPLE OF A DRAMA COACHING STRATEGY: HISTORY, THEATER, AND HOLLYWOOD

Which of the images make you think history and which Hollywood? Why?
    Which of the images provide history and which drama: are both possible together?

Figure 4.6:   Portrait of Cleopatra VII in marble, 1st century B.C.

(Altes Museum) photographer: Anagoria GNU Free documentation license/Wikipedia.

Figure 4.7: A drawing by A. M. Faulkner of Cleopatra greeting Antony, in Shakespeare's Antony and Cleopatra (1906).

Folger Shakespeare Library Digital Image Collection http://luna.folger.edu/luna/servlet/s/55ved8. This file is licensed under the Creative Commons Attribution-Share Alike 4.0 International license.

Characters in Antony and Cleopatra

Cleopatra: The queen of Egypt and Antony's lover. A highly attractive woman who once seduced Julius Caesar, Cleopatra delights in the thought that she has caught Antony like a fish. In matters of love, as in all things, Cleopatra favors high drama: her emotions are as volatile as they are theatrical, and regardless of whether her audience is her handmaid or the emperor of Rome, she always offers a top-notch performance. Although she tends to make a spectacle of her emotions, one cannot doubt the genuine nature of her love for Antony. Shakespeare makes clear that the queen *does* love the general, even if her loyalty is sometimes misplaced.

   Octavius Caesar: The nephew and adopted son of Julius Caesar. Octavius rules the Roman Empire with Antony and Lepidus. Relations between Caesar and Antony are strained throughout the play, for the young triumvir believes that Antony squanders his time and neglects his duties while in Egypt. Ambitious and extremely pragmatic, Octavius

Figure 4.8: Actress Theda Bara playing Cleopatra in the 1917 film *Cleopatra*, Fox Film Corporation, work in public domain.

lacks Antony's military might as a general, but his careful and stoic reasoning enables him to avoid Antony's tendency toward heroic or romantic folly. Destined to be the first Roman emperor (later renamed Caesar Augustus), he symbolizes 'Western' values in the play, which stand opposed to the exotic lures of Cleopatra's.

Enobarbus: Antony's most loyal supporter. Worldly and cynical, Enobarbus is friendly with the subordinates of both Pompey and Caesar, yet stays faithful to his master even after Antony makes grave political and military missteps. He abandons Antony only when the general appears to be completely finished.

Marcus Aemilius Lepidus: The third member of the triumvirate and the weakest, both politically and personally. Lepidus's rather desperate attempts to keep the peace between Caesar and Antony fail when Caesar imprisons him after the defeat of Pompey.

Pompey: The son of a great general who was one of Julius Caesar's partners in power. Pompey is young and popular with the Roman people, and he possesses enough military might to stand as a legitimate threat to the triumvirs. He fancies himself honorable for refusing to allow one of his men to kill the unsuspecting Caesar, Antony, and Lepidus when they are his guests.

Octavia: Octavius Caesar's sister. Octavia marries Antony to cement an alliance between the two triumvirs. She is a victim of Antony's deception, and her meekness, purity, and submission make her the paradigm of Roman womanhood, and Cleopatra's polar opposite.

Charmian and Iras: Cleopatra's faithful attendants.

The Soothsayer. An Egyptian fortune-teller who follows Antony to Rome and predicts that his fortune will always pale in comparison to Caesar's.

A Bare-Bones Description of the Cleopatra VII Story Danger

Many accounts and interpretations and images exist of and about Cleopatra, Queen of Egypt.

Cleopatra VII Philopator was number 7 in a line of Greek-Macedonian rulers of Egypt all descended from Ptolemy I, a top general in Alexander the Great's army. Cleo was the closing act on the Ptolemy family ruling Egypt for about 300 years. Egypt was a valuable prize because it was a land of rich agriculture and large populations, a very productive and powerful kingdom. Though the Ptolemies ruled for three centuries, Cleo was the first and only member of the family to learn the Egyptian language. She was proud of her people and their culture and could perform her Queenly role in two cultures or more.

Cleopatra lived in Rome for a while because there was a revolt in Egypt against her father, Ptolemy XII, and he fled with her and the family to Rome in 58 BC because Egypt was already a state under Roman protection. The King's daughter Berenice claimed the throne of Egypt and ruled three years until killed in 55 BC when Ptolemy returned to Egypt with Roman help and took back his kingdom. A complicated family struggle followed with Cleo's brother Ptolemy XIII ruling with her but ending in a civil war between them, that ended with his death at the hands of Romans. All through this time, Roman Senators Julius Caesar and Pompey were involved in court intrigue with Greeks and Egyptians until their deaths during a very unstable time in the Roman Republic which ended with Romans on both sides of a civil war.

Cleopatra walked a tightrope between opposing Roman, Greek, and Egyptian forces, proving herself a rather capable foreign policy expert playing with famous Roman leaders like Julius Caesar, Mark Antony, and Octavian (Caesar's nephew). The Queen had a love affair with Mark Antony in 41 BC, funding his army and navy to oppose Roman forces led by Octavian, who later became the first emperor Augustus. Antony was originally married to Octavia, sister to Octavian, but divorced her to marry Cleopatra.

Cleopatra ruled well and fought well, until one fatal error: betting on the wrong leader, Antony, during the Roman civil war. He was defeated in 31 BC at the battle of Actium and lost the Egyptian navy, then committed suicide before capture. Octavian declared war on Cleopatra and threatened to bring her back in chains to be publicly led in a triumphal procession through the streets of Rome. Cleopatra took poison and killed herself in 30 BC thus ending Egypt's independence, which became a province of the new Roman Empire.

AUTHOR'S SUMMARY AND SIMPLIFICATION, BASED ON A VARIOUS SOURCES.

Plutarch (1920) *Plutarch's Lives*, translated by Bernadotte Perrin (Cambridge, MA: Harvard University Press) Perseus Digital Library, Tufts University.

Jones, P. J. (2006) *Cleopatra: A Sourcebook* (Norman, OK: University of Oklahoma Press), ISBN 9780806137414.

Tyldesley, J. (2008) *Cleopatra: Last Queen of Egypt.* (Basic Books). ISBN 9780465018925.

Volkmann, H. (1958) *Cleopatra: A Study in Politics and Propaganda*, translated by T. J. Cadoux (New York: Sagamore Press).

TO DO

Select a primary source, documentary, movie, docudrama, or Hollywood film on an Asian topic (compare the *Last Emperor of China* to a textbook account of the Chinese Empire's end), zeroing in on a short dramatic scene, with Pu Yi's memoirs. Compare a Roman primary source describing the life and death of Julius Caesar with Shakespeare's play *Julius Caesar*. Compare the Biblical story of the Jewish exodus from Egypt led by Moses with the Cecil B. de Mille film, *The Ten Commandments*. Design your lesson for accurate content and for comparisons with literary, film, and other media sources. After studying WWI, ask students to write skits that dramatize life in the trenches and then show them *All Quiet on the Western Front* or if you are brave, *Paths of Glory* or one of the latest flicks available like *War Horse* or *Saving Private Ryan*.

Walk into class one day and after no more than ten minutes of background, re-enact one scene from the Civil Rights Era events, e.g., March on Selma or Martin Luther King's "I Have a Dream" speech. Have a contest for best actor and actress. Make social studies part of showbiz!

SUMMARY

Lower levels of the new Bloom's taxonomy and Common Core goals were discussed in this chapter, and suggestions presented for gathering data and promoting understanding through comprehension, comparison, and contrast, and drama coaching. *Data gathering* was defined as a strategy focused on collecting accurate and interesting information (scour The NET); *comparison and contrast* was defined as building and testing definitions of terms (what are revolts?) into like and unlike examples. Using data and understanding of the past and present, students can engage in a drama strategy bringing the past to life through role-play, skits, and dramatizations. Three easy strategies were suggested to build knowledge, understand definitions, introducing learners to stimulating but not highly demanding intellectual and theater skills. Practice checking content, classifying, and applying definitions to serve as a base for more demanding activities of strategies of multiple perspectives, mystery, and controversy in the chapter that follows.

NOTES

1 Alexander, P. A. and Judy, J. (Winter, 1988) "The Interaction of Domain-Specific and Strategic Knowledge in Academic Performance," *Review of Educational Research*, 58, 4, 375–404.

2 Chi, M. (1985) Interactive Roles of Knowledge and Strategies in the Development of Organized Sorting and Recall. In Chipman, S. et al. (eds.) *Thinking and Learning Skills*, Vol. 2 (Hillsdale, NJ: Lawrence Erlbaum Associates), 457–484.

3 Brown, A. L. (1978) Know When and Where and How to Remember: A Problem of Metacognition. In Glaser, R. (ed.) *Advances in Instructional Psychology* (Hillsdale, NJ: Lawrence Erlbaum), 319–337.

4 Gagne, R. M., Briggs, L. J. and Wager, W. (1988) *Principles of Instructional Design* (New York: Holt, Rinehart & Winston).

5 Rohwer, N. D. and Thomas, J. W. (1987) The Role of Mnemonic Strategies in Study Effectiveness: Theories, Individual Differences, and Applications. In McDaniel, M. A. and Pressley, M. (eds.) *Imagery and Related Mnemonic Processes* (New York: Springer-Verlag), 428–450.

6 MacLeish, J. (1968) *The Lecture Method* (Cambridge, UK: Cambridge Institute of Education).

7 Reigluth, C. M. et al. (1978) "The Elaboration Theory of Instruction," *Instructional Science*, 7, 107–126.

8 Klausmeier, H. et al. (1974) *Conceptual Learning and Development* (Orlando, FL: Academic Press).

9 Endacott, J. and Brooks, S. (2018) Historical Empathy: Perspectives in Responding to the Past. In *The Wiley International Handbook of History Teaching and Learning* (New York: Wiley-Blackwell), 203–226.

10 Brinton, C. (1952) *The Anatomy of Revolution* (New York: Prentice-Hall).

11 Weiner, B. (1986) *An Attributional Theory of Motivation and Emotion* (New York and Berlin: Springer-Verlag).

12 de Charms, R. (1983) Intrinsic Motivation, Peer Tutoring, and Cooperative Learning. In Levine J. M. and Wang, M. C. (eds.) *Teacher and Student Perceptions: Implications for Learning* (Hillsdale, NJ: Lawrence Erlbaum Associates), 391–398.

13 McCaslin, N. (2006) *Creative Drama in the Classroom and Beyond*, 8th Ed. (Boston, MA: Allyn and Bacon).

FOR FURTHER STUDY: TEACHING STRATEGIES FOR LOWER LEVEL SKILLS

Cruz, B. (2006) "Breathing Life into History: Using Role-Playing to Engage Students," National Council for the Social Studies, *Social Studies and the Young Learner* 19, 1, 4–8.

Hidi, S. "Interest and Its Contribution as a Mental Resource for Learning," *Review of Educational Research*, 60, 4, 549–573.

Hollingsworth, J. R. and Ybarra, S. E. (2018) *Explicit Direct Instruction: The Power of a Well-Crafted, Well-Taught Lesson* (Corwin Teaching Essentials).

Jennings, S. (2017) *Creative Drama in Groupwork*, 2nd Ed. (New York: Routledge).

Mace, J. H. (2010) *The Act of Remembering: Toward an Understanding of How We Recall the Past* (New York: Wiley-Blackwell).

Marzano, R. J. (2017) *Art and Science of Teaching* (Bloomington, IN: ASCD Solution Tree Press).

Rose, G. (2012) *Visual Methodologies*, 3rd Ed. (Thousand Oaks: CA).

Rubin, L. J. (1985) *Artistry in Teaching* (New York: Random House).

Tonjes, M. J. and Zintz, M. V. (1987) *Teaching Reading, Thinking, and Study Skills in Content Classrooms* (Dubuque, IA: Brown).

Wilen, W. W. (1991) *Questioning Skills for Teachers*, 3rd Ed. (Washington, DC: National Education Association).

Willis, S. (1992) *Teaching Thinking. Curriculum Update.* (Alexandria, VA: Association for Supervision and Curriculum Development).

Zevin, J. (2010) *Teaching on a Tightrope: Diverse Roles of Great Teachers* (Lanham: MD: Rowman & Littlefield).

TEACHING STRATEGIES FOR LOWER LEVEL SKILLS

BUILD YOUR OWN LESSON

The challenge: thinking 'on your feet.'

Interact with a new piece of evidence, data, issue, or problem.

Design a lesson of your own using different materials (newly discovered art, music, literature, history, geography, etc.).

Worry not about what you know, but react by thinking about how you would teach the data. Improvise!

Write a didactic, reflective, and affective goal for each document or picture, then add a low, medium, and high order question.

Choose one of the six strategies.

Pick a brief method of evaluating success (verbal, written, and tested).

What questions do the data support? Where do they fit in history?

What is the source and context: time and place? And how does that matter?

Did you find improvisation for the classroom easy or difficult? Why?

Document Text

Olympe de Gouges, a female French political activist and playwright, wrote the Declaration of the Rights of Woman and of the Female Citizen in 1791 in direct response to the Declaration of the Rights of Man and Citizen. The document sheds light on the failure of the French Revolution to extend its ideals beyond men and demands political and legal equality for women. De Gouges was an outspoken critic of the government during the revolution's "Reign of Terror" from 1793 to 1794. As a result, she was the only female to be executed for her political writings during this period.

DOI: 10.4324/9781003026235-11

For the National Assembly to decree in its last sessions, or in those of the next legislature:

Preamble

Mothers, daughters, sisters [and] representatives of the nation demand to be constituted into a national assembly. Believing that ignorance, omission, or scorn for the rights of woman are the only causes of public misfortunes and of the corruption of governments, [the women] have resolved to set forth a solemn declaration the natural, inalienable, and sacred rights of woman in order that this declaration, constantly exposed before all members of the society, will ceaselessly remind them of their rights and duties; in order that the authoritative acts of women and the authoritative acts of men may be at any moment compared with and respectful of the purpose of all political institutions; and in order that citizens' demands, henceforth based on simple and incontestable principles, will always support the constitution, good morals, and the happiness of all.

Consequently, the sex that is as superior in beauty as it is in courage during the sufferings of maternity recognizes and declares in the presence and under the auspices of the Supreme Being, the following Rights of Woman and of Female Citizens.

"A Declaration of the Rights of Woman and the Female Citizen," Rutgers University, https://andromeda.rutgers.edu/~jlynch/Texts/degouges.html.

How would you teach about women's rights? What are Olympe's main points? Would this provide material for a Perspectives strategy?

5

TEACHING STRATEGIES FOR HIGHER LEVEL SKILLS

"History repeats itself, but in such a cunning disguise that we never detect the resemblance until the damage is done."

Sydney J. Harris (1917–1986)

D2.His.10.6-8. Detect possible limitations in the historical record based on evidence collected from different kinds of historical sources.

D2.His.10.9-12. Detect possible limitations in various kinds of historical evidence and differing secondary interpretations.

D2.His.11.6-8. Use other historical sources to infer a plausible maker, date, place of origin, and intended audience for historical sources where this information is not easily identified.

D2.His.12.6-8. Use questions generated about multiple historical sources to identify further areas of inquiry and additional sources.

D2.His.12.9-12. Use questions generated about multiple historical sources to pursue further inquiry and investigate additional sources.

C3 Framework, 48

OVERVIEW

Three more advanced and challenging strategies are offered for unit planning, perspectives, mystery, and controversy, discussing the advantages and disadvantages of each approach.

This chapter presents three higher order strategies aimed at promoting (a) multiple perspectives (complementary and clashing views), (b) mystery (the unknown and puzzling), and (c) controversy (issues and value judgments). All three demand a good deal more of students than previous strategies, and each promotes more divergent forms of reasoning.

DOI: 10.4324/9781003026235-12

At higher levels, students are encouraged to examine many alternative hypotheses as they work toward a conclusion or decision. *Analysis, synthesis, evaluation,* to use Bloom's terms, and now *creating* are prominent components in the three new strategies. When using these strategies, you and the students may sometimes find it almost impossible to reach more than a settled conclusion! Examination of an emotionally charged or complex controversy or clashing views may end in a draw. As in the previous chapter, examples of lessons are provided for perspectives, mystery, and controversy strategies.

A PERSPECTIVES STRATEGY

Playing with perspectives employs multiple viewpoints of an event, problem, or person to provoke discussion. Perspectives require seeing the same phenomenon *through two or more different lenses.* This strategy is related to comparison and contrast, but pushes beyond to include many perspectives and viewpoints. Perspectives use a series of accounts that offer complementary, overlapping, and/or conflicting versions of an event or problem, providing a range of views.

Perspectives help students see the world through the eyes of others. Literature often employs this technique, for example, when an author describes events as different characters live them. The play *Rashomon* is a classic example of perspectives in which each character's account is either self-centered or self-serving in some way and does not agree with the others.[1] This makes the 'truth' difficult to discern, the drama's point, much like 'fake' vs. 'real' news.

Biographies of American presidents, for example, frequently give us sharply contrasting viewpoints of a leader's personality and actions, disagreeing on the facts, as well as causes of actions taken. A perspectives lesson immediately causes students to raise questions: What's the truth? Whose word can I believe? How do I judge among the different versions? Historians and social scientists constantly have to deal with eyewitness problems when they judge accounts or face conflicting reports or explanations.

Usefulness of a Perspectives Strategy

Perspectives are especially powerful in demonstrating how upbringing, politics, social status, and culture can shape perception. Employ the perspectives approach to teach students how to look for subtle, underlying biases and distortions in the way people think and view one another and history. Provide practice in interpreting conflicting and debatable viewpoints. Discover the variety of frames or viewpoints that exist in a series of perspectives. Observing how values and motives shape worldviews is a frightening and enlightening process.[2]

Like good detectives, students will begin to see values, theories, and biases embedded in historical and literary accounts. They will increasingly judge sources on logical criteria like consistency, and by cross-checking other sources. Eventually they will identify a set of working rules for separating reliable and valid conclusions from shakier ones.

Encourage students to purposely adopt others' viewpoints, to walk in their shoes, seeking explanatory power of an unfamiliar, perhaps even disturbing, perception. Many anthropological studies employ this method of entering the worldview of other cultures; e.g., Native American, and U.S. Army accounts of General Custer's last stand offer clashing perspectives that merit demanding historical evaluation.

Problems with a Perspectives Strategy

The perspectives strategy takes students out of a narrow, personal, or ethnocentric pattern of thought opening up new doors to thinking and decision-making. The surprise and subsequent fascination for those who encounter multiple perspectives, clashing viewpoints, and strikingly different interpretations, can spark vibrant, lengthy discussions. The nature of evidence is called into question, raising issues of objectivity and subjectivity in drawing conclusions. At first, some students may be shocked by views and arguments that run counter to personal or mainstream traditions, but later they are frequently motivated to find answers. Why can't witnesses agree?

A perspectives strategy often produces a high degree of frustration and maybe a touch of cynicism: "There is nothing to believe, and no one to be trusted." This, in turn, leads students to review data and positions as suspect, and that is all to the good. To counteract possible student frustration and cynicism, direct the discussion toward defining criteria or making rubrics to interpret evidence. Assist students in creating a rationale for their work. Students may settle on a few operating principles or rules to follow, e.g.: expert testimony is better than that of novices; outsider eyewitnesses are more objective than participants; logical accounts are better than inconsistent or emotional accounts, etc. Recycle these ideas over and over because this is critical to higher level thinking, reinforcing the notion of criteria to test evidence and arguments for 'truth.'

Multiple Perspectives Teaching Techniques

As students become comfortable evaluating multiple viewpoints, they can decide that some perspectives are more reliable than others and more defensible in public debate. Given a set of agreed-upon criteria, students will pick and choose from among many accounts to build the 'truest,' 'best,' or 'most probably so' version.

Different newspaper accounts, or documents, or texts of an event can easily be used to build a perspectives strategy. Textbook accounts may be paired to illustrate subtle or not-so-subtle differences in reporting data, characterizing events, and describing personalities. Literary excerpts, YouTube clips, and films may also serve as examples of conflicting and convergent perspectives, pro- and antiwar views of famous battles. Filmmakers could be used who created examples that glorify human conflict; others could be shown deriding war, *The Green Berets* versus *Full Metal Jacket,* Vietnam being a wonderful minefield of contradictory examples. In addition, primary and secondary sources describing the same event sparks students' insights into the way historians and social scientists draw different conclusions from the same data.

Thus, a perspectives strategy introduces students to the interpretation of multiple views ranging across sliding scales of accuracy and bias. There can be stark differences and outright disagreements about interpretations and judgments, or a series of overlapping witnesses. It is a lot like estimations of crowd turnout by different parties. Using perspectives ultimately breeds a healthy skepticism, particularly when dealing with two competing authors who make claims for accuracy and truth. Learning to keep open minds about views and viewpoints may be troubling, unusual, or unpopular, but in the long run will help us understand facts and issues better than bland textbooks. The power of taking multiple perspectives demands independent thought and careful decision-making.

An Example of a Perspectives Lesson

American and British Versions of the Battle of Lexington[3]

The Battle of Lexington, the "shot heard 'round the world," offers a ready-made perspectives lesson because so many witnesses left behind so many contradictory accounts of both the event and its underlying causes. As might be expected, many of the British versions imply or directly state that the Americans provoked the fight, whereas American sources portray the British as having caused the fracas by miscalculated or willful aggression. Terrific stuff for classroom debate!

In one eyewitness account written by an English seaman to a Dr. Rogers on the British warship *Empress of Russia*, the Americans are described as firing the first shots in the battle and cruelly harassing English troops every step of the way, while the soldiers were simply carrying out their orders to "destroy some guns and provisions." Even "weamin" (women) took part in the attack by firing on the English, who, of course, had to respond in kind. A second witness, the Rev. Jonas Clark, pastor of a church in Lexington, counters the seaman's views in a sermon, reporting that the British troops cried, "Damn them. We will have them!" According to Clark, when the British sighted the patriot soldiers, they charged, although the American militia had been instructed "to disperse" and "not to fire." The English troops are viewed as aggressors who exceeded accepted standards of warfare, behaving brutally toward their American brethren. You can also have fun with the spellings, so ask the students to correct the colonials. Which account do you think is the most truthful, and how can you decide as you prepare these documents for class?

Document A: John Crozier to Dr. Rogers

Empress of Russia, Boston, April 23, 1775

> On the 18th instant between 11 and 12 o'clock at night I conducted all the boats of the fleet (as well men-o-war as transports) to the back part of Boston, where I received the Grenadiers and Light Infantry amounting to 850 officers and men and landed them on a point of marsh or mudland which is overflowed with the last quarter flood; this service, I presume to say, was performed with secrecy and quietness, having oars muffled and every necessary precaution taken, but the watchful inhabitants whose houses are intermixed with the soldiers' barracks heard the troops arms and from thence concluded that something was going on, tho' they could not conceive how or where directed. In consequence of this conception, a light was shown at the top of a church stiple [steeple] directing those in the country to be on their guard.

> The intention of this expedition was to destroy some guns and provisions which were collected near Concord, a town 20 miles from where the troops were landed. Colonel Smith, a gallant old officer, commanded this detachment and performed the above service. A firelock was snapt over a wall by one of the country people but did not go off. The next who pulled his trigger wounded one of the Light Infantry company of General Hodgsons of the Kings Own. The fire then commenced and fell

heavy on our troops, the militia having posted them selves behind walls, in houses and woods and had possession of almost every eminence or rising ground which commanded the long vale through which the King's troops were under the disagreeable necessity of passing in their return.

Colonel Smith was wounded early in the action and must have been cut off with all those he commanded had not Earl Percy come to his relief with the First Brigade; on the appearance of it our almost conquered Grenadiers and Light Infantry gave three cheers and renewed the defence with more spirits.

Lord Percy's courage and good conduct on this occasion must do him immortal honor. Upon taking the command he ordered the King's Own to flank on the right, and the 27th on the left, the Royal Welsh Fuseliers to defend the rear, and in this manner retreated for at least 11 miles before he reached Charlestown—for they could not cross at Cambridge where the bridge is, they [the colonists] having tore it up, and filled the town and houses with armed men to prevent his passage; our loss in this small essay amounts to 250 killed, wounded and missing. And we are at present kept up in Boston, they being in possession of Roxbury, a little village just before our lines with the Royal and Rebel centenels [sentinels] within musquet [musket] shot of each other.

The fatigue which our people passed through the day which I have described can hardly be believed, having marched at least 45 miles and the Light Companys perhaps 60. A most amiable young man of General Hodgsons's fell that day, his name Knight, brother to Knight of the 43 who was with us at Jamaica.

The enthusiastic zeal with which those people have behaved must convince every reasonable man what a difficult and unpleasant task General Gage has before him. Even weamin [women] had firelocks. One was seen to fire a blunder bus between her father and husband, from their windows; there they three with an infant child soon suffered the fury of the day. In another house which was long defended by 8 resolute fellows the Grenadiers at last got possession when, after having run their bayonets into 7, the 8th continued to abuse them ... and but a moment before he quitted this world applyed such epethets as I must leave unmentioned. God of his infinite mercy be pleased to restore peace and unanimity to those countrys again, for I never did nor can think that arms will enforce obedience. ... The number of the country people who fired on our troops might be about 5 thousand, ranged along from Concord to Charlestown, but not less than 20 thousand were that day under arms and on the march to join the others. Their loss we find to be nearly on a footing with our own.

Three days have now passed without communication with the country; three more will reduce this town to a most unpleasant situation; for there [their] dependence for provision was from day to day on supply from the country; that ceasing you may conceive the consequences. Preparations are now making on both sides the Neck for attacking and defending. The Hampshire and Connecticut Militia have joined so that Rebel army are now numerous. Collins is well and stationed between Charles Town and the end of this town to assist in the defense..."[4]

Document B: From a Sermon by the Reverend Jonas Clark, Pastor of the Church in Lexington

April 19, 1776

Between the hours of twelve and one, on the morning of the nineteenth of April, we received intelligence, by express, from the Honorable Joseph Warren, Esq., at Boston, "that a large body of the king's troops (supposed to be a brigade of about 12 or 1500) were embarked in boats from Boston, and gone over to land on Lechmere's Point (so called) in Cambridge; and that it was shrewdly suspected that they were ordered to seize and destroy the stores belonging to the colony, then deposited at Concord." … Upon this intelligence, as also upon information of the conduct of the officers as above-mentioned, the militia of this town were alarmed and ordered to meet on the usual place of parade; not with any design of commencing hostilities upon the king's troops, but to consult what might be done for our own and the people's safety; and also to be ready for whatever service providence might call us out to, upon this alarming occasion, in case overt acts of violence or open hostilities should be committed by this mercenary band of armed and blood-thirsty oppressors

…. The militia met according to order and waited the return of the messengers, that they might order their measures as occasion should require. Between 3 and 4 o'clock, one of the expresses returned, informing that there was no appearance of the troops on the roads either from Cambridge or Charles-town; and that it was supposed that the movements in the army the evening before were only a feint to alarm the people. Upon this, therefore, the militia company were dismissed for the present, but with orders to be within call of the drum—waiting the return of the other messenger, who was expected in about an hour, or sooner, if any discovery should be made of the motions of the troops. But he was prevented by their silent and sudden arrival at the place where he was waiting for intelligence. So that, after all this precaution, he had no notice of their approach till the brigade was actually in the town and upon a quick march within about a mile and a quarter of the meeting-house and place of parade.

However, the commanding officer thought best to call the company together; not with any design of opposing so superior a force, much less of commencing hostilities, but only with a view to determine what to do, when and where to meet, and to dismiss and disperse.

Accordingly, about half an hour after four o'clock, alarm guns were fired, and the drums beat to arms, and the militia were collecting together. Some, to the number of about 50 or 60, or possibly more, were on the parade, others were coming towards it. …meantime, the troops having thus stolen a march upon us and, to prevent any intelligence of their approach, having seized and held prisoner several persons whom they met unarmed upon the road seemed to come determined for murder and blood-shed—and that whether provoked to it or not! When within about half a quarter of a mile of the meeting-house, they halted, and the command was given to prime and load; which being done, they marched on till they came up to the east end of said meeting-house, in sight of our militia (collecting as aforesaid) who were about 12 or 13 rods distant.

Immediately upon their appearing so suddenly and so nigh, Capt. Parker, who commanded the militia company, ordered the men to disperse and take care of themselves, and not to fire. Upon this, our men dispersed—but many of them not so speedily as they might have done, not having the most distant idea of such brutal barbarity and more than savage cruelty from the troops of a British king, as they immediately experienced! For, no sooner did they come in sight of our company, but one of them, supposed to be an officer of rank, was heard to say to the troops, "Damn them! We will have them!" Upon which the troops shouted aloud, huzza'd, and rushed furiously towards our men.

About the same time, three officers (supposed to be Col. Smith, Major Pitcairn and another officer) advanced on horseback to the front of the body, and coming within 5 or 6 rods of the militia, one of them cried out, "Ye Villain Rebels, disperse! Damn you, disperse!"—or words to this effect. One of them (whether the same or not is not easily determined) said, "Lay down your arms! Damn you, why don't you lay down your arms?" The second of these officers, about this time, fired a pistol towards the militia as they were dispersing. The foremost, who was within a few yards of our men, brandishing his sword and then pointing towards them, with a loud voice said to the troops "Fire! By God, fire!" which was instantly followed by a discharge of arms from the said troops, succeeded by a very heavy and close fire upon our party, dispersing, so long as any of them were within reach. Eight were left dead upon the ground! Ten were wounded. The rest of the company, through divine goodness, were (to a miracle) preserved unhurt in this murderous action! … One circumstance more before the brigade quitted Lexington, I beg leave to mention, as what may give a further specimen of the spirit and character of the officers and men of this body of troops. After the militia company were dispersed and the firing ceased, the troops drew up and formed in a body on the common, fired a volley and gave three huzzas, by wash of triumph and as expressive of the joy of victory and glory of conquest! Of this transaction, I was a witness, having, at that time, a fair view of their motions and being at the distance of not more than 70 or 80 rods from them.[5]

The two accounts (and there are many others) are contradictory and contain a good deal of dramatic language. The battle raises numerous issues about truth in history and the reliability of evidence. Both accounts are first-hand or nearly so, and should in theory at least be more accurate than accounts drawn from memory. However, differences of fact and interpretation make it difficult to decide which version is the most truthful, a nasty problem that gives you a marvelous opportunity to ask a range of questions about the American Revolution in particular, and about the nature of the evidence in general, e.g.:

Why do accounts differ and sometimes contradict each other? Are one-sided views heightened or lessened in a conflict?

Are conflicting views deliberately created by opponents as propaganda to justify their own actions? How? How can you be sure?

Can propaganda be separated from genuine differences in perception?

What rules may we use judging documents? Should more emotional stories be discounted in favor of the coldly objective views?

Should the logical story be given greater credence than a confused account? Should we believe the more detailed story? (What if both sides offer equally specific accounts?)

Should more consistent stories be believed than contradictory stories?

How can we decide what to believe when faced with different perspectives? What are the best *rules for truth* in considering conflicting accounts?

Students might suggest that more eyewitnesses are always needed. They might add that rules of logic should apply equally to all stories, causing the least reasonable to be tossed out. Some could argue that motives also should be considered in any interpretation, mistrusting those who seem to have produced propaganda for one side or another. Students might also conclude that there may be no conclusions we can believe with 100% certainty. Even the best decision must be made in terms of probabilities based on a preponderance of evidence. With these conclusions, you've done well!

LET'S DECIDE

Military actions seem to breed distortion. Iraqi leader Saddam Hussein was once a close ally of the United States. Yet three times in our history, we went to war with Hussein, finally toppling his regime in 2004. Our putative reason was that he possessed weapons of mass destruction that posed an immediate threat to the United States. Although no weapons were found after invasion, our government continues to claim that Hussein was a dictator and that world safety demanded his ouster. But was Hussein really a threat? How can we find out: from U.S sources alone? Arab or Iraqi sources? International? Others? Find and compare different sources on the 2003–2004 Iraq conflict and on a current conflict as well. Are sources predictably in opposition or are there a few surprises?

Perspectives are historiography problems that can be reinforced during the entire year returning to the same powerful, thought-provoking questions, issues of truth, method, and interpretation. These are essential questions that never go away in social studies and are part of real-world practical problems. Once a perspective is adopted, begin to look for opportunities for discussions of multiple views in every aspect of the curriculum—media, Internet, and current events to historical documents and textbooks. Accounts that clash, complement, and contradict are naturals in provoking and sustaining inquiry.

TO DO

Develop a lesson in which perspective plays a vital role. Select one or two cases for the same event seen from the eyes of observers representing diverse interests and cultures. Would Spanish and Aztec sources describing the conquest of Mexico agree? Would British colonial representatives and Africans agree on what happened during the 19th century colonial period? Would Muslims and Christian knights agree on the value and purposes of the Crusades? Research primary and literary sources showing two or more views of an event—for example, *The Broken Spears*, Aztec accounts of Mexico, the Aztec poet, Nezahualcoyotl, and the diaries of Bernal Diaz del Castillo or Hernan Cortez presenting Spanish points of view.

MYSTERY STRATEGY

A 'mystery' strategy is powered by a search for unknowns, missing data and puzzling clues, to solve a problem. The mystery strategy relies on a sense of puzzlement and curiosity, drawing on deep wells of playfulness. Much like a good detective novel, plot, character, and evidence all conspire to drive people to discover the ending, whether by inductive or deductive means.[6]

History and the social sciences contain a wide variety of mysteries, from the classic archaeological find to philosophical disputes with no solution. There are real mysteries, humankind's origin and evolution, still partially understood (calling for inference and synthesis), and there are mysteries with multiple interpretations (calling for judgment and decision) of clues.

The mystery strategy requires *open-ended problems* that encourage many interpretations. For example, archaeological reconstructions based on fragments of artifacts or bones have built-in unknowns to hypothesize about using available evidence. However, the evidence may be insufficient for a definitive answer, and that makes a perfect classroom mystery. Cahokia (a temple mound city in Illinois) was one of the largest native settlements in North America, but declined before Europeans arrived for reasons still not understood, thus a real mystery. Cahokia may have been the center of a Mississippi trade network or an empire or both.

Why would people build mounds in the shape of animals, shapes best seen from the air? Why would people build shapes that they couldn't see, or could they? The Moundbuilder peoples present many mysteries in terms of artifacts that would provide a profitable archeological 'dig' for secondary student discoveries. Based on what you know so far predict what Moundbuilder pottery might look like, then look below for an example. Was your prediction on target or way off? Why do you think Moundbuilder peoples took on nature totems? What was their lifestyle?

Many subjects in history/social sciences contain built-in mysteries ripe for student solutions. Create mysteries of your own by leaving out bits and pieces of information for students to infer or track down, a search for cues and clues. Overall, classroom mysteries encourage students to play detectives to exercise higher-order thinking.[7]

Usefulness of a Mystery Strategy

Mystery is most powerful when you want to heighten student interest in a topic and promote inference and synthesis of clues to reach 'Aha!' conclusions. Mysteries are usually successful in arousing interest because learners become detectives relentlessly attempting to solve cases.[8] Drive to gather knowledge, piece together clues, compare and contrast finds, develop and test multiple hypotheses to complete or nearly complete a puzzle, an investigation.

Mysteries, checking claims, need not be confined to simple 'whodunnits?' Rather focus on questions of what, when, where, how, and why in much the same fashion as any top-notch example of the mystery genre. Popular computer simulation games, *A Plague Tale:*

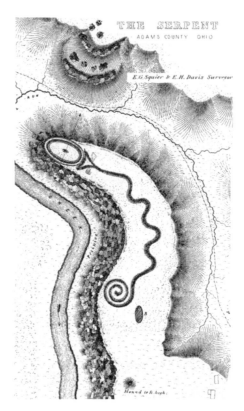

Figure 5.1: Effigy mounds built by Native Americans related to the folks at Cahokia are found in many areas of the United States from Louisiana to Minnesota following the Mississippi River system.

Innocence or Myst III, or *Age of Empires IV,* play on curiosity and love of the unknown to teach geographic and investigative principles.[9] Students are role-playing historians and detectives and may pick up skills, though most games seem aimed at warfare and winning.

Solving mysteries is a process that aims at reinforcing student confidence in using formal and informal logic to test hypotheses and interpret evidence. If the case is incomplete, and information is unavailable, data have been lost or obliterated, then a problem becomes all the more appealing. When too much is known, the fun goes out of it for everyone!

History can present a real mystery and an intellectual puzzle at the same time, rather than a solution. Science often involves mysteries or unknowns that must be solved by painstaking research. The knottier the problem finding causes of the COVID-19 virus, the greater the challenge. Science and social science can combine in studying the reasons for a cure or a plane crash: Was it an accident or an act of terrorism? Once involved, students willingly throw themselves into the effort of solving a puzzle; going to the library or Internet becomes fun when research is applied to solutions. A discovery approach is similar to mystery strategy because both encourage the student to make leaps in thinking from limited evidence to hypotheses or generalizations.[10]

A mystery strategy as a research process begins with evidence and a set of assumptions, proceeding in steps toward a defensible conclusion. Mystery as a strategy is most useful for teaching students problem-solving skills that dovetail neatly with research procedures. Research problems, the cause of a disease, the spread of an innovation, the way humans adapt to environments, are ultimate mysteries. Mystery promotes skills easily applied to many fields or situations—like figuring out why Napoleon lost to Wellington—identifying crucial links in a chain of human conflict.

Problems with a Mystery Strategy

A mystery problem carries with it a number of potential difficulties, e.g., confusion, frustration, and jumping to conclusions. Mysteries must be carefully constructed for maximum effect generating student ideas and reinforcing reasoning skills. The mystery must be real even if partially set up to allow two or three solutions. Difficulties develop if the problem is either too complex or too simple. Directions can confuse and students may lack self-confidence to deal with difficult problems, with no clear answers.

Like a good game, a mystery should be engaging, not trivial; it should not have an easy solution.[11] If the outcome is too easy students will lose interest. In contrast, a problem that is too confusing, difficult, or ambiguous will lead to frustration. Students may give up their search before even a tentative solution appears. Teachers must fit the mystery to the abilities of audiences they know and understand, but always pushing the envelope of inference a bit. A mystery needs audience testing.

Investigations shape students' responses. For beginners a problem-solving strategy is preferable to asking them to invent their own. Generally, the greater the structure (more facts, clues, and guidance) provided by the teacher, the easier it will be for the students to come up with a solution, but at a motivational cost. Interesting and complex problems will produce the greatest motivation and challenges but may also frustrate learning efforts.[12] Your audience brings a mind-set to a lesson that can enhance or retard learning. A class that is unfamiliar with problem-solving strategies or lacks self-confidence will need more practice than a group that is accustomed.[13] Audience is critical to any mystery, so experimentation is necessary to find the right balance.

Problems and students range across a continuum of skills. Therefore, design a mystery lesson or unit sufficient to involve a class in high-level thinking, but not at a level that will overwhelm or defeat them. Try a few mystery strategies until you discover a level at which your students feel successful and grow, building confidence along the way.

Mystery Teaching Techniques

A mystery strategy requires assembling data, making certain that alternative hypotheses are likely, and enough clues to work out hypotheses but not certain conclusions. Develop key or central questions at a level of difficulty suitable for the skills and experiences of your audience. Design a mystery lesson or use an actual problem or event that already contains one or more unknowns. Mysteries range from specific to general questions, "Why didn't Japan surrender before the atomic bomb was dropped?" or "Why did President Truman order the bomb dropped on Hiroshima and Nagasaki?" to more complex problems like understanding the context for WWII. You may use a mystery strategy for a particular topic or for a full-fledged research assignment.

Stimulate investigation by building a game-like classroom atmosphere suitable for sleuthing. The questions posed should be open-ended and thought provoking, divergent, and designed to sustain students' curiosity. The data provided must be rich enough to suggest problems without providing quick, linear conclusions. As a rule of thumb, a problem that can be solved in the first half of a class period is too easy a mystery.

Above all, the whole concept of a mystery strategy, like a game of Clue, is that students should work out their own (not your) solutions to questions of who, what, when, how, and why. Research clearly demonstrates middle school students can be excellent historical detectives, so why not secondary students?[14] You may certainly offer advice (but not too quickly!) suggest sources of data and references to help students define their terms. Your true objectives are to arouse students' curiosity and free their imaginations to sustain problem solving. They need to develop a sense of pride and confidence reaching a hard-won conclusion.

Perhaps the easiest way to evoke a mystery is through questions that ask students to identify causes and consequences. Examples might include the following:

1. Why, when, and where did the women's movement develop in the United States?
2. Why is a dictator able to control a nation for a long time?
3. Is there really a relationship between race, social class, and voter participation in elections?
4. Is industrial pollution creating global warming? And here's a mystery: Do we know what to do about it?
5. How do we know when leaders are telling us the truth?

Challenging mysteries are designed from a body of evidence, accompanied by thought-provoking questions. Answers develop slowly because data and resources needed are sometimes missing or only suggested. Pressing students to subject the data and clues to intense scrutiny guarantees more careful reading and observation than where large portions of the outcome are already known. The "missing pieces" technique may be illustrated by lessons in which students analyze incomplete primary sources, piecing together available clues to place literature, letters, or speeches in context.

Examples of Mystery Lessons

In a mystery lesson, students grapple with words in documents or objects in archaeological finds while searching for clues that will reveal function or purpose, and yield solid interpretations. Poetry is very Common Core and can work well as historical documents. A poem by the well-known 7th-century Chinese poet Du Fu is presented for your enjoyment as a 'manufactured' mystery with names, dates, and places blanked out. In this poem, issues of war and peace are raised by the story of an old man who deliberately broke his arm to evade a military draft. The elderly survivor explains why he injured himself and what happened during and after the war, while the poet comments on life and politics in the China of his time. Proper names, dates, places, and Chinese phrases are omitted to intensify reading and bolster a sense of mysteriousness.

The Old Man with the Broken Arm

At ____an old man—four-score and eight; The hair on his head and the hair of his eyebrows—white as the new snow. Leaning on the shoulders of his great-grandchildren, he walks in front of the Inn.

With his left arm he leans on their shoulders; his right arm is broken. I asked the old man how many
    years had passed since he broke his arm; I also asked the cause of the injury, how and why it
    happened.
The old man said he was born and reared in the District of ___; At the time of his birth—a wise
    reign; no wars or discords. "Often I listened in the Pear-Tree Garden to the sound of flute and
    song;
Naught I knew of banner and lance; nothing of arrow or bow. Then came the wars... and the great
    ley of men; of T___ of three men in each house—one was taken.
And those to whom the lot fell where were they taken to? Five months' journey, a thousand miles—
    away to. We heard it said that in ___ there flows the River.
As the flowers fall from the pepper-trees, poisonous vapors rise. When the great army waded across,
    the water seethed like a cauldron; When barely ten had entered the water, two of three were dead.
To the north of my village, to the south of my village, the sound of weeping and wailing, Children
    parting from fathers and mothers; husbands parting from wives.
Of a million men who are sent out, not one returns. I, that am old, was then twenty-four; My name
    and fore-name were written down in the rolls of the Board of War. In the depth of night not dar-
    ing to let any one know,
I secretly took a huge stone and dashed it against my arm. For drawing the bow and waving the banner
    now wholly unfit; I knew henceforward I should not be sent to fight in ___.
Bones broken and sinews wounded could not fail to hurt; I was ready enough to bear pain, if only I
    got back home. My arm—broken ever since; it was sixty years ago.
One limb, although destroyed,—whole body safe! But even now on winter nights when the wind and
    rain blow, from evening on till day's dawn I cannot sleep for pain. Not sleeping for pain is a small
    thing to bear,
Compared with the joy of being alive when all the rest are dead. For otherwise, years ago, at the ford
    of River___. My body would have died and my soul hovered by the bones that no one gathered.
A ghost, I'd have wandered in, always looking for home. Over the graves of ten thousand soldiers,
    mournfully hovering." So the old man spoke, And I bid you listen to his words. Have you not
    heard.
That the Prime Minister of K___ did not reward frontier exploits, lest a spirit of aggression should
    prevail? Not heard that Prime Minister of T__,
Desiring to win imperial favor, started a frontier war? But long before he could win the war, people had
    lost their temper; Ask the man with the broken arm in the village of___![15]

A triple problem is presented by the poem. First, there is a mystery about its origins—time and place; second, there is a problem interpreting its meaning; and third, there is the potential for controversy over the issue of lack of patriotism. Patriotism, from the old man's viewpoint can be a springboard for discussion of more modern events and values, such as antiwar protests and draft evasions that characterized the Vietnam War period as well as the Iraq War, and many others as well. Why are some wars supported enthusiastically but others hated?

Ask students to search the poem for clues that could shed light on its origins: Where in the world are pear-tree gardens and pepper trees? Why did the old man break his own arm? Is he happy or sad about his decision? Why? How did he feel about family? What does the old man feel about government exploits at home and at war? Is he for or against wars? All wars? Why or why not? Using the war issue, extend the discussion to moral or ethical problems related to support for or rejection of governmental foreign policy. For example, under what conditions might it be ethical to resist a nation's decision to attack another nation: offense, defense, both, or neither? What arguments could be offered to support the old man's views or to oppose them? What form did his protest take? Did he have regrets? Ask students to write their own poem or story about war. (Would they glorify or disapprove of it—for example, the Iraq or Afghan Wars?)

Arguments for or against war might include love of family over nation, reverence for the elderly, and the wandering of ghosts who died away from home. Concrete items 'pear tree garden,' 'bow and lance,' 'pepper trees,' 'village,' 'five months journey, a thousand miles,' and 'rolls of the Board of War' could serve as geographic, cultural, and historical clues. Add up a picture of a big country with strong family values, widespread village life, and a well-organized central government whose decisions are sometimes contrary to popular opinion. A benefit of poetry gives the China of long ago a human face through Du Fu's story. The real goal is for students to discover meanings and insights of their own through close reading. Debating the old man's ethics and the poet's message may help the class arrive at an accepted overall interpretation. Then you can offer the knowledge that the poet was a Chinese scholar of the 7th century named Du Fu who frequently protested against government decisions and was banished from home as a result. Rule by an emperor was far from freedom, therefore opposition took a good deal of courage.

Opportunities for a mystery strategy abound in social studies across disciplines, but has to be set up and guided. Students must identify a mystery question, perhaps in groups, and collect the data needed to prove or reject its conclusions. A good research study should permit alternative theories, allow a fair test of competing interpretations, yet defend interpretations with evidence and logic, for example:

1. How can we trace origins, e.g., of foods like oranges, tomatoes, potatoes, and rice? Can origins always be pinpointed or are results unsure?
2. Why are competing causes and explanations offered of the same people, places, and events?
3. Can we trust identifying the motivations of historical figures from their own writings and the writings of others?
4. How can we make sense of a culture leaving us only artifacts and no written records?
5. Do we believe Sherlock Holmes for every single case, or do we need to do some detective work of our own?

TO DO

Create a mystery: Develop a real mystery around an unsolved controversy. You might consider John Brown, the abolitionist who conducted a pre-Civil War raid on Harper's Ferry, Virginia, to free slaves. For this action, he was sentenced to death and hung by the U.S. Army. Southerners portrayed him as a madman and a villain, whereas northern abolitionists portrayed him as a hero and leader. Read John Brown's last speech in court, and decide if he is raving or makes sense. What was the truth? Were his motives noble or evil? Were his methods defensible? Did President Lincoln support Brown or condemn him? Is violence ever reasonable and defensible? Why not? If so, when?

You might ask students to conduct their own investigation of the causes of World War I. Do they really think that the assassination of Archduke Franz Ferdinand was enough to set off a worldwide conflict? Have them check on the German, French, and English armament situation at the time. Were these peaceful states armed at the last minute or had there been a buildup of many years? Which nations really wanted war and which did not?

What claims are made about the origins of COVID-19 virus? Was China a source? Is it easy or difficult to trace a virus and its spread? Were previous plagues, pandemics, and diseases clearly mapped out or was there confusion and counter-claims? Why might diseases be difficult mysteries to trace back to their beginnings?

CONTROVERSY STRATEGY

Controversy rests on values and philosophies about morality, justice, order, and the 'good life.'

Controversies arise out of clashes concerning basic values that guide human aspirations, codes of daily behavior, and guides to right and wrong.[16] Because value disputes draw on emotional commitments, they inherently involve a strong hold on attention.[17] Controversies range from attempts to hammer out compromises among contending positions, choosing the better of many evils, to taking a stand based on universal truths.

What makes value discussions so interesting is the chance to hear different sides of issues. However, discussions of value are difficult because there are no definite answers; sometimes no resolution is possible. Methods of adjudicating disputes, getting to 'Yes,' or analyzing values may be called into question, challenging basic notions of truth. Judgments, based on ethics and evidence ought to be our goals at examining controversy.

A strategy of controversy is a most productive and powerful tool for teaching and discussion. But there is also no strategy more fraught with pitfalls and problems. A successful discussion of values, issues, and debates must incorporate cognitive and affective domains, data and analysis, theory and practice to arrive at well thought-out decisions or recommendations. You may also induce conversational warfare.

Fairness is difficult to achieve when people are inflamed about a subject, defending beliefs they hold sacred, or have an ideological commitment to one position. Teachers must try to lead discussion and debate in ways that are balanced, allowing consideration of opinions. The free flow of views is sometimes painful when individuals express opinions you view, rightfully as crude, retrograde, or socially explosive.

At these times, you desperately want to tell students what is 'right!' Yet to do so may quash unpleasant or unpopular views, and is undemocratic, suppressing conversation. To favor one position over another is to diminish or destroy the whole strategy, thereby also diminishing freedom of expression, the very skills students need to think through a problem. Thus, the social studies teacher's dilemma is how to handle values and hot topics in class in a professional manner that is exciting, fair, and civilized. Why do disputes or protests or differences develop? Why do people hold different beliefs on important topics? How are exchanges of opinions expressed in a courteous and productive way, so all voices are heard? A difficult problem in teaching, indeed!

Usefulness of a Controversy Strategy

A controversy strategy is most useful for illuminating choices between and among alternative values. Values can be immediate and practical, or long range and philosophical, directed toward down-to-earth matters like selecting the 'best' car based on gender issues, equality between men and women at work in the U.S., or world society. If women are valued as much as men, why do they make up so few corporate heads or political leaders? A much knottier problem than cars.

Difficult choices revolve around universal values, the relationship between rich and poor, elite and underdog, unequal nations. Here arguments can focus on issues of responsibility, charity, self-help, individualism, need, ability, dignity, and social discord to name but a few values. Income and wealth inequality are deep and difficult issues worthy of discussion, perhaps by raising the idea that we live in an age of the 1% and the 99%. Welfare, tax reform, food stamps, medical treatment, and health care are socioeconomic issues that engender heated disagreements over who deserves help and by what methods aid should be delivered. A serious discussion of poverty and wealth would demand considerable data, careful analysis of policy choices, and an agreement to delay judgment until all sides are heard. Tough, you might say, but well worth it in terms of impact on student interest, perspective, and choice.

Problems with a Controversy Strategy

Interest generated by a controversial issue can also sow the seeds of its own destruction. So powerful may the arguments become that passion and heat will overwhelm reason and light in searching for a defensible solution. More sensitive issues result in greater likelihood of discussion/debate getting out of hand. Students may strongly prefer that only one of the sides in a debate wins, creating a hostile climate for minority views, or minority supporters may be so loud and intolerant that they destroy a discussion. Our party politics is like this nowadays, with the middle disappearing. Examination of ideas is difficult to sustain in an atmosphere of controversy seen strictly in win-or-lose terms.

Your deepest objective in using a controversy approach is to encourage critical thinking and choice, asking students to judge alternative viewpoints on logical, philosophical, and evidential criteria. More than any other strategy, controversy needs time to develop and deepen through review, debate, and reflection on major positions. Premature decision-making mocks issues by promoting a rush to judgment rather than an intelligent rationale. You must always, however partisan you are, give a fair representation or sampling of views on an issue.

Problems develop when personally affected by an issue. We are all human and we have feelings, students and teachers alike. Difficulties may arise when you have strong feelings about an issue, e.g., wishing to condemn or praise a political figure, an act of Congress, or a Supreme Court decision. Even more potentially explosive are situations in which students become shocked or angered at hostile remarks, racial slurs, or stereotypic thinking made by and directed at classmates. Examples of controversy gone awry might be anti-Jewish remarks offered, wittingly or unwittingly, by a student during a discussion of the Holocaust, or racist remarks during a discussion of civil rights.

How then can strong personal views be controlled, limiting conflict, prejudice, and bias? Potentially volatile issues and strong personal beliefs, thus a system for discussion is necessary, perhaps signing a new Mayflower compact to listening and taking notes before any response to antagonists. Teachers' aim must be a balanced, thoughtful manner that combines didactic, reflective, and affective components, focusing students on respectfully presenting positions, not resolving all.

Controversy Teaching Techniques

Problems generic to a controversy strategy (and its motivational power) may be kept under control using a variety of techniques that harness energy yet produce balanced understanding. As much as possible, controversy must allow competing interpretations, accompanied by sufficient data, and a format for discussion that gives students the time and opportunity to weigh differences and come to a reasonable decision.[18]

For a successful controversy lesson, any issue or difference of opinion must offer alternative viewpoints. If the issue is stacked in one direction or another, students will lead to a conclusion rather than engage philosophical argument. Perhaps with your help class can draft a compact for discussion that is read aloud and procedures agreed upon before discussion begins, each member signing on to signal acceptance?

Debate and discussion can employ a variety of formats, including research, debates, panels, devil's advocacy, committees, mock trials, investigative journalism, and editorial writing. Debates and panels, if properly prepared, allow a two-sided or multifaceted approach in a structured format that constrains personal emotions and puts a premium on justifying positions. A well-prepared debater, for example, supports their arguments with detailed data, research findings, expert opinions, and logical arguments against opponents' positions. Alternative approaches for a controversy strategy include:

Simulations: Play general and specific roles that relate directly to issues through the medium of a game or game-like series of moves and countermoves, making choices to win, lose, or stalemate.

Debates: Students engage in a formal exchange of ideas in teams that research opposing sides and present their views by defense, cross-examination, rebuttal, and concluding summary.

Panels: Students research a variety of views and solutions that they present to others as members of an expert panel.

Investigative Reporters: Students role-play newspaper reporters studying origins, development, and present status of a controversial topic to write a story that is fair to all sides.

Devil's Advocates: You and/or one or more students argue positions that are either unpopular or overlooked by most because these views should be heard and evaluated.

Mock Trials: Students organize a lengthy role-play in which they reenact either an actual or a fictitious court case playing parts: lawyers, judges, witnesses, defendants, plaintiffs, etc. How about the case of Citizens United?

Social Science Researchers: Students collect, analyze, and evaluate evidence and arguments used to support different positions on an issue, concluding with a report to the class and an assessment of the evidence and arguments by each side.

Poll Takers/Interviewers: Students develop, write, and field test a survey of attitudes and opinions (following Pew, Gallup, or other pollsters) on a topic of importance and value, to peers, sharing findings and errors.

Councils/Committees/Policymakers: Students serve as policymakers, role-playing a real group or committee responsible for settling a dispute.

Role-Reversals: Students take the position of an 'enemy,' the opposing side, in an argument, at the beginning of a lesson or after completing an argument for their side.

Once issues have been thoroughly examined, discuss the whole experience in a debriefing. Review data acquired, reasons heard, and pros and cons thrashed out. At this point, specifics have been added to general principles, putting flesh on the bones of abstract values. There may, of course, still be students offering ideas that fly in the face of all evidence or reason, but their problems will become rapidly evident to peers who have carefully deliberated a case.

Thoughtfulness and knowledge put pressure on everyone to be fairer and more understanding than at the beginning of the lesson or unit. As members of the class offer competing views or puncture poor defenses and illogic, you need not intervene.

If, however, a majority of students adopt a stand you see as stereotypical, unethical, or indefensible, then offer arguments and evidence in support of alternative views. Convey to students positions that run directly counter to theirs and point them to better evidence. If they thoroughly review a controversy or value problem and still refuse or are unable to consider the views of others, you must *respond strongly and with feeling even if they find the other side disturbing.* Taking a public stand against majority or mainstream values is a time-honored democratic tradition that has been nurtured by both political and cultural leaders, so talk to Thoreau. Students may accept or reject what you see as the better position, but at least they do so with the understanding that there is no absolute, unchallenged truth! Within the context of legitimate disagreement, opposition to students' opinions can be voiced without fear.[19]

The doctrine of defensible partiality first described by Massialas and Cox offers a series of guidelines when you:

(a) wish to express an opinion or deeply held belief of your own,
(b) need to offer an alternative position that competes with narrow or biased student views, or
(c) must counter student views that seem unreasonable prejudice.[20]

You do not want to be in the position of promoting your personal views because this will lead to making decisions for the students. But neither do you have to express unnatural neutrality. The rationale for defensible partiality is that imposition of value choices diminishes the learner's independence of thought and reduces decision making to a farce, which is likely to promote political apathy and indifference. Students who are trying to build identities in a complex, democratic social order do not need input that promotes a sense of powerlessness and disrespect of opinions.[21]

It is far more preferable that young people make choices on clear, publicly stated issues and policies in their own best interests or as logically and morally correct.

Defensible partiality means that you can express ideas and ideals, but you must **explain the basis of your viewpoint** to the students. Expression of your views must also be timed (not too early on, please!) in a manner that does not diminish student opportunities to develop and promote their own ideas. Introduce your values and preferences at points where students are deadlocked on an issue or wrapped up in their own emotions. Interfere on occasion, but this should happen *after* students have grasped the issues and are psychologically prepared to take a policy position—for example, while studying the political process during an election campaign. As a member of society, you may be for or against someone in an election, or you may decide to abstain or vote for a third-party candidate, or no one at all. Share views with students at many points in a discussion as a demonstration showing you care about election outcomes.

However, if your view is offered too early or argued too strongly, students may agree to an idea that is not really theirs, falling silent out of respect, or they may be persuaded by the intensity of your feelings. If you advance your views after students have already argued, or partially argued, about candidates and issues, then the psychological impact will be quite different. Yours is now one among many developing views—a more mature view, but not one that will overwhelm others.

Play devil's advocate for a position or candidate that is not popular or well understood. Advocate for climate heroine Greta Thunberg or someone in class. Recent studies demonstrate that the issue of teacher[22] closure of views is still very much around and may inhibit controversial conversations. Defensible partiality gives you a reasonable plan of action that avoids hands-off neutrality and active intervention on giving values to students. Students are expected to identify issues in a controversy, research the evidence, analyze the alternatives, make judgments and perhaps take action.

Examples of Controversy Lessons

Use primary and secondary sources in coordinated sets of pros and cons to raise moral or ethical issues. Introduce multiple viewpoints and alternatives to each. Debating issues sets up built-in confrontations with already well-formulated arguments and supporting resources. However, formal debate usually involves a two-sided argument, rather than a continuum of views, and limits group interaction to face-offs. Consider employing a panel for a sliding spectrum of views on a tough issue, e.g., gun control laws, or taxing the rich, or climate change.

Statistics can be a basis for raising issues although this requires careful preparation and selection on your part using numbers, charts, and graphs or if equipped draw from the Internet. For example, the U.S. and many nations and international organizations keep records of the distribution of wealth and income among different populations. The Bureau of the Census is a good source, so are foundations like the Pew Research Center. Often this information is given in graphic form, i.e., the example in Figures 5.2 and 5.3 below.

Both charts represent a reading challenge, an interpretation, and raises questions of inequality, public policy, the economy, and social class. Ask students to interpret, analyze, and synthesize the figures for each year, each bracket, and overall. After interpretations are offered, ask students to make a bold leap beyond the information given to the realm of policy considerations, by asking a series of reading, judgmental, and ethical questions.

This complex chart gives a lot of data about the U.S. population from 1959-2019 about raw median household income. It also gives dollar figures for each group, and charts the ups and downs of each group over 60 years. The chart raises many questions about income equality and race, and ethnic distribution over time, and provides dollar amounts over the historical period.

Groups include Asians, White/non-Hispanic, all races, Hispanics/any race, and blacks to 2019. Each category needs discussion about who is in or not in each statistical definition with attention to direction (most going up) and amounts from a low of about $45,000 for black people to a high of $76,000 for White/non-Hispanic people.

Questions based on Figure 5.2:

1. Are incomes generally rising or falling from 1959?
2. Are all groups beginning as equals, ending as equals? Why not?
3. What is median income—an average, a middle, a total?
4. Why does each group earn different average incomes?

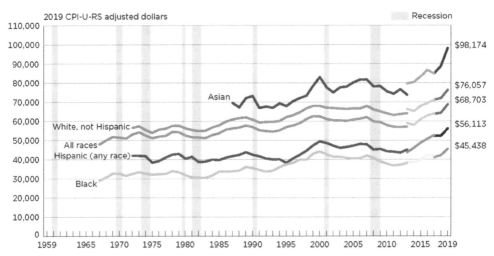

Notes: The data for 2017 and beyond reflect the implementation of an updated processing system. The data for 2013 and beyond reflect the implementation of the redesigned income questions. See Table A-2 for historical race footnotes. The data points are placed at the midpoints of the respective years. Median household income data are not available prior to 1967. For more information on the CPI-U-RS dollar adjustment and recessions, see Appendix A. For information on confidentiality protection, sampling error, nonsampling error, and definitions, see <https://www2.census.gov/programs-surveys/cps/techdocs/cpsmar20.pdf>.

Source: U.S. Census Bureau, Current Population Survey, 1968 to 2020 Annual Social and Economic Supplements (CPS ASEC).

Figure 5.2: Income and poverty in the United States: 2019 Current Population Reports.

Jessica Semega, Melissa Kollar, Emily A. Shrider, and John Creamer, Report Number P60-270. September (2020).

---

5. Which groups have the best and the worst incomes in 1959 and 1999 and 2019?
6. Why are some enjoying high incomes while others have lower incomes? Can you guess an explanation?
7. Do you think it is okay to have widely different incomes by group?
8. Does inequality promote trust and friendship, or competition and hostility? Why?
9. Why might some groups be higher earners than others: is it historical, sociological, racial?
10. Based on this chart, would you vote for laws that promote raising lower income levels, raising higher levels, or do nothing at all? Why?

Questions based on Figure 5.3:

1. How much was earned by each fifth of the population in 1968 and in 2018?
2. Is inequality increasing or decreasing?
3. How much (shaded top) was earned by the top 5% in 1968 and in 2018?
4. How much was earned by the lowest and middle 20% over the years?
5. Does this chart show an increasingly equal or unequal income for each fifth?
6. Why does the top 5% and top fifth probably earn so much? Who is each fifth?
7. How do you feel about a country in which 20% of the people earn more than half of the total income in 2018?
8. Is the income distribution fairly or unfairly, and what can be done about it?

The highest-earning 20% of families made more than half of all U.S. income in 2018

Share of U.S. aggregate household income, by income quintile

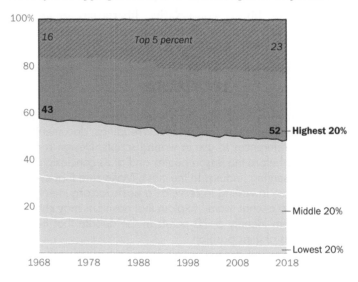

Note: Figures may not add to 100% due to rounding.
Source: U.S. Census Bureau, Income and Poverty in the U.S.: 2018, Table A-4.

PEW RESEARCH CENTER

Figure 5.3:   Pew Research Center (2020) www.pewresearch.org.

9. Would you argue for taxes for the rich or against more taxes? Why?
10. Is it healthy for so few to have so much, and for others to have so little?

SUMMARY QUESTIONS

1. Based on Figures 5.2 and 5.3, what might you recognize as income inequality issues in the U.S.? Would tax solutions improve the situation?
2. Based on both charts, is income inequality likely to get worse or better, and why?
3. Based on both charts, how would you describe the U.S. social economy and divisions?

Many Americans are concerned that income inequality and social is a growing problem for the country. Greater inequality distorts the economy giving less spending money to the poor and middle class and more to the rich and very rich. Some feel this is fair if the funds are earned by hard work, others feel that no one should go hungry and that all should earn a decent pay guaranteed by a minimum wage. Ask students to research ideas about wealth and income and present arguments for and against higher taxes for the rich and/or higher minimum wages for the poor and working poor. To enrich the historical knowledge underpinning this controversy, present ideas from sources including Rawls' *Theory of Justice*, Smith's *Wealth of Nations*, Marx's *Communist Manifesto,* or Wilkerson's *Caste: The Origins of Our Discontent*. Offer newspaper and online quotes about income inequality to spark and sustain discussion.

Encourage students to decide which kind of distribution would be fairest: one that is more equal or more unequal. As discussion progresses, students will identify and develop alternative positions on socioeconomic fairness, but not necessarily consensus. To round out the issue, create a formal debate or role-play Congress to set a tax and minimum wage policy—*laissez-faire*, socialist, liberal, conservative, libertarian, or green party, with students finally stating their preference for or against income inequality in the United States.

LET'S DECIDE

Choose a popular controversy for discussion. Develop roles to play for a panel discussion or debate on a highly charged issue. Offer students readings, documents, online statistics, Internet resources, and references to use in writing scripts. Design a survey that will be administered to students before the lesson begins and at its conclusion. Students assist in tabulating data and presenting findings to the class. Make sure that everyone submits an initial position on the issue in writing to serve as a basis for argument. Perhaps you can send positions by email to a 'chat room.' Explain that positions may change after the final arguments and have them identify 5–10 points in the debate that they think everyone needs to know regardless of their position.

Controversies could focus on (a) international terrorism, (b) national health care in the U.S., (c) tax reform, (d) government tapping of Internet communications, (e) extending women's rights, or (f) economic inequality within the U.S. and/or among the nations of the world. Within these topics, more specific issues could be identified, aimed at particular areas, actions, or legal decisions. What current events and issues are ripe for a controversy strategy in your school and community? How would you try to obtain student cooperation in taking the range of arguments on an issue? Are there any issues that you might want to avoid discussing at the middle or high school level? Which issues would resonate *best* for teens, for pre-teens? Are any local issues open to debate, like a new power plant or sports stadium or gun laws, drinking ages, or perhaps you might like to try out dietary issues, controlling fat and sugar overload, cholesterol and diabetes prevention?

SUMMARY

Perspectives, mystery, and controversy are three higher order strategies used to move social studies classes toward meeting C3 and Common Core goals of interpretation and judgment. Fueled by interesting data, thought-provoking questions, and role-playing, student interest and insight should grow significantly. Mix the three or the six strategies to suit your goals. The more powerful strategies encourage analysis, synthesis, and judgment. The less-powerful strategies—data gathering, comparison and contrast, and drama—involve valuable but somewhat less complex cognition and affect (i.e., recall, comprehension, and application). Strategies can be combined to create a more powerful effect than a single approach.

Greater power and impact may create more difficulties for students, for example, greater frustration. Strategies must be assessed in terms of intended audiences and applied accordingly. Prepare students to think, on a daily basis not irregularly. For example, you might want to hold informal practice debates before fielding full-scale teams. As students become

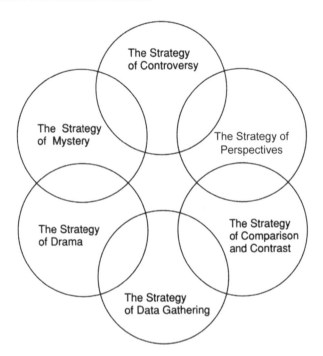

Figure 5.4:   Six strategies for teaching social studies.

familiar with the more exacting, complex, challenging strategies, they will increasingly be able to take on harder issues and feel quite comfortable.

Building thinking skills in social studies attracts student interest in proportion to the intriguing qualities of the problems provided. The more curiosity and interest aroused, the greater the potential for growth of rich and varied ideas, reaching the highest levels of the new taxonomy, *creating*. In the act of creating, learners take the initiative inventing maps, projects, ideas, and products of their own designs. Our six strategies, seen as part of our overall repertory, are portrayed in Figure 5.4 as a series of overlapping sets or circles.

Each is independent yet complementary, working together to build the didactic, reflective, and affective goals we hope to achieve in social studies, forming a hierarchy from lower to higher levels including:

Data-gathering, comparison, and contrast are aimed at didactic goals; drama and controversy are oriented toward affective goals; and mystery, controversy, and perspectives strategies build reflective thinking. Your choice of a particular strategy will inevitably influence and be influenced by topic selection and sources, questions, activities, and assessment. In the chapters that follow, the six strategies will be applied to commonly taught middle and secondary courses, world/global studies, U.S. history, economics, government, and other social sciences, sciences, and humanities.

TO DO

Prepare a list of topics commonly taught in U.S. history, global studies, civics, or economics. Write each topic on a 3 x 5 index card or on your electronic notepad or computer. Sort the topics according to the strategy that would seem most appropriate. For example, would the Civil War best lend itself to a perspectives' strategy or to a mystery strategy? Would the Civil Rights Movement of the 1960s be most appropriately presented as drama or controversy or a mix of the two? Would current party politics fit a perspectives approach?

Might preparation of a website rating current Latin American or African governments be best suited to data gathering or perspectives? Are particular topics always suited to a single strategy? Can the same topic be developed in several ways? Is the way you present a topic more dependent on your view of the subject or the subject itself? Discuss this question in a brief written essay. Purposely choose a topic, such as the Mexican Revolution, the British conquest of India, or the power of the U.S. Presidency in the American system of government. Create plans to teach it by preparing a mini-unit you think is nicely suited to using *each of the six strategies* discussed in this and the previous chapters.

Questions to Think about Strategies for Future Teaching

When are there too many perspectives? How would you judge a mystery that was too easy or difficult for your audience? Are there any sensitive controversies that should be avoided in your view? Why or why not? Are there any controversies for which you would not follow a defensible partiality approach? Why? How would you approach higher order thinking in preparing for classes?

Questions to Consider in Choosing Content

How would you react to the question of knowing truth? Do you think that facts are always true? Do you think that conclusions are always true? Can facts or conclusions be less than 100% true but still be acceptable? For example, if 70% of economists agree on the value of a free-market system over traditional or command systems, is their conclusion true? Are high probabilities acceptable? How about data on the most successful economies, would that prove best system awards? Why or why not?

Are all conclusions questionable, to what degree? When you teach a topic in social studies, any topic, how certain are you that the facts are accurate? How sure are you that the conclusions offered are valid? Will you share with students any doubts or questions you have about evidence? Will you teach the knowledge contained in the texts, on the Internet, or in documents as factual and proven? Write a brief essay discussing how you would present social studies issues—as fact, as probability, or as subjective material. Defend your position. Review yourself: are you comfortable with perspectives, mystery, and controversy strategies? Which would you find most difficult to implement: perspectives because you might be confused by multiple views; mystery because you would worry that the answers are never quite certain; or controversy because you will have to play referee in a game of clashing sides and deeply held arguments on hot topics?

NOTES

1 Akutagawa, R. (1959) *Rashomon and Other Stories* (New York: Bantam Books).
2 Husserl, E. (1931) *Ideas: General Introduction to Pure Phenomenology*, trans. from German by W. R. B. Gibson (New York: Macmillan).

3 Commager H. S. and Morris, R. B. (1975) *The Spirit of Seventy-Six: Primary Sources* (New York: Harper & Row), 77–78, 80–82.

4 Tyler, J. E. (ed.) (1953) "Account of Lexington," *William & Mary Quarterly,* 3rd series, 10, 1, 104–107.

5 Hudson, C. (1913) *History of the Town of Lexington*, Vol. 1 (Boston: Houghton Mifflin), 527–529, 530.

6 For a discussion of strategy theory see Dewey, J. (1913) *Interest and Effort in Education* (New York: Houghton Mifflin). For a hands-on approach, go to Gerwin, D. and Zevin, J. (2010) *Teaching U.S. History as Mystery* (New York: Routledge).

7 Parenti, M. (1999) *History as Mystery* (San Francisco: City Lights Books).

8 Berlyne, D. E. (1965) *Structure and Direction in Thinking* (New York: Wiley), 236–276.

9 Russell, W. B., III (ed.) (2014) *Digital Social Studies* (Charlotte, NC: Information Age Publishing).

10 Bruner, J. (1965) *On Knowing: Essays for the Left Hand* (New York: Atheneum).

11 Hidi, S., and Renninger, K. A. (2006). "The Four-Phase Model of Interest Development," *Educational Psychologist*, 41, 111–127.

12 Yazzie-Mintz, E. (2010). *Charting the Path from Engagement to Achievement: A Report on the 2009 High School Survey of Student Engagement* (Bloomington, IN: Center for Evaluation & Education Policy).

13 Weinstein, C. E. and Mayer, R. E. (1986) The Teaching of Learning Strategies. In Wittrock, M. C. (ed.) *Handbook of Research on Teaching*, 3rd Ed (New York: Macmillan), 315–327.

14 Van Sledright, B. (2002) *In Search of America's Past: Learning to Read History in Elementary School* (New York: Teachers College Press).

15 Waley, A. (1964) *Translations from the Chinese* (New York: Knopf).

16 Massialas, B. (Sept./Oct. 1990) "Educating Students for Conflict Resolution and Democratic Decision-Making," *The Social Studies,* 5, 202–207.

17 Festinger, L. (1964) *Conflict, Decision, and Dissonance* (Stanford, CA: Stanford University Press).

18 Lockwood, A. and Harris, D. (1985) *Reasoning with Democratic Values: Ethical Problems in United States History* (New York: Columbia Teachers College Press).

19 Shaver, J. P. and Strong, W. (1982). *Facing Value Decisions: Rationale-Building for Teachers,* 2nd Ed. (New York: Columbia Teachers College Press).

20 Ross, E. W. (2017) *Rethinking Social Studies: Critical Pedagogy in Pursuit of Dangerous Citizenship* (IAP Press).

21 Rossi, J. A. (Spring, 1995) "In-Depth Study in an Issues-Oriented Social Studies Classroom," *Theory and Research in Social Education,* 33, 2, 88–120.

22 Parker, W. (2010) "Listening to Strangers: Classroom Discussion in Democratic Education," *Teachers College Record*, 112, 2815–2832.

FOR FURTHER STUDY: TEACHING STRATEGIES FOR HIGHER LEVEL SKILLS

Beyer, B. K. (1997) *Improving Student Thinking: A Comprehensive Approach* (Boston: Allyn & Bacon).

Fisher, R. and Ury, W. (1991) *Getting to Yes: Negotiating Agreements Without Giving In* (Boston: Houghton-Mifflin).

Grant, A. (2021) *Think Again* (New York: Viking Press).

Hartoonian, M. (1989) Social Content and Higher-Order Thinking. In *Teaching Complex Thinking in School Subjects.* (Alexandria, VA: Association for Supervision and Curriculum Development).

Hess, D. (2015) *Controversy in the Classroom: The Democratic Power of Discussion* (New York and London: Routledge).

Laurel, B. (1991) *Computer as Theatre: A Dramatic Theory of the Interactive Experience* (Reading, MA: Addison-Wesley).

Lipman, M. (1991) *Thinking in Education* (New York: Cambridge University Press).

Massialis, B. G. and Zevin, J. (1983) *Teaching Creatively* (Malabar, FL: Kreiger & Sons).

Newmann, F. (1988) *Higher-Order Thinking in High School Social Studies* (Madison, WI: National Center on Effective Secondary Schools).

Raths, L. (1986) *Teaching for Thinking: Theories, Strategies, and Activities for the Classroom*, 2nd Ed. (New York: Teachers College Press).

Richards, R. (ed.) (2009) *Everyday Creativity and New Views of Human Nature: Psychological, Social, and Spiritual Perspectives* (Washington, DC: American Psychological Association).

Ruggiero, V. (1988) *Thinking Across the Curriculum* (New York: Harper & Row).

Samuelson, M. (2016) "Education for Deliberative Democracy: *Democracy and Education*, 24, 1, Article 5, www.democracyeducationjournal.org.

Starko, A. J. (2010) *Creativity in the Classroom: School of Curious Delight* (New York: Routledge).

Stitztlein, S. M. (2020) *Learning How to Hope: Democracy through Our Schools and Civil Society* (UK: Oxford University Press).

Wiggins, A. (2017) *The Best Class You Never Taught: How Spider Web Discussion Can Turn Student into Learning Leaders* (Washington, DC: ASCD).

Winne, P. H. (Winter, 1979) "Experiments Relating to Teachers' Use of Higher Cognitive Questions to Student Achievement," *Review of Educational Research*, 49, 1, 13–49.

TEACHING STRATEGIES FOR HIGHER LEVEL SKILLS

BUILD YOUR OWN LESSON

The challenge: thinking 'on your feet.'

Interact with a new piece of evidence, data, issue, or problem.

Design a lesson of your own using different materials (newly discovered art, music, literature, history, geography, etc.).

Worry not about what you know, but react by thinking about how you would teach the data. Improvise!

Write a didactic, reflective, and affective goal for each document or picture, then add a low, medium, and high order question.

Choose one of the six strategies.

Pick a brief method of evaluating success (verbal, written, and tested).

What questions do the data support? Where do they fit in history?

What is the source and context: time and place? And how does that matter?

Did you find improvisation for the classroom easy or difficult? Why?

Why were locomotives invented? How old might be the one shown? What ideas could you develop around this very old engine? How is it put together? Write the role you'd play presenting the locomotive in class. Which unit of study would the engine best fit?

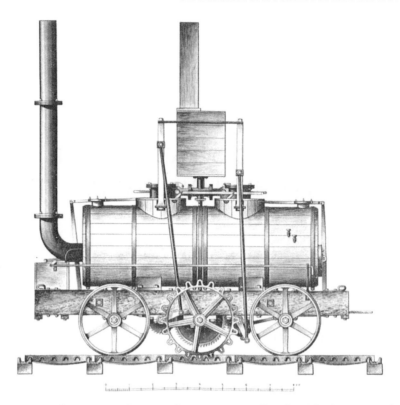

Figure 5.5: Early Locomotive Made From a Boiler in 1812 (engraving 1829). Blenkinsop's rack locomotive ran from 1812-1859, Salamanca UK, coal tramway. The Mechanics Magazine, 1829, author unknown. Wikipedia, public domain, commons.

6

ASSESSMENT IN SOCIAL STUDIES

D4.4.6-8. Critique arguments for credibility.

D4.4.9-12. Critique the use of claims and evidence in arguments for credibility.

D4.5.6-8. Critique the structure of explanations.

D4.5.9-12. Critique the use of the reasoning, sequencing, and supporting details of explanations.

C3 Framework, p. 61.

OVERVIEW

This chapter aims at examining the process and techniques, and issues in evaluating learning by a variety of methods.

INTRODUCTION

Teachers need feedback on student learning, formally and informally, and student opinion is critically important too. Asking and diagnosing how you are doing is a continuous process. This chapter examines diagnosis, testing, and measurement of student performance along the three dimensions from lower to higher levels of thinking.

There are several issues that Social Studies teachers need to be aware of when making evaluations. These issues may be listed as:

(a) selecting assessment tools based on topics; does one size fit all?;
(b) applying evaluation as a part of instructional activities in order for learning to occur;
(c) not only assessing the product, but also the process;
(d) using traditional and alternative evaluation methods;

DOI: 10.4324/9781003026235-14

(e) aiming to improve divergent thinking when using even traditional evaluation aimed at convergent thinking;

(f) being able to use a variety of evaluation tools together.

An assessment method which is developed based on the above issues will be in line with educational constructivism. Consequently, constructivist Social Studies teachers have to implement alternative assessment techniques and traditional assessment methods together. Social Studies teachers are able to use alternative assessment tools as effectively as they use traditional assessment tools. As a result, Social Studies teachers' opinions of alternative assessment are important. Cognitive (didactic and reflective) assessment provides indicators of performance in terms of remembering and understanding, up through reasoning and insight. Information-based questions (IBQs) can be posed on paper, online, and in conversation to assess knowledge and comprehension. Document-based questions (DBQs), formal and informal, call upon students to reason, interpret, and infer answers from evidence and source material posed to assess reflective learning. Perception-based questions (PBQs) ascertain students' attitudes about social studies that apply to historical figures, controversial issues, or popular opinion, part of the affective domain.

If your purpose is clear and sharp, a wide variety of assessments can be applied to almost any aspect of performance across the range of Bloom's cognitive and affective taxonomies, across the C3 Framework, and across a wide swath of multiple intelligences. The same principles hold for all. Teachers need a variety of test devices for a comprehensive view of instructional impact, and this can take many forms, from simple fill-in-the-blank home-made questions to sophisticated Advanced Placement-style DBQ questions and essays on new primary source material presented on the examination. Or you can ask for portfolios of work with samples of student writing aimed at expressing a firm grasp and understanding of historical materials.

The more techniques a teacher used in assessment, the greater the range of capabilities that will emerge and the more reliable the results. High-stakes testing is not an evil in and of itself, but it is damaging to faculty and students because it seeks to assess long-term learning in one-shot assuming that this single examination can validly and reliably provide insight into all taxonomic levels and all intelligences. Actually, with the recent emphasis on reading and mathematics, more and more tests focus on only verbal and numerical skills but there are a dozen intelligences to ask about.

The vast majority of formal test questions—short answer, multiple choice, essay, standardized, or written by teachers—fall into one of the three categories described. Categories may also be mixed in a 'portfolio' that includes a broad range of student work demonstrating many different skills and intelligences. These portfolio collections are often called *authentic* or *performance assessments* because the contents include a student's actual production over a semester or a year, in contrast to achievement extrapolated from performance on a brief standardized test.

How evaluation instruments are used depends on school climate, teacher, subject, and the school or state requirements involving formative, ongoing, as well as concluding, summative, testing. Regardless of format, evaluation may be used to diagnose student and class development, suggesting changes in teaching methods and materials, as well as helping teachers in grading.

Diagnosis is particularly important in deciding on quality and quantity of student learning across the didactic, reflective, and affective dimensions. Quantity alone is unlikely to be sufficient in determining success because memory/recall represents the lowest level of Bloom's taxonomy of objectives, and memory evaporates quickly. If a student does or does not know an answer, this tells us little about comprehension or skills. Therefore, we need to diagnose levels of understanding and affect from low to high, LOT, MOT, and HOT to find elements of the curriculum the students view as successful and engaging.

Note that we seek to learn if students absorb a good portion of the material taught, and understand and reason, and we want feedback on how they perceive and feel about the curriculum and teaching methods. In the Internet Age, knowledge can be easily accessed, so why is memory especially important anymore? What Common Core and the C3 Framework hold dearest is the growth of reasoning processes, particularly the ability to use historical and social science methods of inquiry to pull hypotheses out of evidence and compare explanations from different sources and directions.

At the end or top of the food chain, students are assessed on their ability to make and defend conclusions, take stands, support them with reasons and evidence, and create new constructions and projects with researched materials. Application and insight are what we hope to find expressed in student work, not names, dates, and places we can look up in ten seconds.

THE ASSESSMENT PROCESS

Purposes of Assessment

Every day of teaching, you must make decisions about student progress and attitudes. Problems abound in making a sound judgment because students and teachers get nervous during testing, especially formal examinations.

Did Jimmy have a breakthrough into high-level analysis in our conversation about clashing views of Reconstruction today? Did Matilda wreck her test of Civil War facts because she didn't study or because she didn't feel well? Should Jose receive a higher grade than usual because of a rapid rate of progress, though he is not completely up to standard? Should Mai-Lin be given a lower grade on her essay about World War I because her English is poor, even though most of her information was correct? These are the little problems of assessment that often make teaching complex and difficult. In its broadest sense, evaluation is the organized way we gather and interpret evidence to decide if students are meeting the objectives set for them.

Evaluation encompasses not only measurement and testing, but also opinion polling and self-assessment. *Measurement* is a numerical representation of how much or how well a student has absorbed a specified level of knowledge, skills, or attitudes. Scores express the degree a student holds a particular belief or the amount of facts recalled. The most common form of measurement is *testing. Polling* (surveys, questionnaires, and self-reports) is a way of estimating the strength or weakness of someone's perceptions, values, and feelings. Testing is largely used to assess didactic and reflective abilities, while surveys and self-reports assess affective expression, views, and perspectives. Evaluation may also be informal—your perception performance on everyday class assignments, written or oral, perhaps artistic or musical. Ultimately, evaluation is intended to give you a broad picture of achievement that will serve as a benchmark for individual students or a whole class.

Figure 6.1:   Keying the right answer?

Benchmarks set a baseline for comparing mid and final assessments. If students don't know anything about the history of Latin America at the beginning of your World History course, well, that is fine, and you have nowhere to go but up. But if you did not administer a pretest, mental map question, or survey of knowledge, you have nothing to use for later comparisons in judging progress.

Thus, a variety of methods should be employed as a measure of a *range* of knowledge, skills, views, and abilities.

You may also ask students to produce many different kinds of work, written, drawn, acted, filmed, and spoken, added to an ongoing portfolio to assess as the semester moves along to a conclusion. Howard Gardner points out that it is important to vary assignments and assessments so that several of a student's 'multiple intelligences' come into play.[1] Eventually, you will use all of the data collected to judge overall performance. The more performances you have and the greater its variety, the more valid your judgment will be, of everyday and over-all outcomes.

Ideally, evaluation should be closely tied to curriculum, instructional techniques, and course goals. First, decide on goals. Which content knowledge and attitudes are most desirable? Second, find out what students know and believe: Do students already know/ understand the material you intend to teach? Third, design curriculum and methods to match your goals: Are you using student feedback to monitor progress, readjust schedules and assignments, and judge the level of understanding and thinking? Fourth, prepare a summative test and course survey that reflects goals, ongoing analysis of student performance, and the material you taught.

The final product (a portfolio perhaps?) or written examination should pull *together a fair sample* of what was presented. If you taught a unit on China and Indian civilizations, the exam items and essays should match what you taught. For the best results, goals, curriculum, methods, and assessments should dovetail closely to ensure a fair test of students' knowledge and development. Evaluate a variety of skills, such as test-taking, map-making, narrative, and argumentative writing. A defensible and meaningful grade, interpretation or judgment is the final award of an assessment process.

Assessment provides valuable diagnostic information, not just scores. It also helps you judge a student's output or product, ongoing and at the end of a course. Regardless of how you feel about assigning grades, grading is usually an important, inescapable part of school life. Parents, students, and school officials all expect examination and evaluation. In fact, standardized tests have become virtually synonymous with student achievement, only questioned now because of online learning issues caused by the COVID-19 pandemic.

Testing is frequently narrow and misapplied, diagnosis often confused with judgment, and results taken too seriously. There is always a degree of error, particularly in high-stakes examinations. The question is how much?

Test performance should always be compared with classroom performance for a comprehensive picture of work. Some students are great participants live, online, and on a call, but poor test takers, or vice versa. Therefore, testing should be used as carefully as possible to ensure a fair result from a wide sample of student work and motivation, leading to an honest evaluation of audience progress.

Types of Evaluation

Most assessment is designed to measure learning goals in terms of cognition, knowledge of facts, or a range of reasoning skills from lower to higher levels. Social studies tests, for example, typically assess growth in knowledge of U.S. or world history, ability to apply economic concepts to new data, or skill in writing an argument defending or attacking a controversial position. However, there are also facets of social studies for which affective measures are appropriate—measures of attitude, opinion, and perception. These are psychological instruments that are interpreted differently from tests used to assess cognitive outcomes, views count, not data alone.

Responses on cognitive examinations, because they measure factual knowledge (IBQs) and analytical skills (DBQs), can usually be judged as correct or incorrect, better or worse, yielding scores based on established criteria. Attitudes, by contrast (PBQs), involve perceptions about the world, classroom, or personal opinions. Attitudes may be *scaled* (ranked) according to their emotional strength or weakness, but cannot be graded numerically or evaluated in terms of right and wrong. There are also 'gray areas,' questions that are difficult to classify, particularly involving judgments that incorporate cognitive and affective components, perceptions, and knowledge together, e.g., a judgment of a U.S. President.

There are several ways to classify evaluation methods involving concepts of centrality and quality. *Centrality* constitutes the 'normal' or average achievement levels of students. Cronbach has distinguished between *maximum* performance and *typical* performance.[2] Both are vital to evaluation because the typical, average, or central is what you can expect from most of your students. A normal curve demonstrates centrality, with most students performing above or below the average. Maximum performance might plot the growth in verbal and writing skills from the beginning to the end of the term. Quality or 'maximum' measures reflect the upper limits of knowledge, ability, and skill, or rapidly changing opinions and values. To adequately evaluate students, you must be able to identify each of these criteria.

WHAT DO YOU THINK?

Consider the ways that different types of tests are developed and administered. What could you learn from each kind of test?

Standardized or Informal Tests/Polls: Standardized tests and surveys are constructed by experts and given field tests; informal tests or polls are created by a teacher and/or a team of students.

Group or Individual Tests/Polls: Tests or polls administered to individuals one at a time (e.g., a personal interview). More commonly, these are administered to groups.

Norm- or Criterion-Referenced Tests: A norm-referenced test measures performance against a comparison group such as students who have already completed the course, or the entire school, or students throughout the state. Raw scores (number of correct or incorrect answers) are then compared to the norm to create a grade. The score is thus comparative 'on a curve.' Criteria-referenced tests, in comparison, are absolute measures that demonstrate mastery of a certain body of knowledge.

Selection or Supply Tests: Selection tests or polls ask students to choose from ready-made alternative answers, whereas supply tests, such as fill-ins or essays, require students to provide the answers.

Power or Timed Tests: Power questions (usually reflective) provide students with enough time to reach their highest level of performance, whereas with speeded tests students must complete the exam working a specified time.

Objective or Subjective Tests: On objective tests, there are right and wrong answers usually in multiple-choice format. Students receive the same grade regardless of who is scoring the exam. In contrast, subjective tests use evaluator's opinions to determine the final scores or grades.

Product or Performance Tests: Product or performance work means that a student must complete written, artistic, or active/oral presentations in a form, package, or portfolio that can be judged against set or established criteria (like rubrics) or in comparison with the work of others.

Questions:

1. In what ways are polls and surveys like or unlike cognitive tests? Are student views important to check?
2. Why have many tests been field tested for use on a national basis?
3. When might you want students to complete an oral examination or present a portfolio of their hands-on work?

Would such material be easy or difficult to grade in comparison to standardized objective/multiple-choice tests?

When you set a standard for passing a test, 75%, you are establishing a bar for performance.

However, if you assess scores in terms of averages, you are measuring typical results, using the mean/mode/median as a central standard. Actual student performance vis-à-vis others in the group determines passing and failing scores. A bar holds students to a predetermined standard, whereas typical performance measures the individual against the distribution of group scores. Neither method is better than the other. Each has a place in a social studies classroom depending on goals and diagnosis of students' skills and capabilities.

In recent years, authentic or alternative forms of assessment (so called because these reflect the actual, ongoing activities of a learner) have been gaining ground. In contrast to formal standardized tests, these evaluation techniques represent an attempt to look at a wide body of student work as achievement. The most common means of achieving this is via a student built portfolio on a negotiated topic.

For an authentic approach, develop a series of related assignments and exercises that call on students to demonstrate different forms of knowledge and skills. The goal is to obtain a holistic picture of 'the student,' not simply their test performance on an examination.[3] Because each student is growing, changing, and absorbing new ideas, portfolio assessment gives teachers the opportunity to assess development. Portfolios are formative measures based on criteria set by you and your students, a committee of colleagues, or based on national subject matter standards like the C3 Framework.

A well-designed portfolio assessment should:

(a) be purposeful, systematic, and meaningful,
(b) promote student selection and judgment of products,
(c) permit input from parents, teachers, and administrators,
(d) reflect daily assignments and activities,
(e) accumulate over a long period of time,
(f) encourage revision and rethinking of contents,
(g) include many different media.

Portfolio/authentic assessment takes a broad view of development and focuses on growth over time, with participation in setting evaluation standards. There is no 'rush to judgment' by you or anyone else. Students may select their best work for inclusion in their final portfolio, tidying up and revising any products they see as weak before submitting the total package for a mark or grade. This is different from a quick quiz or a standardized test and tells you a great deal more about what is going on in a student's mind. The contents of the portfolio can include everything that teachers and/or students believe will reveal evidence of progress. Portfolios in social studies, much like those in the arts, might include notes, reflective writing, arguments and essays, peer reviews, videotapes, photographs, paintings and drawings, musical or audiotapes, descriptions, rough drafts, diagrams, graphs or charts, group products, and computer-generated materials.[4] To the extent possible, items selected for the portfolio should be 'authentically' that of students, individuals and groups. Copied or plagiarized materials have no place unless clearly used or reinterpreted by the student for a public reason. Internet checking is easy now to identify copycats. With this wealth of product to choose from, the portfolio permits you and the student to diagnose how far and how deeply the student has progressed.

Portfolio quality is measured against established criteria shared with (and sometimes developed by) students. Students are allowed to choose projects and review their own performance before submitting their portfolio to the teacher or committee for assessment. Experience with portfolios often produces more critically minded students who are often harder graders than teachers! Although *typical* performance is frequently hard to identify using authentic assessment, maximum performance is relatively easy to measure because effort is continuously evaluated from a baseline of agreed-on criteria or rubrics that all share at the beginning of a unit or course. Perfecting a portfolio on work on, say, the powers of the President, is continuous and demanding.

Rubrics. Rubrics are a set of evaluation criteria established to rate, rank, and analyze assignments. In recent years, rubrics have become all pervasive in popularity, though most in my view are rather primitive and 'additive' rather than 'categorical.' Additive rubrics basically assess in terms of complete, mostly complete, poorly complete, student performances, begging the question of what 'complete' means. More is not better, but it is quality that counts. Many rubrics are generic and barely relate to the content of lessons and units. They could be about anything, reading better, thinking cleverly, etc. Rubrics should specify levels of performance as outstanding, acceptable or substandard. In a history class these might involve:

(a) understanding and explaining cause and effect,
(b) drawing inferences from primary sources and artifacts,
(c) comparing and contrasting sources with secondary historical interpretations and tertiary textbooks.

The best and most useful rubrics are detailed and specific to the curriculum goals. Whatever the topic, teachers would be a lot better writing their own rubrics than swiping them from the Internet. Each category of the rubric should represent a different dimension, a different aspect of Bloom's taxonomy, and/or a different multiple intelligence. Rubrics should move from lower to higher order goals and criteria for outcomes, not simply add a bit more on each level.

Adding on is not bad, but it is all about performance levels, not different kinds of skills like applying, analyzing, and then creating. A sample rubric is shown below in Figure 6.2.

High-quality performance: Knowledge of history is extensive (six sources or more), and student can draw inferences using primary and secondary sources; students can *consistently* judge reliable and unreliable historical witnesses; student can *regularly* point out cause–effect relationships; students can develop projects like two or more travel brochures that accurately and imaginatively reflect research on time and place using multiple media.

Medium-quality performance: Knowledge of history is modest (three to six sources) and students can support ideas with texts and sources, drawing several inferences and judgments; students can sometimes separate reliable and unreliable sources; students understand cause–effect relationships half of the time; and can develop a project that uses either primary or secondary sources, constructing a 'Blast from the Past' newspaper.

Substandard performance: Knowledge of history is limited (three sources or less) and is factual rather than inferential; students can understand the concept of bias and reliability, but confuse primary and secondary sources; students can partially interpret original sources, but are more comfortable taking notes from textbooks used as a guide to events; students are capable of a small-scale project such as creating a postcard from the past.

An example of a scoring rubric for a U.S. history class project is given in Figure 6.2.

Assessment rubric for The New Deal	Connections between sources	Connections between supporters and critics	Connections between past and present
Affective/HOT	Students will make judgments of two or more New Deal sources by rating their arguments: based on logic, based on evidence, based on emotion.	Students will infer democratic Ideals that motivated critics and supporters about government policies that they saw as fitting or not fitting civic ideals.	Students will conduct brief research projects demonstrating how New Deal policies connect to present day civic life are connected, government vs. private control of the economy by integrating pro and con sources.
Reflective/MOT	Students will interpret at least two sources for and two sources against New Deal policies, explaining the main reasons for agreement or opposition.	Students will connect sources to issues of the time, explaining the major argument posed by critics and supporters of FDR/New Deal.	Students will apply at least two New Deal policies from the past to at least two current economic issues (wages and taxes) reported in the daily news.
Didactic/LOT	Students will identify at least one source for and one against the New Deal.	Students will note at least three key words used by critics and by supporters.	Students will point to at least three examples connecting present events to past New Deal events.

Figure 6.2: Sample rubric demonstrating levels and kinds of performances assessed.

Understanding Student Outcomes. Three ways are available to understand student outcomes. One is norm-referenced relating the individual's performance to that of a group, for example, Elliot's map interpretations were better than 80% of his classmates. Performance is judged against a 'normal' or 'typical' result we actually know about based on previous measures of other student groups. A second way of interpreting results is measuring the extent outcomes match pre-specified criteria. Performance is measured against a specific teaching objective, a criterion, or rubric for success. Melanie correctly identified 18 nations on an outline map, with 20 the maximum possible, so a good job!

A third way of interpreting results involves measuring a student's performance against a baseline for that student. For instance, you and the student could compare three attempts at drawing a map of the world from memory or contrast written arguments for or against a given issue from the beginning, middle, and end of the school year. Performance is observed and measured against a student's earlier or ongoing performance. This is a measure of a student's evolution.

Function of Assessment. Overall course objectives are keys assessment. Objectives, general and specific, apply to class as a whole, and to each individual within. Thus, we are dealing with function rather than form, the uses of a survey or test directed to classroom achievement. Bloom and colleagues have suggested several major functions: placement in a class, ongoing assessment (formative), diagnosis, and (summative) end of unit or term evaluation applications.[5]

Tests, surveys, or self-reports can be used to judge student operational levels before placement in a new setting or program. Knowing an individual's predisposition, interests, and mastery of a body of material is key to understanding the tasks they need to master in a learning sequence. Placement procedures might involve determining individual learning style, or finding out how much a student already knows about a social science or history topic.

Teacher-made pretests, standardized aptitude tests, cognitive mapping or semantic webbing, surveys of feelings about a subject, observations, portfolios of student work, or a combination and interview might be used for placements.

Tests to acquire feedback from students about ongoing work and attitude development are part of *formative evaluations*. Examine small changes in student performance so you can adjust your program.

Quizzes might show students needing more or less data on a topic, higher or lower levels of inquiry, a faster or slower pace of instruction. A test in economics might show widespread misunderstanding of personal finance including confusion over credit, implying the need for review. A test on the U.S. Civil War could show a solid knowledge indicating moving on to the Reconstruction unit. If a portfolio is being accumulated, each essay could be compared with the previous one to discern improvements in knowledge, reasoning, and interpretation of primary sources. Awareness of sources, especially bias and exaggeration, is an indicator of deep reflection.

Different ways of thinking about assessments, as in Figure 6.3, shows the ways assessments and observations intersect and dovetails with three categories of assessment. Evaluation goals intersect with didactic, reflective, and affective dimensions. Finally, assessment takes place at all levels as ongoing and end-of- course procedures. Students are measured against absolute standards (criterion-referenced) or against means, modes, and

---

Document-Based Essay

The task: You will work with seven primary source documents. Using the information in the documents, explain why certain people criticized President Franklin D. Roosevelt and the New Deal while others enthusiastically supported it.

In your essay, you should:

Develop a thesis (point of view) with a major or essential question.

Use information from **at least three documents** to support your main idea or answer any questions.

Incorporate and identify other, outside historical sources to support your argument.

Reach a conclusion: Answer the question or explain why the criticism was, or was not, justified.

How your essay will be scored:

90 or above: You began with main idea and/or essential question. You used information from at least three documents and included additional information from identified sources. You reached and defended conclusions.

80–89: Fewer than three documents used. **Or** you did not reach a conclusion. **Or** you didn't understand part of the information in the documents.

70–79: You did not begin with an idea or essential question. You did not reach any conclusion. Your essay contained some errors.

60–69: You used fewer than three documents/you didn't understand the documents. Essay contained several errors. Summarized the documents and the background information but you didn't put these to use to make a point. Your essay did not begin with an idea or question. No conclusion.

No grade: You're having trouble with essay writing. For a next essay, you will be teamed with a "buddy" to help you complete the task.

Figure 6.3: Scoring rubric for a document-based essay in U.S. History.

medians derived from 'normal' performances (norm-referenced). Greater variety of testing leads to a broader and more comprehensive picture of individuals and groups in your classroom.

WHAT DO YOU THINK?

Which types of tests have you taken or given recently: norm-referenced or criterion-referenced; using a 'bar' or a mean; summative or formative assessment? What, are the advantages and disadvantages of each type? Which standards would you favor in your own classroom: those based on absolute levels, bars, such as 75% to pass, or those based on a normal curve, where student performance sets the mean? What if your class usually achieves a mean of 50% or 60%? Is this acceptable? Why or why not? What if 75% is achieved by only half, on any one test? How will your answers change (if at all) when 80% of your class scores 90% or above?

Will you give those below 90% Cs and Ds? Why or why not? Describe your personal policy for giving grades.

ISSUES IN EVALUATION

We are faced with serious problems each time we attempt to judge student progress or the quality of student work either in groups or as individuals. Testing, diagnosing, or surveying students' knowledge, understanding, and/or values is a fine art that is often distorted by problems concerning validity and reliability, formal versus informal assessment, how to measure the quality of student work, and standardized testing.

Reliability and Validity

Reliability means that measurement instruments (tests or polls) yield similar results each time they are given. This enables us to compare findings in a meaningful way. If results vary widely, the test may not be measuring what we intended (i.e., the test is not reliable). Using the same or a similar test to measure cognitive changes before and after a unit or course, or employing correlated forms of the same survey to assess shifts in opinion or behavior, are means of ensuring reliability. However, this type of controlled testing does

Table 6.1 The structure of evaluation.

Evaluation Levels	
Formative	*Summative*
Didactic	Didactic
Reflective	Reflective
Summative	Summative
Evaluation Purpose	Diagnosis of Learning
Assignment of Grades and/or Scores	
Criterion-Referenced	Norm-Referenced

not reflect a student's many different abilities and talents in the same way an alternative or authentic assessment of portfolio work.

Thus, you face a dilemma choosing between self-expression and standardization, measuring growth and measuring achievement. This dilemma can be resolved by asking students to do a variety of related tasks, which, although judged in different ways, add up to a more complete and realistic picture of ability and accomplishment than test scores alone. Keep in mind, too, that a portfolio of projects and student work can include traditional tests and essays, as well as art, oral history, cartoons, or museum projects. Some students can be artistic, others musical, and some great interpreters.

Test validity is a term that asks: Are we measuring what we really want to measure? More frequently than we would care to admit, there is often little congruence between what is taught and what is tested. Tests may differ from assessment. For example, a teacher or test-maker may decide to measure thinking skills but construct a test that, on careful review, contains items that mostly require the recall of information rather than comprehension, inference, or analysis. This is a quintessential validity problem: The goals and the content of the test do not match, therefore the test results lead to incorrect conclusions.

TO DO

Review dictionary definitions of *reliability* and *validity*. Compare these definitions to those offered in a test and measurement textbook, or online. Do definitions differ substantially, or are they similar? Define validity and reliability in your own terms.

Informal Assessment: Dialogue and Discussion

Informal assessment is the ongoing process by which you try to find out what students know and how they feel. Your focus is on current capabilities and students' attitudes and values. Evaluation in this sense is continuous because it is a way of establishing benchmarks—points at which students show they have achieved a new, higher plateau of learning. Based on responses to classroom questions, you can make important decisions about what the future pace of instruction should be, which materials to assign, and what level of difficulty is next in the sequence of events.

Frequent questioning matched by a high response level also improves achievement.[6] If you are using authentic portfolio assessment, you might ask students to record their questions or answers in a log for future reflection, adding these to their portfolios for later consideration. In any event, diagnostic evaluation helps you know where students are in achieving classroom goals; you can miss this if you only use tests to measure expected outcomes. So, ask and listen!

For example, if a teacher sets a standard of 75% correct answers on an exam for passing, less able students who have made great progress but cannot achieve this level will fail. In addition to examining how we should test, we should also consider when we should test. The notion that a test should follow a given unit of work is dangerous. First, we have no idea of the students' starting point, and thus cannot accurately assess their progress. Second, if the goals are set too low or too high, students will seem brighter or slower than they really are. Third, individual strengths and weaknesses are obscured if you use a group mean or norm. Group norms may conceal serious problems within groups or among individuals. Therefore, regular informal diagnosis of progress is vital to obtaining an accurate view of students' individual strengths and weaknesses, and their place in a group.

WHAT DO YOU THINK?

Would verbal feedback be a way of judging student growth on an informal basis? Do classroom responses indicate students' thinking levels? How much or how little would you trust verbal reasoning as a guide to student progress? What could students say during a lesson that would show insight or lack of understanding? Give two examples.

You can get a pretty good sense of students' comprehension and analytic ability by tracking their thinking through a series of questions and answers. Questions, directions, and the use of students' ideas through redirection and paraphrase will usually elicit enough feedback for you to decide how to proceed. For instance, a preliminary discussion of foreign policy may reveal that 10 or 12 students cannot define the concept. Many others are silent. Such poor reactions indicate that you must backtrack to the comprehension level and define basic terms.

Or, if a number of students seem unable to use new evidence about Russia to test a theory of conflict and cooperation, then a practice session on application is in order. Demonstrate through an example how to use evidence to build or critique a hypothesis, theory, or generalization, e.g., are all revolutions violent? Students' early, midterm, and concluding attempts at developing a theory might be saved and noted as a measure of growth.

Pretests and Correlated Surveys

A second, vital link in diagnosis is a pretest or measure that establishes a benchmark of knowledge or skills.

The same instrument could also serve as a source of information and/or attitudes once the unit is completed. The pretest could be a cognitive map, check- list, questionnaire, drawing, quiz, or information-based test. If the next month or so will be spent studying Latin America, you could offer students an outline map of that continent and ask them to write in the names of all the countries they can identify in a span of three minutes. Student helpers could then tabulate results, counting accurate and inaccurate identifications for each country. The class could then *compare the students' mental map of Latin America to an up-to-date wall map* or website. (This could be done for any country or region.) Toward the end of the unit, the same test could be given again to discover whether the range and accuracy of students' identifications have improved.

Attitudes can also be diagnosed through survey instruments in which students are asked whether they think they will find (and whether they did find) a topic worthy of future study. Students might be polled concerning which subject they would like to study, for what reasons. They might feel they already know a great deal about the U.S. Constitution and prefer to go into greater detail on the Bill of Rights. A preference poll offers insights into student interests and encourages student involvement by showing them that you take their views seriously. Demonstrate that you care to know more about students' views before planning a next unit.

SAMPLE LESSON PLAN

Coffee spilled all over your test ...the Internet is down... Oh no! What can you do while the tests are drying and electricity is back? How about an essay instead of multiple-choice questions on the history of India? The students saw the film *Gandhi* and read some of his speeches, so put this to good use by asking them to explain Gandhi's role in creating a large independent nation. Was Gandhi a great leader in theory, in practice, or both? How do you define a great leader and defend your definition?

Measures of satisfaction or agreement can be used to ascertain student interest in a topic or identification with a position or feeling. Likert scales,[7] such as the one shown in the Bill of Right Opinion Poll, are built for polling. Students are asked to use the scale to answer a series of survey questions on the Bill of Rights as an example.

To use the information collected, calculate the number of students choosing each response SA to SD, and then compute the averages for each response to uncover trends in thinking. This provides you with feedback about student perceptions of the Bill of Rights. You can also have the students' tabulate answers and present the data in a table or graph to foster mathematical intelligence and research skills.

Giving Final Grades

Remember, grades and scores may be based on personal growth, class norms, or absolute standards of achievement. Share your criteria and a rubric right at the start. Regardless of the standard you choose, be as consistent as possible. Unless you explain beforehand what you are going to do, switching from one approach to another confuses and seems unfair to students.

Grading on a curve (norm-referenced) determine grades because based on students' performance, with groups setting the mean. However, studies have shown that absolute (criterion-referenced) standards tend to produce higher achievement, at least for better performing students.[8]

Those doing poorly who need more assistance often give up altogether with a strict criterion for success. Perhaps less able students need a standard that sets successive personal benchmarks allowing students to self-assess learning, comparing their output against a baseline.

The decision to establish grades depends on the type of class you have and your goals. Grading has a direct effect on motivation, so it is probably best to assess student audiences against themselves and their group norms. Whenever possible, I think you should give less able students the benefit of the doubt on a grade and watch the effect. If the effect is positive as hoped for, then your standards and/or norms can safely rise. If negative, you have reinforced one student who will not have a minor overall impact on group averages per semester or year.

BILL OF RIGHTS OPINION POLL

1. The Bill of Rights is familiar to me and I can explain most of its content.
    SA _ A _ U _ D _ SD _

2. The Bill of Rights is the most interesting part of the U.S. Constitution.
    SA _ A _ U _ D _ SD _

3. The Bill of Rights is just on paper; it doesn't tell what's really happening.
    SA _ A _ U _ D _ SD _

4. The Bill of Rights should be well understood by all Americans.
    SA _ A _ U _ D _ SD _

5. The Bill of Rights is the part of the Constitution that I want to know more about.
    SA _ A _ U _ D _ SD _

Strongly Agree (SA) Agree (A) Undecided or Don't Know (U) Disagree
(D) Strongly Disagree (SD)

Figure 6.4:   Bill of Rights Opinion Poll

Formative and summative grades should reflect a wide mix of measures: classroom questions, true–false quizzes, oral presentations, projects, multiple-choice tests, essay. Variety allows students with different multiple intelligences, strengths and weaknesses, the opportunity to perform better on some measures and worse on others; eventually everyone has a roughly equal chance to succeed or fail. Authentic or portfolio assessment seeks to create a broad measure combined into a cumulative record unique to each student.[9]

Overall, grades should reward insight, cooperation, and not quantity. Special encouragement should be given to those who are willing to move from surface to deeper thinking on a topic, whatever form this may take.[10] You can promote student interest by choosing topics that have appeal introducing lessons that are thought-provoking and setting standards that emphasize reflective and affective responses.

When grading time arrives, be a bit wary of the numerical results and, when warranted, be a bit generous. Daily, weekly, and monthly performance should add up to a summative judgment that accurately reflects students' work and ability. As noted before, Tests for diagnostic or grading purposes should measure students' growth from an established baseline. Results may be set against class norms or absolute passing standards.

Whether you use popular standardized computer tests or write your own examinations as summative or formative evaluations, assessment should be tied to your grading objectives. Clearly distinguish between those tests and portfolio selections that will be graded and those used for diagnostic or self-assessment purposes.

Ideally, goals and concepts, data and questions, and tests and surveys should be integrated with grading criteria made explicit to students at the beginning of the course. Timing and content are important. The final must fairly reflect the curriculum that was taught. Otherwise, students will deal with information that may be unfamiliar. If a summative test is geared toward information covered early in the course, students may have forgotten the details they once knew, yielding an inaccurate picture of knowledge. Thus, your final test should include a balanced selection of key LOT, MOT, and HOT questions based mainly on covered data with only a few *new examples* that seek to extend creative insights and theories.

TO DO

How much faith do you have in standardized tests? Teacher-made tests? Opinion polls? What factors increase your respect for a test or poll? What factors reduce your estimation of test reliability or validity? Write a brief two- or three-paragraph essay stating your views on testing online and on paper, and how seriously scores should be taken. Would you base a student's grade *entirely* on scores? Why or why not? Would you include credit for class participation? Why or why not?

DESIGNING TESTS

Information-Based Questions

The most familiar kinds of test questions are those designed to elicit what a student knows in terms of data. These questions are almost always convergent, cognitive, and didactic.

Answers tend to be either correct or incorrect. Students usually get the answers from reading textbooks and listening to classroom lectures. Information-based questions (IBQs) are also the easiest to write for a classroom test; they may be objectively graded because they tap few of the complexities that characterize higher-order thinking. If you administer an IBQ pretest before a unit of instruction and a similar posttest afterward, you will have a sample of student knowledge in your classroom—assuming that your test, instructional goals, and curriculum materials match one another and the students' ability levels.

Even with excellent IBQs, however, you will not be able to diagnose or assess higher levels of student understanding or affect. Typically, IBQs are online tests using a matching, true–false, fill-in, or multiple-choice format supplemented by ongoing recall questions during daily lessons. Samples of each type of IBQ are offered next.

Short-Answer Tests. These tests are designed primarily to assess 'remembering' of information. Short-answer or multiple-choice tests are popular because of ease in scoring, reliability, and direct tie-in to textbooks lists of names, dates, and places. Typically, short-answer questions leave students a blank space to fill in or ask for the correct answer from four or five provided. Items from a unit on Rome are offered as examples of the fill-in-the-blank type of test question:

1. The representatives of the Plebeians in Republican Rome were called_____ .
2. The representatives of the Patricians in Republican Rome were called _____.
3. When the Roman Republic collapsed after the assassination of Julius Caesar, there was a period of civil war followed by a new leader who was titled _____.

Each open blank asks for specific terms or names, which students presumably discussed in class or read about in textbooks. Short-answer questions are easy to invent, but their limitations must be kept firmly in mind. Students are placed in the position of either knowing or not knowing, repeating the key words exactly as taught. There are only right answers and wrong answers, not discussable answers.

In addition to (or instead of) writing questions, you may choose to use published items or online standardized tests, generally in a short-answer format. Standardized tests are often given at the conclusion of a lengthy sequence of instruction, but can and should be used on a pretest–posttest basis, providing comparisons over time.

A great many textbook publishers provide online tests geared to the material covered for typical social studies units and at the end of books. These are easy to use, but vary greatly in quality, so read them carefully before using in class. State-mandated tests, such as the New York State Regents Examinations, are made public after each administration and are another potential source of questions. Most states have tests available to teachers, although these vary by state curriculum. (In New York, there are fully prepared units and exams on EngageNY).

Matching. Matching items also involve recall of information, but can demand a higher levels like comprehension and application by emphasizing elimination strategies. To work well matching lists should not be overly long and should hold to the same categories on both sides of columns. Overall difficulty level can increase by offering a longer list of items, or presenting some that are indirectly, rather than directly related to each other. The matching format is also relatively easy to prepare and grade, but omits much insight into student reasoning.

Examples of matching items on Roman history might include:

1. Patriarch	a. the father or head of the family
2. Monogamy	b. the son or inheritor
3. Tribune	c. judges the laws of the country
4. Consul	d. creates laws for the country
5. Polygamy	e. decides on what laws are best
6. Plebian	f. marriage to more than one wife
	g. one husband and one wife in a marriage

Notice that there are more responses (7) than possible matches. This makes elimination more difficult and causes students to compare and contrast possible answers. Greater disparities raise the difficulty level.

True–False. True–false items are a series of statements that students must evaluate as either correct or incorrect. Statements are almost always factual, formulated on the assumption that the knowledge included has been properly validated and is not open to question. (Of course, this may or may not be true because distinctions may become invalid as student knowledge deepens.) We are also assuming the makers know the facts.

True–false tests are easy to score, but probably more difficult to prepare than one might think; great care must be taken not to give the answers away with qualifiers, such as all, none, some, few, or many. Furthermore, students guess their way through many of the items by deductive or syllogistic reasoning. True–false items can be made much more exciting through the concept of *probabilities—that is, some answers are* **more likely** *to be truer or falser than others.* For instance, conclusions that are neither completely true nor completely false may be offered, asking students to categorize these as generally true, sometimes true, or seldom true. Students identify and judge items using more discriminating classifications thus converting the lowly true–false item into a vehicle for more elegant medium-order responses that require understanding.

Examples of standard true–false items from a teacher-made test on China are presented next.

Directions: Mark T for True or F for False in each blank provided.

____1. The Great Wall of China was constructed during the Ch'in Dynasty.

____2. The Han Dynasty was a period of constant warfare and dissension.

____3. Confucius believed that under no circumstances should young people argue with their elders.

____4. Confucius, although very influential in China, was not able to convince any of the rulers of his time to adopt his ideas.

____5. Chinese language reform, the pinyin system, involves using Chinese characters as a new alphabet.

To answer these questions, students must have stored the knowledge about China and be able to recall it. For example, Item 3 is probably true, although it is stated as an absolute, 'under no circumstances,' which may be changed after careful study of Confucius's writings. Item 4 is true because it is supported by available records of the time. Item 5 is most likely untrue because language reform in China uses Latin letters, not characters, to express Chinese sounds. Although memory is a key element in successful responses to true–false quizzes, close reading and definition also play important roles. Much depends on the way items are written and what is taught in class. A true–false format can be used to evaluate didactic and the lower end of reflective goals.

Multiple Choice. Multiple-choice items are among the most flexible of test formats. Virtually every level of didactic and reflective thought can be measured depending on item writing skills. Multiple-choice items can easily be adapted to measure reflective and affective goals: application, analysis, synthesis, evaluation, and creating. However, items that measure thinking skills are more difficult and time-consuming to write. Reflective questions may be worth the extra effort because multiple-choice results are easy to score, allowing comparisons among responses, and permit detailed analysis of how students and classes performed on each item and as a whole.

Multiple-choice responses can be recorded on special sheets read by electronic scanner that totals up the results, making the scoring process even easier. Numerous computer programs are available to assist you in creating and storing test items on different subjects. Programs are also available to provide statistical analyses using normal curve design as a basis for diagnosing student performance. You may want multiple-choice results to grade on the curve—that is, using a 'normed' sample to establish grades and means.

As is true of other types of questions, multiple-choice items may be well or poorly written. Items should be field tested several times before adopting them for your standard repertory. New questions should be given to several classes, and answers carefully analyzed for signs of misunderstanding or simplicity indicated by very low or very high percentages of correct responses. Experts suggest that multiple-choice items consist of a stem and three to five responses.[11]

The stem is the question portion that requests one or more correct or 'most reasonable' answers. The responses include from three to five choices, one or two of which are designated as correct or best. Distractors are wrong answers, although, depending on the purpose

of the test and level of the test takers, at least one of these may be *very close* to correct. An example of a didactic IBQ, four-response item is given next (* indicates the correct response):
Stem: What is the capital of Botswana? Responses:

1. Johannesburg
2. Gaborone *
3. Cairo
4. Ouagadougou

In this geography example, assuming students have done homework on Africa, Cairo should be a far-fetched choice because it is distant from Botswana, a sub-Saharan nation. Ouagadougou is somewhat closer, but in West Africa, while Johannesburg is very close and thus the most difficult of the distractors, but in the wrong country. In addition to knowledge of specific facts, IBQs can also ask for knowledge of political procedures or principles, as in the following example:
    Which of the following principles guided the framers of the U.S. Constitution in choosing a government with three branches?

a. the need for separate meeting places
b. the need for checks and balances among powers *
c. the need for reverence for the law
d. the need for expertise in law, legislation, and leadership

Again, note that two of the answers, (a) and (c), are improbable or irrelevant, while (d) is an excellent principle that does apply to American politics. However, expertise was not the rationale for a three-part system of government. So, that leaves checks and balances (b) as the correct selection.
    Good distractors are vital to the game of successful multiple-choice items because they help to differentiate between those students who understand the material and those who do not. However, care must be taken in choosing these items. If distractors are too illogical, the right answer will be too easy to select; if the distractors are too much alike, the right answer will be difficult to select. Therefore, distractors should be designed along a continuum: one being obviously wrong, a second being almost as good a choice as the correct answer, and a third somewhere in between.[12] Multiple-choice questions used effectively test knowledge of specific facts, principles as well as rules. This type of question requires recall and comprehension, middle order thinking.

Document-Based Questions

Document-based questions (DBQs), also called evidence-based questions (EBQs), seek to assess students' reflective skills and reasoning ability. DBQs are designed to promote skills: application, analysis, and synthesis for both convergent and divergent problem solving. These questions ask students to read documents and evaluate art and artifacts. Thus, DBQs require problem-solving strategies. A DBQ should not be answered on the basis of knowledge alone, although some knowledge may be useful for understanding definitions and interpreting clues. If an item called a DBQ is easily answered from memory, then it is masquerading under a false name.

Answers to DBQs are drawn from information presented on the examination; this may be a historical document, quotation, graph, chart, photograph, painting, song, or research report. Students interpret the material presented to answer the question, drawing on prior knowledge as well as information presented. Thus, there is a range of potential responses, none of which is specifically or clearly right or wrong. The standard for a good answer to a DBQ is reason—the argument or response that makes the most sense given the data. Thus, DBQs generally assess higher order thinking.

DBQs are more difficult to write than fact questions requiring more subjective grading, but do evaluate richer and deeper levels of student understanding, such as how and why students have drawn conclusions, rather than what they know. The document can be a written excerpt, cartoon, graph, or other visual representation. Most commonly, a primary source is used for this purpose. The most important aspect of this type of question is that it allows for students' interpretations. Two examples are given next.

"That government is best which governs least." —Thomas Jefferson

3. What does Jefferson mean by this statement?
4. What kinds of responsibilities would a government have in Jefferson's statement? What responsibilities would be excluded?

"All communities divide themselves into the few and the many. The first are the rich and well born, the other the mass of the people. … The people are turbulent and changing. … Give therefore to the first class a distinct permanent share in the government. They will check the unsteadiness of the second." —Alexander Hamilton

3. Based on the quote, what type of government would Alexander Hamilton advocate?
4. Hamilton served in George Washington's cabinet. Is this quote consistent with the beginnings of U.S. democracy? Why or why not? Does it apply now?

CLASSIC RESEARCH REPORT

Using Bloom's taxonomy as a framework for coding 8,800 test questions developed by teachers in 12 grade and subject combinations (mostly upper elementary through high school), researchers estimated that approximately four-fifths of all questions were at the recall level, the lowest of the six levels.* The social studies test items within this pool were, on the whole, more oriented toward recall of information than were mathematics and language questions; oddly enough, the latter involved more higher level queries. Teacher emphasis on recall questions has been explained by poor training in measurement, the difficulty of writing questions aimed at evaluating higher level problem-solving skills, and fear that more open-ended items will promote student confusion and anxiety, and increase failure rates.[+]

* Fleming, M. and Chambers, B. (1983) Teacher-Made Tests: Windows on the Classroom. In Hathaway, W. E. (ed.) *New Directions for Testing and Measurement, Vol. 19, Testing in the Schools* (San Francisco: Jossey-Bass).

[+] Doyle, W. (1986) Classroom Organization and Management. In Wittrock, M. C. (ed.) *Handbook of Research on Teaching*, 3rd Ed. (New York: Macmillan), 392–431.

Teacher Questions and Oral Diagnostics. Students' questions and answers are valuable sources for evaluation. What students say indicates the extent and depth of knowledge, and sometimes their feelings, about a topic. The more they say and the lengthier the exchanges (up to a point of course), the better your sample thinking for diagnostic and evaluative purposes. Research suggests that frequent questioning by the teacher is generally related to improved academic achievement, particularly when there is a high level of student responses.[13] To promote frequent responses at a higher order, ask many probing questions and allow students enough time to think through answers.

If you have a good memory, you can keep track of the quality and frequency of student responses as you move through the course. If memory is crowded with other business, you may want to keep a diary or log of response levels You might also build a checklist into your grading procedures on which you can record examples of students' thinking styles. For example:

Response Levels	Respondents
High: Makes and defends judgments. Hypothesizes about causes and theories for events; draws inferences and conclusions.	Mary Jones
Medium: Offers reasons for statements; analyzes underlying motives for actions. Understands and applies concepts and definitions.	John Smith
Low: Accurately recalls or offers information on a subject. Presents a list of names, dates, or places.	

A log of this type would aid overall evaluation of individuals and the course as a whole. You can also build verbal responses into your courses in the form of speeches, role-plays, or oral tests. Students can be called on to do a bit of public speaking to demonstrate their knowledge and skill at putting ideas together. As an example, ask each student to prepare and present the answer to a reflective question as a short speech or perhaps reenact a speech by a famous person (e.g., Daniel Webster, Abraham Lincoln, or Barack Obama).

LET'S DECIDE

1. Design an oral examination with a group of students on a critical issue such as the bombing of Hiroshima and Nagasaki, or the Cuban missile crisis. Stress friendly public speaking skills.
2. Ask students to develop and submit in writing a list of questions they would like to see discussed in class. Have them set up their own procedure with a checklist that distinguishes better from worse answers, resulting in a grade for each speaker. They'll love it!

Questions for Complex Reasoning. Multiple-choice question formats are well suited to test reflective thinking. Variations include: (a) missing answers (excluding a key factor), (b) two 'best' answers, (c) one 'best' or one 'worst' answer, or (d) a single worst answer—that is, the only answer that is wrong out of the four or five choices. More creative questions can be developed supplying students with documentary, graphic, or text materials *on the test*. In other words, students are given new data to interpret—data similar to or identical with studies they have completed at home and in class. You may also present data analogous to the work students have grown familiar with, pushing them to apply past learning to new similar content. When developing best-answer items, you should make clear to the respondents that, although many of the responses are reasonable in some sense, one is best in the light of evidence or through logical inference. In the item that follows, the same basic concept is handled in two ways: Which do you think promotes more reasoning, Type 1 or Type 2?

1. Correct-Answer Format	2. Best-Answer Format
The capital of a country is a location that serves as:	The main reason for choosing a location as the capital of a country is probably:
1. The cultural center	1. The need for a home by the leader
2. The economic center	2. The need for a political center *
3. The government center *	3. The need for a national symbol
4. The population center	4. The need for a geographic heart

Each stem and the accompanying distractors are quite different in intent and phrasing in each format. The correct-answer set aims to assess knowledge; the best-answer set seeks comprehension and application, an inference game. Phrasing is also dissimilar, with the best-answer format asking for the main reason, rather than the one right bit of data. None of the best-answer distractors is 'wrong,' but offers more or less logical choices.

   Challenging questions can also be created using charts, graphs, quotations, pictures, and documents. Readings and visuals should be reproduced on the test. Difficulty can be varied by selecting lengthier and more complex or shorter, simple readings. A complex multiple-choice example is created using an old woodprint showing Queen Elizabeth hunting deer in 1576 (see Figure 6.5). A wide range of items could be generated from this print because it is rich in meaning and amenable to many interpretations.

   Sample questions are given next.

1. This woodcut is most probably *a hunting scene by upper class people* because:
    a.   they have horses and dogs to hunt deer
    b.   the style and fanciness of suits and dresses *
    c.   the kind of forest where they are hunting
    d.   the quality of the weapons used
2. The most important person in this woodcut is most likely:
    a.   the noble and beautiful horse
    b.   The dead deer shown upside down
    c.   The Noble Lady with hat and gloves *
    d.   The man kneeling before the Noble Lady
    3. From a social and historical point of view, this woodcut is *most surprising* because:
    a.   There are so many members of the nobility in the picture
    b.   The hunting action takes place in formal and expensive clothes
    c.   A woman hunting with men is the most important figure *

The booke of Hunting.   133

that the Prince or chiefe (it to please them) doe alight and take
assaye of the Deare with a sharpe knyfe, the whiche is done.
L.iij.   iij

Figure 6.5: Turbervile's Booke of Hunting (1576) p. 135. Thinkstock Item No. 92833121.

d. Men are wearing funny looking skirts and tight stockings
4. In general in historical pictures, the best clues to date a work of art or photograph is probably:
   a. the kinds of birds and animals shown
   b. the kinds of transportation included
   c. the dress and style of clothing worn *
   d. the type and health of the environment

All four questions demand visual literacy and interpretation asking students to discriminate between less and more reasonable answers based on one piece of evidence. But this evidence demands several intelligences, reading, artistic, and interpersonal.

For Question 1, (d) is clearly a poor choice, while two of the four answers, (a) and (b), are reasonable in showing class status. Only one, (b) follows from the woodcut, since clothing expresses status in this time period. A great many people could own dogs and horses but be lower in status than those shown. Question 2 asks for understanding of the woodcut's design with the first two choices somewhat lacking in conviction since these are not about people, while (c) and (d) focus on the characters. Of these two, (c) is better than (d) because the kneeling man is paying homage to the Queen, and not the other way round, though he is clearly an important figure of high status.

Question 3 asks for inferences from the woodcut, drawing attention to the unusual, a most surprising result. The question demands fairly high order analysis and insights into social relations. Students can demonstrate historical knowledge by eliminating choices, surmising that people wore lots of odd things in history, so out goes (d) and formal dress was often worn in hunts (think *Downton Abbey*), so out goes (b). (a) doesn't make much sense so that leaves (c) the mixing of the sexes and woman on a hunt, which is quite surprising long ago, but Queen Elizabeth loved to hunt, boat, and dance, and was allowed since she was the boss.

Question 4 pushes students into the realm of generalization from data already carefully analyzed. They must link a concept of historical time from common activities, dress, transport, environment and applying these across time. Choices (a) and (d) are not well supported by the evidence because animals have been similar for long periods and environments are hard to read from one forest setting, while (b) is a distractor that is reasonable if you consider horses transportation. But (c) is left as the best fit for the data and thus the most reasonable answer. Dress and style are powerful indicators of time and often can be used to date sources *if* you know the styles, but even if you don't, most students might reasonably conclude we don't dress like those in the woodcut anymore, especially to go hunting. Thus, test items measuring middle and higher order document-based objectives should be designed and posed on a regular basis because they are thought-provoking and a form of inquiry training. Students should be encouraged to argue over answers and write their own DBQ items.

Great care must be taken in selecting artifacts and reading materials for student analysis and response. Nevertheless, it is worth the trouble to write your own DBQ questions as practice because this reinforces understanding of student expectations, and helps formulate higher order questions. An easy way out is to search the Internet for examples of complex and demanding questions to encourage critical thinking of a high order and tie in with stated reflective goals. If you regularly write and use document-based questions, your skill will increase markedly and the questions will become easier to create.

Remember to save your test items in folders organized by subject; file standardized tests in a test bank for the different courses you teach and swap items with colleagues to make your life easier and to improve your tests. Bookmark best items and add to your collection when opportunities arise. Standardized tests that include higher order questions are also available for purchase through textbook companies and test developers for many subjects, from U.S. History through Economics. Particularly well-developed economic reasoning tests are available for the middle and senior high schools.[14] Some excellent geography examinations are online from the National Council for Geographic Education and Association of American Geographers.[15]

Consider the following when constructing DBQs:

1. Match tests with reflective objectives.
2. Design questions that humanely reflect the state of student knowledge and skill.
3. Prepare questions drawn from what was taught in the course.

4. Insert new (but analogous) data and questions to promote critical thinking and application.
5. Choose pictures and readings that are dramatic, puzzling, and interesting.
6. Keep introductory material brief so students can retain or easily glance at it, then carefully concentrate on the actual documents for potential answers.
7. Place most material in the stem portion of the question, keep the choices relatively brief.
8. Check questions, stems, and alternatives to make sure you are not leading students, or that a single correct answer is built into the question.
9. Choices for each set of questions should be homogeneous, standard, and mutually exclusive, and the format for responses identical. Students must direct efforts toward answering questions, not trying to figure out what you are asking or how to answer.
10. Try out new items with a group you are teaching, analyzing responses. If responses are inconsistent, seemingly random, or generally wrong, then discuss the item with students to revise or discard. Save successful items most students select as the logical choice, when next highest numbers choose the major distractor and the fewest choose the incorrect or illogical responses.[16] With practice, develop a battery of test items for the major course: global history, U.S. history, economics, and government.

SAMPLE LESSON/TEST PLANS

1. Using a multiple-choice, best-answer format, write a series of at least six related document-based items on portions of George Washington's "Farewell Address." Increase the difficulty level of each question, beginning with comprehension and analysis and concluding with a judgment and creativity question.
2. Select a famous European painting or sculpture such as Picasso's *Guernica* or Rodin's *The Thinker* and devise at least three higher order multiple-choice items compare and contrast inferences about society and politics from art.
3. Choose a graph or chart that you believe illustrates valuable data, such as Chinese and American economic growth from the 2000s to the present. Create at least four questions that ask students to use the graph's statistics as a basis for analyzing (reflectively) economic trends.
4. Research secondary-level standardized tests in at least two subjects, such as global studies and geography. Evaluate the questions according to level (lower, middle, higher), and calculate the percentage of each type on the test. Are there enough higher-level items to challenge students?
5. Have students complete a set of homemade items and analyze the results, noting percentages of correct and incorrect answers. Be prepared for criticism, and revise items to the students' and your own satisfaction.

Essay Tests: Writing Skills in the Social Studies. Generally, essay tests allow greater opportunity to elicit reflective and affective responses from students than other formats. Using the ability to develop a full line of reasoning as a criterion, essay questions are by far the best tools to assess student thinking. However, there are problems with essay tests: (a) variability of response (Do you judge quality of response against set criteria or average responses? You could write a 'perfect' essay yourself as a standard or model, using a rubric you invented as a guide!); (b) interpretation (Does each student interpret the assignment in a similar way?), and (c) the assignment (Is the problem clear or ambiguous?).

Thus, although essays allow students a great deal of freedom and flexibility in terms of length, complexity, and creativity of response, there are problems of interpretation and standardization. In addition, an essay format does not, in and of itself, guarantee reflective thinking because the directions may ask for what is essentially recall listing of information or conclusions. We have all seen essay questions that are really no different from matching or fill-in items except that full sentences are required. However, essay examinations may be highly creative and difficult, requiring students to interpret and synthesize large amounts of data, develop logical arguments, or speculate creatively about the future.

Compounding the problems of assessing the content and reasoning in an essay is the reaction to the way language is used. Poorly written but thoughtful essays are often graded lower than less thoughtful well-written essays. For example, Figure 6.6 demonstrates a high school student's thinking in the form of a handwritten in-class essay. The orthography is interesting, with big headings, and smaller writing. The student provides considerable factual information about Solon's Laws and shows a fairly high degree of comprehension, in my opinion. However, the student does not go very far in reflecting on Solon's ideas, offering no feelings or judgments.

For essays there is always a conflict between teachers who want to encourage good writing and those who primarily seek knowledge of subject matter. Because of these problems, it is important that you make criteria (rubrics?) for assessment clear to students indicating:

(a) how much content or evidence is expected, specifying a minimum amount,
(b) what types of data are valued most and which least,
(c) types of reasoning process expected (argument, narrative, description), and
(d) the degree that literacy and style will count in the total grade.

If criteria for essay questions are established early in the semester with frequent practice and feedback, student writing and thinking skills are likely to improve. Conversely, the more ambiguous the criteria and the less specific the feedback, the less students' skills are likely to improve. Many rubrics are additive and exact in number but use language that is inherently subjective leaving open wide interpretation of results.

Despite these problems, to promote critical literacy, essays should be a regular and integral part of social studies coursework and evaluation. Ideally, a typical unit or course should contain a mixture of essay questions—short or long, with definite word limits, and open-ended or creative exercises. Reliance on only one type of essay penalizes some students while rewarding others with the knowledge and skills to fit. Essays assess learning at virtually every level, from didactic to affective across the full range of thinking. Vary goals and length of essays to promote a broad range of abilities.

Essay questions aimed mainly at assessing comprehension might include:

6. Explain three key causes for the Civil War in complete sentences in your own words, adding a fourth possibility in an essay of no more than 200 words.

The Greek Word
Solon and his plan for a better life!

Today at noon, Solon was elected the chief government official. He was given the authority to change the laws. Solon came up with new political and economic reforms to help Athens

During one of his assemblies we heard a woman say "Solon was born in Athens and now he's here to help it? Athens today, is badly in need of his reforms. The power is in the hands of the wealthy citizens and Solon is changing that. The farmers who had been forced to mortgage their lands and to borrow money don't have to do that anymore. He also freeded the people who became slaves. In addition he changed the money system to make foreign trade easier, and he made a law banning the export of grain.

Solon's constitutional reforms redivided the citizens into four classes according to income. Citizens of all classes participated in the assemblies and the public law courts. He also established the Council of 400 to take over the political powers of the Areopogus and he set up courts. In these courts citizens can appeal the officials decisions. The only law that wasn't changed by Solon, was the old provisions that allowed only three higher classes to hold public office. This is the change, Athens was waiting for

Figure 6.6: Student essay on ancient Greece.

7. Describe the reasons for including the Bill of Rights in the U.S. as far as you remember, adding your own opinion with reasons in an essay of at least 250 words.

Essay questions assess students' reflective skills, as the following examples illustrate:

1. Compare Athens and Sparta telling how they were similar and/or different in political, social, and economic lifestyles, and culture.
2. Explain how U.S. foreign policy has changed security in the wake of 9/11. Choose one security measure, like airports or phone tapping, and explain whether or not you think this is the best course for American democracy.

The construction and grading of essay questions can be clarified by establishing a rubric and criteria for success to interpret and judge results. Assigning an essay about conflict in the Middle East as a case in point, apply following rules for essay writing:

1. *Recapitulate the Goals You Want to Assess.* To judge how well students have understood the cultural, economic, social, and political problems Middle Eastern countries share. Define the specific goals students should achieve:
   a. collect relevant statistics about per capita income and technological capability of Egypt, Iraq, Iran, Syria, Israel, The Palestinian Authority, Jordan, and Saudi Arabia.
   b. explain how great powers set the stage for clashes among nations in the Middle East.

c. analyze and synthesize the reasons for conflict: religious identification, imperialism, diversity, government authority, territorial ambitions, economic conflicts over oil, and other resources.

2. *Provide Detail and Direction in the Essay Question.* Rewrite essay questions providing data with questions that refer directly to examples and cases. Prepare students for the essay by asking them to submit questions they want answered or questions they believe make people think about the Middle East. Reformulate the original question into a more specific problem.

How can conflict in the Middle East best be explained: in terms of religious and cultural differences, interference by foreign powers, economic and territorial competition, and historical development, or a combination?

Write an essay of approximately 500 words discussing whether the political situation now is related *most* to political, historical, cultural, or economic problems. Save about 50 words or so at the end for your own clearly labeled judgment of causes for problems.

3. *Specify Size, Structure, Time Allotment, and Grading Standards for an Essay.* Direct all students to write an essay of between 400 and 500 words in a specified time, such as one 40-minute period. Be clear about what you want students to include: a conclusion, an expression of opinion, or a defense or attack of a hypothesis. Indicate which points are considered most valuable, and provide at least a few examples showing how the essay will be graded. Identification of relationships such as cause and effect, or judgments about which problems are more or less important, are highly prized and likely to receive more points than general theories or vague unsupported reasons.

Make clear that points will also be given for accurate and reliable information. If students correctly identify several events and nations, their political leaders, and the current economic situation, their scores will increase by 10, 20, or 30 points. Those who tie examples with explanations and judgments will receive still higher totals. This information helps students know where to invest their greatest energy for the highest possible return.

4. *Analyze the Answers.* Answers should fit the goals laid down previously as a basis for evaluating essays in a more objective fashion than is usually possible.

In the example given on the Middle East, use five criteria to assess the essays:

a. supplies accurate statistics and other data about Middle Eastern countries,
b. identifies connections between local economic problems and political conflicts,

c. presents two or three clear and specific historical reasons for political clashes,

d. offers at least one major generalization or hypothesis about cultural and social problems, and

e. recommends one or two best solutions to ameliorate the situation and extra credit if they look up or know 'ameliorate.'

Up to 20 points can be given for each criterion that is met, up to 100, with a bonus perhaps added for quality writing:

uses data = 20 points
draws connections = 20 points
presents reasons = 20 points
develops hypothesis = 20 points
offers recommendations = 20 points
writes well = 10 points
Maximum = 110 points (or more?)

By looking at the essays as part and whole, you can identify patterns of excellence or misunderstanding among students, as well as decide on an overall evaluation of each pupil's work compared to either public criteria or class norms.

Perception-Based Questions

Perception-based questions (PBQs) involve the affective realm—how students feel about or view themselves, events, or issues, and their reasons for these attitudes. Affect may range from low-level awareness of feelings about one's self-image to sophisticated defenses of value positions. Psychological assessments of self-confidence and public opinion polls fall within the PBQ category because they assess how people see their world, rather than objectively calculate the amount of verifiable information someone possesses. These types of assessment have become increasingly important in recent years as the focus of social studies teaching and learning has shifted toward an 'arc of inquiry' problem-based learning with answers that offer more than one interpretation. Students may be asked to adopt and to examine positions opposite to their own (i.e., stand in someone else's shoes). They may be asked to understand the reasons for the actions of people who lived hundreds or even thousands of years earlier, in circumstances drastically different from students' encounters on a daily basis.[17]

Such exercises require far more from a student than the mastery of knowledge or even skills. An emotional or empathetic mode of reasoning is required. PBQs can help ascertain the degree a student is able to step into another's shoes, perhaps as a pretest, as well as the degree to which the material and lessons have deepened empathetic ability.

Generally, PBQs focus on three different areas: psychological, attitudinal, and self-evaluative. *Psychological* instruments are used to measure self-perception and feelings about social roles. Thematic-apperception tests, student interest inventories, and self-reports are common examples of measurements. *Attitudinal* measures involve school, society, politics, and social issues as well as use of scales of agreement or satisfaction. Gallup, Roper, or *New York Times* surveys and polls are typical attitudinal measures. *Self-evaluative* measures involve judgments about quality or educational experience in lessons, units, courses, and workshops, or review of courses and teachers. Therefore, polls that ask for subjective opinions, feelings, and viewpoints can be employed to learn more about individual responses and group reactions in a systematic way to guide classroom planning.

MEASURING STUDENT FEELINGS AND VIEWPOINTS

Expressions of feelings, interests, and values indicate how students view themselves and their educational milieu. The focus of evaluation is expression of opinions, issues, and self-reports that express positive and negative feelings about a topic issue to judge the degree of students' feelings and opinions over time. However, note that almost any expression of feeling or judgment is based on experience, knowledge, and reflection as well as preference and perception that encompass the didactic and reflective dimensions.

Nonetheless, affective evaluation is different from the others in its emphasis on opinions and values that do not fit a 'right or wrong' assessment mold. Values are at the heart of social studies instruction, although they are rarely used overtly or acknowledged by either students or teachers.[18] Still, our most important decisions are almost always based on a mixture of facts and feelings, empiricism and phenomenology, reality and perception.

By bringing the assessment of affective objectives into the open, make the expression of opinion legitimate, and diagnose important attitudinal changes with the assistance of your students. Studying students' feelings and attitudes should be part of normal routine, as should student feedback on methods and materials of instruction. There is every reason to include maturing middle and secondary school students in the process of reviewing their own educational experience. Respect the feelings and judgments of your audience by polling reactions and teaching students how to conduct surveys in a careful, scientific manner.

Our perceptions of others often cloud our judgment. We infer beliefs and motives based on these perceptions, yet they are often wrong and biased. Polls and surveys, especially those dealing with feelings, beliefs, and attitudes, are meant as a corrective. If our population is small, such as a single class, we can gather data on the entire group. In most instances, however, it is preferable to survey a representative sample. There are precise statistical procedures and techniques both for choosing those samples and analyzing the results, with easy programs to use online like Survey Monkey (www .surveymonkey.com) and eSurveysPro (www.esurveyspro.com). Depending on interest and the type of information desired, political, marketing, and personal review, there are a variety of survey instruments available, including informal observation, self-reports, attitude scales, peer appraisal, checklists, course evaluations and tests of imagination, creativity, and problem-solving style. Of course, all such polling is subject to errors depending on the quality of the sample and the design of the survey instrument. But let's finally bring baseline review into the classroom for our own diagnostic and professional purposes.

Survey Techniques in the Classroom

Some of the examples mentioned earlier are of use in evaluating affective goals in the classroom.

Student Interest Inventories

To learn more about students' interests and attitudes, why not ask them? One way of doing this is to survey students about their feelings and attitudes on subjects and issues. As an example, a straightforward interest questionnaire follows that could be used before beginning a unit on industrialization:

1. What topics on industrialization would you like to see included in our U.S. history course? Inventions? Big business? Labor history? Personal autobiography?
2. What topics do you feel are already familiar to you that could be shared?
3. Do you see industrialization or technology as important or unimportant history? Why?

Asking for students' advice assists planning and helps you avoid or shorten discussion of topics that are unpopular or already understood. Seeking student advice also demonstrates respect for their views and opinions.

WHAT DO YOU THINK?

What areas of classroom life do you think would benefit from attitude polling or psychological testing? Would you be willing to assist students in preparing an evaluation of your course? Why or why not?

Checklists

A checklist offers students a series of statements about themselves or the class to agree or disagree. A checklist provides students with the opportunity to assess themselves independent of formal evaluation. An example of a self-assessment checklist is given in Figure 6.7. You may let them assess past assignments anonymously, expressing what they did or did not like about methods and materials of instruction. Be willing to stand up to criticism. Be ready to make changes, as suggested by your students or risk loss of credibility. A

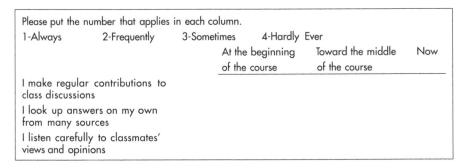

Figure 6.7: Student self-evaluation checklist.

priority checklist allows students to review activities applied to the goals for improving participation.

TO DO

Develop a checklist for students on a topic you would like to teach. What will you ask your critics to judge? What would you like to know about their interests and motivations? What would you avoid asking? Why? If you are having students develop portfolios, which cognitive and which affective measures are included?

TEACHER AND COURSE EVALUATION

In theory, greater student motivation to learn leads to higher levels of achievement.[19] Attitudes toward teacher and course provide valuable insight into student motivation. Didactic and reflective growth is related to a student's feelings about her or himself, the teacher, and the school. You are a vital link in the learning chain, so why not find out how you're doing?

SUMMARY

Assessment includes the identification of three major dimensions of questions: (a) information based, or IBQs, (b) data based or DBQs, and (c) perception based or PBQs, conforming to a full range of thinking and feeling across LOT, MOT, and HOT goals of social studies instruction.

Information-based assessment concerns remembering and understanding of facts and definitions—that is, testing for knowledge and terms that rely on formats like short-answer quizzes, matching tests, true–false, and multiple-choice. IBQ testing is usually criterion-referenced—that is, measured against set standards supplied by teacher, school, or a testing agency. Answers are usually right or wrong, linear, and moving toward a definite conclusion. Theoretically, information can be clearly assessed objectively.

Document- or evidence-based assessment measures reasoning and inferential abilities. These questions, drawn from material supplied on an examination, demand analysis, application, synthesis, and/or judgment. DBQs are presented as multiple-choice or essay questions, a principal means for testing higher order skills and abilities. Essays probably allow for more divergent thinking than do the other types of questions, but are more subjective. All types of products and tests, like rubrics, may be incorporated into a student portfolio for presentation at the conclusion of a course or program. But rubrics too are subjective in design and grading.

Perception-based evaluation covers all types of affective questions in which students or teachers express views, feelings, and judgments about events, issues, or classroom activities. Checklists, surveys, interviews, opinion polls, differential polls, and essays may be employed to probe feelings and values. Surveys and opinion polls dominate attitude measurement because of easy administration and scoring. Affective evaluation is usually norm-referenced, measured against group means. Students should be encouraged to design and write their own opinion surveys or course evaluations using either published or class-created forms because this builds insight into testing as a process. Testing can also be diagnostic, paying close attention to the rise and fall, quantity and quality of conversations and exchanges in the classroom and between and among students. Furthermore, even formal assessment can be creative, by using mental mapping or webbing techniques for pre- and posttest measure of production, encouraging projects and inventions that fit a given topic, and promoting dramatic role-play and skit development demonstrating absorption of historical and social science knowledge now applied to another medium of expression and a different multiple intelligence brought into play.

Based on carefully defined goals assessment should be accompanied by regular and consistent formative (ongoing) measures of student development as well as the usual summative final tests and polls. Evaluation should be seen as a vital part of the teaching process because it affords teachers and students feedback on the level and amount of achievement measured against C3 and other goals. From such feedback, students and teacher form judgments about how well or how poorly they are performing and which learning areas need the least or most improvement. Quality evaluation, varied and creative, results in better planning for long-term, future achievement. Authentic/portfolio assessment was recommended as a means for getting the 'big picture' of a student's performance and for contributing significantly in measuring growth and change over time. Evaluation is a continuing process of diagnosis and judgment, spurring students to change study habits, attitudes, redouble work efforts, seeking additional resources.

Finally, a word of caution for all of us on assessment. Although tests and surveys are useful, probably necessary, and most likely unavoidable given present trends in social studies education, assessment as a set of procedures and tools can at best produce a result that represents only the tip of the iceberg of student knowledge, reasoning, and values. Each self-report, test score, portfolio presentation, or observation can only approximate the true internal state of a student. Variations in test reliability, student health, teaching methods, and a multitude of other factors may lead to accurate or erroneous interpretation of one or more students' real strengths and weaknesses. As teachers, we need to learn what is happening to our students through a variety of evaluation techniques for diagnostic or grading, or through authentic assessment, but we must allow our own compassion and judgment to play a part in all our decisions.

TO DO

1. Write a 20-item multiple-choice test using only DBQs drawn from world studies readings and statistics. Predict student performance on each item: degree of success, percentage of correct responses, and difficulty answering. Administer the test to your class and analyze the response patterns. Were your predictions correct? Why or why not? Did you prepare students to deal with this type of examination? Be fair!

2. Assist students preparing an opinion poll on the power of the U.S. presidency compared with that of Congress and the Supreme Court. Use a Likert scale of agreement or disagreement with a range of positive and negative statements about the three branches of government. Offer students previous surveys and polls of political attitudes to mimic. Select sample responses. Use a computerized item-analysis program to organize the results. What were the averages for each question, the standard deviation from the norm? Were any results significantly different from chance? Why?

3. Prepare pre- and posttests on geographic places in Asia, Africa, or Latin America. Ask students to identify the nations on a blank map. Then tally the results for each student and the class as a whole. Offer two weeks of instruction on the continent in question, providing details about each nation's lifestyle, living standards, weather, and topography. Repeat your identification of places IBQ information test. Did the students improve individually, as a group? Why or why not?
4. Select an online teacher or course evaluation and ask students to respond to the questionnaire anonymously. Leave space at the end for suggestions and criticisms. Did most students enjoy the program? How do you feel about subjecting yourself to an evaluation by students? Would you trust the results? Why or why not? Is it too much like a marketing survey?
5. Select a course and level you would like to teach: 7th or 8th grade U.S. history, civics/problems of democracy/government, world studies, or high school economics. Write a set of didactic, reflective, and affective goals for the course with roughly equal proportions for each dimension. (Which goal[s] will be your highest priority?) Design an evaluation program encompassing IBQs, DBQs, and PBQs. Select or design items for each area and decide how and when you will ask students to respond. Administer pre- and posttests of student knowledge and understanding of a topic. Ask for student attitudes toward the subject: Did they enjoy the civil war unit? Will you offer students the opportunity to review the program? Are you going to give a few major tests unit by unit, many short quizzes, or a mixture?
6. Design an authentic assessment program for a global studies or world history course at your school. Provide students with examples of the rubrics or criteria for a successful portfolio of work and include assignments that involve many of the students' multiple intelligences (i.e., visual, verbal, interpersonal, and written). Make sure that a wide variety of tasks contribute to an overall judgment.

TESTING AUTHENTICALLY: A FINAL CONVERSATION

The Role of Portfolio Evaluation in Social Studies Teacher Education How Evaluation Practices Shape Learning Experiences

E. Wayne Ross

The development of the ability to think is widely acknowledged to be a primary goal of our educational efforts. By enabling learners to acquire and apply information, social studies educators aim to engage them in decision-making and problem-solving about social issues, past and present (Adler 1994).

The concept of reflective thought provides a useful framework for curriculum and instruction in the K–12 social studies classroom, as well as in the teacher education process. As John Dewey pointed out, reflective thought guides us away from routine activities and toward those that stimulate inquiry and consideration (Dewey 1933). The reflective teacher is concerned not only with the subject matter to be transmitted, but also with the activity of the mind.

For reflective teaching to be successful, it must be incorporated not only in a teacher's instructional methods, but also into the system of assessment employed by the teacher. This article explores the utility of portfolio evaluation as a system of assessment that can enhance reflective teaching. It is based on the experience of classes teaching methods to future teachers, but its basic principles can be applied at a variety of other levels in the educational system.

In recent years teachers and teacher educators have been experimenting with a variety of performance-based assessments, including portfolios. 'Authentic' assessments of student learning strive to create natural or real-life settings and activities in order to document how learners think and behave over an extended period of time. The goal of authentic assessment is to reveal not only what students know and understand, but how those new understandings are developed.

Portfolios can take different forms. They are essentially a collection of artifacts documenting students' work and activities over time, either as an alternative to or supplement for testing. There is no standard portfolio format. Products labeled portfolios vary widely from collections of drafts at various stages of development to selections of a student's best work. Portfolios are not ends in themselves, but a means of reflecting the knowledge and activities of students. They resemble real-life tasks; reveal how students solve problems; value solo as well as community performances; recognize that there is more than one acceptable solution, answer or point of view; recognize whole performances rather than fragmented skills; and permit many forms of representation or communication of knowledge and skills (Mathison 1995).

The literature on portfolios identifies a wide variety of benefits and advantages for their use in student assessment. Portfolios are generally intended to:

- illustrate the actual work of students
- illustrate student growth and learning over time
- enhance teacher and student involvement in evaluation
- promote student reflection and self-assessment, and
- provide opportunities for student choice and decision-making regarding the construction and evaluation of portfolios.

ADDENDUM: TEST PUBLISHERS AND DISTRIBUTORS

Test publishers and distributors usually provide online examples and catalogues of their current tests and survey instruments. In addition to those listed, the names and addresses of other test publishers and distributors can be obtained from the latest volume of the *Mental Measurements Yearbook*, which should also be consulted for current addresses and Internet sites.

American College Testing (www.act.com)
800-498-6065

The College Board (www.collegeboard.org)
45 Columbus Avenue
New York, NY 10023-6992
212-713-8060

CTB/McGraw-Hill (www.ctb.com)

Educational Testing Service (www.ets.org/media/Tests)
Princeton, NJ 08540
609-951-1691

Examgen, Inc. (www.examgen.com/social studies)
Data Bases for Teachers
Syracuse, NY 13210
800-736-8172

From Now On: The Educational Technology Journal (www.fno.org)

National Assessment of Educational Progress (NAEP) (www.naep.gov)
Office of Educational Research and Improvement (www.nloe.gov) U.S.
Department of Education: National Library of Education
555 New Jersey Avenue, N.W. Washington, DC 20208-5641
800-424-1616 or 202-219-1651

Scholastic Testing Service (www.scholastic.com) /techtools for test building)
800-642-6787

NOTES

1 Gardner, H. (1993) *Frames of Mind: The Theory of Multiple Intelligences* (New York: Basic Books).
2 Saye, J., Stoddard, J. et al. (2018) "Authentic Pedagogy: Examining Intellectual Challenge in Social Studies Classrooms," *Journal of Curriculum Studies*, 50, 6, 865–884.
3 Damiani, V. (2004) *Portfolio Assessment in the Classroom* (National Association of School Psychologists).
4 Sherrin, D. (2021) *Authentic Assessment: A Guide to Keeping It Real* (New York: Routledge).
5 Bloom, B. S., Madaus, G. F., and Hastings, J. T. (1981). *Evaluation to Improve Learning* (New York: McGraw-Hill).
6 Rosenshine, B. and Stevens, R. (1986) Teaching Functions. In Wittrock, M. (ed.) *Handbook of Research on Teaching,* 3rd Ed. (New York: Macmillan), 376–391.
7 Rensis L. (1967) *Human Organization: Its Management and Value* (New York: McGraw-Hill), 39–43.
8 Arbaugh, J. B. et. al. (2008) "Developing a Community of Inquiry Instrument: Testing a Measure of Community of Inquiry Framework," *The Internet and Higher Education*, 11 (3-3), 133–134, www.ijbssnet.com/journals.
9 Herman, J. L. et. al. (December 2006) "The Nature and Impact of Teachers' Formative Assessment Practices," CSE Technical Report 703, National Center for Research on Evaluation, Standards, and Student Testing (Los Angeles: UCLA).
10 Larwin, K. H., Gorman, J. and Larwin, D. A. (May 2013) "Assessing the impact of testing aides on post-secondary student performance: A meta-analytic investigation," *Educational Psychology Review*, 25, 429–443.
11 ETS (2020) *Understanding Your Praxis Scores* (Princeton, NJ: Educational Testing Service).
12 Miller, D., Linn, R. and Gronlund, N. E. (2015) *Assessment of Student Achievement*, 11th Ed. (New York: Pearson).

13 Hamilton, R. J. (1985) "A Framework for the Evaluation of the Effectiveness of Adjunct Questions and Objectives," *Review of Educational Research,* 55, 47–85.

14 CEE (2020) Test of Economic Literacy and Economic Literacy Quiz, www.councilforec-coned.org/test.

15 Bednarz, R. S. and Lee. J. (2019). "What Improves Spatial Thinking? Evidence from the Spatial Thinking Abilities Test," *International Research in Geographic and Environmental Education,* 28, 4, 262–280. Also see: National Council for Geographic Education Test Development Committee (Macomb, IL: National Council for Geographic Education, Western Illinois University).

16 Miller, M. D., Linn, R. L. and Gronlund, N. (2012) *Measurement and Assessment in Teaching,* 11th Ed. Kindle edition (New York: Pearson).

17 See for example Davis, Jr., O. L., Yeager, E. A., and Foster, S. J. (eds.) (2001) *Historical Empathy and Perspective Taking in the Social Studies* (Lanham, MD: Rowman & Littlefield).

18 Simon, K. G. (2001) *Moral Questions in the Classroom* (New Haven, CT: Yale University Press) presents a strong case for the implicit existence of moral questions across the curriculum.

19 Erickson, S. C. (1983) "Private Measures of Good Teaching," *Teaching of Psychology,* 10, 133–136.

FOR FURTHER STUDY: ASSESSMENT IN SOCIAL STUDIES

Archbald, D. A. and Newmann, F. M. (1988) *Beyond Standardized Testing: Assessing Authentic Academic Achievement in the Secondary School* (Reston, VA: National Association of Secondary School Principals).

Bednarz, S. W. and Bednarz, R. S. (2019). Citizenship Education in a Spatially Enhanced World. In Shin E. and Bednarz, S. (eds.) *Spatial Citizenship Education: Citizenship through Geography* (Routledge), 59–71.

Bloom, B. S., Hastings, J. T., and Madaus, G. F. (1971) *Handbook of Formative and Summative Evaluation of Student Learning* (New York: McGraw-Hill).

Calder, L. and Williams, R. (2021) Must History Students Write History Papers? *Journal of American History,* 926–942.

Davis, K., Christodoulou, J. et al. (2011) The Theory of Multiple Intelligences. In Sternberg, R. J. and Kaufman, B. *The Cambridge Handbook of Intelligence* (Cambridge University Press), 485–503.

Demetriou, A., Mouyi, A., and Spanoudis, G. (2010) The Development of Mental Processing. In Overton, W. F., *The Handbook of Life-Span Development: Cognition, Biology and Methods* (John Wiley & Sons), 36–55.

Gardner, H. (2000) *Intelligence Reframed: Multiple Intelligences for the 21st Century* (Basic Books).

Haladyna, T. M. (1987) *Writing Test Items to Evaluate Higher Order Thinking* (Needham Heights, MA: Allyn & Bacon).

Johnson, E. and Ramos, E. L. et. al. (2020) *The Social Studies Teacher's Toolbox* (San Francisco: Jossey-Bass).

King-O'Brien, K. (2021) "Reimagining Writing in History Courses," *Journal of American History,* 942–955.

Morse, H. T. and McCune, G. H. (1973) *Selected Items for the Testing of Study Skills and Critical Thinking* (Washington, DC: National Council for the Social Studies).

Newmann, F. M. and Wehlage, G. G. (2009) *Five Standards of Authentic Instruction,* www.learner.org /channel/workshops/socialstudies/pdf/session6/6.AuthenticInstruction.pdf (see especially their discipline-based rubric for inquiry).

Penuel, W. R. and Shepard, L. A. (2016) Assessment and Teaching. In Gitomer, D. H. and Bell, C. A. (eds.) *Handbook of Research on Teaching,* 5th Ed. (Washington, DC: American Educational Research Association), 787–850.

Popham, W. J. (2017) *Modern Educational Measurement* (Boston, MA: Pearson Education, Inc.).

Reisman, A. (2012). "Reading Like a Historian: A Document-Based History Curriculum Intervention in Urban High Schools," *Cognition and Instruction* 30, 1, 86–112.

Shepard, L. A., Penuel, W. R., and Pellegrino, J. W. (2019) "Using Learning and Motivation Theories to Coherently Link Formative Assessment, Grading Practices, and Large-Scale Assessment," *Educational Measurement: Issues and Practice* 37, 1, 21–34.

Social Studies Resource Toolkit (State of New York: Engage, NY), www.engageny.gov.

Scheurman, G. and Newman, F. M. (1998) "Authentic Intellectual Work in Social Studies: Putting Performance before Pedagogy," *Social Education* 62.1, 23–25.

Sherrin, D. (2020) *Authentic Assessment in Social Studies: A Guide to Keeping it Real* (New York: Routledge/ CRC Press).

Smith, M., Breakstone, J., and Wineburg, S. (2019) "History Assessments of Thinking: A Validity Study," *Cognition and Instruction*, 37, 1, 118–144.

Tuckman, B. W. (1996) *Testing for Teachers* (San Diego: Harcourt Brace Jovanovich).

Waugh K. C., and Gronlund, N. (2012) *Measuring Student Achievement*, 10th Ed. (New York: Pearson).

Wynne, S. A. (2021) *Praxis II: Social Studies 5086*, Exam Secrets, Mometrix Test Preparation Inc. mo -media.com.

Assessment in Social Studies

BUILD YOUR OWN LESSON

The challenge: thinking 'on your feet.'

Interact with a new piece of evidence, data, issue, or problem.

Design a lesson of your own using different materials (newly discovered art, music, literature, history, geography, etc.).

Worry not about what you know, but react by thinking about how you would teach the data. Improvise!

Write a didactic, reflective, and affective goal for each document or picture, then add a low, medium, and high order question.

Choose one of the six strategies.

Pick a brief method of evaluating success (verbal, written, and tested).

What questions do the data support? Where do they fit in history?

What is the source and context: time and place? And how does that matter?

Did you find improvisation for the classroom easy or difficult? Why?

Could you teach Word War I and its consequences from more than one point of view: German, French, or American? What is the artists' point of view in this drawing? How is the city shown? If WWI is over, why is the soldier still in uniform? Why are there bodies in the river? What does the town look like and why? Is the artist expressing any values? If so, what are these? Can art be valuable as historical evidence?

DOI: 10.4324/9781003026235-15

Figure 6.8:   Woodcut "FINIS" by George Grosz, 1919. Owned by author.

TEACHING THE SOCIAL STUDIES CURRICULUM

7

TEACHING WORLD/GLOBAL STUDIES

"Privileging a global perspective means focusing not only on the relations societies build up with one another and on the way they are articulated to one another, forming a variety of different groups, but also on the way these human, economic, social, religious or political arrangements either enhance the homogeneity of the planet or, on the contrary, resist it."

Moyn, S. and Sartori, A. (eds.) (2013) *Global Intellectual History*
(New York, NY: Columbia University Press), 96.

D2. His.1.6-8. Analyze connections among events and developments in broader historical contexts.

D2. His.1.9-12. Evaluate how historical events and developments were shaped by unique circumstances of time and place as well as broader both clear and surprising ways from time historical contexts.

D2. His.2.6-8. Classify series of historical events and developments as examples of change and/or continuity.

D2. His.2.9-12. Analyze change and continuity in historical eras.

C3 Framework, p. 46.

OVERVIEW

This chapter is about designing the most difficult course in social studies: World Studies. Alternative approaches are examined and evaluated: integrative global, geographic, western history, and cross-cultural.

DOI: 10.4324/9781003026235-17

INTRODUCTION

World, global, international, history is probably the most important course we need to teach because all nations and peoples participate in one and same political, economic, and environmental system. The reasons are clear: the world has coalesced into one interconnected set of populations all dependent on each other. The COVID-19 pandemic makes connectedness as sharp as can be since the virus and variants traveled with their human hosts across the entire planet in less than a year. Much like previous pandemics, but with much greater scientific and medical knowledge, sapiens still suffers all the faults of organization and caring and sharing like most previous human disasters from disease, climate, or ecological destruction. In some ways, the unseen microscopic foe is more disorienting than a full out tidal wave or storm. Therefore, the globe must be taught holistically and with our fates interconnected.

World history was once easy to plan and teach because we pretty much ignored everyone seen outside of 'us' as unimportant or peripheral and that took in *most* of recorded history. The dominant goal was to impart information about the history of Western Europe (mostly England, France, and Italy, a bit of Germany and Russia, and ancient Greece and Rome), those seen as forbearers. Other regions and cultures were mentioned briefly, if at all, and usually from a U.S., Western, or Eurocentric perspective. There was little consciousness that other peoples or cultures had or now have their own views of history.

Chronology was the rule; *world history* was typically defined as a series of set pieces beginning with Greece and Rome, progressing through the Middle Ages and the Renaissance, and concluding with World Wars I & II, or—with great luck—a bit of the present. What happened to the Hebrews or Chinese?

Since those relatively simple days, the world, and world studies have changed a good deal. World history has changed, too, casting a wider and wider net encompassing more and more of earth's cultures. No longer can world studies be taught from a purely Eurocentric or ethnocentric perspective.[1] East and west, north and south, have done more than just meet—each is now interdependent, resulting in a closer and perhaps more sensitive world. There are now international news channels, Canal One, Al Jazeera, BBC, and others if you care to find out what the news looks like from a non-American perspective. We could argue that current events show a disturbing triad of problems for societies across the world, a retreat into narrow national identities, the increase of globally linked trade and commerce, and the most tepid recognition of climate change and world environmental destruction.

This chapter offers an example of what should be addressed in a world or global studies course and some alternative approaches as well. You may choose the one most suitable for your students, school or district, or you may invent a plan taking account of the particular needs of your situation and knowledge level. Teaching the world is no easy task for any teacher and should be viewed as an experiment in providing a more comprehensive and honest view of the world from our own *and* others' perspectives. No single source, certainly not one with a nationalistic bias, should be the base for a global curriculum.

Teachers should take responsibility for presenting a **balanced view of our changing world. That means you must try to be fair to how others view us, and their history, as well as respect the evidence.** Above all, you are invited to experiment with world history while strongly holding onto a few basic principles, mostly missing, from past courses, a true worldview, i.e., create and use materials keeping in mind to:

1. Always include points of view from at least two sources, one of which should represent the 'other' or another viewpoint.
2. Always review lessons, documents, and images for biased reporting, and context (is the source of the time and place?).
3. Never completely trust or believe sources, check them out and leave conclusions open and tentative.
4. Keep your mind open to other viewpoints, especially from critics, and to other historical interpretations.
5. Ask questions about sources, interpretations, and especially conclusions that glorify, privilege, or excuse the speech and acts of people and policies.

SETTING GOALS

The goals chosen for a course sets its direction, organizes its content, and promotes different levels of learning. Within world studies/world history, there are three basic structures for organizing the curriculum: **theme, chronology, and place.** Thematic units are built around general concepts such as revolution or technological change; or nationalism. Chronological units follow a time frame: Renaissance to Reformation, Shang Dynasty to Ming, and go backwards and/or forward in time. A place structure organizes units around areas such as Africa, Asia, or Latin America, or the entire world. Big History can be a variant of the three concepts (fully integrated) that treats all of history within a framework for understanding links between and among peoples. Giving the world its due is not at all easy to pull off because very few have an unbiased grasp of the entire sweep of human history from its humble beginnings to the pandemic present.

The History of the World, as the Globe, the Ecosystem, Sapiens, etc. may be united by adopting a new view of the human story as **one interlocking system dating back to the beginning of evolution in which all humans are descended from the same African ancestors** who crossed almost the entire earth and populated nearly all of it by 50,000 years ago. Even before migrating to the New World, humans and protohumans had penetrated nearly every ecological niche across the planet simply by walking!

To shift your mind to a comprehensive worldview, a true worldview, takes effort and rethinking on a planetary scale. Communities, towns, cities, nations, empires all shape and are shaped by history and all are connected in immemorial. The COVID-19 virus is a good example of our connectivity and its frightening results, and can only be grasped on a planetary level to be fully understood. History often repeats itself in varying ways, and we often forget that diffusion, migration, and invention and plagues share the same spaces. Big events like diseases, storms, and disasters do not respect borders or boundaries. Yet we tend to think locally and nationalistically.

The three curriculum concepts of theme, chronology, and place can be made more specific by recognizing and building upon five concepts to organize our views and enhance our grasp of human and protohuman history and social science. Let us view world, global, international, and ecological history through five lenses:

1. **Evolving pathways and landscapes:** The human and hominid animal expands across nearly all ecological niches with noticeable effects.
2. **Expanding human travel and settlement:** Creates cultures, heartlands, and technologies, beliefs and skills across the world that are easily diffused and shared.

3. **Human and hominid populations move around:** Humans change places and develop lifestyles in larger and larger groups, from bands to groups to villages to towns, cities, nations, and empires.
4. **Social systems evolve and adapt with populations:** Settings and cultures develop different sets of social relations, classes, castes, family relations, and a sense of identity.
5. **Trade, transport and travel sweep the planet:** Hunting, gathering, manufacturing tools, and farming arise and shift toward global economic systems and trade networks.
6. Once you have decided on the theme and structure of your course, you must also **choose specific goals along the three dimensions:** didactic, reflective, and affective. Any of the goals can be used with any of the three structures. The choice of goals is dependent on the abilities of your student audience and what you would like them to achieve, content knowledge and understanding, insight and generalizations, plus, maybe even feelings for others, empathy. In the Internet Age, however, it is the building of thinking skills that is key, not the amount of knowledge collected.

Didactic Goals

World studies naturally demands that a great deal of knowledge is covered—an amount that is nearly impossible to contemplate, let alone teach. Nevertheless, many teachers try to cover the 'facts' as well as they can, often consciously or unconsciously offering students a highly selective list of cases and interpretations drawn from the vast pool available.[2] In planning a course, you should acknowledge frankly the need for selection and thoughtfulness. This is particularly important in establishing didactic goals, perhaps case studies. In fact, given the broad nature of world or global studies, there is a danger, regardless of the goal, of lapsing into generalizations that do little to focus your course. You and your students will drown in data.

To begin, let's look at some examples of didactic goals in need of improvement:

1. Students will gain more information about the world.
2. Students will understand the sweep and grandeur of the contacts between Eastern and Western civilizations.
3. Students will comprehend how Western civilization became unique in comparison with other civilizations.

In the first case, what students will know has not been specified. In the second example, values and judgments have already been identified, leaving no room for student opinions. In the third instance, differences are presupposed, with no possibility of similarities or meaningful comparisons.

More effective didactic or informational goals would focus on a limited number of themes, concepts, and ideas you want students to acquire. Given that most world studies programs require students to be familiar with the major periods of Western history and with cultural landmarks in other cultures, a set of improved didactic goals for world studies might look like this:

1. Students will accurately describe developments during a major period of Western history beginning with a unit on Ancient Greece.

2. Students will correctly identify five enlightenment philosophies and their authors, analyzing and debating their viewpoints.
3. Students will be able to divide the world into specific cultural and geographic regions distinguishing among their physical characteristics and human populations.

Compared with the first set, these goals, although far from perfect, give your students a more concrete notion of what they are supposed to know and be able to do. They also provide insight into the direction and content of the course as a whole. The first goal alerts students to chronological periods in Western history, the second goal asks that students to learn about important philosophers (political 'idea' people), and the third goal requires students to have overview knowledge of regions and populations.

Although at first your didactic goals may be vague and general, you can refine them until you have developed more specific objectives and settle on an outline that defines the precise topics, facts, and areas to be studied in an allotted time frame.

Reflective Goals

Two kinds of reflective goals apply to world studies: those designed to foster understanding of causes and influences, and those designed to develop skills of historical and scientific inquiry. As with didactic goals, there are far too many possible reflective goals for a world studies program, so you must exercise selectivity. You might begin with general goals such as the following:

1. Students will appreciate the contributions of many diverse societies to the world's story.
2. Students will understand why technology may be a major key to history.
3. Students will learn how to think like a historian *and* social scientist in viewing past events.

These three examples are a beginning, but they leave out the specifics of what is to be studied, and which thinking processes students will be asked to use. *Appreciate*, for instance, might mean nothing more than recalling a list of facts, or as much as being able to describe and analyze ideas that have had widespread impact on the everyday affairs of large populations. The second goal assumes an answer (that technology is or is not the key to history) leaving students out of developing alternative theories. The third goal seeks to develop historiography or scientific thinking, but does not give an example of which tools of investigation will be stressed (e.g., checking eyewitness accounts).

After deliberation, you might reshape the three goals into statements with greater behavioral precision:

1. Students will describe and explain at least two different inventions, ideas, or skills from five different societies, Western and non-Western, that they consider contributions to people in the present, and defend their choices with reasons and evidence.
2. Students will examine cultural growth, change, or decline, drawing connections between the economic development and political stability of each society deciding which factors are most important for a *successful* culture (as defined by students).

3. Students will interpret and apply information from primary sources such as statistics, autobiographies, and public documents to test two or more competing theories of historical progress (in excerpted form) by scholars, concluding with written judgments of their own decisions.

Note that the previously stated goals still lack specifics—names, dates, theories, primary sources, and so forth—but they provide far more direction than at first. The first goal asks students to move from description and analysis to evaluation—not only listing contributions, but also defending their choices.

The second goal asks students to consider key or leading ideas (growth, change, and decline) and compare and contrast these in political and economic terms.

The third goal asks student to 'think like historians,' calling on them to use reading and research skills to check the bases of historians' explanations. In short, all three of the expanded, more specific reflective goals (bordering now on what teachers call *learning objectives*) require application and interpretation, with a stress on decision-making and problem-solving rather than only retrieval of information.

Affective Goals

World/global studies programs also seek to develop affective goals that raise problems of ethical choice and decision.[3] Helping students to decide issues and formulate positions without pushing them to adopt any specific viewpoint is difficult, but worthwhile. Your job is to prepare affective goals that support independent judgment and raise issues, but do not easily solve problems. The big question is how to promote caring and empathy without pressing specific values. We are not trying to force values on students!

Affective goals in world studies frequently deal with how students and teachers see other cultures, times, and places. Many world studies programs include aims such as 'building sensitivity to other cultures,' 'seeing ourselves through others' perspectives,' 'evolving open-mindedness or empathy for other cultures,' and 'building cross-cultural awareness.' Implied in goals such as open-mindedness or sensitivity is a commitment to building a sense of empathy for students, encouraging them to feel problems and issues from an insider viewpoint, looking at the world from another's shoes. This is more than simply feeling pride or sorrow for others but less than sympathizing and agreeing. It is really more about being able to step outside of one's own narrow ethnocentric circle. We need an attitude of respect toward others combatting our own prejudices and culturally centered attitudes.

Affective goals share a common commitment to diminishing the prejudice and bias that often seem inherent in the contact among different cultures and societies, allowing students to view those unlike themselves as fully human for whom feelings and understandings can be evoked. A sense of pride in your own culture or country is fine, but it may also work to shape negative or distorting attitudes that everyone else's country and culture is somehow inferior, strange, or pathetic. Affective goals in world studies also encourage students to take positions on issues, especially in the area of international relations and foreign policy. These issues can range from ecology to trade and aid, typically centering on such topics as world hunger, human rights, climate change, and energy exploitation or conservation.

Typical preliminary, general affective goals might include the following:

1. Students will show increasing sensitivity to bias directed at others.
2. Students will compare definitions of the term 'demagogue' and populist, and make judgments about which is best.
3. Students will be able to take a stand on some aspect of foreign affairs.

Sensitivity is not defined in the first goal, nor is it clear how students will demonstrate their increasing awareness of the existence of bias. Empathy is not mentioned, although it is implied in sensitivity. Defining demagogue certainly appears to be a worthy goal improved by a request for multiple definitions of terms. Students have the chance to test and compare definitions and judge the best fit. Finally, taking a stand is always a useful goal in the social studies, and certainly in world affairs, but nothing in the statement suggests how that stand will be created, from what sources, and to what effect.

The addition of specific procedures clarifies these goals and makes them easier to apply.

1. Based on a series of historical case studies, students will develop a list of key words and behaviors that indicate bias and prejudice and apply criteria to two or three present-day examples, deciding if suspicions of bias can be justified.
2. Students will review the United Nations Charter on Human Rights (e.g., rules on the treatment of captured soldiers and torture, or policies of intervention in other nations' affairs), debating which rights they would be willing to defend as universal and which they would not. They will present their arguments in an orderly, organized way and listen carefully to the arguments of those who disagree.
3. Students will collect, analyze, and summarize information concerning an issue from at least three different Web sources (e.g., human rights, immigration, climate change, helping others, international trade, and racial or ethnic prejudice) as the basis for proposing and defending a solution.

These more elaborate goals suggest content students will study, which skills they will be asked to employ, and what kinds of outcomes are sought (e.g., being able to hold and defend a position on a specific issue). All three examples share a commitment both to amassing evidence for or against an issue and deciding which side the student chooses in an argument. Actions supporting these goals might include having students raise money for a worthy organization; participate in a protest march; write a letter to a local, state, or national official; or perhaps send an editorial to a newspaper.

TO DO

Let's say that you are asked to create a unit on one of the following: political leadership, immigration/migration, economic inequality, or cultural contact and conflict.

Write a set of at least one didactic, reflective, and affective goal for one of these units using the criteria discussed in this section. As you develop each goal, think about these questions:

What would you want students to learn about the topic? Which facts, which sorts of data might you present? How would you organize the unit? Which problems and issues should be raised first and foremost?

How will you arrange materials to promote reflective and creative thinking about causes and consequences? What kinds of ethical and moral questions arise from the examples? Which controversies do you think students most need to consider? Offer reasons for your goals and procedures, explaining what you hope to accomplish.

DESIGNING A PROGRAM FOR THE NOW AND FUTURE WORLD

World/global studies programs are typically organized thematically, chronologically, or geographically.[4] Thematic approaches usually have a single major focus (e.g., cultural achievements, social structure, international relations, or political power), but multiple themes or concepts can be used as organizing ideas with which events and people from many different times and places can be studied. A single theme implies a developmental view of events, whereas multiple themes set up a comparative framework; for instance, using the idea of revolution as a concept for side-by-side case studies of the American, French, Haitian, Russian, Chinese, or Mexican revolutions will lead to student hypotheses about revolutions.

Thematic Approaches Emphasize Central Idea as the Heart of a Course

Chronological approaches usually begin at some point in the past and work forward, although occasionally courses begin with an aspect of the present and work backward. A starting point in the past inevitably encourages students to focus on the way events and people develop in historical perspective, whereas a present-day beginning leads students to think about the roots of current ideas and actions. **Time is a key aspect** of beginnings but in many world studies and global courses, starting points are often not clear. Instructors jump around and between cultures and regions, beginning and ending at different time periods (e.g., just what does *medieval* mean in the context of Chinese or Indian histories, as compared with European?).

World studies programs are typically organized around **the idea of place,** usually regions, cultural heartlands, or the historical uniqueness of particular areas. Often world studies programs introduce geographic concepts followed by units on Africa, Asia, the Middle East, Europe, the Americas, and rarely Oceania. Case studies from each area may be compared or followed in time from their historical beginnings to the present, making the material more manageable. However, there is again considerable jumping around in terms of chronology.

The three organizing structures—theme, time, and place—yield quite different world studies courses if followed rigorously. Often, however, the three approaches are mixed or mashed to develop a program that is divided into large themes presented chronologically or a chronologically oriented curriculum that offers flashbacks and fast forwards for comparison and contrast. The permutations and combinations are many and varied, all seeking to solve the problem of integrating vast amounts of data from different histories into a whole. The primary fused approach is chronological, and this is usually the dominant approach to world studies overall, with area studies a runner-up. Whether this makes sense to student audiences is unclear.

The most provocative approach is to develop a comparative structure of your own that emphasizes building familiarity with and comparisons of several cultures and situations without particular regard to chronology or place. For example, think plural: industrial revolutions, political institutions, democracy, autocracy, and oligarchy, Renaissances, trade and travel, etc. **Choose three or so illustrative examples to broaden horizons for both you and students. Note that these are all centered on one or two themes.**

For example, AP world history emphasizes four themes, i.e., students study four separate themes that organize world history:

- **Theme 1: Interaction between Humans and Environment.** Students will learn about diseases and the demographics that affect, the migration of humans across time, patterns of settlement around the world, and the importance of technology in developing civilizations.
- **Theme 2: Development and Interaction of Cultures.** Students will develop an understanding of religions, belief systems, science and technology's effect on government, and the arts and architecture's effect on the general population.
- **Theme 3: State-Building, Expansion, and Conflict.** Students will learn about political structures and their forms of governance, empires, nationalism, and revolutions across different types of government.
- **Theme 4: Creation, Expansion, and Interaction of Economic Systems.** Students will gain an appreciation for agricultural and pastoral production, trade and commerce patterns, labor systems, and industrialization (https://course-notes.org/world_history).

RESEARCH REPORT

Textbooks written for world history are sometimes subjected to review and criticism using content analysis methods of research. A recent report using content analysis of the five most popular World History textbooks in the U.S. demonstrated progress on opening the curriculum to non-Western history but still maintaining a Western worldview nonetheless. The author states that:

> The texts seem caught between two competing conceptions of the high school world history course. Early versions of this course were heavily concentrated in European history, but over time, the content of the course has become more diverse and less Eurocentric. The books' organization shows that they have retained the older, European approach to organization while adding newfangled supplementary materials and addenda onto this structure.[8]

Marino, M. P. (2011) "High School World History Textbooks: An Analysis of Content Focus and Chronological Approaches," *The History Teacher*, 44, 3, 422–445.

The Western History Approach Enlarged

World studies programs are relative newcomers to the global scene. Western history, with a stress on both the West and history aspects, has been common for several decades. Only since World War II has serious national attention been given to the study of non-Western history and culture, ultimately resulting in calls for fully integrated world studies courses. However, no widely popular, well-defined curriculum has yet emerged, although the number of suggestions has grown considerably.

In contrast, most Western/European history courses rest on a well-organized structure and clearly defined body of information. Typically, Western history is presented as a series of chronological periods, each with a distinct character and set of ideas that have contributed to succeeding stages. The course is usually taught as if Western civilization is following its own developmental path marginally influenced by other regions and cultures. Each time period is presented with its own cast of characters and major events, causes, and consequences, although some mavericks do consider an 'outstanding people' or a 'causes' approach unacceptable.[5]

Most Western history courses are Eurocentric, meaning that they are organized from a European or American point of view—America being seen as part of European tradition. This approach can be extremely one-sided.[6] For example, the growth of Islam is often presented almost entirely in terms of the way it affected Western nations. It is rare that more than a few pages are given to important events in Islamic history, such as Iranian Shiism, or the rise of the Ottoman Empire, which lasted 400 years.

Western civilization programs typically begin with ancient Greece and Rome (sometimes the Hebrews or 'early humans'), shown as the foundations of Western tradition, although all societies had connections to the Middle East and Africa. Prehistory and the complexities of cultural diffusion even in the periods studied are often overlooked indeed, history is organized into ages or periods that imply a steady, linear sequence. However, Western history courses persist and are defended on the grounds that students need to understand their own nation's background and cultural heritage. Course organization is quite predictable. Typical Western history courses cover the following major topics:

A. The Foundations of Civilization
   1. Human Prehistory (much changed but little taught)
   2. Cradles of Civilization (fertile crescent)
   3. Greek and Hellenistic Civilizations
   4. Roman Civilization (plus Byzantium?)
   5. The Development of Feudalism
B. Restoration and Continuity
   1. The Renaissance
   2. The Reformation
   3. The Age of Discovery (of others by the West)
   4. Age of Religious Wars
   5. England and France in the 17th and 18th Centuries
   6. Age of Exploration
   7. Period of the Enlightenment
C. The Age of Revolutions
   1. The American Revolution
   2. The French Revolution

  3. Napoleon and the French Empire
  4. Temporary Restoration
  5. Revolutions of 1830, 1848, and 1870
  6. Reform Movements
  7. Industrialization
D. Age of Nationalism
  1. Italian Unification
  2. German Union
  3. The Hapsburg Empire
  4. Russia—Change and Emancipation
  5. British, German, French and a little Italian Imperialism
  6. Ideologies and Social Movements
  7. Alliances and Ententes
  8. World War I
  9. The Peaceful 1920s
  10. World Depression
  11. Rise of Dictators
E. World War II
  1. Prelude
  2. War Breaks Out
  3. The Holocaust
  4. Defeats and Victories
  5. Peace and the United Nations
F. Age of Internationalism
  1. Europe Caught in the Soviet/U.S. Rivalry: The Cold War
  2. Independence in the Third World
  3. Decline of Colonial Powers
  4. Rise of Asian Industrial Powers
  5. Fragmentation of the Communist Countries
  6. Conflicts in the Middle East: The Soviet Union Crumbles
  7. First, Second, and Third Worlds: Dependence and Interdependence
  8. American Hegemony and the Rise of World Capitalism
  9. Globalization, Pandemic, and Climate Change: A Postmodern Condition?

SAMPLE LESSON PLAN

For example, Figure 7.1, The Execution of Charles the First of England, January 39, 1649. The Title Page of The Confession of Richard Brandon, a pamphlet claiming to reveal Richard Brandon as Charles I's executioner. Compare and contrast the executions of the two monarchs: style, image, audience, and manner of execution: King Charles I and King Louis XVI By José-Manuel Benito Álvarez, CC BY-SA 2.5.

What is the artist's view of Solomon and Sheba? Who is more important? How do you know this? Is this what Solomon and Sheba really looked like? Or is this what people

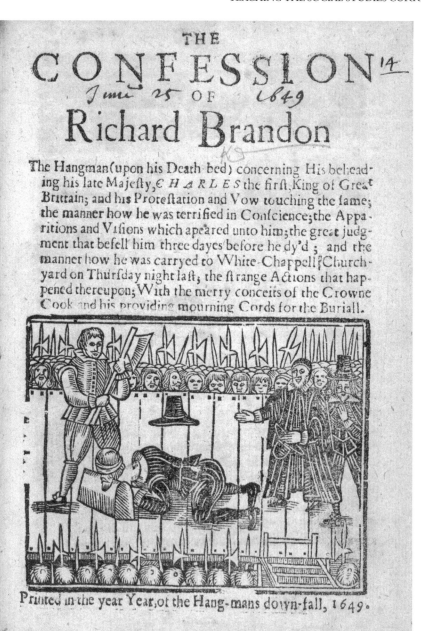

Figure 7.1:   The Execution of Charles the First of England, January 39, 1649 The Title Page of The Confession of Richard Brandon, a pamphlet claiming to reveal Richard Brandon as Charles I's executioner. Compare and contrast the executions of the two monarchs: style, image, audience, And manner of execution: King Charles I and King Louis XVI By José-Manuel Benito Álvarez, CC BY-SA 2.5.

Source: https://upload.wikimedia.org/wikipedia/commons/a/ad/Confession-of-Richard-Brandon-hst_tl_1600_E_561_14.jpg looked like in the artist's times? How can you tell when you have an accurate contemporary depiction?

Western history courses provide students with solid grounding in a line that runs from the Cro-Magnon cave artists to modern times. The program is plotted in terms of events and ideas—Greek philosophy, Hebrew history and the idea of monotheism, the Roman Empire, and the birth of Christianity, for example, as foundations for understanding the Middle Ages and the Renaissance, which in turn lay the groundwork for the nationalism, revolution, imperialism, and wars of the 18th, 19th, and 20th centuries. Proponents of teaching Western history argue that American students need this material (and they do! But it is centered on U.S. history, not us in the globe!) because the symbols, ideas, and ideals of U.S. culture have grown from roots. But this does not solve the problem of placing the U.S. and the West in a global context.

WHAT DO YOU THINK?

How would you expand the list of topics for a World Studies program, especially if you were working on a sensitive topic like Islam? The following is a section from a Western history curriculum dealing with the Age of Feudalism, and 'Threats from the Outside,' one of which is Islam. Assuming you wanted to give fair treatment to Muslims vis-à-vis Europeans, how would you change or rearrange these topics? Would you ask students to read portions of the Koran? Would you offer students Muslim views of Christians and Crusaders? How much time would you deduct from Europe if you had only three to four weeks for instruction? What choices will give students balanced views?

A. Age of Feudalism Across the Globe
    1. The Growth of Christianity and Islam
    2. Threats to Europe from Outside
    3. The Black Death and Plagues Inside
    4. Social Classes and Customs

Expand the brief outline of Western history given and revise it in a fair way for others (e.g., Arabs, Turks, Chinese, North African and Arabs, or Jews) that will diminish student stereotypes (e.g., The Dark Ages, Spread of Islam, or Colonialism). How about doing African Medievalism, e.g. The Epic of Sundiata? Google it!

Criticism. Western history courses are open to attack because we live in a shrinking global community. Recent and ongoing migration has altered the U.S. population mix significantly. This has led to recognition that many people, cultures, and critical events have been seriously neglected promoting an effort to replace Western history with world or global studies programs. At the very least, critics ask that courses be expanded to include more comparative examples from other cultures or that a parallel non-Western studies program is included.

Educators who believe that we are moving closer and closer to one world community argue that Western history programs give students a biased and isolated view of both the past and the present.[7] They argue that cultures have nearly *always* traded, traveled, and borrowed, making Western history an inadequate account of cultural diffusion even within Europe and its colonies. In addition, critics point out that the focus of the course is often narrow, concentrating mainly on a chronology of major political events, slighting technology and science as well as socio-cultural issues. Most courses focus primarily on a few European countries (France, England, Italy, Germany, and maybe Russia), with scant reference even to Eastern or Southern Europe, much less Iran and the Middle East.

Greece never seems to get beyond ancient times. Western history courses may reflect scholarship that is largely (still) the product of a White, male, Christian conqueror's point of view: one that ignores or slights women, non-Whites, non-Christians, the poor and less fortunate, minorities, and the conquered. To understand these arguments, you need only review an outline for a typical Western history course. Africa, Oceania, and Latin America, even Canada, are largely absent. Few women or minorities are mentioned, the conquered rarely have the opportunity to describe their views and feelings, competing cultures are treated as peripheral to events in the West, although some groups (e.g., Byzantines, Turks, Persians) threatened and influenced Europe for centuries.

Defense. Attacks on the role of Western history in the curriculum have been met with equally vehement defenses, such as that mounted by the Bradley Commission on History in Schools, which argued strongly in favor of a focus on European traditions, emphasizing history over the social sciences, and reinforcing students' identification with a common heritage of Western ideas and traditions.[8] The core of the argument is the notion that the United States is largely a product of Western historical development, and all students need to understand that whatever their own backgrounds may be. Many of those who defend the importance of teaching students about the rise of the West nevertheless are displeased with the way they see the course taught, preferring, especially at the secondary level, discussions of great works of literature, philosophy, and art to textbook narratives and lectures. Real familiarity with Western history, they argue, can emerge only from study of the most influential key works: the Bible and Plato through Machiavelli and Descartes to John Stuart Mill and Rousseau.

Powerful arguments for Western history or European studies are countered by equally intense and well-grounded arguments for world or global approaches. The two, of course, are not necessarily incompatible. But a number of problems must be resolved in fusing them into a single, coherent world studies program. Most global history/world studies programs are piecemeal collections of Western and non-Western time periods, famous personalities, and cultural contributions. Often non-Western units are simply added to European history courses without any real integration. Courses stress points of contact—an East-meets-West or North-meets-South perspective—but difficult choices must still be made about what to teach among materials that remain unfamiliar for many teachers. The difficulties are compounded because there is little direct linkage among time periods across cultures; the Middle Ages in European history are not linked to Feudalism in African history, though it could be done through Muslim chroniclers and sources like the Epic of Sundiata.

Additional problems arise because world studies embrace *so much* material, much of it fragmented and distorted, that neither teachers nor students have time to absorb more than a modest amount in the course of a normal year. Selections may not seem approachable to students. As the demand to teach more information grows, teachers tend to use instructional techniques that speed up the transfer—with PowerPoint replacing lectures, Internet searches replacing texts—in a program that would be better served by involvement, discussion, and understanding frequently confusing and unfamiliar ideas and events. Teachers who want students to understand Buddhism or Confucianism, but rush through the 'facts' of Chinese history or condense the Buddha's main ideas into epigrams, lose the chance to reflect on complex and thought-provoking ideas that have influenced millions of people for thousands of years. That teacher is left with a 'cover versus understand' dilemma that can be resolved only by unsatisfactory compromises.

Within world studies, several alternative approaches address this problem:

1. A World Geographic Approach
2. An International Relations Approach
3. A Cross-Cultural Approach
4. An Integrated Whole World Approach

Alternative Approaches to Organizing a Global History Course

As yet, there is no universally accepted structure for teaching world studies, but there has been progress and movement in the direction of greater 'worldview.'[9] There has also been greater integration of regional histories (e.g., recent work on the Atlantic or Pacific World or 'Big' history or fusion approaches).

More and more historians have attempted integrative global histories like Yuval Noah Harari (Sapiens 2018) a best-seller. From these efforts, four major themes have emerged: a geographic approach, which stresses human and physical interactions among the world's regions and climates; an international relations approach, which stresses the relationships between and among the political systems of the world; a cross-cultural approach, which invites comparisons among cultures that have evolved different (or similar) solutions to fundamental human problems; and an integrated or global history approach, which focuses on social, economic, and political change resulting in increasing global interdependence.

Within each of these approaches, teachers make choices and create their own fusion. The three organizing principles outlined at the beginning of this chapter—theme, chronology, and place—can be used to structure any approach. You might even want to work backward (Wow! Would you be different!) beginning with current events, or focus on issues such as human rights, or combine historical topics into themes: social systems, cultural diffusion, or environment. By beginning with now, you might perhaps convince students of the worth and relevance of history helping them view past threads woven into the present cloth.

A Geographic/Geoscience/Science Approach (Regional Studies)

World studies programs may focus on place and ecology, framing everything in a spatial rather than a historical perspective.[10] If you choose this route, introduce students to places by discussing the relationship of sites to other factors such as topography, natural resources, or trade routes. Focus on where innovations began and how they spread, where cities or agriculture first developed, and how new technologies were disseminated. Move on to discuss why the same ideas and institutions took different forms in different locales and regions, viewing variation on a local, national, regional, or worldwide basis. This geographic/regional approach invites comparisons of cities, technology, culture, and political systems, and it raises questions about why some people have achieved great wealth and influence, whereas others cope poorly with their environments and barely survive. Introduce students to physical and human regions as defined by historical and geographical research, usually along cultural or physical lines such as those that delineate Europe, Asia, Africa, and the Middle East. Ask them to use data to discuss the ways which people and ecosystems have interacted on local, national, regional, and social connections creating distinct cultures. National development, its causes and consequences, is a key concept that binds the course. We see the consequences in the modern world. Rich and poor nations are interdependent, sharing a world where economic development brings prosperity to some, but also causes havoc and ecological destruction through pollution, waste, and ecocide—a tough value dilemma for students to wrestle with throughout the course. The Big game is whether we are approaching ecological disaster or speeding up survival technology, or both? With a geographic organization, human-ecological interactions, questions of place and resources, change and climate crises stand out for attention.

With a geographic organization, human–environmental interactions, questions of place and location, change and crisis emerge as dominant themes.

Geographic approaches do not provide a strong historical background for students, nor does it yield a clear picture of periodization for either Western or non-Western history. Nevertheless, if your goals are to build student understanding of the Earth's features and how people have developed in different regions, and to promote a better grasp of current ecological and trade issues, the geographic approach is excellent.

LET'S DECIDE

The idea of place gives world studies a different perspective from that of theme or chronology, yet the latter are important as well. If you and several colleagues or classmates use a place or regional structure for teaching world history, how would you and the group select content for the different regions—by theme, time period, or country? Would your Africa unit begin with a study of culture, prehistory, or case studies of several nations such as Iraq, Egypt, Kenya, and Nigeria? Would the course's organization make a difference to you? How would you solve conceptual problems if you decide to use a geographical approach? For example, are China, Japan, and India comparable to Africa south of the Sahara? Is Central America or the Caribbean a place in the same sense as France and England? Suppose your group decides to use a case studies approach. What choices would you make for each of the following reasons? Why?

An International Relations Approach

An international relations approach to world studies stresses issues that grow out of the political connections among people, groups, agencies, institutions, nations, and worldwide organizations. Generally, an international focus works best if the course begins with or stresses the present and works back to the causes of current events, but could also work as a guide to understanding the interactions between societies and polities from the ancient world to the present.[11] The increasing interconnectedness of our time especially with the Internet and instant global news, helps to justify an international approach. But interconnectedness can also illuminate the past. You could argue that ancient Israel, for example, was just as much a crossroads and battleground for great powers then as it is today (but why?). You could propose that the Roman Empire, at its height, connected four continents, and has many descendants today. Each day events in trade, world debt, diplomacy, human rights, and popular culture demonstrate the influence people and nations have on each other, with distance less important than ever before. Africa was always part of a global network with regular caravans crossing the Sahara to visit West and East African kingdoms, e.g., Ethiopia and Mali.

In addition, students need to be introduced to foreign affairs: to the tools and ideas used by political and social scientists. The issues you select can engage students in debates, discussions, and activities that involve citizenship education with attention to tensions among national and global concerns: Are the interests of my nation the same as those of the region or world? If not, then what, can be done to satisfy the needs of all?

Global citizenship discussions help students to understand their own place in the international system and the role that their nation plays as an actor, for better or worse. Past and present can be seen as part of worldwide power relationships (as proposed by Brown University's Choices program). So, engage students to interpret events through a series of policy 'futures.'[12] An understanding of global policy and its effects will, in turn, enable students taking stands on the vital issues of our time.

WHAT DO YOU THINK?

How far back in time could you travel with an international relations approach? 19th century, surely, and to the 18th, 17th, 16th, and 15th century as well? Some scholars, such as Immanuel Wallerstein in *The Modern World System*, assert that the entire planet has been drawing together into a tighter and tighter single economic and political system since the Renaissance in Europe or perhaps earlier. This debate could be interesting in and of itself.

Using this idea, could you design a global course in which all of the traditional topics of the Western approach are matched with analogous cases from Asia, Africa, and the Middle East? What diplomatic initiatives would the Chinese of the 16th century have to employ to compete with Europe? Why did some nations (Japan) choose isolation for hundreds of years and then suddenly emerge as a world power? Why did Turkey, a great world power in the 16th, 17th, and 18th centuries, decline in the 19th and 20th centuries? How long is the U.S. going to last as the 'hegemonic' global power: less or more than Rome?

Develop an international relations/world history course for only one century, your choice, remembering to keep a balance between East and West in choosing examples.

A Cross-Cultural Approach

Cross-cultural approaches are usually organized around concepts or themes that invite immediate and direct comparisons of institutions, traditions, customs, ideas, literature, art, and music. Themes may be political, social, economic, aesthetic, philosophical, and geographical/environmental. A cross-cultural approach ideally promotes students' understanding peoples around the globe.[13] Further, a cross-cultural view encourages students to look at developments from the perspective of other cultures as well as their own. 'Strange and exotic' customs take on new meaning through comparison with more familiar ideas and practices, whereas familiar customs frequently benefit from the comparison and can be viewed in a new light. You might ask students to compare the American nuclear family with the extended family common to parts of the Muslim Middle East or Africa; students may perceive advantages in the large networks of relatives, and they may also begin to understand the origins and rationale for polygamy and purdah (the practice among Muslim women of wearing veils in public) in Saudi Arabia and other places, even if they disagree.

The cross-cultural framework can also yield a deeper understanding of the relationship between repressive and authoritarian governments and socioeconomic difficulties. By studying relatively wealthy and poor societies side by side, students can develop their own theories of political development—ones in which they see the correlation between juntas or dictatorships and weak economies, high unemployment and ethnic hatred, democracy and relative wealth, strong beliefs in the rule of law, and histories of political compromise. You can ask students to check and recheck hypotheses as they encounter new cases and examples.

Within the cultural themes, data may be arranged with or without reference to chronology and with or without reference to place. In other words, the theme is predominant over other organizing ideas and controls viewing examples. The ancient Greek *Odyssey* and *Iliad* give views of a society that raises questions about the Vikings as an analog. Both societies share characteristics: these people were seafarers, warriors, polytheists, poets, and storytellers. A cross-cultural view of Viking and ancient Greek societies would provide students with more insights into how cultures develop than would the study of their respective differences, despite the fact that the societies are separated by 1,500 years. Thus, a thematic organization involves comparison of societies. The big question is whether a comparison works in producing useful, productive and valid generalizations about two or more cultures. Although the thematic arrangement is infrequently used for an entire course, you can incorporate it by introducing examples representing the same category for comparison and contrast. These categories can range from the very broad political and social systems, to more specific ideas, leadership, class and caste, or family.

This approach also allows you to include art, music, and literature in the social sciences applied to standard historical periods and themes

Belief and Value Patterns

A comparative-thematic structure encourages imaginative leaps in thinking and the generation and testing of hypotheses about large categories of important events in human history. The discovery of parallel cases and/or dramatic contrasts makes this approach exciting and interesting for students. Your students should develop a strong sense of why and how human behavior *shapes and is shaped* by political, social, cultural, economic, emotional, and aesthetic needs. Students are often excited about testing a theory or hypothesis such as why free enterprise systems develop in one set of circumstances while a different set of circumstances produces state-controlled economies. The major problem with this approach is that, although students develop a good sense of past and present-day events and problems, their knowledge is based more on conceptual understanding of human behavior than on either geographic influences or temporal sequences.

More and more global historians are working on comparisons between structures and states, past and present, to test theories about how people respond to changing times and places, for example research a sample:

Manning, P. (2003) *Navigating World History: Historians Create a Global Past* (New York & London: Palgrave MacMillan).

McNeill, J. R. (2000) *Something New under the Sun: An Environmental History of the 20th Century World* (Aldershot, UK: W. W. Norton).

McNeill, J. R. and McNeill, R. H. (2003) *The Human Web: A Bird's Eye View of World History* (New York: W. W. Norton).

Stearns, P. (2014) *The History of Peace* (New York: Routledge).

An Integrative World (Holistic) or Global History Approach

A stimulating and engaging world history program should try to cover the earth's history by giving us a worldview to apply to worthwhile case studies. Since we cannot know everything and have the wonderful Internet to borrow from, why push students or ourselves to memorize so called facts, collect vast databanks, and such.

Rather we can store documents and data in the cloud and draw upon resources as needed. What we need most as teachers is a structurer, a plan, an overview of global history that we can draw upon to guide our discussions and promote historical habits of mind going way back into evolution and forward into the 22nd century.

We need to admit we are part of a big interconnected family of peoples, and always have been. We should draw examples from every continent and region for our history course, not just a Eurocentric, cultural, or U.S. point of view. We can cut across time and space for examples of human behavior in history that are ripe for comparison and contrast. Ripe for making our own generalizations about causes, conduct, and consequences.

There are several global frameworks that we can use to organize our courses through themes rather than chronology or territory,

An integrative approach connects the Earth's development in time and space, specifically focusing on examples and case studies that demonstrate the spread, migration, fusion, fission, and amalgamation of cultures and events. A single theme such as cultural diffusion, ecological disaster, political interaction, or economic exchange may dominate the curriculum, with examples drawn that demonstrate *how we got here* and where ideas originated.

For example, where did the idea of a dozen come from versus counting in tens? How did people obtain water for drinking and farming now and in ancient times? Do we have a local, national, or international diet and when did it develop? You will often be surprised by the answers. Most students have no idea where a potato or an orange were probably first grown and raised, nor how early farmers learned to manipulate and tame wild species of plants and animals.

Clearly, the integrated or holistic course grows out of a cross-cultural global conception, but is more challenging to prepare, teach, and conceptualize, but it is the most potentially useful in understanding the world as a unified interrelated whole. It pulls together theories, events, personalities, and people in ways that students or teachers have not examined before.

Suggestion for a Global Perspective Course

An innovative approach embeds a theme with a beginning, middle, and end illustrated by 'exhibits' across time and space drawing from all portions of our world. We must admit from the get go that we are selecting themes, exhibits, and periods of time to illustrate world history, not trying to teach all of it at once. An overview really helps and guides us but is rather abstract in concept and needs cases, documents, and Internet resources to bring to life.

I.   Beginnings: Hominids to Humans
      Food, Shelter, and Clothing
      Travel and Transport
      Tools and Technology
      Culture and Expression

II.   The Agricultural Revolution
      Settlement
      Farming
      Domestication of Animals
      Herding
      Organization

III. The State Revolution
      Beginnings of Cities and States
      Worship and Identities
      Laws and Values
      Changing the Face of the Earth
      Status and Service

IV.   Empires and Heartlands
      Cultural Identity
      Political Identity
      Stylistic Identity
      Class And Caste
      World Religions

V.   Heartland Expansions and Collapses
      West Asia and Africa
      Fertile Crescent
      The Mediterranean World
      East Asia and South Asia
      Europe and the North
      The Americas and Pacific

VI.   Feudalisms, Renaissances, and Reformations
      Case Studies: France and England, West Africa and Persia, China and India

VII. Travel and Contact
      Worldwide Explorations
      Culture Contacts and Conquests
      Religious Movements and Connections
      Commerce and Industry

VIII. Industrialization and Trade Networks
      Case Studies: England, China, Spain, the Americas, South Africa
      Racism, Gender, and Social Change

IX. Global Economic and Political Movements
     Revolutions and Ideologies
     Capitalism, Socialism, and Communism
     Republics, Dictatorships, and Monarchies
     Diffusion and Exchange of Cultures

X. Globalization and Technological Innovation
     One World Economy, Many Nations
     Heartlands, Empires, and Client States
     Hegemony and Dominance, Big Players and Small
     Cultural Integration and Exchange, Identity and Bias
     Climate Change and the Challenges of Planetary Survival

There are risks employing big ideas. Some comparisons or linkages may produce exciting and mind-blowing insights, whereas others may present many fascinating avenues for investigation for students. Nonetheless, even if Western history is the focus, an integrated approach can offer new insights simply by juxtaposing cases and examples that have influenced the West, or vice versa. As an example, the rise of Islamic culture during the so-called European Middle Ages raises interesting questions about comparative lifestyles as students uncover a diffusion of ideas in science, technology (inventions), the arts, and philosophy that moved from East to West, rather than the other way around.

The contribution of Muslim societies to European culture is, of course, nothing new, but it is rarely emphasized when the course is taught from a narrow Western perspective. As students broaden their perspectives on the world, they find new ideas and connections for study and discussion, and both students and teacher may conclude that interaction in previous eras was undoubtedly greater than commonly assumed. Networks of trade, aid, and borrowing offer a framework for modern development, even when groups and societies were (are) in a state of conflict and expressed hostility toward one another.

Over the several decades, there has been a growing interest in what is sometimes called *global education* or *world studies* and, less frequently, *international education*. In some cases, definitions overlap or supersede international and peace education, but all share a common and strong concern for 'globalizing' American education, placing America and its history in a world context emphasizing how our society is closely linked to the rest of the world politically, economically, and culturally. Some historians argue that the West, including the United States, has *always* been tied to the rest of the world, but that many have chosen to ignore this fact at certain periods of history for a variety of political reasons. Fernand Braudel, a fine French historian, notes that "the modes of production are all attached to each other. The most advanced are dependent on the most backward and vice versa," and he is writing about the 15th to the 18th centuries![14]

This global view of the past, extended into the present, needs to be transferred into day-to-day educational goals and ideas. In a seminal essay on educating citizens for a global viewpoint, Robert Hanvey pointed out five key interdisciplinary dimensions that need to be developed:

Perspective consciousness: an awareness and appreciation for other people's views of the world and its problems.
State of the planet awareness: a deeper understanding of worldwide issues and current events.

Cross-cultural awareness: greater familiarity with the key features of other cultures, especially literature and art, and the similarities and differences between these ideas and
images and our own.

Systemic awareness: the ability to see 'the world' as a system linking all peoples and nations
in patterns of dependence and interdependence.

Options for participation: plans for ways in which individuals, like us, can take part in local,
national, or international issues that we believe affect us for better or worse.[15]

Few will deny that the world is drawing closer together than it has ever been before, and
economic survival and prosperity are more and more the product of trade and aid for both
the United States and much of the rest of the world. Familiar arguments for a 'one-world'
economy and political system are well known, with proof available simply by a visit to
your local supermarket or department store. However, there are also many problems for
education because cultures, including our own, tend to be local in their thinking and concentrate on local affairs, preferring *not* to worry about others until danger is signaled. This
kind of ethnocentric viewpoint seems increasingly out of place because the United States is
perhaps the world power and is involved in the business and politics of almost every nation
on Earth. A second reason we can no longer remain at home alone in our thinking is that
the world has come to our doorstep, producing cities and towns of great diversity in terms
of cultures and populations, customs, and languages. The people of the world are on the
move! Immigration is bringing peoples together in other countries with attendant issues
of assimilation and prejudice, nationality and identity.

Finally, a third reason for supporting globalism is that Americans and American culture
are on the move, traveling to distant lands for business, tourism, and education influencing cultures through products such as autos, foods, name brands, popular music, art, and
literature across the world. Where in the world can Americans travel without meeting
up with McDonald's, popular music, or Hollywood films? Americans have also imported
many ideas and products from influential cultures around the globe!

Thus, the arguments for globalism are strong, leading to the conclusion that schools
must work harder to promote a comprehensive and refined view of other places and people
from their own viewpoints as well as 'ours.' The key to a sensible and meaningful course
of study lies in two decisions:

Which theme(s) will provide a central focus with which to integrate the vast quantity
of material to be discussed?

What balance of cases or events will be selected so insiders and outsiders, friends and
enemies, achieve equal time?

Programs often flounder because they attempt the impossible—a too-brief coverage
of *all* eras and cultures. The usual result is that students memorize disparate facts, strange
names, and peculiar, unrelated events from around the world (i.e., terminology without
understanding). Without central themes, a global approach will not make sense to students, who will drown in a sea of details and trivia, even worse by poorly guided research
on vast history and social science websites. By focusing on selected time periods and a few
themes, especially those that invite comparisons and detective work, you can build depth
and a comparative framework that may be expanded to other cultures and times, giving
yourself time to actually link past to present, to what is currently hot news!

Whatever overall concept is chosen as the focus, serious questions will still arise about
slighting certain cultures in favor of others, distorting one region's history from the point

of view of another, and separating reliable from unreliable evidence and sources. These are always good questions to ask when reviewing or designing world/global history programs because historical habits of mind are promoted and practiced. (Seixas, P. (2015) *A Model of Historical Thinking* (Taylor & Francis) 593–605, www.tandfonline.com.)

CLASSIC RESEARCH REPORT

Using interviews, case studies, and observational data, researchers sampled a number of teachers and students in the San Francisco, Oakland, and Berkeley areas of California concerning their knowledge of international economics and peace/conflict issues. The "Study of Stanford and the Schools," from the mid-1980s, demonstrated that students who were more knowledgeable, felt most free to express opinions that contradicted those of the instructor, whereas those who felt least free to voice their opinions also demonstrated the lowest scores on international economics and peace/conflict items. The findings clearly imply that students who engage the material are better able to both understand and retain it. Those who only regurgitate 'facts' are left with little in the way of knowledge or insight.

Source: Torney-Purtiz, J. and Landsdale, D. (1986) *Classroom Climate and Process in International Studies: Qualitative and Quantitative Data From the American Schools and the World Project,* paper delivered to the American Educational Research Association, San Francisco, CA. Assesses the results of data gathered by Stanford researchers.

Conceptual themes are plentiful. Contact among and between societies or the diffusion of ideas and inventions serves as your guide to choosing periods and cultures. You might select only those times and places that illustrate the effects of contact, positive or negative, and might achieve balance using a case study from two cultural regions: Africa, Asia, the Middle East, Europe, and the Americas. For those with a more scientific bent, why not study diseases and medical treatments around the world? The rise and fall of empires demonstrate political growth and variety, surges and declines in international contacts, as well as the problem of accommodating both freedom and stability.

There are numerous plans for integrated, holistic approaches subject to revision based on research and experience in teaching from a 'world view' that deepens and broadens understanding. Although some fear lack of structure, world historians and many social scientists invite trial and innovation in teaching the world.

SAMPLE LESSON PLANS

Integrating histories is not as easy as it looks: What would the European Middle Ages or feudal period correspond to in China or the Middle East? Was there a frontier in African history, or Russian history, as there was in North America? What would world history look like through the eyes of a Chinese emperor? Can valid comparisons be made among European, Indian, and Native American myths and epics: all epics and myths? What perspectives from the arts and sciences as well as history in bringing disparate histories and cultures together?

Figure 7.2:   Shah (King) Nasser al Din Qajar of Iran, 1831–1896.

Photo in the public domain/Wikipedia commons.

Prepare an outline integrating two or more cultures on the basis of the following:

a. great personalities
b. broad social movements
c. diffusion of ideas
d. diseases and medical innovations
e. technological inventions
f. trade and commerce
g. population changes and pressures.

Develop a lesson around an unfamiliar character's image (e.g., Figure 7.2). What questions might you ask of him: his age, rank, status, origin, time in history, Western or Eastern, or some of both? What does his image project to you: warmth, sincerity, importance, military, ordinary? Why?

KEY QUESTIONS FOR TEACHING WORLD STUDIES

The complexities and the variety of World studies programs make them among the most interesting and worthwhile social studies programs offered. Conflicting views of how to teach these courses, what should be included or excluded, raise a number of key questions and present common themes over vast periods of time, e.g., race, nation, gender, technological change, and ecological exploitation.

SAMPLE LESSON PLAN

How can we teach from different perspectives on the same theme? Consider the warrior knight images presented in Figure 7.3 and compare and contrast the figures. Are all dressed the same or differently? Is each dressed for the same or a different purpose and how can you tell? Are they ready for battle or is the dress probably ceremonial? Who are they in each society: what is their role? Do all fit a theme in history and if so, which is it? Can there be more than one theme expressed by the images? How could you use these images to help students develop multiple visual and historical intelligences?

For extra credit: can you guess which of the suits of armor and images are authentic from the time or have been dramatized, and which are secondary, taken from the original? Is source important in this case: why or why not?

The following list presents a possible thematic organizing framework for global studies.

Interdependence: How and why events and peoples are linked with each other and their environments.

Development: How and why cultures and societies have forged ahead or have fallen back economically and technologically.

Change: How and why different social, economic, and political systems have evolved. How have humans affected the areas they have settled?

Conflict and cooperation: How and why people have often shown hostility toward each other and worked together in peace at other times.

Cultural diffusion: How cultural artifacts—ideas, religious systems, artistic styles, and technology—have spread and changed over time and place.

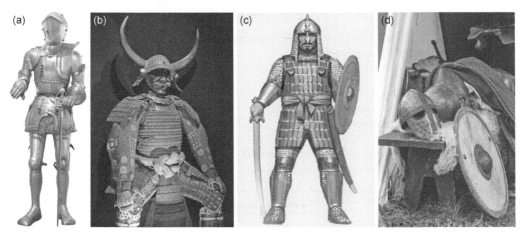

Figure 7.3: Four Knights of Different Origins (a): Knight A: Guess where? Guess when? Guess why? Would you like to be in this suit? Photographer: Herraez. (b) Knight B: Guess where? Guess when? Guess why? Is this suit better or is just the hat? Source: Photographer: Alexey Baskakov. (c) Knight C: Guess where? Guess when? Guess why? Better helmet or do you like the shield? Saracen Warrior. Photographer: Dorling Kindersley. (d) Mystery Knight Trio with great helmets! Photographer: Michal Matlon on Unsplash.

Figure 7.4:   Medieval Knightly armor from 13th Century, Europe.

Diversity and universality: How and why individuals, groups, and people have created distinct life styles and societies to solve problems of security, well-being, making a living, organization, and creativity, as well as the points of communality among societies.

The Bradley Commission on History in Schools has suggested a similar list of themes that its members consider basic to all history:

1. civilization
2. human interaction with the environment
3. values, beliefs, political ideas, and institutions
4. conflict and cooperation
5. comparative history
6. patterns of social and political interaction.[16]

LET'S DECIDE

With at least two colleagues or classmates, develop themes (e.g., political ideas or patterns of social and political interaction) suggested by using films, old and new, with a common cross-cultural and literary theme. These might include titles such as: *The Last Emperor* (1987), the story of Pu Yi, last Manchu royal ruler; *Metropolis* (1926), workers versus managers in a futuristic city; *Shogun* (1980 TV series), British sailor meets

Samurai warriors; *Reds*, John Reed witnesses the Russian Revolution (1981); *Cabaret* (1973), an American woman meets decadence and oppression in pre-WWII Germany; *Amistad* (1997), revolt on a slave ship headed for the Americas; *Gandhi* (1982), the epic struggle for freedom and independence in India; or the 12-part *Untold History of the United States (2012–2013)*, by Oliver Stone that sweeps across U.S. history with trenchant criticisms and astounding footage from Soviet and American footage of WWII.

TO DO

Each culture has had its own view of the world, often differing dramatically from those of other cultures frequently placing that society at the center. It seems that most people have great difficulty imagining the world from any but their own point of view. Likewise, social studies teachers often have trouble imagining world history from any but a Western point of view. To correct this, you are invited to take up action in researching two areas that could use improved attention.

Collect at least a half dozen maps of the world from different nations across all continents, for example, China, Japan, Nigeria, Brazil, Israel, Australia, Iran, and Poland. Is their depiction of the earth realistic? Is each country at the physical center? Do any of the maps view the world from a Chinese or Indian perspective? Discuss why maps and worldviews may differ. Raise questions about the widespread use of the Mercator projection in English-speaking nations. Are there any objections to the Mercator projection? Are there alternatives? Are there any geographic projections entirely fair and unbiased to all sections of the globe? Why or why not?

Select a commonly taught topic such as one of the following:

a. Ancient Greece
b. Imperial Rome
c. The Renaissance in Italy
d. The Columbian exchange
e. The American Revolution
f. World Wars

Search out at least one competing view of time, a Persian perspective on Greece or a Muslim description of Renaissance Italy, a French view of the American Revolution, a Russian view of the Cold War, an Indian foreign policy view of China, an Ethiopian view of its neighbors, etc. Treat events from more than one standpoint, that is, fit and refit the topic you've chosen into a chronological, cross-cultural, thematic, and international relations framework. Do the key questions you might ask change? Is the same set of ideas suggested by each framework, or do interpretations and concepts change? What are the advantages and disadvantages of each of the different approaches for world and global studies?

Share your conclusions with others. Decide which framework may work best for students. Discuss and list the didactic, reflective, and affective questions that are most important for the topic you selected, regardless of the perspective or framework.

SUMMARY

World studies/global history is perhaps the most important, complex, and demanding course to design, prepare, and teach.

You can develop didactic, reflective, and affective goals that engage students in acquiring knowledge, building understanding, and raising ethical questions about the world events. A well-balanced program should ask students to struggle with the dilemmas of human history: (a) self-centeredness, (economic exploitation of each other and the environment, and (c) ethnocentric aggrandizement and a sense of being better than other peoples. World studies/global history courses have usually been Eurocentric, viewing history only in terms of significance to American or Western European development. Traditional topics range from ancient Greece and Rome to the Medieval and Renaissance periods and on to the French Revolution, World Wars I & II, and the Cold War. In response to a growing demand for the study of non-Western cultures, there are many alternatives to the largely chronological Western course structure.

Global/world studies programs attempt to present information about major areas and cultures, focusing on primary sources from other peoples' views. Among alternative approaches are those that unite and compare cultures through themes, over time, and by place or both. These include emphasizing area/regional studies, cross-cultural comparative studies, international relations, or some combination of these into a fully integrated/holistic global structure that does not privilege any particular time or place, but treats all fairly. **All share a commitment to key concepts of interdependence, contact, exchange, economic development, social change, diffusion, perspective, and universality.**

Global Understanding Quiz

What was the first wave of globalization: the second, the third, etc.?

1. What does 'human' mean to you?
2. When was the first state born and why?
3. Where do our favorite foods come from?
4. What may be the top ten 'turning points' in world history?
5. Why is a hero often like a villain, and a villain often like a hero?
6. Why is one person's hero another person's villain?
7. Where are the women and children in teaching global understanding?
8. What makes someone care about others, the world, issues, Greta Thunberg, etc.?
9. How should we think about the globe, as representing the one, few or many?
10. Is there a most powerful underlying motive for human learning?

Extra Credit
11. Draw a picture of global interconnections as a 'mind map' from memory alone: What are the most important places, peoples, and events? Why?
12. Why are humans in arguments, fights, wars, conflict, etc.? Where's cooperation?
13. If you are giving a big dinner, for 10–12, who would you be willing to invite from history? And why?
14. Where are we going in history? How does the past connect to the present and does it offer any advice for future decision-making? What about **climate change**?

NOTES

1 Gaudelli, W. (2003) *World Class: Teaching and Learning in Global Times* (Mahwah, NJ: Routledge).

2 Kreluik, K., Mishra, P., Fahnoe, C. and Terry, L. (2013) "What Knowledge Is of Most Worth: Teacher Knowledge for the 21st Century", *Journal of Digital Learning in Teaching*, 29, 4 ISTE, www.files.eric.ed.gov.

3 Zevin, J. and Gerwin, D. (2010) *Teaching World History as Mystery* (New York: Routledge).

4 Woyach, R. B. and Remy, R. C. (1987) *Approaches to World Studies* (Needham Heights, MA).

5 Allardyce, G. (June 1982) "The Rise and Fall of the Western Civilization Course," *American Historical Review*, 87, 3, 695–743.

6 Samir, A. (2009) *Eurocentrism* (New York: Monthly Review Press).

7 Remy, R. C. and Woyach, R. B. (1984) *Strengthening High School World Studies Courses: Conference Report* (Columbus, OH: Ohio State University).

8 Bradley Commission on History in Schools (1988) *Building a History Curriculum: Guidelines for Teaching History in Schools* (Washington, DC: National Council for History Education).

9 Wallerstein, I, (2004) *World Systems Analysis: An Introduction* (Durham, NC: Duke University Press); Wallerstein's World Systems Analysis (2013) on YouTube.

10 Wiggers, C. (2021) *Trail Guide to World Geography,* www.GeoMatters.com.

11 Remy, R. C. et al. (1975). *International Learning and International Education in a Global Age*, Bulletin 47 (National Council for the Social Studies).

12 Choices for the 21st Century Education Program (2019) *The US Role in a Changing World* (Providence, RI: Brown University).

13 Curtin, P. D. (1984) *Cross-Cultural Trade in World History* (Cambridge: UK: Cambridge University Press). An excellent study of trade in global perspective that is an example of the thematic approach.

14 Braudel, F. (1984, 1992) *The Perspective of the World: Civilization and Capitalism, 15th–18th Century,* Vol. 3 (New York: University of California Press), 70–71.

15 Hanvey, R. (1978) *An Attainable Global Perspective* (Denver, CO: Social Science Education Consortium).

16 Bradley Commission (1998) *Building a History Curriculum*, 10–11.

FOR FURTHER STUDY: TEACHING WORLD STUDIES

Anderson, L. (1979) *Schooling for Citizenship in a Global Age: An Exploration of the Meaning and Significance of Global Education* (Bloomington, IN: Social Studies Development Center).

Barber, B. R. (March, 1992) "Jihad vs McWorld," *The Atlantic Monthly*, 53–55, 58–63.

Braudel, F. (1979, 1981, 1984) *Civilization and Capitalism, 15th–18th Century, The Structures of Everyday Life*, Vol.1, *The Wheels of Commerce*, Vol. 2, *The Perspective of the World*, Vol 3. (New York: Harper & Row).

Choices for the 21st Century Education Programs (2021) Thomas J. Watson Jr. Institute for International Studies, Brown University. Current and historical issues that present a variety of viewpoints. The Institute for International Studies at Brown University. (www.choices.edu).

Contreras, G. (ed.) (1987) *Latin American Culture Studies: Information and Materials for Teaching About Latin America.* (Austin, TX: University of Texas\Institute of Latin American Studies).

Evans, R. (2000) *In Defense of History* (New York: Teachers College Press).

Facts on File Regional History Series (2004–2021) (New York, NY) www.factsonfile.org.

Hanvey, B. (1978) *An Attainable Global Perspective* (New York: Center for Global Perspectives).

Harari, Y. (2014) *Sapiens: A Brief History of Humankind* (New York: Random House).

Harari, Y. (2018) *21 Lessons for the 2st Century* (London: Jonathan Cape).

Kobrin, D. (1996) *Beyond the Textbook: Teaching History Using Documents and Primary Sources* (Portsmouth, NH: Heinemann).

Lindaman, D. and Ward, K. (2004) *History Lessons: How Textbooks from Around the World Portray U.S. History* (New York: Corwin Press).

Merryfield, M. et. al. (January 2008) "World Mindedness: Taking off the Blinders," *Journal of Curriculum and Instruction*, 2, 1.

Metro, R. (2020) *Teaching World History Thematically* (New York: Teacher's College Press).

Organization of American Historians (1990) *Restoring Women to History: Teaching Packets for Integrating Women's History Into Courses on Africa, Asia, Latin America and the Caribbean, and the Middle East* (Bloomington, IN: Organization of American Historians).

Parrish, B. (2020) *Placing Learners at the Centre of Teaching.* (Cambridge University Press) www.cambridge .org.

Wallerstein, I. (1984, 1992) *The Modern World System* (Durham, NC: Duke University Academic Press).

Teaching World/Global Studies

BUILD YOUR OWN LESSON

The challenge: thinking 'on your feet.'

Interact with a new piece of evidence, data, issue, or problem.

Design a lesson of your own using different materials (newly discovered art, music, literature, history, geography, etc.).

Worry not about what you know, but react by thinking about how you would teach the data. Improvise!

Write a didactic, reflective, and affective goal for each document or picture, then add a low, medium, and high order question.

Choose one of the six strategies.

Pick a brief method of evaluating success (verbal, written, and tested).

What questions do the data support? Where do they fit in history?

What is the source and context: time and place? And how does that matter?

Did you find improvisation for the classroom easy or difficult? Why?

What is happening here? Where are we? When are we? Would this fit a good comprehension strategy? What languages appear? What month is it? Which cultures are represented?

DOI: 10.4324/9781003026235-18

Figure 7.5: Print by Guaman de Poma de Ayala (circa 1535–1616?) from Peru's Nueva coronica y buen gobierno (1600–1615). Inca Manco is in a litter with his soldiers.

Wikimedia Commons: free within the United States: public domain.

8

TEACHING U.S. GOVERNMENT AND CIVICS

"…don't ever underestimate the importance you can have because history has shown us that courage can be contagious and hope can take on a life of its own."

Michelle Obama

OVERVIEW

This chapter will examine civics as citizenship, as protest and reform, and as a set of political institutions.

INTRODUCTION

Civics, so called is all about socializing youth into the rules and practice of democratic rule. Yet the curriculum and classroom frequently teach ideals without recognizing the problems we face as citizens in actual practice.

Considering that the National Council for the Social Studies promotes citizenship education as a principal rationale for social studies, the actual state of civics in schools is probably the weakest member of the big history/government trio. And despite public statements of support from government leaders, most financing seems to be pouring into reading and math rather than programs bolstering democratic ideals.

Where there were once many kinds of civics courses, at several grade levels, there is now pretty much a single semester or maybe year, usually in the senior year of high school, rather late in time to implement and influence civic voting habits, particularly if it is merely informative rather than critical. A recent survey by CIRCLE, a civic education foundation, found only about a quarter of civics student reported remembering that they had worked on a community project.[1] Most never saw any action at all.

The results are that new voters who emerge often have the worst voting record of any segment of the population, demonstrating long-term declines in engagement only recently turned around for the 2020 election for President of the U.S.[2]

DOI: 10.4324/9781003026235-19

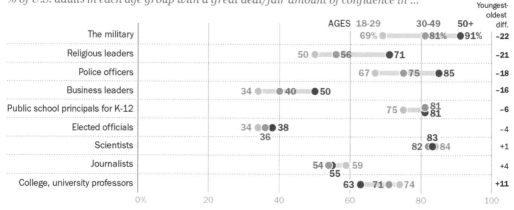

Young adults are less confident in the military, religious, police, business leaders

% of U.S. adults in each age group with a great deal/fair amount of confidence in ...

Note: Statistically significant differences shown in bold.
Source: Survey conducted Nov. 27-Dec. 10, 2018.
"Trust and Distrust in America"

PEW RESEARCH CENTER

Figure 8.1: Pew Research on young adult confidence. Youth opinions can vary widely for role models and career paths.

There are many reasons for the weakness of civics, a course many students report disliking, along with other social studies courses as 'dull and boring.' They also report less trust and confidence in political institutions and leaders.[3] Note that business leaders, elected officials, and journalists receive the lowest rankings.[4]

Civics is an inherently contradictory subject in schools because of its built-in conflicts. Goals are often stated in patriotic tones, with the implication that this is an agenda to be accepted, not discussed and criticized.[5] Aiming at polite discussion and sharing views often becomes contentious and even hostile.

Then there is the problem of aiming at civic ideals, or civic realities, patriotism or criticism. Teaching both side by side is seldom done well, and teachers report high levels of discomfort helping students criticize their own political culture. In a sense, civics is a servant of the state, helping socialize and popularize democratic rule in American and other cultures. And this has a positive side instilling pride and knowledge of the system and how it works. But, if positive is the only view of civics then this is a closed structure without much political science or real-world events to it. Science is about finding truth through observation, experimentation, and examination. Examination of political practices may conflict directly with stated ideals.

Many teachers do not want the pain from critical review and argumentative discussion.

School climate studies indicate that the 'atmosphere' of a school really matters in areas like discipline, learning growth, and democratic practice. In a relatively open atmosphere, school governance, cooperation, discipline, and learning curves all move up and ahead in tandem. By contrast, in relatively closed or authoritarian schools, the 'atmosphere' may produce discipline but foster cynicism, and a sense of discouragement that carries over into adult democratic participation. Engagement by students tends to increase in creative schools where participation in class, in government, in simulations, and in the outside world becomes lived experience that matters.

Students' sense when they are free to choose, free to speak their minds, and when they are repressed and constrained, and they know quite well what taboo subjects include and exclude. Exclusions close off even polite conservation on contrasting or conflicting points. So, as exclusions grow, conversation diminishes in classrooms. Rose tinted history creates a discontinuity, a clash, between stated ideals of democracy and. The real world that often leaves secondary school students bored and disinterested. They've heard versions of this before, and if they want anything, it would be real world political arguments about the here and now political system. Here and now is quite engaging, full of conflict and drama, value clashes, arguments and put-downs, emotions and defeats, much like a good soap opera.

The second model is one that focuses on controversy and issues. Thus, we have a choice between a civics course driven by controversies, where almost everything is on the table and open to multiple viewpoints, and one driven by knowledge and ideals driven by data collection, knowledge of the labels, and workings of the political system. A steady diet of institutions and ideals produces ennui and boredom, while a diet of controversy produces sparks and disagreements but is a lot more exciting. Accepted answers are safe to teach, while debates and clashing viewpoints are much harder to handle and may get you into hot water.

So, in this current climate for civics, we have the new C3 standards and goals to drive us forward (with a few reservations), but we still need a method of inquiry to engage students. Therefore, we need models to follow in terms of content and methods to employ to engage interest and participation. Not an easy mix, but we will try to work it out.

First, let's define quality civics instruction as factual knowledge that provides background and engages students with issues showing casing competing, conflicting, and overlapping perspectives on just about any subject in politics you would like to teach.

What citizenship means is a huge and difficult question for the social studies, and what a teacher should or can teach in civics is often problematic. There seem to be two competing models, one aimed at teaching about government as a perfect invention, usually a standard list of topics known well throughout the United States. How a bill becomes a law, the three branches of government, The Bill of Rights and Constitution, The Supreme Court, The Office of President, and so forth form the spine for the civics program. Usually descriptive, and detailed, but devoid of anything but endorsement, a legalistic formal approach tends to bore students. With proper preparation, however, it is possible to provide both data and ideals in an atmosphere of questioning and discussion where nearly all can participate and offer different views bolstered by reason and evidence. Getting to Yes, well, maybe, but at least to center, agree to disagree, and honor hard evidence.

SETTING GOALS

Secondary school social studies programs usually include a required course or two on government, civics, and/or some version of participation in democracy. Unlike U.S. history courses, government courses have greater latitude to vary in design, content, and conception, but rarely take advantage of the privilege. Courses usually reflect one of two major approaches: a traditional study of structure and function in U. S. government, or a focus on political issues and problems, and controversial topics.[6]

Most textbooks and supporting materials reflect the more traditional civics approach emphasizing patriotism and government structure than hot issues, but many teachers mix modes, switching from *government* to *problems* within the same program. Research indicates that teachers tend to avoid controversies and so-called taboo topics because they cause arguments and disagreements to develop. (Hess, 2017, www.kappanonline.org).

Regardless of approach, actual decision-making by student government or applying democratic principles to school life is largely ignored, although this has changed somewhat for the better.[7] These more recent approaches include a comprehensive and all-inclusive set of standards for civics, including, goals, and content guidelines for Grades 4, 8, and 12.[8] Although not mandated by government (oddly enough), the C3 Framework for college, career and civic standards for states offer a definition and goals and assessments for government courses by any name.

Therefore, we will set a variety of goals from didactic to reflective through affective to offer a full range of skills, abilities, and intelligences in our civics course design.

Civics Defined by NCSS C3 Standards

> Because government is a means for addressing common or public problems, the political system established by the U.S. Constitution is an important subject of study within civics. Civics requires other knowledge, too; students should also learn about state and local governments; markets; courts and legal systems; civil society; other nations' systems and practices; international institutions; and the techniques available to citizens for preserving and changing a society. Civics is not limited to the study of politics and society; it also encompasses participation in classrooms and schools, neighborhoods, groups, and organizations. **Not all participation is beneficial. This framework makes frequent reference to civic virtues and principles that guide participation and to the norm of deliberation (which means discussing issues and making choices and judgments with information and evidence, civility and respect, and concern for fair procedures).**
>
> What defines civic virtue, which democratic principles apply in given situations, and when discussions are deliberative are not easy questions, but they are topics for inquiry and reflection. In civics, students learn to contribute appropriately to public processes and discussions of real issues. Their contributions to public discussions may take many forms, ranging from personal testimony to abstract arguments. They will also learn civic practices such as voting, volunteering, jury service, and joining with others to improve society.
>
> Civics enables students not only to study how others participate, but also to practice participating and taking informed action themselves.

Note that the National Council's C3 definition while comprehensive is rather timid about the benefits of 'all participation,' though this is not clearly spelled out. The arc of inquiry is followed but with amendments and limitations that call for making choices with facility and respect, and concern for fairness. That's fine but indicates a certain nervousness with controversial issues, closely related to teachers' worrying about taboo topics of race, gender, religion, and of course, politics. Why not be willing to engage students in a good hearty 'knockdown, drag out' argument about a topic? Why not promote multilogues, though these will seem rather disorganized and multidirectional?

Lack of confidence in controlling an argument and reaching a good conclusion or a conclusive stalemate seems to befuddle both elite and front line teachers, but there are methods available for handling both civilized and uncivilized discussion (with limits) that can be most productive in providing a real sense of democratic participation in and out of classrooms. These methods depend on careful lesson design using stimulating materials, clearly sequenced questions, lower to higher order, and teacher's role as guide, adjudicator and devil's advocate simultaneously.

Major Topics

The C3 Framework outlines general and specific goals for instruction, more specific about coverage and 'learning civic virtues' including democratic principles, civic institutions, and processes, rules and laws.

Participation and Deliberation: Applying Civic Virtues and Democratic Principles

Civics teaches democratic principles—such as adherence to the social contract, consent of the governed, limited government, legitimate authority, federalism, and separation of powers—that are meant to guide official institutions such as legislatures, courts, and government agencies. It also teaches the virtues—such as honesty, mutual respect, cooperation, and attentiveness to multiple perspectives—that citizens should use when they interact with each other on public matters. Principles such as equality, freedom, liberty, respect for individual rights, and deliberation apply to both official institutions and informal interactions among citizens. Learning these virtues and principles requires obtaining factual knowledge of written provisions found in important texts such as the founding documents of the United States. It also means coming to understand the diverse arguments that have been made about these documents and their meanings. Finally, students understand virtues and principles by applying and reflecting on them through actual civic engagement—their own and that of other people from the past and present.

Civic and Political Institutions

In order to act responsibly and effectively, citizens must understand the important institutions of their society and the principles that these institutions are intended to reflect. That requires mastery of a body of knowledge about law, politics, and government.

Processes, Rules, and Laws

Civics is the discipline of the social studies most directly concerned with the processes and rules by which groups of people make decisions, govern themselves, and address public problems. People address problems at all scales, from a classroom to the agreements among nations. Public policies are among the tools that governments use to address public problems. Students must learn how various rules, processes, laws, and policies actually work, which requires factual understanding of political systems: the focus of this section. NCSS C3 Framework, Civics, 31–34.

C3 Sample objectives by end of Grade 8 and Grade 12 for civic education include:

> D2.Civ.1.6-8. Distinguish the powers and responsibilities of citizens, political parties, interest groups, and the media in a variety of governmental and nongovernmental contexts.

> D2.Civ.1.9-12. Distinguish the powers and responsibilities of local, state, tribal, national, and international civic and political institutions.

> D2.Civ.2.9-12. Analyze the role of citizens in the U.S. political system, with attention to various theories of democracy, changes in Americans' participation over time, and alternative models from other countries, past and present.

> D2.Civ.3.6-8. Examine the origins, purposes, and impact of constitutions, laws, treaties, and international agreements.

> D2.Civ.4.9-12. Explain how the U.S. Constitution establishes a system of government that has powers, responsibilities, and limits that have changed over time and that are still contested.

> D2.Civ.5.6-8. Explain the origins, functions, and structure of government with reference to the U.S. Constitution, state constitutions, and selected other systems of government.

> D2.Civ.6.9-12. Critique relationships among governments, civil societies, and economic markets.

Keep in mind that civics courses are justified as a training ground for students who will function in a democracy, and we should encourage participation by modeling elections and voting *as a minimum* for good citizenship training. Action is a high priority in the C3 Standards but this must be carried out with 'information and evidence, civility and respect.' This is a tall order for classrooms where respect and civility have always been honored more so than in our political life where conflict and hardball seem to be the order of the day.

Nevertheless, civility and respect, while laudable goals, also imply that teachers must keep discussions polite and bloodless, rather than passionate and honest. Thus, there is a contradiction of control underlying the need for building better citizens who must be circumspect in fomenting arguments about issues.[9] Most programs stress a commitment to American political values. Although this does not necessarily restrict student thinking, there is a real danger of espousing a particular partisan point of view.

For example, the concept of national defense may be generally acceptable, but should be open to debate in justifying any specific actions taken by our country, such as military involvement in Afghanistan and Iraq. There should be room in every government course for criticism of policy decisions and examination of 'my country right or wrong.' More than ever, serious debate about the real political world at home and abroad is needed.

In fact, you might even argue that it is of critical importance given the closeness of many recent elections. Ironically, many civics and government courses constrain student time and freedom to debate controversies and participate in community politics. We should bear in mind that coverage of history and government, especially if it is positive and self-congratulatory and/or mechanical (how to register to vote), will not predispose students to become active and involved citizens.[10] As we examine goals for a Government or Civics course, we must bear in mind that controversy and (civilized) argument in a good program are part and parcel of motivating students to participate in and out of class.

TO DO

The Ancient Athenians enjoyed a good argument and would go at it in style, so why can't we, or do we also seek to put Socrates to death for outspokenness? Review the case of Socrates in the context of ancient Greece and in the current U.S. context. How would your class react to Socrates if he came as a guest speaker, and what might he say about the current political situation? Would Socrates be popular today in your neighborhood? Why or why not?

In Figure 8.2, why is Socrates chained? Why is he holding a scroll in one hand and reaching for hemlock (a poison) with the other? Why does everyone but the guard look sad?

He drank the contents as though it were a draught of wine

Figure 8.2: The Death of Socrates. Write your own story of Socrates taking the hemlock and ask a what, why, and should question for the picture, e.g. How does a democracy justify silencing Socrates?

Source: By Walter Crane.

CLASSIC RESEARCH REPORT

A 2001 study of students' knowledge of civics offers good and bad news. Overall, U.S. 9th-grade students were better able to comprehend political messages, interpret political cartoons, and distinguish fact from opinion than were their peers in the 27 other nations studied. Overall, U.S. students scored at or above the mean on all measures of civic awareness in the study. However, results varied by ethnicity and socioeconomic status (SES). White students and students from higher socioeconomic backgrounds tended to score better. In addition, students tended to side with their own kind on certain issues. Female students were more supportive of women's rights than were male students, and immigrants were more supportive of immigrants' rights, leading the authors to ask, "Do students think that rights are a zero-sum game, in which giving others more rights diminishes their own?" U.S. students also reported higher rates of involvement in a variety of civic and cultural activities, and this activity correlated positively with knowledge. Subjects were also more likely to follow the news whether in print or on TV. (The study did not mention Internet usage at the time.) On a less positive note, fewer than 50% of the students reported studying governments other than their own or international organizations. The study found a lack of issues-oriented discussions.

Hahn, C. L. (November/December 2001) "Student Views of Democracy: The Good News and the Bad News," *Social Education, 65, 7*, 456–512.

Didactic Goals

Didactic goals involve acquiring knowledge about the political system. In an atmosphere for coverage teachers are tempted to use a safe *de jure* approach: how a bill becomes a law, the three branches of U.S. government, the Bill of Rights, and voting procedures. Political behavior, however, may also be built into a program. Typical didactic goals often include the following:

1. Students will know how legislation is passed.
2. Students will be able to identify the branches and functions of the U.S. government.
3. Students will learn more about government voting procedures in key states, including their own state.
4. Students will know how local, state, and federal agencies are organized, top to bottom.

These goals are too broad and abstract. Legislation needs specific examples, and identifying the parts of government may give students nothing more than a set of labels. Initial goals should be rewritten in behavioral terms to reflect more fully what students will study and what they will be expected to accomplish. Definitions of terms are part of recall. The same goals can be improved by making each more specific by defining expected results:

1. Students will be able to describe the major steps in moving bills from the House and Senate to the executive branch and back again.
2. Students will be able to identify the three branches of government (executive, legislative, and judicial) and provide at least one example of crossover powers.

3. Students will be able to verbalize formal definitions of government and define the process and meaning voting.
4. Students will be able to chart the hierarchical structure of local, state, national and international agencies of governments and transnational bodies.

Develop more specifics about a topic, perhaps the United Nations, and the way it will be taught, and expected student outcomes. Plan a unit and choose additional materials, making sure to include news reports and literature, as well as YouTube clips. The didactic realm, however, is only one part of a whole set of expectations for student knowledge of government and the problems of democracy. Reflective and affective goals are also needed for higher order thinking, decision-making, and creative action.

TO DO

Would you teach international politics in a civics course? Would you compare the U.S. to other nations that are also democracies or dictatorships? What would be a fair comparison to set up for your classroom? What would be likely to work with the U.S. and France, the U.S. and Russia, the U.S. and Brazil? Try a pair out to see if the analogy works or doesn't work, and make a judgment on the results. Look up *World Affairs* articles on the nations you chose and to get an overall look at U.S. foreign policy issues.

Reflective Goals

Reflective goals move students to higher cognitive ground. Building on the information base already established, reflective goals encourage student inquiry into the reasons behind political decisions and the use of power. Students will explore the relationship between formal written law and informal behind-the-scenes practice: personal, local, state, national, and international.

Reflective goals should stress the comprehension, analysis and synthesis of human political behavior. Conclusions might serve as guides for understanding political trust, participation in political activities, protest, political decisions, and the use and abuse of authority. In general, reflective goals guide students in building an analytical framework, theories and generalizations about the reasons behind political action or apathy, and the way laws are turned into social policy.

You might begin with the following:

1. Students will be able to understand how political decisions are made.
2. Students will be able to discuss ways in which laws are enforced in daily life.
3. Students will be able to develop a definition of political participation and use it to identify the causes of social activism or apathy.
4. Students will be able to identify media influences our knowledge and images of political leaders, events, and policy debates.

These goals target further development: comprehending the process of political choice, comparing de jure (lawful) and de facto (actual) behavior, searching for influences that make people more active or more passive citizens. Each goal demands knowledge about political behavior and a grasp of political terminology. Let's think about filling in the missing elements: materials, techniques, outcomes, and assessment. As each element is identified, rate its importance in politics by giving a plus, minus, or zero to your list of actions.

More specific versions of our goals might look like these:

1. Using a series of case studies on environmental proposals at the community, state, local, and national levels, students will assume the role of legislators who identify and analyze the issues, decide on the cost of each proposal, and choose those most acceptable to voters.
2. Students will examine procedures for a bill becoming a law by comparing the written process with the actual process influenced by public officials and outside participants such as lobbyists, journalists, and civic groups, developing conclusions about which groups are *most important* in forming public policy, e.g., business or labor, rich or poor, etc.
3. After examining types of political participation (e.g., voting, letter writing, protest, volunteer service), students will create their own scale or ranking of political activism, setting priorities for the highest and lowest degrees of participation. Teachers should ask students to consider whether some forms of participation might be considered negative in certain contexts—bullying opponents, destroying property applying conclusions to at least two new political events discussed orally.
4. Students will learn to look at media techniques, signs, and symbols (including radio, newspapers, journals, TV, blogs, and films) that affect feelings and attitudes about politics. Suggest that the students collect photographs, posters, and campaign buttons, evaluating which are most effective in communicating either negative or positive images of political leaders and issues during or between campaigns. Form media consultant groups to create ad campaigns to promote a personality or issue.

Revised reflective goals specify which materials will be used, how students will accomplish each task, and what outcomes are expected. Include some form of evaluation, formal and informal, to include voter participation, Supreme Court decisions, the structure of the American political system, political parties, media influence, pressure groups, community affairs, taxation, social problems, and leadership. Provide Internet sources as the raw material for planning a unit or course. You are invited to write neater goals of your own to fit your needs and audiences.

TO DO

What would you recommend as a general plan to promote reflective thinking in civics by: (a) providing answers, (b) providing guidance, or (c) promoting independence? Can independent thought exist as the same time as you are feeding answers? Can independent thought coexist with poor quality curriculum? Why or why not?

Affective Goals

Affective objectives are vitally important to any civics/government course because political decisions inevitably rest on human judgment and values.[11] Didactic and reflective goals provide a base, but without values politics that turns into a falsely neutral compilation of dry facts and definitions. Even the word 'transparency' allows for criticism. Students, and most ordinary citizens, snap to attention when news reveals the government is not working. Audiences pay more attention to stories of political corruption, conflict, and personality clashes than they do to the details of the legislative process. Why do we then censor such subjects in our classrooms? In fact, efforts to present only uncontroversial ideas and the good side of the American political system offer students a distorted perception and reinforces rather than counteracts cynical, apathetic attitudes.[12]

CLASSIC RESEARCH REPORT

Secondary Students' Attitudes and Knowledge in the Bicentennial Year

During the bicentennial year, 1976, National Assessment of Educational Progress (NAEP) surveyed a random sample of approximately 2,500 American youth ages 13 and 17, asking them for information about government and for attitudes about politics and their classroom experiences. Results were divided into four categories: social attitudes, political attitudes, political knowledge, and political education. Students in both age groups generally agreed (88%) that they were *always, often,* or *sometimes* encouraged to speak freely and openly in class. Very few (12%) replied *never* to this question. Further, about three-quarters of both age groups thought their teachers *usually* respected their views; 69% and 72% of 13- and 17-year-olds, respectively, felt that they *sometimes* were asked to "help decide about school affairs."

Despite this relatively positive picture, results on several knowledge and attitude items were rather poor. For example, only 47% and 41% of the 13- and 17-year-olds, respectively, could correctly identify the powers of the United Nations to settle or intervene in conflicts. Correct answers to questions about the Senate, the House of Representatives, and Congress generally were in the 30% to 50% range. Fifty-six percent of 17-year-olds and only 32% of 13-year-olds were aware that the number of congressional members varies with state population. Of the younger group, 44% agreed that, "a lot of elections are not important enough to vote in"; 32% of 17-year-olds agreed. African-American students indicated more interest in politics overall than did Whites; there was little difference generally between younger and older secondary students on most items, knowledge or attitude, although older students did tend to receive slightly higher scores on knowledge questions.

Source: National Assessment for Educational Progress, *Education for Citizenship: A Bicentennial Survey*, Report No. 07-CS-01 (Denver, November, 1976).

Note: The NAEP is cycled and repeated every few years across a variety of subjects, so research the latest results for civics and compare these to the 1976 results. See what the scores were for history as well. Do you think any surprises await you, or is the system and the result stuck in a rut? What might help students out of the rut of apathy? Visit www.nces.ed.gov/nationsreportcard.

Major goals for all middle/senior high school government courses should concern real world policies, values, perceptions, and decision–making. Although many view values as 'soft' and data as 'hard,' political scientists argue that attitudes are quite real in the sense that feelings are a major factor in tilting a political system in one direction or another.

Important legislation and power often depend on public feelings about a given problem, leader, or issue. A potent example is the Presidential election of 2016. The issues of patriotism, immigration, abortion, and gun control polarized large numbers of voters, making values and 'image' rather than compromise or economics determinant in the election's outcome. Contrary to popular opinion, relatively few votes can and often do drastically change elections and policies. The 2020 election reversed almost all of the policy commitments of the 2016 election! Will this happen again?

Political leaders and social scientists spend a great amount of time acquiring and examining voters' feelings about a variety of issues, most commonly using polls. Poll results often suggest alternative solutions to a problem. Polls and surveys are easily 'Googled' on the Internet for instant examination. Students should be familiar with the process of sampling opinion because it is so prevalent and influential in modern society and because attitudes often influence policy.[13]

We can incorporate polling into course goals such as:

1. Students can use polls to identify major values and rationales for action.
2. Students will develop a tolerance for the viewpoints of other people and groups.
3. Students will debate different sides of an issue, playing roles they may not agree with and deciding where they personally will stand on an issue.
4. Students will discuss how much or how little they feel a part of the political system, their sense of efficacy, trust, and why. (Does their role or lack of it in school governance help or hurt political life, and why?)

Initial affective goals focus on values and policy and involve decision-making skills. Attitudes are studied and formed during class activities, although the specifics of curriculum and group dynamics are missing as yet. Tolerance and empathy are not the same: tolerance gives an okay, a get along, but empathy provides an extension of feeling. Pre and post polls provide insight into growth measured by changes from the first to the last poll. Finally, students are asked to analyze and evaluate their own feelings about the system and whether they intend to participate in it, when and how and for whom. Not only are others' viewpoints and the public's attitudes debated, but students will also probe their own beliefs and emotional states, such as political trust or mistrust, alienation or identification, efficacy or apathy toward political parties, leaders, and legislation.

We can now add more specific features to our affective objectives, refining content and improving planning. The new, improved versions of our original four goals might be:

1. Students will review a recent Gallup or Pew Trust poll of public attitudes toward foreign policy issues, analyze the testimony of at least three experts, and decide where they stand both as individuals and as a group trying to reach a consensus about foreign policy proposals.
2. Prior to the lesson, students will survey (by their design) peer attitudes about a public controversy, taxation, immigration reform, health care benefits. In class, students will examine and discuss the viewpoint most opposed to their own, administering the same survey a second time to see whether any opinions have changed or greater empathy has developed for the contrary argument, and to what degree the shift, on average,

can be considered significant. Note that Survey Monkey (www.surveymonkey.com) and other 'canned' programs are available to design a homemade survey with models to follow.

3. Students will take part in a formal debate or mock trial on a civil rights issue using a recent Supreme Court ruling in a discrimination or affirmative action case as a basis for argument. Prepare and present statements, cross-examinations, and rebuttals rated on a scale of 1 to 10 (best) by a class vote.

4. Using a series of case studies of many forms of political participation: community action, assisting in a campaign, letter writing to officials, voting, taking part in a protest, and abstaining or 'fence sitting.' Students will analyze and evaluate which responses they see as most or least valuable. Explain in writing which types of participation provides the greatest or least sense of belonging to American political culture, concluding with an exchange and critique of each other's stands on the subject.

These rewritten, expanded goals clarify what students and teachers are actually working to accomplish. Activities include self-analysis of political values and attitudes, practice with survey research techniques as a prelude to value formation, making decisions about international issues, and considering others' views even when unpopular, perhaps leading to greater tolerance. Students make decisions based on their study of political behavior, public perception of issues, and examination of their beliefs. Policy formation and value analyses are accompanied at each stage by materials that provide factual data and expert arguments that students may use to build positions. At all times, students may abstain as well as participate, or remain open to revising a stand. Encourage choice and taking a position allow students time to think about their feelings or obtain more information before making a decision. Positive, neutral, and negative aspects of each position should be considered. However, decisions should be left to participants, not teachers.

Ask students to develop positions taking into account one or more of the factors below:

(a) empathy for others' viewpoints,
(b) commitments to consider arguments *before* choosing a stand,
(c) stronger feelings of efficacy—the notion that ordinary individuals like us can make a difference (the Power of One!) in the political process.

TO DO

Write five affective goals that you believe should be part of every civics or government program (e.g., tolerate other views). Will you try to convince students about which values are best or have them develop their own positions? What goals encourage free and open discussion? Are any goals that might inhibit discussion? Is free and open discussion important?

While you think about these questions, write the five affective goals at top speed and share them. Rate each goal according to *its power* for promoting (+) or inhibiting (−) the free discussion of ideas. Was it easy or difficult to decide how each goal would affect discussion? Why?

DESIGNING A CIVICS/U.S. GOVERNMENT PROGRAM

Most civics courses follow a predictable pattern of topics, units and lessons, mostly formal and descriptive, and almost wholly focused on U.S. government. The mainstay topics are largely organizational and historical repeating much of what was covered in U.S. history, particularly the Bill of Rights, Constitution, Supreme Court, President and Congress. Despite stated aims relatively little work is done on political parties and issues, the history of parties, other political systems, or international relations.

A few essential questions can focus course design, particularly if the questions are treated as open to multiple responses and viewpoints. If our goal truly is to motivate students toward greater participation in the political process, they must be invited into the conversation and recognized as worthy participants about to become active citizens.

1. What is a political system and how does it work? Here at home, or anywhere?
2. What are the foundations and evolution of the American political system, and do most civic ideals match most civic realities? Like voting registration rules? Is there a rule for 'one person, one vote'?
3. How effective is the United States right now in safeguarding and extending political liberties, economic opportunities, and social justice within the system of laws and citizen benefits? Can everyone vote easily?
4. What is the relationship of the United States to other nations and to world affairs, and how do other nations and world agencies treat the United States? How many countries are friendly and how many are not? Does it matter?
5. What roles do citizens play in American democracy, and do these live up to standards, like voting, discrimination, taxation, or fall below?[14]

A Traditional Approach to Government and Civics

A typical course in U.S. government or civics, as mentioned, focuses largely on the de jure aspects of how the system functions. In other words, a legalistic rather than a behavioral approach is adopted. An outline for such a course would include the following:

Description: A 12th grade program that addresses state and national standards for Civics and American government that emphasizes foundational philosophies (enlightenment) and documentary records including the Constitution, Bill of Rights, and Supreme Court decisions. Major topics include separation of powers, federalism, civil rights and liberties, responsible citizenship, and the role of the press, media, social media, and Internet communication for news and political campaigning. The U.S. system will be viewed as **an evolving adaptation to changing economic, social, and political conditions within a federal structure composed of state units**.

Unit 1: Principles of American Government
Unit 2: Origins and History of American Government
Unit 3: The U.S. Constitution
Unit 4: Federalism
Unit 5: Political Parties

Unit 6: Voters and Voter Behavior
Unit 7: The Electoral Process
Unit 8: Public Opinion and Mass Media (including social media)
Unit 9: Interest Groups and Lobbying
Unit 10: The Powers of the Presidency
Unit 11: Powers of Congress
Unit 12: Powers of the Supreme Court and the Federal Court System
Unit 13: State and Local Government
Unit 14: Civil Liberties/Individual Rights and Responsibilities
Unit 15: Civil Rights and Responsibilities
Unit 16: Comparative Political Systems
Unit:17: World Governmental Agencies
Unit 18: Foreign Policy and International Relations

A sample of expected learning outcomes might include:

1. Students will be able to discuss and evaluate the different philosophies of government, liberal and conservative, that contributed to the foundation of the nation.
2. Students will be able to discuss and analyze the purpose and function of government.
3. Students will be able to trace the evolution of voting and participation from the beginning to the present.
4. Students will be able to interpret the Bill of Rights and Constitution across time periods up to and including the present.
5. Students will be able to compare federal, confederate, and unitary systems of government.
6. Students will examine the structure of government, the three branches, the process of amendments, and the role of the political parties.
7. Students will be able to identify and distinguish between federal and state powers, federal and state jurisdictions, federal and state issues.
8. Students will be able to read, analyze, interpret, and apply important Supreme Court decisions to current and past issues about the rights and responsibilities of citizens.
9. Students will be able to connect their lives and responsibilities as citizens with past and present political decisions, policies, and laws.
10. Students will be able to recognize, comprehend, and judge election campaigns, in many media forms, assessing the positions, issues, fairness, and statements of candidates for local, state, and national offices.

The course topics outlined above provide the basics of any civics course. This course concentrates on students being able to identify the parts of government and how these relate to each other in a formal, legal sense. A good deal of what is presented overlaps with American or U.S. history materials, but with more attention to current political structures at home and abroad. The emphasis is clearly on the present de jure structure, but with considerable attention to the forces that influence all decisions (i.e., voter groups, media, special interest groups, the economic situation, campaign platforms, and party politics).

WHAT DO YOU THINK?

With a few classmates or colleagues, discuss which areas of government really deserve the most class time—for example, are the three branches worth more than a day or two to tell about? What if the three branches are discussed in terms of power struggles over bills like health care, or laws dealing with money as free speech like the Citizens' United Supreme Court decision? Where do firearm laws come from state by state?

Criticism. The structure described, at best, gives youth a narrow view of politics.[15] Personal politics, community experience, volunteer work (service learning), and precinct-level door-to-door campaigning are barely discussed. Yet these forms of political activity are training grounds for future leaders and probably represent areas that students may find more interesting than voting, which occurs infrequently and at designated places and times. Face-to-face interactions, which may also be viewed as a kind of politics, are almost entirely neglected in most civic courses and texts.

Political conversation is, however, at the heart of daily political life.[16]

Schools are fertile grounds for political activity and training, particularly for young adults, yet this opportunity is almost largely ignored. Mostly, constitutional laws are presented rather than everyday electoral politics.[17] Certainly, high school students are cognizant of their emerging roles as citizens in our society and are capable of assuming a great deal more responsibility than is offered by basically honorific student government offices. How about a discussion of changing the voting age to 16 from 18?

Students could be empowered and socialized by serving on committees that assist teachers in curriculum planning and advisory groups that discuss issues with the school administration, publish student newspapers, and conduct course evaluation surveys and school assessments. Such participation involving real decision-making would reduce students' cynicism about the political process as well as offer firsthand experience with political compromise and the exchange of views.[18]

Also, largely missing from the typical civics course are analyses of vital socioeconomic issues that frequently perplex and divide people. These include frank and open discussions about the place of gender in politics, the role of minorities, and the part religious groups play in the American system. Women in particular, more than half the population, are often mis- or underrepresented in politics, even when issues deal directly with gender.[19]

In general, most secondary school students receive sanitized versions of the political system that are either so boring or so different from reality that their attitudes become more negative than positive as a result of their studies. Lesbian, gay, bisexual, and transgender issues further complicate political conversations, particularly with the rapid rise in acceptance of sexual variation in American life. Gay marriage is now widely accepted both socially and legally in large portions of the U.S. but barely discussed in civics or anywhere else in the curriculum. There are gay members of Congress and the Cabinet from both parties!

Finally, American government courses are accused of viewing the U.S. system in isolation from other systems it could be compared, with such as European parliamentary democracy and the European Union, one-party rule, authoritarian regimes, and military juntas. Students have little knowledge of why different systems exist or how these systems may borrow techniques and institutions (as they always have historically) to achieve social and economic goals. Most students have scant knowledge about the political and economic systems of Mexico and Canada, both of which share long borders and trade heavily with the United States.[20] Students are equally undeveloped in terms of a worldview, or how America fits into the total political scheme as a global power in international affairs. We could argue that even in colonial times, North America was directly connected to international politics with interference by foreign powers, Native American nations, French, English, German, Polish, etc. working on behalf of the revolutionaries or the Tories.

Thus, we can criticize the typical government or civics course on several grounds: (a) formalism, (b) in-attention to personal and school politics, (c) lack of emphasis on social problems, (d) too narrow a definition of participation, (e) little or no comparative framework, (f) an often biased view that we are 'the best,' and (g) little or no attention to the United States as a participant in global politics.

Defense. Students need basic information about their government before they can discuss more sophisticated issues and problems or understand the international scene.[21]

Because there is no widely agreed-on framework for teaching about political values and social issues, it is sensible to stick to government structures, party politics, and the electoral process. The traditional civics course provides information vital to voting, which is, after all, a major form of political expression in the United States. After students have absorbed the basics, you can easily supplement each topic with relevant case studies. Local, state, or national news and supplemental materials can be designed to teach students how to evaluate arguments about social policy. At least students would have a solid grounding if teachers did a good job of covering basic forms and structures, rights and responsibilities.

Because events change rapidly, you must adapt your course to current controversies and political disputes. However, while value issues come and go, the basic structures remain and are of value. Using a traditional course structure, develop a sense of involvement through activities such as student government, mock trials, model United Nations, student review committees, and writing for the school newspaper.

SAMPLE LESSON PLAN

You've left your materials on gender issues at home, alas, but this is the topic for your class today. The students have already discussed the Bill of Rights and the 13th Amendment, but you need something to capture their interest. What can you use as an example? How about sports? Private clubs? The military? Business leadership? Introduce the subject of equal rights by asking about women serving in combat, or being integrated into baseball teams—professional, pony, and little league. Would openly gay students participate? Does the class know that a women's rights amendment, The Equal Rights Amendment (ERA, 1973, fell three states short of the threshold to become law) failed to be added to the Constitution in recent times, and is still waiting approval? Why not look up a copy and find out why it failed to pass approval by two-thirds of the States. That should get a good discussion going. What do you think?

SAMPLE LESSON PLAN

View Figure 8.3. What kind of map do you think this is? Why are the countries of the world shown in blocks? What is the point of the map? Which conclusions do the people who created this map want you to draw from their data? Do you agree or disagree with their conclusions? How would you use this map with students in government, civics, world studies, or global history? Design a lesson using this map.

Alternative Approaches

Traditional government or civics courses focus on the mechanics of politics, legal rights and responsibilities. Alternative approaches stress issues, participation, and political science.

A Problems- or Issues-Centered Approach

Political and social controversies lie at the heart of an issues-centered controversy approach to civics, sometimes titled 'problems of democracy' or 'crucial issues in democracy.' Whatever its name, the content of a controversy course is usually organized around themes or questions that encourage debate about both long- and short-term controversies. Problems and issues can be arranged as debate questions that students use to develop their own positions. The classroom becomes a forum for the free expression of views on political, economic, and social issues. Students are continually called on to collect evidence, analyze data, apply these to current problems and make decisions. Usually, issues are discussed through the media of case studies, simulations, or contrasting positions. Dialogue and multilogue are crucial to the development of skills dealing with controversy as students learn how to argue with each other while respecting diverse and sometimes upsetting perspectives.

Two outstanding experiments issues programs date back to the 1960s and 1970s. The Harvard Social Studies Project and The Crucial Issues in Government series offered teachers easy-to-use pamphlets that provided materials for student discussion and debate focusing on key questions or persisting issues.[22] Both used small pamphlets to provide students with a sample of data and ethical positions involving problems of racism, gender, pressure groups, lawsuits, voter apathy, community participation, free speech, and foreign aid.

A sample controversy or issues-centered course might be organized around themes and questions like the following topics and questions:

1. The Three Branches: Are they in balance?
2. The President: Is the office too powerful or too weak?
3. Should political parties work with or against each other? When does the public good come first?
4. What should States and the Federal Government control separately or together?
5. Lobbying $$$: Should it be controlled for the general good or run free?
6. Free Speech and Assembly: Where should the lines be drawn? Is money free speech? Should the rich count more than other citizens?

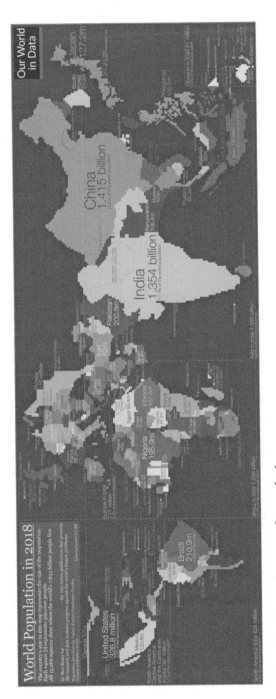

Figure 8.3: A schematic map of population.

7. Participation: Should there be one rule for all giving the vote as equals? Should voters care? Can Whites, Asians, African Americans, Native Peoples, and Hispanic voters have equal voting opportunities in our current system?
8. Political Parties: Work together or compete aggressively?
9. Women, LGBT groups, and minorities: Are they really equal before the law? In practice and theory? How must Black Lives Matter?
10. Rich, Middle Class, and Poor: How should wealth be distributed? Who benefits? Should there be guaranteed assistance for all?
11. International Human Rights: Should these be one standard for all?
12. Foreign Aid: How much for guns and how much for butter?
13. Security: How much security do we need and how much liberty? How far should government be allowed to intrude in private life, business, or other governments?
14. How cooperative or competitive should the U.S. be with other nations: on trade, conflicts, cultural exchanges, and migration laws? Which nations count?
15. What are the best and worst forms of government in history and at present in terms of protecting basic rights, freedoms, and justice?

Underlying controversy approaches is a strong commitment to analyzing and weighing the issues by identifying the causes and consequences, costs and benefits of alternative solutions.

Questions of justice, freedom, and the limits of authority permeate the entire course.

Many other possibilities could be added to the prior list, such as disputes over the death penalty, gun laws, campaign financing, environmental protection, political corruption, and police powers and rights of the accused. Problems and issues are a perfect vehicle for employing computer applications to save, analyze, and crosscheck Internet websites that justify (or fail to justify) a political position.

For example, homicide rates for states with and without the death penalty could be compared statistically, using graphic analysis, to discover whether the death penalty correlates with higher or reduced levels of murder. Rates of participation in elections for different segments of society could be compared to discover which groups vote most or least frequently and for what type of candidates. We could research whether activism correlates with class, race, age, gender, or ethnicity.

From these correlations, identify tentative hypotheses to explain a variety of social patterns. Can party politics be explained by issues, or by demography, geography, or by racial and ethnic associations? Let's find out! Examine a sample of studies, charts, and graphs amassed by Pew Trust, www.pewtrust.org. Choose one to examine closely with your audience.

Sharp Partisan Gaps on Addressing Race, Global Climate Change

In Figure 8.4, which issues and priorities get the best responses? Which receive majority approval?

Are there any sharp divides? And general agreements?

What does this survey prove or disprove about public views of government and social issues?

Is there a question you would like to add? Data you'd like to have? Why?

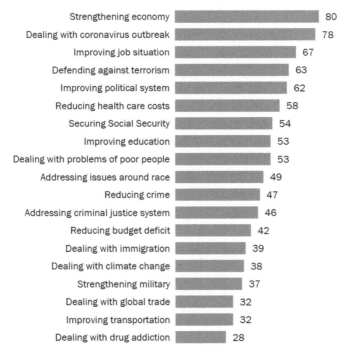

Strengthening the economy and dealing with coronavirus stand out as the public's top priorities

% who say ____ should be a top priority for the president and Congress to address this year

Strengthening economy	80
Dealing with coronavirus outbreak	78
Improving job situation	67
Defending against terrorism	63
Improving political system	62
Reducing health care costs	58
Securing Social Security	54
Improving education	53
Dealing with problems of poor people	53
Addressing issues around race	49
Reducing crime	47
Addressing criminal justice system	46
Reducing budget deficit	42
Dealing with immigration	39
Dealing with climate change	38
Strengthening military	37
Dealing with global trade	32
Improving transportation	32
Dealing with drug addiction	28

Source: Survey of U.S. adults conducted Jan. 8-12, 2021.

PEW RESEARCH CENTER

Figure 8.4:   Economy and COVID-19 top the public's Policy Agenda for 2021.

An issues approach is likely to be far more involving and motivating than a descriptive government class. The basics of government can be worked into the issues and covered as part of each debate. However, there are drawbacks to controversy because not all issues can be neatly divided into pros and cons. Often the issue is complex, and the proposed solutions may involve many distinct positions. Despite the difficulty of splitting issues into neat divisions, this design for a civics/U.S. government program should be given more serious consideration by social studies teachers.

WHAT DO YOU THINK?

Are there other issues that should be added to the course outline? Make a list of those that are 'musts' for discussion. Explain why you feel as you do. Are there any issues you would avoid? Why?

A Political Systems Analysis Approach. Issues- and participation-oriented programs are more common than those based on political science.[23] Political scientists may be avid people watchers, but they do not pay much professional attention to the social studies, although our field has citizenship as its central goal.[24]

However, a political science approach may provide motivation for your students to apply concepts and research methods to the study of political values and behavior. Actual political behavior, rather than formal government structures, is emphasized. The causes and consequences of action or inaction are analyzed to identify patterns in the way people behave, vote, make demands, and assume leadership.

A political science approach might ask questions like, 'How do active citizens compare to apathetic citizens in terms of party membership, socioeconomic status (SES), ethnicity, race, education, or gender? A political science approach involves studying the meanings people give to political actions and symbols so as to understand the factors that influence their decisions. Political scientists interpret and compare events before coming to conclusions. Statistics can be used to support theory, and primary sources, such as eyewitness reports, serving to illuminate different vantage points and value systems.

SAMPLE LESSON PLAN

Studies might focus on democratic and authoritarian regimes, the path of revolutions and counterrevolutions, the development of centralized and federal structures, and the building of ideologies and rationales. Concepts are used to interpret events and test theories that may relate to situations ranging from the local to the international. Throughout any political science-oriented course, you must be conscious of the way an inquiry is undertaken: Research tools, data sources, possible errors, and real or potential biases must be monitored. A political science approach is not 'selling' civics or anything else but aimed at providing a set of analytical tools for studying political power, how it is won, who supports it, and what sorts of decisions are made about who gets what. Students are being asked to adopt a scientific point of view in analyzing human belief and action.

SAMPLE LESSON PLAN

Political cartoons are a longstanding tradition of most democratic and even many undemocratic cultures. Cartoons usually deliver a solid punch of irony, sarcasm, and criticism that many other media may not be able to manage as well. There are now Internet sites featuring political cartoons as well as traditional magazine and newspaper cartoons. Views and controversies are frequently presented directly or indirectly through cartoons, but keep aware that cartoonists also have their political biases and perspectives. In teaching old or new cartoons, you always have to examine for bias and neutrality, asking if the cartoonist is one-sided or open-minded in criticism a political figure or event. Often, cartoonists use symbols to convey messages and turn people into caricatures that they believe suits their behavior and personality. You may, of course, agree or disagree. Old cartoons are free and sometimes demonstrate nearly eternal truths.

But the point is that cartoons make excellent civics lessons. In Figure 8.5, what controversy is the artist raising here? Does the artist take a stand? Why or why not in your opinion?

How can art be used for political purposes? Could you draw a cartoon of your own about political issues and/or personalities?

Find two or three cartoons on your own critical of the ties between wealth and politics. Examine the signs and symbols in each cartoon, and decide if the cartoonist is one-sided or is criticizing all sides or the system in general. How can you tell the nature of criticism?

The 19th Amendment to the U.S. Constitution granted women the right to vote. When the Tennessee General Assembly passed the ratification resolution on August 18, 1920, it gave the amendment the 36th and final state necessary for ratification. Suffragists and anti-suffragists lobbied furiously to secure votes during that intense summer in Nashville. The ratification resolution passed easily in the Tennessee State Senate on August 13, but the House of Representatives was deadlocked. When young Harry T. Burn of Niota changed his vote to support ratification of the 19th Amendment, he broke a tie in the House and made history.

Concepts and methods of political science are useful for interpreting elections, analyzing conflicts, and summarizing patterns of influence. Ideas such as power, socioeconomic status. Ideas including political socialization, efficacy, authority, community, and choice infuse the vocabulary of a social science approach to government that might include the following topics that could be applied to *any* system on earth or outer space.

Figure 8.5: 1893 cartoon that portrays the issues of immigrant and working-class people during the Gilded Age.

Figure 8.6: "His Daughter." A 1915 cartoon by W. E. Hill as it appeared in "The Gracious Road to Battle" by Louise Davis in the *Nashville Tennessean*, January 11, 1948. The cartoon features a young woman standing before a crowd of men, wearing a "Votes for Women" sash and carrying a box with "Freedom" written on it. An older man in a top hat faces the reader with a look of shock and concern on his face. The caption reads: "And he thought she was 'just a little girl.'"

In this example only one of many possibilities, we concentrate on analysis, fitting issues and controversies into larger, more encompassing categories such as conflict and conflict resolution. The U.S. government is viewed as a case study to be compared and contrasted with other systems. Students begin to see the U.S. system as one of many with built-in freedoms that have emerged from English law and custom, codified in the Constitution and Bill of Rights. The system works because of effective socialization methods (education, media, and leadership) and because of the relative wealth of the nation. With this approach, less attention is paid to citizenship values, patriotism, and historical evolution than to a theory about system stability. Students focus on a global perspective, comparative political structures, and political motivation. Personal decisions are linked directly to predictions about how others will act based on social values and previous performance. A political science approach offers a more analytical alternative to the standard, formalized government course.

A Participation or Community Action Approach. American politics may also be presented to secondary students in a 'participation in democracy' format. This approach stresses activism—*firsthand* experience in political situations such as internships, court service, and field trips. Exercises are designed to bring the students out of the classroom and into the real-life drama of politics. This approach shares many goals with the other designs, especially those promoting issues and controversies. Success depends largely on school or a politician's support for field-based experience. Ties to local organizations that can provide a steady stream of visitors to the classroom are also helpful. Participation is an exciting idea, particularly relevant to high school juniors and seniors who will soon vote, but equally applicable to middle and junior high students as a way of bringing abstract ideas and institutions to life.

The possibilities for a participation approach are virtually endless. You could arrange classroom visits by lawyers, lobbyists, politicians, and representatives of different interest groups. You might schedule field trips to courts, political clubs, campaign offices, City Hall, or government agencies. Media consultants and reporters could be asked to discuss how they choose and present stories about candidates or events. Representatives from the League of Women Voters, The Close Up Foundation, The University of Virginia's Youth Leadership Initiative program, or Future Voters of America might speak in class or work with students over Zoom.

Students could apply what they have learned to a school campaign of their own, with permission of the administration. Where possible, students should participate in cooperative work-study programs with elected officials, lawyers, judges, civil servants, or private organizations, getting a chance to observe political action at firsthand. Of course, there are also dangers involved in close contact, such as losing objectivity because the student is working for one side. Other problems may arise when the experience becomes all-consuming, blotting out the curriculum or school work. And be careful that students are not pulled into violent actions under your supervision.

To be keen political observers and decision makers, students still need to know the basic rules of government. They will also certainly benefit from some form of system analysis to understand how and why lines of power and influence develop. Thus, a participation approach requires the same basics as the other approaches, but this knowledge is applied directly to life experiences.

At its best, a participation approach would offer students an overview of constitutional rules, election procedures, legal precedents, and voting patterns while integrating these into carefully selected practical, real-life experiences. For example, a visit to criminal court could yield a sociological picture of the defendants: Are they rich or poor, well or poorly educated, and so on—and why? Theories and rules could then be tested through observation of de facto behavior. To work well, a participation approach must incorporate regular field experiences with presentations about formal government operation and political science research on participation, protest, and apathy. The whole game plan or strategy for a participation course would rest on the juxtaposition of de jure and de facto politics.

If it is well balanced, a participation approach can yield vital and interesting questions for discussion. These would focus on issues of freedom, authority, justice, and conflict that affect every aspect of life.

Participation should be worth several dialogues on didactic, reflective, and affective levels—that is, what is participation? Why do people participate or not? Which forms of participation are most affective for individuals, groups, and society as a whole?

Figure 8.7: March on Washington 1963. In the front row, from left are: Whitney M. Young, Jr., Roy Wilkins, A. Philip Randolph, Walter P. Reuther, Arnold Aronson. Public domain: U.S. government holding.

Figure. 8.7, based on political activism research, could be used as a springboard for discussing participation. Question whether voting really is low-level participation. Should group protests be seen as an advanced form of participation? Which forms of activism are best for most people most of the time? What situations demand a more (or less) active approach by citizens? Furthermore, participation might be discussed. For example, if pro- and anti-abortion factions are active in a divided community, what are the consequences? Often compromises are made and a community lives peacefully, but at other times passions bring a level of activism that tears it apart. A participation program might be thought of as existing on two tracks—the academic and the experimental—with strong connections between service learning and community citizenship.

A CLASSIC VIEW OF PARTICIPATION: WHAT DO YOU THINK?

Query: According to this concept of participation, who are the most active and who are the least active? Do you agree?

Questions:

Why do the political scientists call those on the bottom 'apathetics'?

What are defined as spectator activities?

Which activities are considered 'transitional' and 'gladiatorial'?

Why is high activism compared to the work of gladiators in combat?

Have you ever engaged in any of the activities on the list?

How would you describe your own level of activism?

Why are you relatively active or inactive on Milbrath's 14-point scale?

QUESTIONS ON FIGURE 8.7.

What does this photo show about participation and leadership?

Who are leading and who are following: can you tell?

What are the aims of the March and is there a variety of participants?

Does this March relate to issues and protests of our time now?

How might you teach this photo in the current context of Black Lives Matter?

A participation design, although sometimes touted as a new course structure, can be traced back to much earlier suggestions for socially active programs that involve students.[25]

The examples provided earlier can be emulated, altered, or redesigned depending on the students' needs, the teacher's goals, school mandates, and community issues. Whatever its faults, the participation model does provide an alternative to government courses that mainly offer descriptions of the laws and institutions of federal, state, and local authorities.

KEY QUESTIONS FOR TEACHING U.S. GOVERNMENT

There are important questions that cut across *all the approaches* to teaching about government.

Focus on the central problem of government: deciding how to allocate scarce resources and power among unlimited political demands. Negotiation and compromise make the demands manageable. However, if a satisfactory solution cannot be found, violence may result, especially on the part of those whose demands have gone unmet. A political system with its laws, leaders, and legislators can therefore be seen as a set of institutions created for the purpose of constructively negotiating and channeling social demands. These assumptions lead to a set of key questions:

1. Who gets what, when, where, and how?
2. How is power defined in the system? And practiced? Are power and practice the same?
3. Which groups, classes, sections, or parties have greater power than others? Why?
4. What conflicts seem to be part of the political process? Are all disputes solvable? Why or why not?
5. How much authority are people willing to allow their leaders? How much participation is common?

6. Is the government basically one of laws or one of leaders? How can you tell?
7. To what extent is the political system fair or unfair to each citizen and group? How does the majority view what is fair? What are the views of minorities?
8. Does the system as a whole work to meet all or most demands and advance the interests of its citizens, or are there numerous problems? How are demands negotiated and problems handled by the government?
9. Is the system basically respectful or disrespectful of human life?
10. When is a political decision ethical? Give examples.

Although these 10 questions are by no means exhaustive, any one or all may be applied to cases and examples of your choice that would be common to any government and civics program. Key questions ask students to develop explanations based on observations and generate hypotheses that explain human action. For example, students could attempt answers to tough questions: Why does a law fail to pass Congress? Why may a strongly supported bill like gun control fail to change public behavior? Why do different leaders in the same position achieve a great deal or very little? Why are the political systems of nations so different? Why do economic conditions influence politics, and vice versa? Why do traditions and values shape the way people feel about their governments? In politics, interesting questions are easily formulated and lead to a high amount of student ideas and judgments. Above all, it is your role to encourage students to initiate and follow through on their own ideas, and to avoid communicating either a sense that all government decisions are good or that all leaders are corrupt, ineffective, and cynical.

SUMMARY

A course in civics or U.S. government is commonly required at the middle/junior and senior high school level. Giving students an understanding of U.S. federal, state, and local systems, especially the importance of voting, is central to the mission of such courses, sometimes in a world setting where other governments and the United Nations are included. This understanding can be shallow, fulfilling mainly didactic aims, or deeper, achieving reflective and affective goals.

However, it is difficult to see how politics can be studied without arguing positions and taking sides in the ongoing debates that affect our lives. All civics, participation, and government courses face a built-in dilemma—how to balance socialization into the system and patriotism with criticism protest. Course goals may stress building a commitment to common core values such as the Bill of Rights and patriotic beliefs while simultaneously pressing for independent decision making and full debate of issues. The potential is great for critical challenge of traditional beliefs and strongly held values. You have to build pride and consensus while promoting critical thinking—not an easy task!

Despite polemical problems, in which the textbooks may prompt agreement on a number of issues, government can be taught in a variety of creative ways, ranging from the traditional structural approach to the more flexible issues or participation design. Professional research and analysis suggests that students need far more involvement with government, directly and through role-play and classroom debate, and less instruction concerning formal organizations than is currently the case. Furthermore, schools can support positive values by including students in school decisions through participation in student government and on committees. Politics poses persisting questions for secondary students (who will very soon be legal voters) concerning the uses and abuses of power, who makes decisions, how and why allegiances are formed, and which values should be the basis of social and personal life.

TO DO

Participating in a survey or census is a superb way of engaging students in field-based survey research. Through their own polling efforts, they will learn both the methods and pitfalls of finding out what people know about their society and government, and what issues and beliefs they care about. Computer programs designed for compiling, analyzing, and graphically representing survey data could be applied to a student-designed poll, thereby achieving two goals simultaneously: (a) extending research skills, and (b) putting computer technology into practice.

The Census Education Project (www.census.gov) 2000, 2010, 2020 and beyond incorporates 'teacher-ready' lessons that allow students to plan, conduct, analyze, display, and interpret their own local census data. Students can also play the parts of community planners and market researchers who are preparing government and business plans for the next 10 years. Students' projections represent their conclusions about which changes will be significant in our society in the near future.

The Census Education Project is available from the U.S. Department of Commerce, Bureau of the Census, Office of the Director, Washington, DC 20233.

APPENDIX

Vast Resources for Teaching Government and Civics!

American Bar Association

For teachers and students, the American Bar Association offers a resource guide on how to organize a Civics and Law Academy, which engages middle and high school students in learning about law and society. Most material is free. Level: Middle and high school.

Annenberg Learner

Annenberg Learner develops and distributes multimedia resources for teaching and learning. Level: Kindergarten through 12th grade.

Bill of Rights Institute

The Bill of Rights Institute provides a trove of online educational resources for teachers and students as well as constitutional seminars around the country for teachers and the Constitutional Academy. Companion websites include: **Article II -- Presidents and the Constitution.** This website explores the powers and responsibilities of the President through short videos, explanation of key terms, and extension activities.

Campaign for the Civic Mission of Schools

The goal of this coalition of 40 organizations is to improve civics education in schools. Among its many resources, Civic Learning Online provides free, public materials for educators. Lesson plans and practices for all grade levels, professional development and related resources, and whole school or district models are available online at the website. The Civic Learning Database may be searched.

Center for Action Civics

The Center for Action Civics, the professional development branch of The Mikva Challenge, provides the tools and strategies needed to engage young people in high quality Action Civics programming and experiential learning. The center's website includes a database of free lesson plans and resources; Mikva's Action Civics curricula for purchase; examples of Action Civics projects; and more. Level: Middle and high school.

Center for Civic Education

The Center for Civic Education is an independent, nonprofit organization based in California. A network of program coordinators throughout the United States and more than 70 other countries administers a range of curricular, teacher-training and community-based programs. Some materials are free; other material are available for purchase. Level: Elementary, middle and high school. Highlights include:

We the People: The Citizen and the Constitution: An instructional program on the history and principles of American constitutional democracy for all grade levels. The program is based on curricular materials developed by the Center for Civic Education. A simulated congressional hearing is the culminating activity.

Resource Center: For high school students: links to biographies, historical documents, images and firsthand accounts of historical events. For teachers: free professional development opportunities, free lesson plans, classroom activities.

Podcasts: Users can subscribe to four different podcasts, 60-Second Civics and quiz, Talking Civics, Conversations on Civics and Education for Democracy. Also a series of podcasts supplement text of We the People: The Citizen and the Constitution.

Center on Congress at Indiana University

Directed by former U.S. Rep. Lee Hamilton, the center and its site cover all aspects of the legislative branch and civic involvement. Interactive learning activities are aimed at the general public as well as schools. The online material is free; books available for purchase. Level: Middle and high school. Highlights include:

Interactive Learning Modules

Virtual Congress: This is a fully functional online replica of Congress in which students become lawmakers and propose ideas for legislation, discussing them in-world with other students, and working in realistic 3-D locations that include the House and Senate chambers.

Choices project: Brown University.

Constitute

Developed by the Comparative Constitutions Project, the website contains the constitution of nearly every independent state in the world, as of September 2013. It allows the user to search by country and by topic. The website is free. Level: Middle and high school.

Constitutional Rights Foundation

The CRF is a nonpartisan, nonprofit community-based organization that focuses on law and government and civic participation by young people. Its site pulls together resources for curriculum and professional development. Its outreach programs include a Mock Trial competition and other academic competitions and Courtroom to Classroom outreach. Free lesson plans are available on U.S. history, world history, and government. Some materials are free; others available for purchase. Level: Primarily for middle and high school, but also some material for younger students. Companion websites include:

Educating about Immigration: An information clearinghouse on topics of U.S. immigration, its history, and current controversies.
Civic Action Project: A practicum for high school students in civics and government in which they integrate the content of a government class with hands-on learning about public policy in the real world.
Judges, Courts, and the Law: Activities, games, and stories instruct students on the courts' role in our government.
CFR Blog: This site features discussion and information for all social studies educators.
CRF Forum: A site for young people who want to voice their opinion on current events.

Constitutional Rights Foundation Chicago

This nonprofit and nonpartisan organization provides resources for teachers to develop critical thinking skills, civic involvement, and commitment to the rule of law by young people.

Constitutional Sources Project

This project, also known as ConSource, is a free online library of constitutional history. ConSource contains an educational program called Primary Sources in which educators share lesson plans that use primary source documents. Level: Upper elementary, middle and high schools.

Courts in the Classroom

Created by the State of California's judicial branch and the Constitutional Rights Foundation, this site uses animated story videos and quizzes to teach students about Big Ideas, such as due process, free expression, and checks and balances; the Third Branch. The site is free. Level: Middle and high school.

C-SPAN Classroom

The cable channel's site features a wealth of audio and video clips, both current and historical, related to government, history, other civics topics, and news abroad. All resources are free. The site also contains TV and radio programs that feature recordings of past presidents and oral history interviews with presidents; Supreme Court oral arguments in landmark cases and videos of justices; and interactive Supreme Court timeline. The resources are free. Level: Middle and high school.

Dirksen Congressional Center

Named for Everett Dirksen, who served in the U.S. House and Senate, the site promotes civics engagement by providing a better understanding of Congress and its members. Extensive information covers modern and historical information, the legislative process, the current Congress' activities, and lawmakers' duties. The site has comprehensive coverage via Congress Link, which provides up-to-date information about the current Congress; About Government. Level: Elementary, middle and high school.

First Amendment Center

A Vanderbilt University site funded by the Freedom Forum, the First Amendment Center provides current news and information about First Amendment issues. Lesson plans, videos, RSS feeds, podcasts, and an interactive glossary are provided. The content is free. Level: Primarily for middle and high school, but also some resources for younger students.

iCivics

An initiative of retired Supreme Court Justice Sandra Day O'Connor, this site features online lessons covering the three branches of government and interactive games that cover citizenship and participation, the Constitution and Bill of Rights, separation of powers, budgeting, and the executive, judicial and legislative branches. Online discussion forums allow teachers and students to give feedback on various topics. Resources are free. Level: Middle and high school.

Library of Congress: America's Library

"America's Library" provides classroom materials from a vast array of primary sources (documents, photos, objects) about events and significant figures in U.S. history. Two sections are particularly relevant for educators: America's Story from America's Library and for Teachers. The resources are free online, and some material is downloadable. Lesson plans on American history are supplemented with primary sources from the Library of Congress collection. Class starters include Today in History and American Memory Timeline. Interactive learning activities are available for younger children. Several professional development programs for teachers are offered. The content is free. Level: Elementary, middle and high school.

National Archives

The National Archives and the Center for Civic Education partnered to create Docs Teach, a series of lesson plans that use primary sources to teach about different periods of U.S. history and the Constitution. The material is free. Level: Middle and high school.

National Constitution Center

The National Constitution Center site addresses topics related to the Constitution as well as civic participation and responsibility, and the executive branch. Printed materials include lesson plans. Online resources are interactive games, videos, webcasts, primary and secondary sources, Constitution Fast Facts, biographies of Constitutional Convention delegates, and an interactive Constitution guide. Resources are free. Level: Elementary, middle and high school.

National Endowment for the Humanities

The organization's EDSITEment project provides comprehensive lesson plans on American history, social studies and civics, government and society, among others. Its Introduction to Advanced Placement U.S. History Lessons contains scholar-reviewed website and primary sources; lesson plans focused on the Document Based Questions in the AP exam; and lesson plans based on active learning, mastery of content, and engaging the student. Resources are free. Level: Kindergarten through 12th grade.

New York Times Learning Network

The *New York Times*' content, current and historical, is the basis for teacher and student resources on this site. The Teaching Topics page is a living index page of links to resources on frequently taught subjects. For each topic, collected resources include lesson plans, related articles, multimedia, themed crosswords, and archival material. The site also provides a daily news quiz, Word of the Day, Student Crossword, Today in History, and more. An online forum invites students to post their opinions on issues in the news. Resources are free. Level: Middle and high school.

Newseum/Newseum Institute

This organization's website contains a Digital Classroom, which offers video lessons and viewing guides, primary sources, standards-aligned content, and integrated activities that support media literacy, critical thinking skills, and civic engagement. Level: Middle and high school.

Office of the Clerk, U.S. House of Representatives

Lesson and activities that teach about the legislative branch are offered at the Office of the Clerk's Kids in the House. Resources are free. Level: Preschool to high school.

Online Newshour Extra: For Students and Teachers

This PBS site uses current events as the basis for educational content revolving around news categories such as health, science, U.S., and history. Lesson plans based on current events contain videos, audio and photo essays; a forum for students to post essays, articles or comments on issues in the news. The material is free. Level: High school

PBS Teachers

The Public Broadcasting Systems' site for teachers covers all subject areas, including civics participation, community, the three branches of government, politics, economics, current events, the courts, and history. Lesson plans are free, with some material downloadable. Videos and audio recordings supplement lesson plans; interactive activities for younger children are available in the Democracy Project. Teachers have access to discussion forums, online professional developments courses, and an archive of webinars. Level: Preschool, elementary, middle and high school

Presidential Libraries

The National Archives offers a list of links to the presidential libraries that have resources for students and teachers. The material is free. Level: All grades

Rock the Vote

This organization uses pop culture and music to draw young people into the election process and engage as active participants. Democracy Class covers the history of voting rights and helps students identify national and local issues that affect their daily lives. The class ends with a mock election in which students seek office based on a platform of issues that they support.

Street Law

Street Law and the Supreme Court Historical Society partnered to create Landmark Cases of the U.S. Supreme Court, which explores 17 key cases. In-depth information about each case, related activities that involve interactive teaching strategies and external resources are provided. A Resource Library has compiled hundreds of teaching activities, case summaries, mock trials, and articles. The material is free. Level: Middle and high school

Sunnylands Classroom

A project of the Annenberg Foundation Trust at Sunnylands, this website hosts a multimedia curriculum on the Constitution containing award-winning documentaries, videos with Supreme Court justices, interactive games and downloadable books. Many of the materials have been close-captioned in 14 languages. The material is free. Level: Middle and high school.

U.S. Courts

This government site focuses on Court Literacy, featuring free, downloadable in-depth resources to help students understand how the courts work, key amendments to the Constitution, federal court basics and fast facts, legal concepts, legal landmarks, and Supreme Court cases. Classrooms to Courtrooms provides real-life teen-related scenarios to stage in-class or in-court simulations of trials with accompanying scripts. You Be the Supreme Court features comprehensive material for a class to simulate Supreme Court deliberations. Sections on the First, Fourth, and Sixth Amendment gives teacher a variety of formats to present to a class, including Oxford-style debate or a Supreme Court case conference. Homework Help is a set of links to related websites. Videos and podcasts are also provided. Material is free. Level: Middle and high school.

U.S. Government Printing Office

This comprehensive site, called Ben's Guide to U.S. Government for Kids, features information about all aspects of government, citizenship, elections, and voting. It also provides links to kids' sites for most government agencies. Activities include print games, interactive games and activities; information pages; links to other government agencies' curriculum; and a glossary. Content is free. Level: Elementary, middle and high school.

WhatSoProudlyWeHail.org

This site focuses on literary-based curricula for instruction of U.S. history, civics, social studies, and language arts. Resources include lesson plans, video seminars, and primary resources. Content is primarily free. Level: Middle and high school.

Youth Leadership Initiative

The University of Virginia Center for Politics' Youth Leadership Initiative has created three interactive simulations. E-Congress, a free, interactive, and national online simulation lets students play the part of a member of the House. They research issues, write legislation, debate bills in committee, and work to move their bill to the House floor. Students use innovative technology to interact with their legislators and to connect with their peers around the country. Mock Election is conducted each fall by the Youth Leadership Initiative for students around the nation using electronic ballots designed for each student's home district. A More Perfect Union simulates an actual campaign for Senate. The site also provides teacher-developed lesson plans and a service-learning program called Democracy Corps. Level: Middle and high school.

NOTES

1 Godsay, S., Kawashima, Ginsberg, K., Kiesa, A. and Levine, P. (2012) *That's Not Democracy: How Out-Of-School Youth Engage in Civic Life and What Stands in Their Way* (Medford, MA: Center for Information and Research on Civic Learning) www.ciircle.org.

2 Snell, P. (2010) "Emerging Adult Civic and Political Disengagement: A Longitudinal Analysis of Lack of Involvement with Politics," *Journal of Adolescent Research*, 25, 258–287.

3 Chiodo, J. and Byford, J. (2006) "Do They Really Dislike Social Studies?: A Study of Middle and High School Students," *The Journal of Social Studies Research*, 28, 1, 16–26.

4 Kahne, J. and Middaugh, E. (2010) "High Quality Civic Education: What Is It and Who Gets It?" In Parker, W. (ed.) *Social Studies Today: Research and Practice* (New York: Routledge), 140–150.

5 D'Allesandro, A. (September, 2013) "A Review of School Climate Research," *Review of Educational Research*, 83, 3, 357–386.

6 Hess, D. (2009) *Controversy in the Classroom: The Democratic Power of Discussion* (New York: Routledge).

7 **Gramlich, J., Pew Research Center (June 7, 2019)** *Young Americans Are Less Trusting of Other People – and Key Institutions – Than Their Elders.* www.pewresearch.org.

8 Saye, J. (2013) "Social Studies Research Collaborative and the Authentic Pedagogy: Its Presence in Social Studies Classrooms and Relationship to Student Performance on State-Mandated Tests," *Theory and Research in Social Studies Education*, 41, 1, 89–132.

9 McNeil, L. M. (1986) *Contradictions of Control* (New York: Routledge).

10 Pratle, R. (1988) *The Civic Imperative* (New York: Teachers College Press).

11 Massialas, B. (Sept.–Oct. 1989) "The Inevitability of Issue-Centered Discourse in the Classroom," *The Social Studies*, 80, 5, 173–177.

12 Garrett, H. J. (2017) *Learning to Be in the World with Other: Difficult Knowledge and Social Studies Education* (New York: Peter Lang).

13 Mueller, D. J. (1986) *Measuring Social Attitudes* (New York: Columbia University Press).

14 NAEP Civics (2022) *Civics Results for the 2018 National Assessment for Educational Progress* (Washington, DC: National Assessment Governing Board, U.S. Department of Education) www.nces.ed.gov.

15 Newmann, F. (Oct. 1989) "Reflective Civic Participation," *Social Education,* 53, 6, 357–360.

16 Conway, M. M. (1985) *Political Participation in the United States* (Washington, DC: Congressional Quarterly).

17 Coplin, W. D., O'Leary, M. K. and Carroll, J. J. (1988) *Effective Participation in Government: A Guide to Policy Skills* (Croton-On-Hudson, NY: Policy Studies Associates).

18 Jennings, L. (1988) "Learning About Life: New Focus on Service as a Teaching Tool," *Education Week,* 8, 8.

19 Bernard-Powers, J. (1996) The 'Woman Question' in Citizenship Education. In Parker, Walter C. (ed.) *Educating the Democratic Mind* (Albany, NY: SUNY), 287–308.

20 The Gallup Organization (1988) *Geography: An International Gallup Survey: A Summary of Findings* (Princeton, NJ: Gallup Inc.).

21 Remy, R. (1980) *Handbook of Basic Citizenship Competencies* (Alexandria VA: Association for Supervision and Curriculum Development).

22 Oliver, D. W. and Newman, F. M. (1969–1974) *Public Issues Series* (Middletown, CT: American Education Publications).

23 Gross, R. E. (Spring, 1987) "Citizenship Education: Global Challenge for the 1980s," *Social Studies Review,* 26, 3, 47–52.

24 Butts, R. F. (1980). *The Revival of Civic Learning: A Rationale for Citizenship in American Schools* (Bloomington, IN: Phi Delta Kappa,

25 Hepburn, M. A. (1980) "Improving Citizenship Education," *The Social Studies,* 71, 1, 8–13.

FOR FURTHER STUDY: TEACHING U.S. GOVERNMENT

Boulding, E. (1988) *Building a Global Civic Culture: Education for an Interdependent World* (New York: Teachers College Press).

Center for Civic Education. (2020) *National Standards for Civics and Government.* We the People (Calabasas, CA: Author) www.civiced.org.

Character Education: Markkula Center for Applied Ethics. (2021) With lesson plans "*a pro-con discussion of speech codes and free speech.*" www.scu.edu.

Eldersveld, S. J. and Walton, H., Jr. (2000) *Political Parties in American Society* (New York: Palgrave).

de Blij, H. J. (2009) *The Power of Place* (London: Oxford University Press).

Federal Election Commission (2020) Black Lives Matter PAC online, Global Network for Black Lives Matter, www.Blacklivesmatter.com.

Hearst Report (1987) *The American Public's Knowledge of the U.S. Constitution* (New York: Hearst Corporation).

Kendi, I. X. (2020) *Summary: How to Be an Antiracist* (New York: Knowledge Tree).

Kendi, I. X. (2017) *Stamped from the Beginning: The Definitive History of Racist Ideas in America* (New York: Bold Type Books).

Kennedy, P. (1986) *Rise and Fall of the Great Powers* (New York: Random House).

Loewen, J. W. (2007) *Lies My Teacher Told Me: Everything Your American History Textbook Got Wrong* (New York: The New Press).

Loewen, J. W. (2018) Sundown Towns: The Hidden Dimension of American Racism (New York: The New Press).

Lyons, S. R., and Arrington, T. S. (1990) *Who Votes and Why*, 3rd Ed. (New York: Taft Institute for Two Party Government).

Martell, C. C. (2020) *Teaching History for Justice: Centering Activism in Students' Study of the Past* (New York: Teacher's College Press).

Newman, M. and Zevin, J. (2017) *Geography as Inquiry* (Latham, MD., Rowman and Littlefield).

Parker, W. C. (ed.). (1996) *Educating the Democratic Mind* (Albany, NY: State University of New York Press).

Quigley, C. N. and Bahmueller, C. (eds.) (2007). *Civitas: A Framework for Civic Education*. (Calabasas, CA: Center for Civic Education).

Quigley, C. N. et al. (2017) *We the People*, 3rd ed. (Calabasas, CA: Center for Civic Education).

Scheidel, W. (2017) *The Great Leveler: Violence and the History of Inequality from the Stone Age to the Twenty-first Century* (Princeton, NJ: Princeton University Press).

Wallerstein, I. (1974, 1980, 1984) *The Modern World System*. 3 vols. (London: Methuen).

Teaching U.S. Government and Civics

BUILD YOUR OWN LESSON

The challenge: thinking 'on your feet.'

Interact with a new piece of evidence, data, issue, or problem.

Design a lesson of your own using different materials (newly discovered art, music, literature, history, geography, etc.).

Worry not about what you know, but react by thinking about how you would teach the data. Improvise!

Write a didactic, reflective, and affective goal for each document or picture, then add a low, medium, and high order question.

Choose one of the six strategies.

Pick a brief method of evaluating success (verbal, written, and tested).

What questions do the data support? Where do they fit in history?

What is the source and context: time and place? And how does that matter?

Did you find improvisation for the classroom easy or difficult? Why?

The Second Amendment

> "A WELL-REGULATED MILITIA, BEING NECESSARY TO THE SECURITY OF A FREE STATE, THE RIGHT OF THE PEOPLE TO KEEP AND BEAR ARMS, SHALL NOT BE INFRINGED."

How about a comprehension strategy for the 2nd Amendment to the U.S. Constitution? What does it actually say: Everyone can and should own a gun? Who is permitted to carry a gun? Who is not? What is meant by 'infringed,' exactly? Is the language clear?

DOI: 10.4324/9781003026235-20

PART

V

MULTIPLE MEDIA FOR MULTIPLE INTELLIGENCES IN THE SOCIAL STUDIES

9

TEACHING IN THE INTERNET AGE
Multiple Literacy for Many Media

"The real problem with humanity is that we have paleolithic emotions, medieval institutions, and godlike technology."

E. O. Wilson, 2009.

OVERVIEW

This chapter offers guidance for using the Internet to teach most aspects of social studies: print and Internet sources, visual and auditory, seeking alternative views and checking sources for authenticity. Everything's on the Web!

PASSIVE AND ACTIVE ROLES: INTRODUCTION

Like some fuzzy New Age music, it is often difficult to decide how social studies should adapt to the much-hyped electronic, website, blog, instant news era in which we live. The concept of *media* has been expanded to include a wide array of sources and technologies all competing for time in the classroom. In schools where funds are frequently short, it may be very difficult to decide what to buy and what to use. Vast assortments of blogs, websites, podcasts, dramatizations, history channel recreations, and serious scholarly sites make the bases of history are all documents, and some seem pretty dull. After all, the originals pretty much lie there and the images are still.

There is also the problem of content: what some authors refer to as *facts*. Older media, such as print, may seem boring to media-obsessed young adults. Newer media, such as streaming, blogs, podcasts, and webinars may be shaped for entertainment as much as or more than mere reflection. The newer media have added vast quantities of knowledge and material, creating the potential for information overload (IO).

Too much knowledge is being offered and with a speed that may be overwhelming to the average student and perhaps to us teachers as well.[1] Teachers should choose several media offerings from different views.

DOI: 10.4324/9781003026235-22

There is considerable evidence that many teachers are having trouble finding time for more than a few morsels of new media on the Internet, or conducting classes online with paper, podcasts, PowerPoint, and YouTube.[2] Clearly, there is great potential for using new media for content and communication, but there are also difficulties. Secondary and college faculty and students virtually rely on the Internet for information and communication.[3]

Remember that moving, animated media are much harder to analyze and reflect upon than stationery media. The way we use media in class raises a host of questions about our resources from documents to multimedia that might include the following:

- Should traditional teaching materials be supplanted by the Internet for data, insights, communication, and theory?
- Is there still a place for reading and lecture?
- Does technological change content, meaning, and message?
- Should simulations be offered as 'edutainment' or serious curriculum? Or should fun stuff be a supplement?
- Should students prepare research reports drawing on the Internet alone? How can plagiarism be controlled, and do we teachers have time to check students' suspiciously wonderful reports?
- Where do films, theater, music, and documentaries fit into the curriculum now that we have such easy access? How many times a week should teachers show a movie, video, a podcast, and which are most useful in promoting critical thought?
- Are students more or less able to discern reality from imagination, fact from fiction, history from propaganda?
- What should be done with older media such as literature and maps in developing class-room assignments and activities? What relationships ought to be developed between newer and older media?
- How do we introduce students to large and varied websites that require a roadmap to navigate, such as History Matters (www.historymatters.or) and American Memory (on the Library of Congress site, www.loc.gov)?
- How do we prepare for website student access so time is not wasted and higher order thinking develops?

In this chapter, you are offered ideas for using both 'still' and 'moving' media, textbooks, and primary sources as well as active websites, for an overall goal of provoking thought rather than compiling data. The value, motivation, and seductiveness of media will be explored within a framework of five general categories: (a) textbooks; (b) print sources for primary source documents; (c) still images: photographs, paintings, charts, and maps; (d) moving images, webinars, films, and sounds; and (e) interactive computer programs.

Recurring questions focus on audience suitability, narrator roles, medium of delivery, and message (yes, there is always a message!). The particular capabilities of each type of media will be analyzed and debated, with practical suggestions for secondary social studies.

Throughout this chapter, examples are offered to illustrate how media can be used to promote higher order thinking and stimulate student imagination. Always, we need to ask if what we are seeing, hearing, and reading is authentic, edited, or concocted. A bibliography of resources concludes the chapter, keeping in mind that media sometimes change rapidly, requiring almost continuous updating.

TO DO

Do you have any favorite historical dramas/films that you use in your classroom or that you like to watch? If you do, think of two or three examples, e.g., the civil war epic *Glory*. Choose two or three others that you might like to use. Decide those you consider most trustworthy, closest to the historical facts, and those most fanciful and farthest from the facts. How do you decide when moviemakers are being 'authentic,' faithful to history, and when they are inventing dramas to please a modern audience? Do you check sources?

Can a bad film be useful? How or how not?

PASSIVE AND ACTIVE ROLES IN THE MEDIATED SOCIAL STUDIES CLASSROOM

Didactic, Reflective, and Affective Goals

Media invite attention, but allow little input from viewers, listeners, or readers. In some instances, analysis is actually diminished or excluded by the emotional and ideological nature of the programs. Young people, and adults too, may be drawn into a drama, game, or music without much demand on thinking abilities. This is a kind of passive participation, far from an 'optimal flow of data,' in which audiences may make little or no contribution to the performance.[4]

People seeking entertainment who paid for it are usually interested in enjoyment, conceived largely as a sensual or emotional experience, rather than one that promotes reflection. Of course, nothing is inherently wrong in being entertained, but in a classroom setting educational goals should take first place. Primary Sources may not be as inviting as media, but are easier to deal with because they allow the viewer a good, long look or read. Perhaps not as entertaining as media, documents (including images, drama, literature, music, and scholarship) may be approached with greater deliberation and revisited.

Media need to be slowed down and broken apart to subject to the same kind of analysis as still life documents and images. But both are valuable and necessary to social studies instruction. On what platform or through which delivery system content is presented still faces all the usual problems of bias, truth, distortion, and outright fakery in history.

RESEARCH REPORT

A review of research concerning the effect of media on children and adolescents reinforces views that the media, particularly TV and films, and now media on the Internet, are critically influential in ways that promote product demand and commercialization of activities that we expect, but that frequently distorts history, politics, and economics. Presentations may be in a documentary style that blurs the distinction between fiction and nonfiction, with few audience members invited to check out the content. As a consequence, many adolescents believe in 'historical images' drawn from TV or films, rather than historical sources. However, although influential, the media do not seem to have a great deal of direct impact in terms of immediate behavior—that is, they do not necessarily result in spending, civic action, or gender-related action. Rather, media generally shape ways of thinking and imagining that influence on decisions at later points in time. Media are portrayed as 'fragmented and fighting' increasing the rationale for teaching media literacy.

TV, streaming, and radio (still here) present documentaries about people and places that are very engaging especially to young adults, and these could be 'test' cases for checking accuracy and historical truth.

Source: Strasburger, V. C. (2016) "Children, Adolescents and the Media: Ten Mistakes We've Made and How to Fix Them," *Clinical Pediatrics*, 55, 6, 509–512.

In a school setting, educational goals should take priority. However, entertainment may make a valuable contribution in motivating students to learn content, consider ideas, and practice skills. The educational/entertainment functions of a lesson must be balanced to serve didactic, reflective, and affective goals. In an age of 'docudramas' and 'edutainment' this is not always easy but we *must* try.

Particularly in social studies, Students need support in questioning and reflecting on their media experiences, most especially film, musical, Internet, and cell phone experiences. Powerful dramas and striking images may reinforce stereotypes or promote distorted identification with historical times and places. Many stories are shrewdly put together by producers and directors to heighten emotions and deliver propaganda, but teachers can use these disadvantages to promote critical thinking about how media are' fooling around' with us. This is a historical replay of the influence of 'snake oil salesmen' offering tonics to cure nearly everything. But what is the question: is it believable?

TO DO

Poll your colleagues or classmates about how much TV, phone websites, videos, and screen programs they watch during a typical week. Which are their favorite programs? Why? Are any of these historical or political or economic? Do they prefer fact or fiction or both? There are instant online polling surveys usable on Zoom or Google Meet or you can create your own.

Poll at least two groups of secondary students and ask them what TV or Internet news or views they trust most. Tabulate the results and calculate the average amount of TV time spent by each group. What percentage of time is spent over a week watching TV? Which shows are viewed as trustworthy and why? How many of these shows are entertainment and how many educational? Share your results with others! Ask students to think about potential agendas and biases, if any, expressed by photographers, artists, or historians, and how our beliefs and attitudes are formed. How do media influence the 'images in our minds,' the beliefs we hold about historical events and personality, i.e.:

- Have the media helped us to feel happy or sad about people, places, and events, and how have they have influenced us weakly or strongly?
- Is the image or document we all enjoyed true or is it hiding a bias?
- Does the program present more of a balanced or a biased message about an important social problem?
- Should we applaud a masterpiece that has touched our deepest emotions and most positive values, or worry about its power to mislead us?

- Should we write letters of protest to our local TV or radio station letting them know how offended we are by a recent program we hated, or ignore it as a necessary part of free speech?

Offer guidelines, a rubric, or criteria for students to judge the difference between fact and fiction in film. Can they define the differences between a documentary and a Hollywood creation, between a documentary and a docudrama, or between recorded oral history and an invented theater piece? If you feel really ambitious, select a few problematic films to view (*Reds, The American Dream, Rosie the Riveter, Hoffa, The Untold History of the U.S.*) and have students watch all or part of the films, then ask for sharp judgments about effects: bias, underlying values, implied politics, open preaching.

Narrator and Audience

The roles of narrator and audience are key to understanding textbooks, documents and media, on screen or off. Many of us lose track of author or creator and become the believing audience. Secondary students, much like their adult counterparts, frequently suspend judgment when they come into contact with media, particularly well-designed and effective presentations. With daily messaging rising to epic proportions, we all tend to postpone testing sources for truth and we 'buy it all.'

Enjoyment takes precedence over thoughtfulness, and the message or meaning of the presentation is absorbed uncritically. Using media, still or moving, is a major way of calling attention to performance goals and message by making the audience conscious of creators/writers/directors/producers and their roles in designing and authoring the script or image, Remember, in the arts and sciences as well as history, the *author* is the controller and chief influencer.

The audience, even the silent and passive, still plays a role in the drama. We all receive messages and develop visceral feelings about what we are reading or watching that leads to judgment, like it or not! Audiences soak up experiences, evaluating knowledge and feelings consciously or subconsciously. In an interactive setting, the audience plays a far more conscious role in making decisions by being drawn into the action. Both passive and active media require several degrees of reflection about story, and characters, and eventually the creator.

WHAT DO YOU THINK?

Some teachers suggest that media programs be preceded by 'advance organizers'. AO's are questions that guide note-taking and call attention to events, characters, speeches, sounds, and images as they move along screens or soundtracks. Which is preferable: beginning with questions, ending with questions, or guiding along?

Advance organizers can help students thoughtfully consider the role of narrator. The give and take of discussion and debate with students creating their own 'counter' narratives. Raising consciousness about the role of narrator encourages the power of interpretation. As students begin to think about narrators and creators, they may see themselves in that role and realize that the story-maker is infusing an account with their own views and attitudes. Teachers can help students construct their own narration of events, factual or fictional, or both. Information, for better or worse, is edited and filtered through a lens of personal and social values that shape accounts and artistic creations.

The sense or awareness of one's role as a creator—whether painter, narrator, photographer, author, inventor, artist, or filmmaker—is exactly what we seek for students in secondary social studies classrooms. A first step toward interpreting media is asking the question, "Who created this _____ and why?" From this beginning, you might call on students to create a series of products of their own by writing a script or an historical play, by re-creating characters in history, and by designing their own media presentation using PowerPoint and other classroom technologies that are available.[5]

RESEARCH REPORT

Digital History (www.digitalhistory.org) presents work on how families are presented in media. A recent essay indicates that family portrayal on television and in films generally reflects shifts in social values illustrating key issues of an historical period, e.g., ownership by women, the feminist movement, anti-racism, and Black Lives Matter. Women, in particular, are given a more prominent role since the 1970s as workers, economic partners, job seekers, and leaders. Digital History website is interesting for secondary student research on popular culture, a neglected subject in social studies.[6]

LET'S DECIDE!

Have you ever read or shown *Ragtime* by E. L. Doctorow, the well-known play about New York a century or so past? Is the story, made into a novel and film musical, true to history? Why did the author, decide to mix historical characters like Houdini, JP Morgan, and Emma Goldman, mixed in with fictional characters. Can we simply assign *Ragtime* as a unit on 19th century American history or can it raise other questions as well about class and race? Is a historical novel produced during the civil rights 1960s also history? Discuss this issue with at least three classmates and record your decisions.

Audience's Role

The role of audience is a second key concept in approaching and understanding media.

Audiences are usually thought of as consumers of programs and presentations, silent and smiling. They are the ones for whom the narrators created a product. An audience can be an individual, a particular group, a gathering, an assembly, a nation, or even the world. Students are our audience, but can also be teachers, playing interchangeable roles. Audiences may be seeking a pleasurable experience: satisfaction, entertainment, fun, and catharsis.

Others may be seeking information to accomplish practical goals. Some may be seeking intellectual stimulation—ideas and techniques to think about problems. A number may be seeking personal growth, self-enhancement, and/or a moral vision. Every audience reads the 'signals,' but may not be ready to interpret a program by reading the creator's signs and symbols to achieve a deeper understanding. Audience and actress/actors can change roles at will, and it is creative for students to play teacher and teachers to play student.[7]

Many audiences prefer to remain passive (the silence of Zoom), perhaps absorbing the narrator or actor's messages while anonymous. Others prefer involvement, making suggestions, and shaping both the content and style of a presentation. For example, sports can involve many levels of participation from sitting at home at the TV munching snacks, through applauding and cheering attending a live game, to getting out there and playing. The active or passive nature of an audience influences a narrator's creation, players have a much more involved experience than spectators.

Furthermore, an audience can also shape the narrator's view of popularity. What works with certain audiences helps the creator or producer understand their situation growing out of social class; political and moral beliefs; ethnicity, age, and gender; education; as well as tastes, customs, preferences, and culture. Assumptions, correct or incorrect, may be made on both sides, with a narrator constructing media for an intended audience, while the audience has constructed an image of what they expect from the narrator, producer, director, etc.[8]

Frequently, age, social class, and economics produce a set of expectations leaving audiences divided, some participating in certain media forms, like conservative news, that the others will pass over. Experienced teachers approaching 'young' students can turn prejudices around, like introducing old films like Charlie Chaplin's *Modern Times* to work in our favor. Uninformed students may be quite surprised by old media forms.

Popular songs, one old and one new on the same topic, may be the basis for a provocative social studies discussion that bridges the generation gap. You can also widen the concept of audience by providing students with one of your favorite 'old' songs, a springboard to another time (but familiar emotions?), asking students to suggest a match with one of their current favorites. Find out where your students are coming from and share where you are coming from—an even exchange.

TO DO

Select a popular civil war song (e.g.. *Battle Hymn of the Republic*) that you think would make a great discussion starter. Think of it as a historical document, as a primary or secondary source. What questions would you ask about it? How does it reflect its time? Now select a really old song (e.g., *Dixie*) on the same topic. Think of questions that draw analogies to songs and history, and how about national anthems as a world history unit?

Combining Roles

A last step in thinking about audience and actress/actor is to combine the roles in considering any text, work of art, music, literature, history, or social science. Questions about audiences and narrators may be applied to media from print and paintings through music and film to websites and simulations.

Purpose and style influence our perceptions. For instance, narrators may tightly control a story, game, or image making everything predictable and safe, and boring. An audience with strong biases can shape a narrator's product conforming almost totally to expectations, so there is only one answer, and few disturbing questions Other creators of images and documents may seek to disturb, infuriate, provoke, and stimulate, offering historical dramas that attack current prejudices. Audiences may react by rejecting messages or by opening their minds to new interpretations, or both. Some audiences may even break out of the commonly accepted molds of tradition and changing views about the minimum wage or who matters. Narrator and audience are deeply connected and interactive, a yin and yang of overlapping goals and interplay of ideas neither of which exist without the other, a circle of mutual knowledge and comprehension.[9]

TO DO

Do you like to stick with tradition or try something new? Would you include Native American speeches? Would you assign West African epics, like the story of Sundiata; might you tell the Ramayana story from India of love between the God Rama and Sita?

Get together with a few classmates or colleagues and develop your own list of the kinds of media (e.g., graphic novels, poster art, interviews on video, podcasts) and develop this for classes, pick the courses and topics.

Media, Meaning, and Message

Contrary to Marshall McLuhan's famous dictum that "the medium is the message,"[10] is quite wrong for social studies; messages really count whatever the medium.

Information in Media

All messages require interpretation and attention to bias at some level. Political and historical sources call for more caution than average.

Even didactic messages, simple lists of facts, dates, names, and places, can cause problems because the audience must have a way of understanding the data for long-term memory. Classifying, sorting, organizing, and labeling data give meaning to what would otherwise be a confusing mass of largely useless information, like names of Turkish Sultans. Of course, classifications can also lead to trouble if the categories are fuzzy, overlap, or contain biases.

For instance, the debate over what constitutes Western civilization often focuses on definitions either too rigid or too loose. Must we always begin with the ancient Greeks? What of the Hebrews, the Sumerians, the Hittites? Can none of these be considered Western? Just what is Western and what is Eastern or non-Western? Definitions, vocabulary, can be applied to new information, but may collapse as new interpretations emerge, i.e., the East and the West have always been a neatly divided invention rather than a series of meeting grounds.

LET'S DECIDE

Media come with labels people use to define tastes and identities, e.g., research definitions in music: Country and Western, Rock & Roll, Soft Rock, Hard Rock, Heavy Metal,

Soul, World Beat, Classical, Jazz, Blues, Hip Hop, Rap, Reggae, and so on. But which categories have meaning? Ask a group of students to define each category and decide on examples that could be taught in history classes.

Reflection in Media

Messages may also be intellectual or reflective—that is, aimed at improving thinking. These messages offer explanations and evidence that help us understand phenomena: people and events. Data are still important, but meaning is derived from of formal or informal logic as we begin to understand correlations, causes, and consequences. Determine how events are connected, which steps lead to a conclusion, and what changes produce significant effects.

In economics, we may learn that low supplies of a product coupled with high demand cause prices to rise. We can apply this rule to wheat, corn, rice, orange juice, computer chips, basketball tickets, cell phones, anything in a market system. Meaning depends on how well supply and demand are interpreted in relation to price. Note that messages involving reasoning assume that the audience *already* has a grasp of basic definitions (which is not always so), and that data are available. Does a pandemic change economic rules, effects, costs?

Strong feelings on both sides may prevent understanding of or agreement on the message's meaning, or lead to serious misinterpretations. An ideal is an attempt to understand or empathize with different even disturbing opinions. This is often easier said than done, getting to an agreement. It may be more realistic to approach opposing views as part of a continuum, a variety of approaches possible, not simply two sides. Getting to YES is not easy.

TO DO

Select two different posters or ads for the same product (cars, phones, pizza) and check out the line of reasoning (if any) used to sell the product. Is the appeal price, efficiency, durability, or emotional, safety, family? How is meaning conveyed in each ad? Are leaders sold like pizza or by different appeals?

Impact may be diminished if the audience or narrator uses neutral, technical or ideological language, or sharp exaggerations.[11]

TO DO

Pick an issue or controversy (was Columbus genocidal towards natives?), then seek examples of what the opposition thinks. Force yourself to study this material, comparing it to the position you favor. Can you stand in another's shoes? Have you changed your attitude toward the other side as a result? When planning a lesson, will you present both sides fairly, or give more attention to views you favor?

Values in Media

Explicitly or implicitly, affective messages are built into most messages and invite judgments from an audience.

Beliefs (deeply held values) are the deepest and most profound sort of 'sale' to an audience. Values may range from advertisements asking you to purchase a product to demands for immediate action on a serious social issue. Messages range from sales pitches to blatant political propaganda; from simple slogans and common clichés to artful subliminal symbols, and carefully polished arguments.

For example, a powerful artistic film can achieve an emotional hold on an audience through clever combinations of images, actions, characters, and music. Audiences must be wary of both an author/narrator's purposes and methods, sorting and weighing facts, judging arguments, and evaluating emotions. Facts offered by a narrator must always be checked out (can we find time?). The reasoning employed must be carefully and critically evaluated for logic and fairness. Otherwise we may jump to weak or false conclusions that collapse with the first criticism.

TO DO

Find Internet political cartoons (e.g., www.cagle.com) that really got your attention! Consider questions as you read the content:

What images is the site offering? Who is the probable audience? Do you regard the ad as likely to be effective or ineffective and why? Does the cartoon you chose promote reason and choice, or draw you in through emotions? Why believe one advertisement, but reject others?

PRINT MEDIA STAND STILL FOR SOCIAL STUDIES

Fiction and Nonfiction: Literature, News, and Views

Print media, documents, posters, art, photographs, cartoons, etc., are a basic diet in social studies, however presented online or on paper.

These appear in a variety of formats, including newspapers, journals, magazines, pamphlets, and books. Readers usually hold the pages in some format and scan them for information, feelings, reasons, and judgments. Some formats, print or electronic tablets, encourage personal involvement and deep study; others like cell phones encourage rapid viewing and quick decisions.

Traditionally, we distinguish between fiction and nonfiction in print media.[12] Fiction usually encompasses products of the imagination. The narrator or author is the inventor of a story that does not require proof, footnotes, or references. A major goal of fiction is to entertain, interpret, and engage our interest. Nonfiction encompasses research composed of observation, analysis, and conclusions. A major goal of nonfiction is to inform and educate the reader as truthfully as possible about people, places, and events. The author or narrator of nonfiction is a compiler and reporter basing conclusions on real sources.

Categories of fiction and nonfiction are used to determine genres and classify print media. For purposes of social studies and history education, however, this neat and clean distinction causes problems. First, there is the problem of deciding what is real and what is imagined, what is fact and what is opinion. A work of imagination, for instance, is also a product of a particular time, place, and culture just as much as a work of nonfiction. Modern media tend to blend these into recreations, facsimiles, role-plays, and docudramas, like *Downton Abbey*.[13] Although based on factual evidence, these are dramatic reenactments partially driven by researched content and partially by entertainment values.

Narrators (e.g., historians and historical fiction writers) have goals and intentions that shape the content and the message they wish to convey. In other words, all writers have values and beliefs, and these are expressed in their works regardless of whether they are acknowledged. Many well-known and beloved novelists use their art to promote social causes or attack social problems. George Orwell (*1984*) and Aldous Huxley (*Brave New World*) are two are obvious examples of social criticism disguised as science fiction.

Many nonfiction works are subject to similar goals, for example, biographies that seek either to enshrine or demonize their subject. Consider *Frederick Douglass: Prophet of Freedom* by David Blight, and Robert Caro's treatment of Lyndon Johnson. Social scientists and historians, as serious scholars, generally explain their intentions, methods, and positions so a reader will know where they are coming from and judge their research accordingly. However, clarity is not always the case with either form.[14]

Author/narrators draw on historical sources for inspiration and scholarship, news and views. Their works are supposed to be based on evidence, proof, and verification. We should be able to check details against other sources to verify or reject conclusions and judge arguments. In some cases, the authors of historical novels may have done as much or better historical research than their professional counterparts, and may be as good or better than a historian at picturing a time and place. However, historians or social scientists may write so well, and use such charming similes and metaphors, that interpretations of data are obscured by work is as entertaining and emotionally satisfying as efforts by literary cousins. Thus, lines of demarcation blur!

Nonetheless, students must understand that good research is still and will likely always be based on references, sources, and footnotes—in short, on solid homework and a well-developed bibliography of supporting material. This is critically important to classroom work that helps students verify and test historical and scientific conclusions, particularly as presented in textbooks, even those by noted experts in their fields.

Otherwise, why believe what any author says or tells us? In a work of fiction, by contrast, no such constraints apply; history can be made and remade, told and retold, to make a point, dramatize an event, or preach a moral. However, a writer of fiction must follow rules of plausibility, consistency, and context if the work is to make sense. Therefore, the distance is short between style and data, fiction, and nonfiction, with borrowings on all sides.

TO DO

Select a work of historical fiction or nonfiction by a popular YA author, like *Flygirl* by Sherri Smith or *The Astonishing Life of Octavian Nothing: Traitor to the Nation* by M. T.

Anderson, and write a book review noting purpose, style, organization, characters, and historical sources. Be critical!

Within social studies teaching, the vital difference between fiction and nonfiction is the degree and quality of proof that is offered. Standards for excellence are different between literature and social science, between poetry and history. However, any work of art or science can be judged on the basis of solid evidence backing up assertions and conclusions. Common Core calls for students differentiating fact from opinion, evidence from interpretation. Much like the sciences, social studies is all about the real and authentic evidence.

Social studies, particularly history, fiction, and nonfiction, can illustrate the past and bring it to life. Many important facts flow from works of fiction that provides social meaning or historical recreation of a time and place, and many important values can be gleaned from works of nonfiction. As teachers we need to build student awareness of author intention and assess quality and quantity of research in any work: literature, newspapers, poetics, even historians' scholarship. Fiction and nonfiction can be woven into a rich tapestry for students that simultaneously engages students' interests and intellects. But evidence must in the long run be scientifically verifiable. Agreed?

WHAT DO YOU THINK?

Can a work of fiction or film provide historical insights? Do works of imagination offer clues to the values and beliefs of other times and places? Do stories tell us something about the time, place, and culture that produced them? Make a list of books, novels, biographies, or autobiographies vivid in your memory. Write down a few reasons that you think these books and movies made a strong impression.

PRIMARY SOURCES

Primary sources are accounts narrated by first-hand witnesses (as far as we can tell) to the events described. These works are usually straightforward narratives describing what happened from an observer's point of view. The author or picture maker or documentary director is reporting and commenting on the events of the day, sometimes with an eye to history and at other times simply to record events. Usually a primary source is a message describing an event and/or making an argument. The author may, of course, have a point of view that must be taken into account when forming opinions.

Sources that can be cross-checked against other contemporaneous accounts are generally more trustworthy than those that provide the only source of information. The more an account is consistent, comprehensible, and unbiased, the greater its reliability. Beware the author 'selling' a particular (and the 'only true' or 'dramatically faithful') interpretation of events, leaving the reader to separate fact from interpretation. Help students test for truth based on details, consistency, and author bias.[15] Basic standards of judgment involve the degree to which an author is reliable (fits with what we know from other sources) and valid (appears logical and reasonable).

Literary Sources

Literary and film sources are works of imagination, fiction writing, primary and second-ary, reflecting an author's view of people, places, and events.

These works of imagination are often expressed in a personal style designed to make a point or engender a feeling. Words convey emotions and values through characters, signs, and symbols as well as descriptions. Fiction is believable depending on how well the author does her homework, portrays characters, develops the plot, and expresses concepts through the mouths of his cast. The skill an author applies to achieve artistic and emotional goals may be judged by aesthetic and storytelling criteria.

From a social science point of view, the words used and style may provide information about standards of beauty and insights into what people saw as entertaining or pleasing at a given point in time. In addition to using internal criteria, we can also evaluate a work based on external history—other works or precedents and against the standards of the par-ticular time, place, and culture. Historical novels, re-creations of the past, may be assessed on the basis of faithfulness to sources and fidelity to the era. To judge a work, you must know both the history and styles of the time, comparing both to present interpretations. The script for the film *Lincoln* by Steven Spielberg can be profitably compared to Lincoln's own writing, keeping in mind that each is an original of its time.

Scholarly Sources

Scholarly sources are secondary sources based on research on primary, literary, and other secondary sources.

Authors usually develop hypotheses or theories about people, places, and events based on a thorough review of available evidence, footnoting to support their interpretations. Assumptions are identified as much as possible, and research methods are laid out in detail to use in judging conclusions. Scholars demonstrate proof by describing both their sources and rules for drawing conclusions. Historians, for example, should be clear about their sources and their degree of trustworthiness and truth.

Readers may judge a scholarly work by evaluating the author's goals and theories, sup-porting data, research methods, and conclusions. Scholarship is not often seen as recrea-tional reading because it requires attention to the way in which data support a chain of reasoning. Research can be complex and sometimes confusing because theory, goals, data, methods, and conclusions must all be factored into the final work.

But it is through research that we can decide which sources, documents, news reports, films, and literature are most accurate, trustworthy, believable, beautiful, and emotionally satisfying. Primary sources provide eyewitness accounts, images, and literature that draw you into an imaginative experience, but scholarship takes you into the realm of critical thinking, looking for proof.

Current Events/News Sources

Now that we have nearly worldwide electronic transmission, news is reported more quickly and distributed more efficiently than at any time in history, repeated over and over.

The author (reporter) may actually be at a base of operations when filing the story. News is an eyewitness document for classroom purposes, but presents some problems.

News stories are influential but subject to all of the problems that plague historical documents generally, including questions of accuracy, corroboration, and bias. News also presents difficulties that historical documents generally do not because it is fast-moving, developing every day, and often very political in contrast to still documents that may be studied at leisure, researched, checked, and revisited.[16]

News is almost instantaneous now on iPhones, iPads, and apps, offering little or no clear research basis or source or even author. Many news programs currently available quite openly present a biased view of events, and many self-censor, mixing in film clips, content, and quotes available on other channels. In many societies, governments may monitor programs and demand editing. For example, compare an American, Canadian, British (BBC widely available), or Al Jazeera TV news program to notice rather sharp differences in reporting events.

RESEARCH REPORT

How Students Engage with News

The Pew Research Center's Project for Excellence in Journalism report Project Information Literacy focused on three questions:

1. How do students conceptualize what constitutes 'news' and how do they keep up, if they can?
2. How do students interact with and experience news when using social media networks?
3. How do students determine the currency, authority, and credibility of news content they encounter from both traditional news sites and new media sites?

A summary of findings concluded that: "Most significantly, this study's findings suggest the news diet of young news consumers is both multi-modal and multi- social; news comes from their peers and professors about as much as from social media platforms during a given week. Most students know a free press is essential in a democracy, and, yet, the deep political polarization occurring in this country has made them suspicious of biased reporting. Some question the proliferation of 'fast news'—oversimplified and fragmentary coverage spewed across social media platforms. And, for many, engaging with news has become hard work, requiring students to evaluate everything they hear or read for truth and objectivity, whether it's from a Facebook post, a conversation with a friend, or a news tweet on their smartphones.

The News: Study Report (October 16, 2018) and Pew Research Center, Pew Trust, www/stateofthe-media.org. The Drum, top global media consumption trends for 2021, www.thedrum.com.

News reports may be difficult to check or analyze except on the basis of plausibility. Furthermore, a news reporter 's affiliation may shape their view of the world, adding or filtering out items important to us, or other people in other places. When using a news report, we must ask whether the report is giving accurate facts that can be compared to other accounts, and whether the reporter's viewpoint is free from ideology (party allegiance) or prejudice. Because all people have deeply held convictions and emotions, these may color their descriptions of events.

The same set of facts may be reported in different ways on different channels. Sometimes important details are omitted, at other times unimportant details are included. We might also ask whether the author's style and wording affect our interpretation of events. Reporters and editors may, consciously or subconsciously, use 'loaded' words in descriptive reports, making it hard for readers to separate story from interpretation. Many reporters explain their purposes to readers, but many tell their tale with hidden agendas.

The explainers are usually seen as more trustworthy, particularly in these days of rapid communication. Regardless, it is vitally important for teachers and students to critique and carefully analyze the words and images used in news reports. "All the news that's fit to print" may contain biases, inaccuracies, and hearsay accounts that raise questions about believability. News, like other print media, past or present, must be analyzed and criticized; but the good news is that this type of careful reading is just the ticket to instill historical habits of mind and critical thinking into student experiences.

Still Life with Meaning: Reading Images from Past and Present Reality and Imagination

Social studies is greatly enriched by art and photography to teach about past and present. Art includes objects, artifacts, maps, charts, graphs, paintings, sculpture, and other moving and nonmoving media. Images, in particular, open up many possibilities for classroom interpretation and discussion, even if reading levels are poor.

Images are powerful tools in gaining students' attention and capturing their interest. Inherently attractive images can be seen, touched, and stir the imagination. Still images have several advantages in classrooms, the first of which is they don't move and can therefore be studied carefully and in great detail. Of course, you need ideas and techniques for making sense of images, and methods are readily available. Images provide insights into places and cultures that words cannot easily convey. Students can immerse themselves in another time and place by looking at paintings, sculptures, artifacts, and photographs.[17] Pictures put flesh on the bones of history and life, offering students, especially poor readers, the chance to gain insights difficult to obtain from written sources. Finally, images are dramatic and colorful, adding visualization to many historical documents, and scholarly works are not.

Sources particularly visuals develop mental images or pictures of people, places, and events in the mind. However, thoughtful selection is vital, because we usually have time for a sample, no more, and because some sources may promote stereotypes or inaccurate views. The advantages of images also create disadvantages as well. The static nature, power, and drama, if uncritically accepted, interpretation of events can lead to questionable or false conclusions. In some cases, images are so powerful that they have become icons of the past, clichés that we fail to take seriously or reinterpret.[18]

Therefore, like print media, images must be viewed, understood, analyzed, and interpreted. Interpretations are facilitated when additional written, visual, or auditory materials are used to supplement and verify conclusions. Images of the same or related subjects can also be compared and contrasted to build hypotheses and strengthen conclusions. In other words, a sample of images can give us a range of evidence to draw from that a single image simply can't provide. Just as we need two or more eyewitnesses to corroborate an event, we need several images to support an insight or interpretation.

TO DO

What are the subjects of Figures 9.1 and 9.2? What theme can you invent to teach for both? Are there similarities? What about differences? What story does each tell about social conditions? Are social classes presented? How can you tell? Can you explain the attitude of each artist to the subjects? Can you use these images in a lesson?

Tempted as we are to think of the arts as corresponding to fiction and photography to nonfiction, this distinction is not very useful for social studies. Photography may be just as artistic (and fictional) as painting because the creators of both have their own styles and purposes. Artists and photographers are using reality and precedent (works of earlier artists) as a base and source of inspiration giving us a visual invention of past, present, or future.[19]

Data are collected in ways that are realistic or imaginative, literal or figurative, or a mixture. Artists are usually seen as having more freedom to imagine but with digital photography, the potential for manipulating images is now virtually unlimited. A painted or photographed portrait, for example, may convey how someone looks, but may also be subtly shaded, controlled, colored, cut, and posed to create a particular feeling about a figure.

The image might suggest time period, social status, personality, or beliefs, giving us clues to interpret. Sometimes a creation is so clever that we are unaware of being manipulated by the author/artist. Even amateur painters and photographers convey feelings and send messages, purposely or inadvertently, through their lenses and drawings. With the Internet, teachers can juxtapose images, ancient and modern, suggesting comparison, or

Figure 9.1: "Laid Off." Photograph by Benjamin Disinger on Unsplash.

Figure 9.2: **Life of Immigrants, Lower East Side, New York. Photograph by Jacob Riis from his book *How the Other Half Lives* (1890).**

lift competing timelines, suggesting that dates are artificial, or for revenge, place a student's head in a French revolutionary guillotine.

As always we must be careful when using images to draw conclusions about people, times, and places. Remind our students to remember that images were created for a purpose and have probably been shaped, posed, and presented in ways designed to influence attitudes and conclusions. Art and photography are marvelous ways of enhancing our historical understanding, but must be viewed as evidence open to interpretation and revision. Students need help to develop techniques for analyzing images, to supplement documents and scholarly works. Pictures and photographs build a more complete sense of people and places. Concrete examples of art, artifact, and photography follow with suggestions for classroom applications.

SAMPLE LESSON PLAN (USING WORLD WAR I PHOTO)

Photographs can be very striking, but we forget to ask whether they are candid or posed. Because pictures may lead us to important conclusions about events, how the image was made may be a serious issue. The photograph in Figure 9.3 dates from World War I. What questions would you ask before you used it in a lesson? How would the answers change the ongoing use of a photograph? Is war fun?

Figure 9.3: Death in the Trenches. Battlefield photo by an anonymous WWI photographer.

Interpreting Historical Figures

Paintings of historical figures are rich sources of insight into past and present eras. Portraits encourage discussion of personality and artistic style, pose, dress, ornament, facial expression, placement, mood, color scheme, and more. Students put a face to a name, giving historical personalities meaning and a clearer identity. Too many students don't even know what the most famous folks looked like! Art communicates context in ways that words alone may not. For instance, a teacher tells a class about Napoleon Bonaparte's achievements and downfall, but it is quite another to see paintings of Napoleon as a citizen rebel, general, first consul, and then emperor. These evoke a style and grandeur that testify to his power and the French fascination with their great leader. Pictures like Napoleon's evoke power, social class, political leadership, and sometimes criticism and satire.[20]

Portraits may also raise questions about authenticity.[21] We often take for granted that pictures in books or online are from the time and place we are studying, but that is not always true. Students with an appreciation for art and an understanding of styles may be able to detect anachronisms when these appear. For example, nearly every history textbook includes a picture of Christopher Columbus, but none of these is authentic because all were painted after his death. Some texts admit this, whereas others say nothing at all about sources, implying accuracy. Students who want to discover more about how Columbus was portrayed could work together to research historical paintings, collecting examples and carefully recording dates and artists for contrast or comparison. Nice idea? They might discover that his features and dress vary considerably depending on the nationality and the period of the artist. Columbus portraits offer an opportunity to discuss the problems of historical research and the era of European exploration. Other historical figures (Cleopatra, Genghis Khan) could easily be subjects for integrating art and history nicely into your classroom.

SAMPLE LESSON PLAN (USING ROYAL FIGURES)

How did this artist want to portray British King Charles II (see Figure 9.4)? Is he kingly? How do you know a king when you see one? Why is King Charles armored? Why is he carrying a baton? What is the meaning of the wig, cross, and the crown? Would you see him as a leader? Why or why not?

Using Photographs in a Social Studies Classroom

Photographs may be used as sources of information about history, just as you might use a painting or document, focusing on details, symbols, pose, and overall design.[22]

You might consider how an image was processed, use of light and shadow, pose and setting. Encourage students to think of drawing, paintings, and photographs as valuable historical documents, including their own family. Ask them to bring in family/vacation photos to construct their own story or family history. If time permits, students could

Figure 9.4: Etching of Charles II, King of England.

construct a vacation story or family history from the photographs. They may be surprised at how many people and places they do not recognize or are unsure about as time passes. Alas, the memory is weak, which is exactly why we, as good historians, label and care for our photographs like two from my own family, shown in Figures 9.5a and 9.5b. Think about how much we can learn about family and history from old photos and think about a family photo to show.

Figure 9.5:   a (top) and b (bottom) Family photographs: A portrait and a wedding.

Photographs can also be used for analysis and interpretation of the photographer's viewpoint.[23] Photographs serve aesthetic and social or political and business purposes. Students need to develop sensitivity to a photographer's goals and styles, including their own.

TO DO

In Figures 9.5a and 9.5b, what can you learn about past clothing styles? Can styles date pictures? Why or why not? How would you date these two pictures?

Why photograph someone alone or as a couple? What stories do photos tell? Which photo was probably taken first? Are multiple narratives possible? Why are the subjects posed ? Create a narrative for these photos?

Invite analysis and comparison of photos; pictures may be organized into categories *illustrious* and *anonymous* people emphasizing a group vs. individual portraits from a variety of times, places, and photographers. Daguerreotypes from the Matthew Brady collection make a fine introduction to portrait styles.[24] Portraits can be analyzed for clues to social status, religion, technology, psychology (self-consciousness), attitudes, dress, and cultural values. How people *want* to appear and how the photographer *presents* them may be in conflict.

With careful observation, you may find evidence of a desire to appear important or to communicate status or an emotion, like love. For example, during most of the 19th and early 20th centuries, broad smiles and direct eye contact were frowned on as immodest and self-important. Many people were purposely posed in partial profile, looking away from the viewer, averting or lowering their eyes. Photographers, painters, and cartoonists shaped these poses based on the prevailing social values. Now we value shots where everyone appears or is made to appear as happy as possible, smile, say cheese! But we are still posing and directing people, shaping images to conform to *our* prevailing customs and sensibilities.

Photographs can also be used to raise debate of the problem of verification in history and social science. Because all photographs grow out of a historical context and are taken by fallible witnesses, we might question their accuracy and meaning. Photos in particular are often viewed as 'true' as opposed to paintings, though the style and view of the photographer can be as artsy and edited as a painter. Have these been retouched, faked, or altered to change our view to reflect a specific point of view. Is a photo political, like Stalin ordering comrades airbrushed out of his portraits until he alone remains?

Given the unlimited possibilities offered by digital photography on cells or cameras, these questions will become more complex as both historical and contemporary images may be altered in any way desired. Assign students to take digital portraits and draw comparisons with the archives available for American history, creating their own historical records. Now we have the ability to do much more sophisticated manipulations of materials, adding, subtracting, and reshaping. So, how will we be able to authenticate historical accuracy?

SAMPLE LESSON PLAN (MATHEW BRADY'S CIVIL WAR PHOTOGRAPHS)

Employ Brady war photos below (see Figs. 9.6a and 9.6b), raising questions about both his overt and covert purposes and beliefs. For instance, was Brady simply trying to show the facts of war or was he editorializing about the Civil War in particular, and war in general, anti-war or pro-war? Were the photos natural, taken just as they were, or rearranged to dramatize aspects of war? Did Brady glorify war or show it as hellish and brutal? How could you use photos, contrasting the parade with the battlefield, the glory of going to war with the results for the grim reaper? Make up a plan of your own. How can you decide an artist's open or hidden goals?

Art as Artifact

The arts may be used as archeological artifacts that tell us about a time and place. The pictures may be discussed from an aesthetic point of view involving color, texture, shape, size, structure, but also in terms of symbolic meaning, function, status, context, economic well-being, and cultural values. Coins offer many possibilities for discussion (as we noted in Chapter 7) on design and the symbols. You do something as simple as ask a student to find an old quarter out of her pocket then decode its signs and symbols. Do you know the origins of the eagle symbol and the meaning of object the eagle is holding? Why the wreath and what does 'e pluribus unum' mean? Is that English?

Figure 9.6:   (a): Parade at the beginning of the U.S. Civil War. (b): Dead soldiers on a Civil War battlefield.

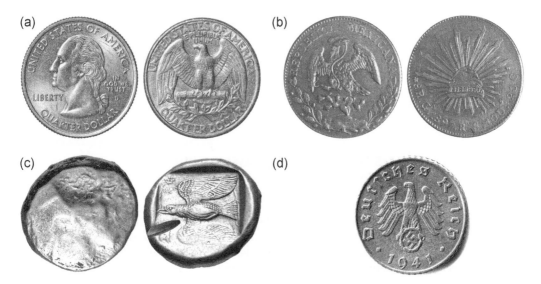

Figure 9.7: Eagle coins past and present. (a) U.S. quarter. (b) Mexican 50 centavos. (c) Ancient Greek eagle. (d) German Republick eagle coin.

Questions:

Why eagles?
Why the tradition of birds of prey as symbols?
Why place eagles on widely used money?

You could go further and set up a comparison of Roman, Medieval, and modern eagle coins, noting differences and similarities in the design and messages. Look at other artistic products: vases and urns (ancient Greek vases make great discussion items); sculptures and statues (Remington's work is an exciting introduction to the Wild West); or arms and armor (Medieval European, Samurai, and Islamic outfits stimulate interesting comparisons). Often museums and galleries have teacher's guides and packets available for purchase or go to online exhibits for classroom use. Large museums offer reproductions of historical items, Egyptian statues, or Mesopotamia cylinder seals, useful as tactile and visual springboards for discussion.

Art and Material Culture as Aesthetic

Art and artifacts are part of a material culture, and have an almost unlimited potential for use in the social studies classroom, making for livelier and more colorful discussions.[25] Material culture is art, and even lowly industrial objects like spoons, knives, cups, machinery, bathroom contraptions, etc., can be interesting and offer insight to lifestyles past and present. Do your own mysteries by bringing in ordinary objects, old and new, into your own classroom, spur discussion of technological, scientific, and stylistic change. The fine arts offer clues to interpreting a time and place based on materials and design. As still images, the fine arts permit slow, careful analysis and thus quiet reflection on the past. Each image can be viewed overall and in great detail, thereby becoming more familiar and understandable. If you regularly include art and artifacts in your lessons, students will become comfortable with learning how to look and will begin to develop insights into the meanings and messages of artists with an appreciation of styles and techniques. Students may develop a sense of the times from artists' styles and subjects, learning to recognize individual artists' work. Students will also be able to date and place a work based on color, texture, subject, goal, and social setting.

SAMPLE LESSON PLAN (MATERIAL CULTURE/ TWO INDUSTRIAL ARTIFACTS)

Artifacts are not all ancient (see Figures 9.8a and 9.8b). Are your students able to tell you about this industrial object? What was it made from? Would this provide a clue about its time? What it was used for? Does the shape provide any clues? Are modern objects more or less difficult to identify? Is it more difficult to identify an object when it isn't in context? Why? Does material culture provide insight into historical change?

TO DO

As you wander around a museum, take note of possibilities for American or world history, civics, and economics lessons. Begin your own collection of slides, posters, and reproductions for classroom use. Take a good close look at paintings like *Washington Crossing the Delaware*, or *Guernica*.

Maps, Charts, and Graphs

Maps, charts, and graphs online or on paper are rich and compact sources of data for social studies and history. Maps and charts condense a large amount of information onto a page

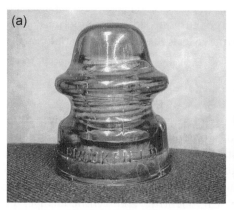
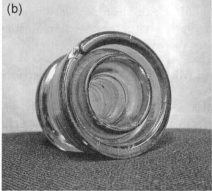

Figure 9.8: **(a): Photograph of a 'mystery' industrial object: Purpose undetermined (top view). (b) This is a wire insulator used on utility poles from the early 20th century (side view).**

or two provoking numerous student hypotheses and interpretations. Each map, chart, or graph is a complex visualization of myriad observations and a great deal of research. Maps, for example, can communicate enormous amounts of data succinctly, including settlement patterns, topography, climate, environment, political boundaries, economics, and even mental knowledge. Social studies students should be comfortable with maps and charts because these are part of daily life in classes, key assists to historical and geographic knowledge.

Statistics and maps are frequently offered as evidence in support of assertions or to attack claims.[26] Increasingly, publishers, newspaper columnists, and political leaders employ maps, charts, and graphs to make points with the public. The assumption is that the public can comprehend a chart, graph, or map, but that is not always true. Even when the information is intelligible to the audience, charts and graphs, in particular, have an aura of truth about them. A graph accepted as accurate by viewers and readers, may pass without much criticism, like unemployment figures. Herein lies a vital role for social studies instruction: teaching students how to critically read and interpret rich, condensed visual representations, statistics, charts, graphs, tables, figures, and maps.[27]

The richness and complexity of maps, graphs, and charts is a problem for many teachers and students because they must make sense of numbers, signs, and symbols to interpret information.[28] The more abstract and symbolic a visual representation is, the longer it takes most students to understand. Conversely, a more realistic and concrete representation is usually easier to understand. Abstractness versus concreteness can be used as two poles along a scale that can be used to predict probable difficulty levels for students.

For instance, an easy map might contain topographic information only (mountains, rivers, plains, forests) shown photographically or in drawings. A difficult map might include three, four, or five major factors with political boundaries crossing topographic features, and weather patterns in isobars running across the face of the landscape. This multifaceted map may morph or change with time in a computer display, confusing a large percentage of students, particularly beginners with low-level skills. Interpreting a complex map, a time changing map, takes close attention, but the rewards are great because, in the process, students will extract much information and learn *how* to read a map, graph, or chart, viewing change across time, then drawing useful conclusions.[29]

We hope that once students learn how to read a map or chart they will transfer skills to other maps and charts, becoming more comfortable with abstract visuals. Assist students in constructing a visual representation of their own, a treasure map, or their neighborhood, actually drawing in landmarks and stores. Provide students with statistical information to convert into a table, or you could provide them with the results of a study that they might convert into bar, pie, or line graphs. Creating graphs is even easier if a computer program is available.

If you are really ambitious, ask students to draw maps using a computer-generated program like GIS, using an agreed-on symbol system, key, or legend for cities, towns, topography, etc., as it is technically called in geography. An aerial photograph of a region from Google Maps, for instance, might serve as the basis for a mapping exercise. Direct them to draw maps that are realistic—a tree symbol standing for a forest of 20 square miles and a few snow-capped mountains standing for a chain. As students gain skills, these features can be shown as green shadings and colors. In addition to a mastery of geography, students will understand the concepts of correspondence and representation: how symbols serve as a metaphor of imagination and reality.

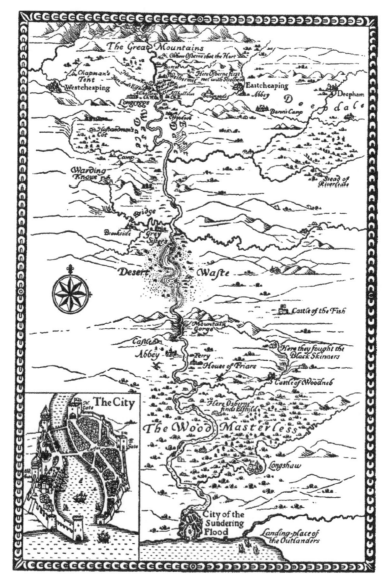

Figure 9.9: Frontispiece map to *The Sundering Flood* by William Morris, 1898.

Source: http://ebooks.adelaide.edu.au/m/morris/william/m87su/.

SAMPLE LESSON PLAN

Once students have acquired a grasp of the purpose and structure of maps (or charts, graphs, and tables) move on to more abstract representations. For example, give regional weather data to students and ask them to use symbols to demonstrate rainfall, temperature, and seasonal patterns. Political boundaries, capitals or voting affiliations could also be placed on maps, with students following tradition or devising their own methods of representation. Capitals might be depicted as small public buildings, as circles with stars inside, as state flags, or whatever is decided. The red and blue states, so popular in recent U.S. presidential elections, might provide a model students could improve on, adding information about the states or refining the distinction by adding symbols for 'swing' states. A major question is whether maps clearly communicate important and meaningful information. Each map, graph, or chart-making exercise should strengthen and extend student understanding. As an adventure, show how maps can be used as moving images (www.socialexplorer.com) to show growth and change in a major city (e.g., New York) for 200 years, or so.

Draw students into the world of mapping and graphing through controversy. Many students and citizens tend to view statistical presentations and maps as basically correct and factual. Because numbers are seen as proof, for claims, they are accepted without question.[30] But maps themselves may represent a political claim, for example, maps of Palestine and Israel that do not agree on boundaries.

Maps of India and China claim different parts of the Himalayas. In some cases, maps can also be used to make points or to promote views of the world that stir emotions or raise social issues, like gun sales, poverty, inequality, and the size of armies. Take a look at building 'mental maps' with students, that is, maps in their minds of say, the 20 most important historical events, or the 25 best places to visit, or the worst and best countries in the world. You collect data from the students and then compare these with reported statistical studies from sources such as the Penguin books mapping section, or for a wilder approach look at Mindmeister.com to create your own versions.

On paper direct students to take 1 or 2 minutes, that is all, and write down everything they remember about important places in history, then tally the results and post it on the Smart Board or Overhead for analysis. The last time I did this with my methods students, Western Europe, West Asia, the Middle East, and the U.S. were huge, while the rest of the world—Africa, South American, Oceania, and the rest of the East—were tiny, alas, hardly a comprehensive world view. This could also be a research study of your own!

SUMMARY

In this chapter, the potential of media from print to Internet was surveyed for use in social studies classrooms. Although still and moving media offer enormous potential, they also present a variety of problems that carry over into Internet and film sources.[31] Media can be exciting, dull, misleading, and absorbing, but for each effect caution is recommended. Student roles across didactic, reflective, or affective goals offer different views of narrators and audiences as interpreters of symbols, subjects, messages and meanings.

First, *print media*, as written words, can be expressed in terms of fiction and nonfiction, distinctions made between primary sources and secondary scholarship; journalistic and literary reporting. The categories of fact and fiction can be viewed as overlapping, not all that different, with different forms often employing the same styles or modes of presentation borrowing from art, storytelling, and mystery.

Teachers are invited to create lessons from a wide range of materials, websites, Internet databases, eyewitness accounts and news reports, journal or diary entries, scholarly sources, fine arts, photographs, and maps, charts, and graphs. Teachers are encouraged to be aware of and suspicious of *all* sources, particularly on huge government, Smithsonian, and university websites that provide a vast range of historical and social science materials. There are persisting issues of quality and reliability of websites and plagiarism dating back well into the beginning of the great era of technology for social studies.[32]

Whatever the sources or styles or delivery system involved, teachers should take full advantage of both still and moving media on reliable historical and social science and humanities websites: reinforce critical thinking and improve appreciation for the vast storehouse of rapidly growing data faced by all of us.

Above all, it is our mission to attune students and ourselves to investigate and assess the goals, messages, and agendas, hidden in plain view, of all communications, regardless of format or medium. Seeking hints of bias and checking claims and absorbing styles is part of the fun of investigation: answers can wait for a while.

NOTES

1 Rosenzweig, R. (2006) "Can History Be Open Source? Wikipedia and the Future of the Past," *Journal of American History*, 117–141.
2 Saye, J. W. (2016). Disciplined Inquiry in Social Studies Classrooms. In Manfra, M. M. and Bolick, C. M. (eds.), *The Handbook of Social Studies Research* (Boston, MA: Wiley-Blackwell), 65–73.
3 McGrew, S., Smith, M. et al. (2019) "Improving University Students' Web Savvy: An Intervention Study," *British Journal of Educational Psychology*, 89, 3, 485–500.
4 Norman, D. A. (1993) Experiencing the World. In *Things That Make Us Smart* (Boston: Addison-Wesley), 19–41.
5 Berger, A. A. (2019) *Media Analysis Techniques*, 6th Ed. (Newbury Park, CA: Sage Publications).
6 Mintz, S. (September 1, 2013) *The Modern Family*. www.digitalhistory.org.
7 Zevin, J. (2021) *Suspicious History* (Lanham, MD: Rowman & Littlefield).
8 Rosenzweig, R. (2011) *Clio Wired: The Future of the Past in the Digital Age* (New York: Columbia University Press).
9 Minor, C. (2019) *We Got This! Equity, Access, and the Quest to Be Who Our Students Need Us to Be* (Heinemann Publishing).
10 Paris, D. and Alim, S. M. (2017) *Culturally Sustaining Pedagogy: Teaching and Learning for Justice in a Changing World* (New York: Teachers College Press).
11 Banks, J. A. (2017) "Failed Citizenship and Transformative education," *Educational Researcher*, 46, 7.
12 Downey, T. and Long, K. (2015). *Teaching for Historical Literacy: Building Knowledge in the History Classroom* (New York: Routledge).
13 Zevin, J. (2021) *Suspicious History* (Lanham, MD: Rowman and Littlefield).
14 Gaudelli, B. (2003) *World Class: Teaching and Learning in Global Times* (Mahwah, NJ: Lawrence Erlbaum Associates).
15 Merryfield, M. (2002) "Rethinking Our Framework for Understanding the World," *Theory and Research in Social Education*, 30, 1, 148–151.
16 National Council for the Social Studies (2013) *College, Career, and Civic Life C3 Framework for Social Studies State Standards* (Silver Spring, MD) 12–13.
17 Sarason, S. (1982) *The Culture of the School and the Problem of Change* (Boston: Houghton-Mifflin).
18 Ravitch, D. and Finn, C. (1987) *What Do Our 17-Year-Olds Know? A Report on the First National Assessment of History and Literature* (New York).

19 Rafferty, M., Warrington, M., Dodson, K., & Faust, D. (2020) "4 Educators' Keys to Connecting STEM and Social Studies," The Journal.com.

20 Rembis, M., Kudlik, C., and Nielsen, K. (2018) *The Oxford Handbook of Disability History* (New York: Oxford University Press).

21 Dewey, J. (1919). *New Schools for Old* (New York: Dutton).

22 National Archives (1979) *The American Image: Photographs from the National Archives, 1860–1960* (National Archives: Washington, DC).

23 Provenzano, E., Jr., Provenzano, A. and Zorn, P. A., Jr., (1989) *Pursuing the Past: Analyzing Pictures and Photographs* (Boston: Pantheon Books).

24 Trachtenberg, A. (1989) *Reading American Photographs* (New York: Hill and Wang).

25 Taylor, J. C. (1976) *America as Art* (Washington, DC: National Collection of Fine Arts).

26 Krantz, L. (1993) *America by the Numbers* (Boston: Houghton-Mifflin & Co.).

27 Berson, M. "Digital Images: Capturing America's Past with the Technology of Today," (April, 2004) *Social Education*, 68, 3, 214–219.

28 Britannica Digital Learning (2021) *Classroom Technology: 5 Ways to Teach Social Studies with Digital Resources*. https://britannicalearn.com/blog/get-more-from-classroom-technology/.

29 Cox, K., Low, M. and Robinson, J. (eds.) (2008) *The SAGE Handbook of Political Geography* (London: Sage).

30 Paulos, J. A. (1995) *A Mathematician Reads the Newspaper* (New York: Basic Books).
    Porter, T. M. (1997) The Triumph of Numbers: Civic Implications of Quantitative Literacy. In Steen, L. A. (ed.) *Why Numbers Count: Quantitative Literacy for Tomorrow's America* (New York: College Entrance Examination Board).

31 Scheuerell, S. K. (2015) *Technology in the Middle and Secondary Social Studies Classroom* (New York: Routledge).

32 Diem, R. (2003) "Technology and the Social Studies: Issues and Responsibilities," *Social Education*, 47, 5.

FOR FURTHER STUDY: ORGANIZING FOR INSTRUCTION

Bennett, W. L. (1988) *News: The Politics of Illusion* (New York: Longman).

Berger, J. (1972) *Ways of Seeing* (London: Penguin).

Boorstin, D. J. (1962) *The Image* (New York: Athenium).

Calkins, S. and Kelley, M. (2009) "Who Writes the Past? Student Perceptions of Wikipedia Knowledge and Credibility in a World History Classroom," *Journal on Excellence in College Teaching*, 30, 3, 123–143.

Ewen, S. (1988) *All Consuming Images* (New York: Basic Books).

Graeber, D. and Wengrow, D. (2021) *The Dawn of Everything: A New History of Humanity* (New York: Farrar, Straus, & Giroux).

Harari, Y. N. (2019) *21 Lessons for the 21st Century* (New York: Random House).

Keen, S. (1987) *Faces of the Enemy* (New York: Harper & Row).

Loewen, J. (2015) *Teaching What Really Happened* (New York: Teachers College Press).

McCall. J. (2011) *Gaming the Past: Using Video Games to Teach Secondary History* (New York: Routledge).

McGuire, S. Y. and McGuire, S. (2015) *Teach Students How to Learn* (Sterling, VA: Stylus Publishing LLC).

Wald, C. (1975) *Myth America: Picturing Women, 1865–1945* (New York: Pantheon Books).

Wineburg, S., Martin, D., and Monte-Santo, M. (2013) *Reading Like an Historian: Teaching Literacy in Middle and High School History Classrooms*. 2nd Ed. (New York: Teachers College Press).

Zevin, J. (2021) *Suspicious History* (Lanham, MD: Rowman & Littlefield).

TEACHING IN THE INTERNET AGE: MULTIPLE LITERACY FOR MANY MEDIA

BUILD YOUR OWN LESSON

The challenge: thinking 'on your feet.'

Interact with a new piece of evidence, data, issue, or problem.

Design a lesson of your own using different materials (newly discovered art, music, literature, history, geography, etc.).

Worry not about what you know, but react by thinking about how you would teach the data. Improvise!

Write a didactic, reflective, and affective goal for each document or picture, then add a low, medium, and high order question.

Choose one of the six strategies.

Pick a brief method of evaluating success (verbal, written, and tested).

What questions do the data support? Where do they fit in history?

What is the source and context: time and place? And how does that matter?

Did you find improvisation for the classroom easy or difficult? Why?

Maybe a good mystery lesson? Who and what is the elegant black man and why is he dressed in european style? What is he reading? Dramatic? What feelings is the painting probably meant to convey to an audience? Who was the audience likely to be? If you turned him into a movie or tv series what might the script dramatize?

DOI: 10.4324/9781003026235-23

Figure 9.10: Toussaint L'Ouverture, general and revolutionary of Haiti, early 19th century. The General reads the Declaration of Independence dressed in a French-style uniform.

Schomburg Center for Research in Black Culture: New York. Artist unknown. Wikipedia commons public domain.

THE SOCIAL STUDIES CLASSROOM
Professional Issues and Trends

10

A FUTURE FOR THE SOCIAL STUDIES CLASSROOM

"Everybody gets so much information all day that they lose their common sense."

Gertrud Stein

OVERVIEW

This chapter will examine professional organizations across a range of subjects that apply to the social studies.

What does it mean to be a professional social studies teacher in a secondary school? Professionalism generally means remaining current in your field, subscribing to a few journals, like *The History Teacher, Archeology*, and *The Social Studies*, in terms of both content and instructional strategies; taking advantage of opportunities and resources to make yourself a better teacher; participating in one or more professional organizations. Checking out history materials from leading websites, reading a history and/or historical novel.

With the advent of the NCSS C3 Framework and Common Core Standards as well as other standards, there are more than enough goals to shoot for as a teacher.

In this chapter, look at your professional identity as a social studies teacher, and at the resources available and constraints imposed on instruction and professional growth. Part of your identity should be keeping abreast of our field, social studies, and extending attention to cognate fields like history, the social sciences, arts and humanities, and the sciences. This is a tall order, but to start perhaps one or two fields of interest like geography will suffice alongside history.

TRENDS AND COUNTERTRENDS

With the Internet Age upon us in full force, a whole new world has opened up for students and teachers. This is a world where almost everything is available almost instantaneously, yet this has created an enormous burden in terms of attention, review, and skill

DOI: 10.4324/9781003026235-25

development. There is too much knowledge, and the problem is to make sense of it as instructors, and to make use of it in classrooms for 'real live audiences.'

Several waves of reform have led to the imposition of evaluation systems that make new demands on teachers of all subjects and levels. Where teachers once took evaluation upon themselves, there is now no shortage of agencies and administrations willing to criticize teaching ability and student results. Change in the direction of more control and higher standards for social studies began as far back as the 1960s with the New Social Studies, an effort to change how and what teachers taught. Much attention was paid to curriculum in the 1960s and '70s and perhaps through the '80s. At that point a flood of reports was issued aimed at restructuring schools and building academic excellence. By the 1990s and 2000s there was a search for standards, criteria, and measures of school success.[1] The result: a lot of examinations of both teachers and students. COVID-19 has left us in a kind of limbo where exams and grading are in flux or postponed because of limitations of online study, and lack of direct onsite observations and assessments. Even with the restoration of onsite education, there are shortages of material, teachers, and up-to-date curricula.

The last few decades brought with it programs of testing and evaluation as a means to improve teaching and school choice as the vehicle for rewarding 'successful' schools while punishing those whose students fail. Reports in the 1980s, particularly *A Nation at Risk* (1983), portrayed American students as having seriously fallen behind their counterparts in Western Europe and Japan. The fear was that the United States would no longer be economically competitive globally. Although employment levels generally rose throughout the decades, educators and employers lamented the poor training students were receiving for careers in an increasingly complex, sophisticated 'Information Age.'[2] Demands for excellence gave way to 'restructuring' proposals for education as a whole. As the economy of the 2000s prospered, grew, and became increasingly dependent on technological growth, the demand for more highly educated workers also rose, with more pressures on the schools to adapt to the new Internet Age.

The Internet has affected politics, law, education, and daily life, with schools relatively slow to adapt.[3] One response to the putative educational crisis was preparation of a spate of standards issued voluntarily by professional agencies and organizations. Although these standards represented an honest effort to define 'what students should know and be able to do' up through high school, many were met with criticism.

American history standards were developed by the National Council for History Education (NCHE) but censured by the U.S. Congress for failing to incorporate enough patriotic material that many Senators and Representatives regarded as crucial to the nation's history. Given the criticism, by the mid-1990s, the attempt to create national standards was partially abandoned, and with the passage of national Goals 2000: Education America Act legislation, responsibility for improving education devolved in individual states. Although many states attempted to reform their curricula, they also introduced standardized testing as a way of proving that standards had been met. By about 2000-01, 44 states had introduced some form of standardized tests for history and social studies. Such tests moved even further toward center stage with the 2002 passage of No Child Left Behind, which tied federal funding more closely to performance on standardized tests.

Thus, for social studies teachers in most areas of the country, culminating examinations have become the engines that drive the 7–12 curriculum. We could argue that, in practice, a set of national standards is actually in place because almost the entire nation is following the same curriculum using the same basic U.S. and world/global textbooks from a few large publishers.[4] In effect, we are living in a new world of educational achievement with de facto standardization, to a large extent, and growing compulsory testing as a measure of instructional prowess in social studies, and in general.

We must, therefore, *walk a tightrope between teaching to the test(s) and attempting to engage our students in meaningful higher-order learning.* The tightrope has become longer as we move into the 2020s and beyond, with communities, states, and the federal government all contributing to the examination craze up to and excluding the pandemic crisis.[5] Meanwhile, the curriculum has largely remained unchanged. It is still a predominantly 19th and early 20th century curriculum mutated to incorporate the Internet and classroom technology, like cell phones, Smartboards, podcasts, and electronic tablets. There is much talk of global studies, but little interconnection globally; much talk of anti-racism and gender equality, but little in the way of curriculum reform.

In response to tests, the social studies curriculum has been restructured in largely conservative ways, with basic courses in civics, U.S. history, and world civilization, and sometimes geography and economics. A movement away from the electives and issues-centered courses that emerged in the 1960s and 70s has faded, though there are survivors. Although the general trend is in a more conservative and reduced direction, many states have attempted to include a more global perspective in their curricula. Global/world studies have grown enormously with the recognition that the world is shrinking, interconnections are necessary economically, and the climate is changing due to human interference.

There has been a strong interest in social studies among both researchers and curriculum developers seeking to enhance a global perspective.[6] Many argue that the entire curriculum needs to be redesigned from a truly global, integrative, and interactive perspective, rather than just adding on more topics, areas, and regions.[7]

World studies/world history has developed into a much more inclusive and less ethnocentric course along with a new preeminence of history in the social studies curriculum. A concerted effort has continued for students to engage in 'authentic' hands-on historical tasks using primary materials that represent conflicting viewpoints and scholarly disagreements.

The goal is for higher-order thinking and meaningful student involvement with historical sources. The C3 Framework enshrines critical thinking about history and the social sciences across middle and high school courses. Sophisticated thinking tasks, for example, have been inserted into state-mandated examinations. The New York State Regents Examinations in global and U.S. history regularly include a document-based section that requires students to analyze a series of primary and secondary documents to construct an essay.

Testing often dictated what is to be taught at least before COVID-19. Examinations combined with a rather self-centered curriculum would seem to clash with long sought-after social studies goals calling for critical thinking, social issues, and respect for primary sources. It is interesting to note that as the pace of testing has grown, the social studies has presented an integrated set of new teaching standards that stress an 'inquiry arc.'[8] Teaching to the test produces conformity and a sense of responsibility for students to succeed. This may not limit *how* a teacher adapts the curriculum to the examination but it does cause worries about being evaluated and measured by the standards, even if criteria clash with goals emphasizing inquiry, one among many contradictions in our field.

Technology, meanwhile, is galloping on and offers a vast array of means and media for classroom use. The Internet provides access to films, TV programs, theater performances, concerts, simulation games, YouTube clips, podcasts, tests, diagnostic devices, do-it-yourself rubrics, and more. Entire programs are encapsulated on DVD or CD disks. Computers offer interactive, searchable resources across time zones, and interactive programs that can enrich any lesson. There are teacher blogs affectionately called webinars, training videos, and lectures. Technology provides access to music and pictures, past, present, and future. The Internet is a vast resource for original materials and interaction. PowerPoint allows a mix of these resources to create a presentation that can be every bit as boring as lecture notes or as engaging as the best MTV show.

All of this is happening within the confines of a still relatively 'traditional' curriculum, one whose bottom line is still gathering knowledge, the lowest level of Bloom's taxonomy, not critical and creative thinking, the highest level. We are at a critical juncture for social studies and related disciplines, pushed by reformers for concrete results, pushed by professional associations for deeper and more thoughtful results, and pushed by legislation for better and cheaper results in every direction.

Thus, quite a dilemma exists in our field, a philosophical struggle for the heart and soul of teaching social studies as we progress into the next decades of the 21st century. Shall we teach historical truth or narrow national pride avoiding 'difficult' topics like slavery, conquest, and racism? All of these forces of change and demand are held in abeyance by the terrible year or two of worldwide pandemic in which most schooling was done via Zoom, Google Meet, and other electronic websites, none originally designed for educational purposes. Onward to live classrooms but what to teach?

PROFESSIONAL IDENTITY

For social studies teachers, our subject, similar to the sciences, is not singular, as it is for most other secondary teachers. Social studies teachers according to a national survey, see themselves primarily as social studies generalists, rather than specialists in a single discipline like history or economics.[8] Social studies teachers support professional organizations like the National Council for the Social Studies, but they do so in somewhat smaller relative numbers than colleagues in English or science. Findings suggest that activist professionals make up only a fraction of secondary social studies teachers, and that the potential for growth is sizable.[9] Professional identity is not limited to membership in a professional organization, of course; another measure may be ongoing participation in seminars, institutes, workshops, and other programs that enrich knowledge and upgrade instruction.

A number of programs were offered by national and state organizations, notably the National Endowment for the Humanities, the National Endowment for the Arts, Constitutional Rights Foundation, American Social History Project, Center for Civic Education, Taft Institute for Government, The Center for Politics at the University of Virginia, the Council for Economic Education, The Gilder/Lehrman Institute, as well as many colleges and universities. The Council for Economic Education offers a vast array of lesson plans, courses, simulation games, and other materials for hands-on economics. These programs may return as real classroom life resumes.

See the Appendix in Chapter 8 for a resource list of such programs.

TO DO

Define what you see as professionalism in social studies education. How does this concept affect teaching? Write a statement listing at least five ways in which you would develop professionalism in or out of online teaching or live classrooms. Share your ideas with colleagues. Do they agree or disagree with your views?

Social studies receives little specific publicity, positive or negative. However, the 1980s and 1990s brought a series of attacks on textbooks, the teaching of history, with accusations of inadequacy in high school students' knowledge in geography and economics.[10] The most recent national social studies test was given in 2018 to 8th graders in history, civics, and geography.[11] A Gallup survey on geography in 1990 commissioned by the National Geographic Society found that American students had a relatively poor sense of place, identifying important terms, and generally produced a lower average on the survey's test than students of most other nations tested.[12]

For example, the most recent report by the National Assessment of Educational Progress (NAEP Report Card: U.S. History), showed that a modest drop in scores had occurred on the 8th grade test, a drop of 4 points from 2014. This result was significant statistically for all but the top level of students in the 2018 8th grade cohort. Only about 15–20% of the sample was above the level of U.S. history 'proficiency.' Declines cut across all thematic subunits of the test, i.e., questions about democracy, culture, technology, and world role. The test sample representative of student populations totaled approximately 13,000 8th graders.

Scores in U.S. history were highest for White and Asian samples, lower for Black and Hispanic and American Indian/Alaska Native samples. All categories fell at a significant level for all but Asian/Pacific Islander groups. Female scores were a bit lower than males, and differences were calculated to be significant statistically. Interestingly, students below the 25th percentile engaged in much less inquiry activities than those at or above the 75th percentile. Inquiry activities are defined as:

(a) Examining causes and effects of important events in U.S. history (25% to 56%);
(b) Analyzing the relationship between two or more historical events (30% to 41%);
(c) Comparing and evaluating different points of view of the past (29% to 48%).

Students had been asked to identify causes related to specific historical events, such as the Civil War or migration movements, and explore the perspective of historical actors related to these events. Students have also been asked to support historical arguments using source materials such as excerpts from texts, photographs, drawings, or cartoons, or have been asked to identify and evaluate different views expressed in historical documents or about historical events.

On the Civics examination for 8th grade, there were no significant changes reported for all groups tested, although scores were lower for Black and Hispanic students than for White and Asian/Pacific Islander groups.

On the Geography assessment, scores trended a bit lower than in 2014, and were not statistically significant. But overall average scores were a bit lower on two of three content areas:

a) space and place
b) environment and society
c) spatial dynamics and connections (no change).

On the Geography report card, White and Black samples declined significantly while Hispanic, Asian/Pacific, and American Indian groups remained steady, no change. In the assessment, 63% report learning geography in the 8th grade, but only 20% reported a whole course in geography.

What questions looked like you might ask? Take a look by exploring the 2018 history, civics, and geography website questions and results.

NAEP reading scores were collected for a random sample nationally, and one fell across all groups between 2017 and 2019. Since the COVID-19 pandemic, we probably will see a greater decline than before, but data are not published as of this writing.

Source: *National Assessment for Educational Progress, Report on History and Economics (2019) www.nationsreportcard.gov.*

WHAT DO YOU THINK?

1. If you could design your own award for excellence in social studies instruction, what criteria would you follow? Would that include an 'inquiry arc' called for in the C3 framework?
2. If you could design your own award for excellence in classroom performance by a social studies student, what criteria would you follow? What would the student have accomplished to win?

PROFESSIONAL ORGANIZATIONS

The National Council for the Social Studies (NCSS) is the major professional organization for elementary and secondary social studies teachers. Based in Silver Spring, Maryland, NCSS represents the interests of social studies groups throughout the country and encompasses a network of regional, state, and local social studies councils and associations. Membership includes all levels from elementary and secondary teachers through supervisors and college/university faculty. Teachers also belong to major teachers' unions— the American Federation of Teachers (AFT) and/or the National Education Association (NEA). Once rivals, now linked, these two organizations speak for teachers' interests in general, there is general cooperation now. The AFT is affiliated with the AFL-CIO umbrella organization, whereas the NEA tends to stress teachers' professional roles, rather than the functions it performs as negotiator or arbitrator for salary and working conditions. Rivalry has given way to coexistence and cooperation in the face of legal, reform, business, and budget confrontations. Overall the AFT tends to be more urban oriented, more attentive to social problems and job stress, while the NEA tends to attract more suburban and rural teachers favoring professional issues over labor conditions.

The National Council for the Social Studies

NCSS sponsors an annual national convention for social studies teachers and college faculty, cosponsors regional programs and meetings, and publishes a national journal called *Social Education* and offers a wide-ranging series of books, pamphlets, and articles to assist teachers. Publications are designed to help teachers plan lessons, create programs, and keep up with issues that affect the field. NCSS has developed a series of policy statements on censorship, academic freedom, and curriculum, as well as a code of ethics, and the integrative C3 Framework for college, careers, and civic life that encompasses the entire structure of social studies, history through the social sciences. Teachers wishing to participate can do more than simply join by responding for committee service, leadership, as well as attending workshops, conferences, and an annual convention (www.ncss.org).

State and Local Organizations

NCSS networks with local councils in every state in the union, as well as internationally. Most follow the lead of the parent body in developing conferences, promoting publications, arranging teacher awards, and defending common interest. Much of the work of state and local associations is curriculum and testing oriented, especially establishing course requirements and reacting to evaluation standards. State and local associations often argue in favor of more course requirements in social studies, but against the loss of electives and student program choices. Over the years, many school districts have developed innovative electives or programs only to be squeezed out by additional course requirements or budget cuts imposed at local or state levels.

ETHICAL RESPONSIBILITY REPORT

1. It is the ethical responsibility of social studies professionals to set forth, maintain, model, and safeguard standards of instructional competence suited to the achievement of the broad goals of the social studies.
2. It is the ethical responsibility of social studies professionals to provide to every student, insofar as possible, the knowledge, skills, and attitudes necessary to function as an effective citizen.
3. It is the ethical responsibility of social studies professionals to foster the understanding and exercise of the rights guaranteed to all citizens under the U.S. Constitution and of the responsibilities implicit in those rights.
4. It is the ethical responsibility of social studies professionals to cultivate and maintain an instructional environment in which the free contest of ideas is prized.
5. It is the ethical responsibility of social studies professionals to adhere to the highest standards of scholarship in the development, production, distribution, or use of social studies materials.
6. It is the ethical responsibility of social studies professionals to concern themselves with the conditions of the school and community...associated.

Source: A Revised Code of Ethics for the Social Studies Profession (Washington, DC: National Council for the Social Studies, 1996)

Local social studies associations are usually represent towns or states, or urban centers. Local organizations vary greatly in size, range of activities, and effectiveness. Some large cities like Los Angeles, Chicago, and New York have active councils that sponsor annual conferences, develop publications, and conduct programs; smaller groups typically offer more modest programs. The name, address, and telephone number of any local or regional association should be available through NCSS and State Social Studies organizations.

Social Science Discipline Associations

In addition to the network of NCSS councils, social studies teachers have a rich base of support in subject areas. Professional groups like the American Historical Association (allied with the Society for History Education, publishes *The History Teacher*, to which all should subscribe), the Organization of American Historians, the National Council for Geographic Education, the American Bar Association Division for Education, the World History Association, Council for Economic Education, the American Geographic Society, and American Association of Geographers typically publish one or more bulletins, newsletters, and online or printed journals serving as the cutting edge of research and thinking across disciplines. There are also fine online materials available from the social science and humanities groups like the American Psychological Association, American Sociological Association, and the American Political Science Association, as well as other associations. Membership keeps you in close touch with the field or fields that interest you most and to keep abreast of current controversies and changes. What is taught in schools, and what serves as the basis for scholarly debate, in any given field can be quite different, so membership in both NCSS and a scholarly association is vital to keeping up with the research world applied to classroom teaching. For example, a recent volume of *The History Teacher* offered prize-winning student essays, book reviews, and fascinating articles on gaming in history.[13]

Special Interest Groups (SIGS) and Foundations

Special interest groups (SIGS) and foundations offer supportive materials for instruction, information on particular issues, and programs open to social studies teachers on a long-term or temporary basis. Some organizations focus on particular countries or cultural regions (the Asia Society, the China Institute), or on a concept like peace education (Teach Peace Now), environmental studies (Greenpeace), or foreign affairs (Foreign Policy Association). Some centers and programs offer valuable opportunities for after-school or summer study for both students and teachers.

PUBLICATIONS FOR THE SOCIAL STUDIES TEACHER

Social studies is rich in resources because it draws from so many different fields for its supply of ideas, methods, and materials. In addition to its own scholarly and organizational base, social studies calls on a broad range of related disciplines, including history, humanities, the social sciences, and the sciences, with attempts at fusion programs like STEM and STEAM. Online materials are readily accessed and in many cases articles, research, and lesson plans are available at no cost.

Major Journals

Journals and newsletters are a way of maintaining contact among professionals about the latest materials, issues, theories, and research in a given field. The two major social studies publications are *Social Education*, which represents the interests and concerns of NCSS and is part of its membership package, and *The Social Studies (TSS)*, a loose network of administrators and college professors, published by Taylor and Francis online (www.tandfonline

.com) and in print. Both journals cover a wide range of topics and offer special issues. Journals also regularly present features for teachers and reports on the latest curricular projects and research in the field. Other publications include the *University of Georgia Journal* (www.coe.uga.edu/gss) or the totally online *Social Studies Research and Practice* (www.soc-strp.org

Research Literature

For deeper insight into research findings than the social studies journals provide, a number of other important publications include *Theory and Research in Social Education*, published by NCSS. *Theory and Research* incorporates findings based on survey and experimental studies with debates on controversial issues. More modest but useful is the *Journal of Social Studies Research*, published by the University of Georgia. *Social Education* and *The Social Studies* also offer occasional research sections as well. Social studies researchers publish articles in one of the three publications of the American Educational Research Association (AERA): *Review of Educational Research, Journal of Educational Research,* and *The Educational Researchers.*

Social Science Publications

Each social science professional organization publishes one or more journals that report current research findings. You may find these valuable, particularly if you are offering electives or wish to introduce current debates and controversial issues. You should also be aware of the wide range of popular publications like *Psychology Today, National Geographic, Smithsonian Magazine, Archeology Today, Consumer Reports,* and *Mother Jones* that address social studies topics, as well as those publications that cater directly to teaching concerns such as *Teaching Political Science, The Journal of Environmental Education, The History Teacher,* and *The Magazine of History.* These sources often provide whole articles for discussion as well as tables, graphs, and pictures to be examined. There are also foundations that provide lessons through subscription newsletters, for example, Bill of Rights in Action offered by the Constitutional Rights Foundation (www.crf@crf-usa.org).

OTHER INSTRUCTIONAL RESOURCES FOR SOCIAL STUDIES TEACHERS

With Internet and library resources available, classroom work can be screen-enriched from a wide range of original documents, artifacts, art and music plus outside experts, field trips, innovative resources of all kinds. There are so many websites available on everything that we need a guide to resources, a website for searching websites. And that has already been provided, but may change because the Internet is also ephemeral, sites coming and going down all the time, resulting in messages like 'This site is empty!' If you need help, look at recommended websites.[14] A small sample of top choices includes:

www.sweetsearch.com (ask for social studies and you will be directed to 101 sites for social studies class)
www.socialstudieshelp.com (course outlines, links to other sites, evaluations)
www.socialstudies.org (NCSS website where you can read the new and old standards, newsletters, lesson plans, reviews, and a host of additional material)

www.world-newspapers.com/alternative-news (search through stories from newspapers around the world and think about alternative views to the top three U.S. sources)

www.cagle.com (cartoons galore on topics of the day organized by dates, subjects, and styles, great for instant discussion of the intersection of art and politics)

For real live entertainment, turn to state and local historical societies for speakers whose knowledge can enliven a classroom; local history can demonstrate how great historical movements of national or international character are reflected in places people take for granted. We often overlook our hometowns as places of historical importance, yet much can be discovered about their role in the past. Ask students to design and carry out an oral history project in their community: have them research citizen roles in the Civil War or Vietnam conflict. Take a look at monuments, plaques, posters, public buildings, etc.

Not every class can visit Williamsburg, Virginia; Sturbridge Village in Massachusetts; or the Alamo in Texas, but virtually every class has some site of historical significance—a beautiful old church or synagogue, the site of a revolutionary war or frontier battle, or one of the nation's first steel mills or industrial plants. Let your students discover what sites are important. Take advantage online even if students cannot be there to smell, touch, and look. Plan a simulated Zoom trip to the Alamo, with sound effects and a video that let students take the roles of Jim Bowie and Colonel Travis. Check if the stories are authentic, and don't forget to include a few Mexican characters like General Santa Ana. Work out an itinerary for a trip to China or the Middle East with a list of places to visit and people to interview. Have some fun with this. Bring in people who lived history, like a WWII, Vietnam, or Gulf War veteran; a holocaust survivor; a local campaigner or a businessperson willing to tell about personal economic choices.

The primary lesson is to understand that resources are everywhere, often right next door or on screen, and many of them are free and underused. Finally, develop a major 'Kids Make History' project of your own by encouraging use of cameras and cell phones to make a record of problems and prospects in and around their own communities. Take a walk around your neighborhood or town center and look for underappreciated monuments and memorials; look at old and new buildings for design flourishes and signs of technological change. Document pollution, decay, and areas that need attention. Publish a chapbook of results: Make history come alive!

BEYOND THE SOCIAL STUDIES: INTEGRATING OTHER DISCIPLINES

Art

In Figure 10.1, what kind of teacher image is shown here: positive or critical? Are the activities familiar still, from the 15th century to today? How can you decide? This is a faithful photographic reproduction of a two-dimensional, **public domain** work of art. The work of art itself is in the public domain for the following reason.

Art museums offer prime field trip possibilities, offering architecture, paintings, and sculpture in the round not available from the Internet or textbooks alone. In addition to museums, private archives can sometimes supply slide collections (although often at some cost), and art history textbooks often have plates that can be reproduced. Sometimes, there are opportunities for connections, such as the New York Historical Society's special Luce collection of art and artifacts that students can walk through and ponder over as products

Vocabularius rerum

Figure 10.1: Woodcut from the title page of Wenceslaus Brack: *Vocabularius rerum*, 1487. The picture shows the teacher of a Latin school and two students; one of them following the teacher's reading from a book.

Source: Unknown author.

of the past. There are also numerous online searches that can be conducted for art materials that illuminate history and for history that brings art and music into a social, political, and economic context.

Music

Music provides an extraordinary insight into the circumstances of a given time—folk music and social protest songs work for social studies, but opera, gospel, and popular song also increase our range of historical emotions.[15] If your students are willing to participate in a performance, even better. Encourage them to analyze the purpose, meaning, and function of music in history; build a lesson, for example, on national anthems designed to build national identification. Play marches and parade music intended to build enthusiasm for military campaigns, or social protest songs aimed at building ire against social injustices. Plan a series of songs to enhance and focus teaching about the Civil Rights Movement or Black Lives Matter. Play two or three off your list, handing out words so everyone can analyze the ideas and sing along for some fun. For civil rights, here are examples:

"If I Had a Hammer (The Hammer Song)," Peter, Paul and Mary (Warner, 1962)
"The Lonesome Death of Hattie Carroll," Bob Dylan (Columbia, 1964)
"Keep on Pushing,"" Curtis Mayfield and The Impressions (ABC-Paramount, 1964)
"People Got to Be Free," The Rascals (Atlantic, 1968)
"Respect Yourself," The Staple Singers (Stax, 1971)
"Say It Loud—I'm Black and I'm Proud (Part 1)," James Brown (King, 1968)
"Stand," Sly and the Family Stone (Epic, 1969)
"Think," Aretha Franklin (Atlantic, 1968)
"We Shall Overcome," Joan Baez (Vanguard, 1963)
http://rockhall.com/education/resources/lesson-plans/sti-lesson

Use folk music to show students how cultural styles, forms, and instruments can diverge or converge in different patterns over time and geographic territories. Use topical or campaign songs as a springboard for talking about political issues or popular songs as indicators of changing class or sexual mores. Use hip-hop and rap as social commentary in the here and now. Build a special project with "Sounds Around the World: The Geography Game for the Global Era," a geography game that links place and space to time and sounds, identifying cultures through music (jabaker@getsoundsaround.com). Or create a project of your own, musical comedy as social criticism, or rock n' roll music as expressions of freedom. Perhaps you might like to sponsor a 'Decades Program' where everyone learns the dances of an era like the 1920s or the 1960s or the 2010s? Use what is current and shock the students into finding out the teacher has knowledge of their musical culture!

Film

Films are democratic by design, easy to assimilate and enjoy, made for an adoring public, and often a rich source of material for discussion and interpretation. A quick retrospective of scenes from old Westerns can stimulate thinking, comparing *Little Big Man* or *Dances with Wolves* with older films like *General Custer in 7th Cavalry* or *She Wore a Yellow Ribbon* will open students' eyes to the ways in which movies reinforce and/or attack stereotypes. Comparative films or clips are perfect to test what students see as authentic. Have students watch *Glory,* then read the letters on which the narrative is based. Let students compare a film treatment of a historical episode, such as *Nixon* or *Braveheart* or *Twelve Years a Slave* with primary and secondary accounts, and develop their own version of events. Line up several editions of the same movie, or different topics, the original *All Quiet on the Western Front* and remakes. If you are willing and a bit brave, discuss films as allegories, helping students to interpret signs and symbols in popular films.

   Science fiction is often social criticism in disguise, so show something imaginative like *Lord of the Rings, Star Wars, District 9,* or *Wonder Woman*. After all, who is Wonder Woman? What is the story? Who is guiding the battles, the people or the gods? Collect a history of Wonder Woman as a topic to measure growth or lack of recognition for the accomplishments of female heroines and culture figures.

Literature

Short stories, novels, folk tales, poems, and plays all *illuminate the time in which they were composed*. These are springboards for the discussion of history's social, political, and economic issues. Fiction often gives students insights into history that are unobtainable from public documents or narrative history because texts often suppress the emotional and dramatic qualities that make literature so compelling. Using literature in the classroom is an instructional strategy that comes into its own because you can teach interpretational and reading skills at the same time.

Comprehensive collections specifically designed for schools include: *Literature: World Masterpieces* that moves across time and regions to provide a rich resource of songs, poems, stories, and documents for global/world history courses.[16] In addition to literature as story, there are numerous works of philosophy that represent important changes in thinking and ideology and have had a wide influence on the course of world history. Some philosophers, like John Stuart Mill or Jean Jacques Rousseau (the Enlightenment) are important developments of social thought and should be part of every social studies program so that students understand key ideas as models for important historical movements. Thinkers whose works could profitably be discussed for history and civics classes include Plato, Seneca, St. Augustine, Machiavelli, Ibn Khaldun, Avicenna, Descartes, Locke, Rousseau, Marx, Engels, Foucault, Confucius, Mo Tzu, and Gandhi. Philosophical writings can be particularly illuminating because they combine historical, literary, and ideological elements. They are also critically important in understanding historical development and intellectual controversies. But make sure you have excerpted and edited selections that will not overwhelm students, and remember that philosophical discussion takes time—no easy right answers!

Science and Technology

Much of human history is the story of technological change impacting economics, culture, and social relations. The argument can be made that scientific literacy is crucial to make sense of an increasingly technical world. Social studies in particular provide an atmosphere conducive to discussing and evaluating science-related issues, science history, and the analysis of artifacts of science as indications of advancement or decline.

Take a look at mass production in the Roman Empire versus Medieval Europe. Take a look at the Sung and Tang Dynasty's scientific materials versus European technology in the 8th–10th centuries. Advocates of interdisciplinary approaches like STEM/STEAM argue for the inclusion of science issues in the curriculum.[17] The NCSS developed a rationale and guidelines for infusing STEM ideas, materials, and issues throughout the social studies curriculum.

Science literacy in the social studies demands that students be prepared to keep their minds open to issues allowing time for reflection, resisting quick pro and con judgments about scientific and technological questions. Consider how many modern problems and issues, such as birth control, computer literacy, gender, and industrial pollution, have technological aspects. Go wild and combine film, literature, and science with history and teach parts of the old *Frankenstein* film that mixes philosophy with a mad scientist and a traditional village. Call out the key line "He's alive!" followed by a discussion of its meaning in the context of the 19th century Industrial Revolution. Or, if you don't like Frankie, teach portions of Fritz Lang's *Metropolis* or the newest *Dune* version (2021) with your favorite class.

LET'S DECIDE

1. Compare yourself as a social studies teacher today with you in the future or during student teaching. What do you see as becoming most important? How will you seek to grow in both knowledge and skills after recovery from the pandemic? What kinds of experiences will you pursue—travel, study, reading, webinars, online training? Compare your vision of teaching with those of several colleagues or students.
2. What kind of teacher do you envision yourself becoming in the next five years? Do you see yourself as active and passive, intellectual and practical, avant-garde and conservative, didactic and reflective, individual and cooperative, meeting content goals, student needs? What are your colleagues' views?
3. What mix of goals and methods will be suited best to changing student audiences, new technologies, and political atmospheres, like supporting discussion of. Controversial issues? Make a list of your choices to share. Join a blog for teachers to exchange views and news. Get active in a local association.

SUMMARY

Two major tenets of professionalism are continued growth and interest in social studies, and a caring, attentive attitude toward your audience. Professionalism is a commitment to continuously update your knowledge of the social sciences and history, and to keep abreast of changing educational methods. Reading history and social studies journals is a good way of keeping up to date providing great teaching ideas almost instantly. Professionalism is helping your audience to achieve didactic, reflective, and affective goals to empower thoughtful, productive, and ethical people.

The philosopher John Dewey pointed out around the turn of the 20th century that effective teaching represents a balance between subject matter and student understanding woven into a meaningful whole.[17] The students pay attention to the subject while you, the teacher, treat their ideas with interest and respect.

As the experience of teaching grows, you should become an active member of one or more organizations. You should attend conferences, seminars, and summer institutes that deal with topics of interest and deepen your understanding of people and events. Read at least one or two journals regularly. Consider research findings as these apply to teaching. Develop materials and lessons of your own unique design and share these with colleagues. Seek out the adventure of learning, and don't go stale teaching the same topics in the same way every semester.

Above all, think of your audience as young adults and adults who have ideas to contribute, decisions to make, and problems to contemplate. Build feedback into your programs, and take the results seriously as bases from which to improve your choice of subject matter and techniques. Be open minded—incorporate new technologies, texts, and points of view, e.g. history games or critical revisions of women's place in the curriculum. Share new ideas, critiques, and difficulties with your audience, demonstrating that knowledge is never completely settled. Above all, bring your audience into the fray, and take them as they are rather than as 'idealized' students. Be willing to analyze the potential and deficiencies of your audience, keeping a watchful eye on learning problems.

Make use of a wide variety of resources to enliven your teaching, including drawing from the humanities and the sciences. Employ film, art, music, literature, and other resources to enrich the documents, texts, and historical narratives that form the typical social studies curriculum. Seek traditions, literatures, and histories from unfamiliar viewpoints (e.g., Muslim, African, Latin American, and Asian sources); select some sources that are countercultural and critical of prevailing ideas, customs, and attitudes. Look at the overlooked and give those left out a chance.

Throughout your teaching career, keep working on a style and method that best suits the educational philosophy you find most effective for students in achieving didactic, reflective, and affective goals. Set a few goals for building values and character defined as people willing to hear all sides and agree nicely to disagree, maybe even get to YES. Ask students to provide suggestions that complement or challenge and invite them to be creative, critical, and philosophical, too. Philosophy is an inherent feature of professionalism because it is these higher principles that guide what to teach, how to teach, and why to teach. May the facts be with you.

NOTES

1　Viadero, D. (December 2, 1992) "First National Standards Bring Anxiety to Social Studies Educators," *Education Week*, 5.
2　Benjamin D. and Schneider, D. D. (April–May 1983) "Patterns of Work Experience Among High School Students: Educational Implications," *High School Journal*, 66, 267–275.
3　American Bar Association Division for Public Education (Winter 2004) "The Internet, Law, and Culture," *Insights on Law and Society*, 4, 2, 11–15.
4　Sewall, G. T. (March 2005) "Textbook Publishing," *Phi Delta Kappan*, 498–502.
5　Zevin, J. (2021) *Suspicious History* (Lanham, MD: Rowman & Littlefield).
6　Gaudelli, B. (2003) *World Class: Teaching and Learning in Global Times* (Mahwah, NJ: Lawrence Erlbaum Associates).
7　Merryfield, M. (2002) "Rethinking Our Framework for Understanding the World," *Theory and Research in Social Education*, 30, 1, 148–151.
8　National Council for the Social Studies (2013) *College, Career, and Civic Life C3 Framework for Social Studies State Standards* (Silver Spring, MD), 12–13.
9　Sarason, S. (1982) *The Culture of the School and the Problem of Change* (Boston: Houghton-Mifflin).
10　Ravitch, D. and Finn, C. (1987) *What Do Our 17-Year-Olds Know? A Report on the First National Assessment of History and Literature* (New York: HarperCollins).
11　*Bradley Commission on History in Schools* (1988) (Educational Excellence Network).
12　The Gallup Organization (July 1988) *Geography: An International Gallup Survey* (Princeton, NJ: National Geographic).
13　Putnam, J. C. (August, 2013) "To Boldly Go Where No History Teacher Has Gone Before," *The History Teacher*, 48, 4, 9–19.
14　Riisinger, C. F. (November/December, 2013) "What's New and Updated…Teaching Social Studies with the Internet," *Social Education* 77, 6, 314–315.
15　Soden, G. J. and Castro A. J. (Summer 2013) "Using Contemporary Music to Teach Critical Perspectives of War," *Social Studies Research and Practice* 8, 255–267. www.socstrp.org.

16 Bowler, E. et al. (eds.) (1996) *Prentice-Hall Literature: World Masterpieces*, 4th Ed. (Upper Saddle River, NJ: Prentice-Hall).

17 Dewey, J. (1919) *New Schools for Old* (New York: Dutton).

FOR FURTHER STUDY: THE COMPLETE PROFESSIONAL

Austin, B. and Grundy, P. (eds.) (2019) *Teaching U.S. History* through Sports (Madison, WI: University of Wisconsin Press).

Binkiewicz, D. M. (2006) "Tunes of the Times: Historical Songs as Pedagogy for Recent United States History," *The History Teacher*, 39, 4, 515–520.

Brkich, C. A. (2012). "Music as a Weapon: Using Popular Culture to Combat Social Injustice," *The Georgia Social Studies Journal*, 2, 1, 1–9.

De Chantal, J. (August, 2021) "Digital Storytelling: A Beneficial Tool for Large Survey Courses in History," *The History Teacher*, 54, 4, 709–731.

Evans, R. W. and Saxe, D. W. (eds.) (2007) *Handbook on the Teaching of Social Issues* (NCSS Bulletin 1993) (Washington, DC: National Council for Social Studies).

Lieberman, A. (ed.) (1988) *Building a Professional Culture in Schools* (New York: Teachers College Press).

Mangram, J. A. and Weber, R. L. (2012) "Incorporating Music into the Social Studies Classroom: A Qualitative Study of Secondary Social Studies Teachers," *The Journal of Social Studies Research* 36, 1, 3–21.

Melber, L. M. and Hunter, A. (2009, 2015, 2021) *Integrating Language Arts and Social Studies: For Intermediate and Middle School Students* (Sage).

PBS Learning Media (2021) *Social Studies and World History through Music and Dance* (KQED Education) www.ny.pbslearningmedia.org.

Pellegrino, A. M. and Lee, C. D. (2012) Let the Music Play! Harnessing the Power of Music for History and Social Studies Classrooms (Charlotte, NC: Information Age Publishing).

Social Studies Success (2017) *The Power of Music in Social Studies* www.socialstudiessuccess.com.

Spring, J. (2021) *American Education* (New York: Routledge).

Taylor, J., Monck, T. and Ayoub, S. (January 2014) "Arts Integration in the Social Studies: Research and Perspectives from the Field," *The Councilor: A Journal of the Social Studies*, 75, 1, 5, www.thekeep.eiu.eduthe_councilor.edu.

Von Tunzelmann, A. (2017). *The Reel History of the World: The World According To The Movies* (London: Atlantic Books).

White, C. and McCormack, S. (2006). "The Message in the Music: Popular Culture and Teaching in Social Studies," *The Social Studies*, 9, 3, 122–127.

Wineburg, S. (2018) *Why Learn History (When It's Already on Your Phone)* (Chicago, IL.: University of Chicago Press).

A FUTURE FOR THE SOCIAL STUDIES CLASSROOM

BUILD YOUR OWN LESSON

The challenge: thinking 'on your feet.'

Interact with a new piece of evidence, data, issue, or problem.

Design a lesson of your own using different materials (newly discovered art, music, literature, history, geography, etc.).

Worry not about what you know, but react by thinking about how you would teach the data. Improvise!

Write a didactic, reflective, and affective goal for each document or picture, then add a low, medium, and high order question.

Choose one of the six strategies.

Pick a brief method of evaluating success (verbal, written, and tested).

What questions do the data support? Where do they fit in history?

What is the source and context: time and place? And how does that matter?

Did you find improvisation for the classroom easy or difficult? Why?

Confucius Speaks

1. The Master said, He that rules by mind is like the north star, steady in his seat, whilst the stars all bend to him.
2. The Master said, The three hundred poems are summed up in the one line, Think no evil.
3. The Master said, Guide the people by law, align them by punishment; they may shun crime, but they will want shame. Guide them by mind, align them by courtesy; they will learn shame and grow good.

DOI: 10.4324/9781003026235-26

Tzu-Chang said, What are the four evil things?

> The Master said, To leave untaught and then kill is cruelty; not to give warning and to expect things to be done is tyranny; to give careless orders and be strict when the day comes is robbery; to be stingy in rewarding men is littleness."
>
> *Book II and XX: Analects of Confucius (*The Sayings of Confucius *(1908) translated by Leonard A. Lyall, Longmans, Green and Co., London · New York · Toronto, reissued by www .gutenberg.org).*

INDEX

Please note that page references to Figures will be in **bold**, while references to Tables are in *italics*.